D0851276

A GUIDE TO THE

TOP
100 COMPANIES
— IN —
CHINA

A GUIDE TO THE

TOP
100 COMPANIES
—— IN ——
CHINA

Editors

Wenxian Zhang & Ilan Alon

Rollins College, USA

World Scientific

NEW JERSEY · LONDON · SINGAPORE · BEIJING · SHANGHAI · HONG KONG · TAIPEI · CHENNAI

Published by

World Scientific Publishing Co. Pte. Ltd.

5 Toh Tuck Link, Singapore 596224

USA office: 27 Warren Street, Suite 401-402, Hackensack, NJ 07601

UK office: 57 Shelton Street, Covent Garden, London WC2H 9HE

Library of Congress Cataloging-in-Publication Data
A guide to the top 100 companies in China / edited by Wenxian Zhang & Ilan Alon.
    p. cm.
  Includes bibliographical references and index.
  ISBN-13: 978-9814291460
  ISBN-10: 9814291463
  1. Corporations--China. 2. Business enterprises--China. 3. China--Commerce. I. Zhang, Wenxian, 1963–
II. Alon, Ilan. III. Title: Guide to the top one hundred companies in China.
  HD2910.G85 2010
  338.0951--dc22

                                     2009053135

British Library Cataloguing-in-Publication Data
A catalogue record for this book is available from the British Library.

In-house Editor: Juliet Lee Ley Chin

Typeset by Stallion Press
Email: enquiries@stallionpress.com

Printed by FuIsland Offset Printing (S) Pte Ltd. Singapore

From Wenxian

To My Parents

From Ilan

To Joseph and Sophia

Contents

Foreword

China remained closed to the West until the late 1970s, but with the normalization of trade and diplomatic relations foreign multinationals began entering the China market in droves. In these early days, foreign multinationals were required to form joint ventures with Chinese companies selected by the Chinese government — there was no shopping for the best partner in an industry or searching to identify a supplier network to support the investment. Government supervised contact with these hand-picked partner companies was the first encounter with Chinese companies by business people or scholars in several decades. In these joint ventures, a foreign partner's access to information, even information about their partner, was extremely limited. This access required government approval from the government that tightly controlled information — and one that shunned transparency and frequently did not even collect the information requested by outsiders.

To be fair, frequently, the Chinese government or the Chinese joint venture partner did not know what they did not know, especially about contemporary business. They were not necessarily trying to be opaque. They were experiencing a clash between planned economy realities as they opened to the West and realities of foreign companies from capitalist countries. The Chinese partner may not have had more than rudimentary knowledge of their suppliers, competitors, or customers! Both sides, Chinese and foreign, assumed that theirs was the way to approach doing business. Chinese businesses were primarily large, state-owned enterprises whose activities had been guided by consecutive 10-year plans. Much of their technology and manufacturing had been adapted from Soviet counterparts or pre-dated the People's Republic of China's founding several decades earlier. Chinese companies had a lot to learn before they could compete internationally, much less as world-class competitors.

To say that China has changed in the three decades during which it has been open to foreign investment is an understatement. When I walked through the Beijing Jeep factory in the early 1980s — one that had been specifically selected for this showcase joint venture because it was a leader in China — the factory floor was dirt. Engines were moved on donkey carts. The assembly line could barely be called that — it resembled none I had ever seen with no mechanization and a lot of chaos. Access to a local supply infrastructure was an aspiration. The government was Beijing Jeep's only customer. Today, in this same factory, there is state-of-the-art technology, world-class management, equipment and techniques, a well-developed local supply infrastructure, and a facility that replicates automotive facilities in Japan, Europe, or the United States. This story is repeated a thousand times over for other Chinese companies that are not only producing for Chinese consumption but also for international markets.

Despite more than 30 years of active business engagement with foreigners, excluding a few notable exceptions, Chinese companies remain almost invisible in the West. While foreigners may have heard of Lenovo and their highly visible purchase of IBM's personal computer business or their support of the Olympics, or CNOOC's or Haier's failed attempts to acquire American businesses, the majority of scholars and business people know little about China's top companies. China's companies represent at least a third of those counted in an important phenomenon, emerging market multinationals. Two centuries ago Napoleon Bonaparte cautioned that when China awakes, the world will tremble. China is not only awake; its top companies are joining the global economy along with other emerging market multinationals.

Emerging market multinationals are drawing increased attention from business people, academics, and the business media. They are major players in big emerging markets such as China, India, Brazil, Korea, and Mexico, not to mention growth and natural resource rich regions such as Southeast Asia, Africa, and Latin America. They are buying North American and European businesses at an increasing rate. Some are going head-to-head with foreign multinationals in a variety of industries and many others are positioning to do so in the near future. Regardless, most business people and academics do not know much about these companies that are shaping the business landscape of the 21st century — even in a context where information now flows fairly freely in China.

The rise of emerging market multinationals parallels the rise of emerging markets in the global economy. This rise of emerging market economies has been identified as the greatest shift in global economic power since the Industrial Revolution. The parallel rise of emerging market multinationals might well portend the greatest shift in the global competitive landscape in this century. It is likely to prove more significant than Japan's internationalization given China's sheer size, growth rate, and economic power. Far beyond the perception that they engage primarily in resource seeking activities, these Chinese companies are shooting past their foreign counterparts in business practices and their ability to serve what C.K. Prahalad coined, the "bottom of the pyramid". More importantly, they are leapfrogging foreign counterparts in technology and innovation — consider the accomplishments of Korea's Samsung, Brazil's Embraer, Mexico's Cemex, or China's Lenovo.

A quarter of a century ago, I began working with Chinese companies, government officials, and university students to help them understand foreign business and contemporary business practices, and have continued to do so since. In these early days, it was apparent that Chinese companies — many featured in this book — were extremely curious, willing to learn, very ambitious, and highly motivated to take their place in the global economy. China began to prepare the soil to support future economic growth, internationalization, and global engagement. The seeds sown in these early days have blossomed. Today, many of these companies are nothing short of world-class. Government officials are sophisticated, highly educated and highly capable of making sense of the global economy. Chinese students consistently exceed my highest expectations. China has evolved from a planned economy to a private-sector-led economy and their growth performance has been spectacular. I am honored to have witnessed this transformation.

This is not to say that China is without challenges — there certainly are many. The successes outlined above have benefits that apply to 20 percent of China's 1.3 billion people, those who live in first tier cities along the coast where many of China's top companies are located. However, in China's rural interior, the remainder of the population has not experienced the same benefits of China's opening to foreigners. Many live in farming communities much like their ancestors with similar standards of living. The banking system is burdened with non-performing loans, and allegations that corruption is rampant. There has been a failure to develop robust capital markets. The Chinese government is engaged in a delicate balancing act to continue to encourage the successes and figure out how to better share the economic benefits with the remainder of China's people. They also struggle to ensure that the institutions critical to business success are in place throughout the country. It is in this context that Chinese companies have flourished and developed unique capabilities.

China's top companies have learned to leverage their knowledge of local consumers, especially those at the "bottom of the pyramid". This gives Chinese companies an advantage over foreign multinationals entering the China market as well as those competing in emerging markets around the world. China's top companies also have access to a vast supply of local talent, especially scientists and engineers, and can offer growth opportunities that foreign multinationals do not offer through innovative training and development and upward facing career paths for top performers. China's top companies have mastered the art of improvisation when faced with difficult situations, high levels of risk, and resource scarcity. As a result, China's top companies have competitive advantage in most of the growth markets in the world — a fact that makes this book an important starting point for business people aspiring to compete in these markets.

Understanding who these top Chinese companies are, what they do, and how they do it is an important first step for foreign companies. Being able to identify the competition and understand the lay of the competitive landscape is the second step in developing a competitive strategy for foreign firms hoping to compete or partner with top Chinese companies in China or elsewhere on the global playing field. This book allows companies to do both. Additionally, China's top companies form a significant part of the foundation of the recent emerging market multinational phenomenon which is, or should be, of great interest to international business scholars. *A Guide to the Top 100 Companies in China* provides a solid reference and starting point for Chinese and foreign scholars researching this emerging phenomenon. The editors, Wenxian Zhang and Ilan Alon, make an important contribution to our understanding of the Chinese companies that inhabit China's competitive landscape.

A Guide to the Top 100 Companies in China could not have been written three decades ago. Chinese companies would not have been forthcoming in sharing "sensitive" information. The Chinese government would have been reluctant to allow scholars or outsiders access to these companies and even to information about these companies — if it existed. However, China has evolved dramatically in the last three decades. Today, this book can be written. Today, China has taken its place on the global stage. Today, China's top companies are taking their place among the world's leading emerging market multinationals. This century promises to become the emerging economies century with China playing a major role alongside India, Brazil, Korea, and Mexico. China has awakened and is ready for business!

Dr. Mary B. Teagarden
Professor of Global Strategy
Editor of Thunderbird International Business Review
Thunderbird School of Global Management, USA

Chinese-English Company Name Index

Company-Industry Index

Industry-Company Index

Industry	Company Name	Page Number

Introduction

While it is common knowledge that China has the largest population base in the world, with over 1.3 billion people, not many people know that when measured by international dollars (purchasing power parity gross domestic product), China is already the second largest economy in the world, quickly narrowing the gap with the United States of America. Part of the growth story is based on the development of the Chinese multinational company, with a unique mixture of government involvement and private initiatives. The top Chinese 100 firms, coined Dragon multinationals, are a distinguishing characteristic of 21st century globalization. State-based capitalism has played a role in this development. This book uniquely packages information on the top Chinese 100 firms by providing concise insight into their formation, development, and structure. The top 100 Chinese firms account for about a third of the total GDP in the country.

Under the label of "the socialist market economy with Chinese characteristics", the government has made firm commitment to economic reform while still retaining tight political control. In retrospect, the third plenum session of the 11th Congress of the Chinese Communist Party held in Beijing in 1978 marked a major milestone in contemporary Chinese history, as the decisions made at that historic meeting changed both China and the world. Under the pragmatic leadership of Deng Xiaoping, China opened its doors and marched into a new era. Over the past three decades, the transition from a planned to a market economy unleashed an extraordinary series of changes in China: private enterprises have sprouted, foreign investment has soared, the standard of living has improved, the regional disparity has grown, the urban–rural divide has widened, and corruption has increased (Alon and McIntyre, 2008).

The country's remarkable development over the last 30 years has puzzled many Western observers. The new Chinese economy is not only massive and with huge growing potential but also complicated, perplexing, and packed with controversies and pitfalls. For example, while the quality of life for many people has noticeably been changed for the better, certain groups have inevitably become the victims of economic reform and income gaps are drastically widened. Although the private sector booms, many large state-owned enterprises struggle to cope with market competition. As a sustainable business growth demands a large supply of human and natural resources, the economy in full gears for an extended time has put substantial strains on the already fragile environment, and a large number of migrant farmers and laid-off workers have also threatened the social stability.

Several factors have given rise to the motivation of this book. Because of the rising influence of the Chinese economy in the global market, more and more people have begun to take interest in the country and its business development over recent years. For example, international business is one of the fast-growing undergraduate majors among academic institutions across the United States, and a significant portion of that group are students seeking to specialize in China. Consequently, there is a large and growing need for quality materials on the Chinese economy to enhance the mainstream reference literature. However, currently most of the relevant information is scattered in newspapers, magazines, web pages, journals, and scholarly books that are not readily accessible to average college students studying international business, or individuals seeking information on certain Chinese enterprises. Though a few are presented in English as case studies for MBA students, a vast amount of information are available in Chinese and therefore beyond the reach of typical readers living in the Western world. Undoubtedly, with China's growing importance in the global economy, there is a genuine need for a compatible research tool to be presented in a format that can be easily accessed by students, librarians, business professionals, or anyone interested to learn more about the country's economy and its key businesses.

While much has been written about China's overall economic growth in recent years, much less is known about the companies helping to generate it. In particular, there is no existing reference work devoted exclusively to the top Chinese enterprises that is aimed for college students. Therefore, to help people gain a better understanding of the country's corporate sector, we believe the publication of *A Guide to the Top 100 Companies in China* will be a welcome addition and likely fill the gap in the current reference literature market.

In recent years, both *Fortune* and *Standard & Poor's* have developed lists of China's 100 largest publicly traded companies, with selection criteria based on the latest available revenues. According to the Chinese edition of *Fortune* magazine, while the country's GDP increased by 11.4% to RMB24.7 trillion in 2007, the total revenues of the top 100 companies rose by 22.7% to RMB7.9 trillion, which amounts to 32% of China's GDP that year (财富, 2008). Clearly as a gauge of the country's overall economy, those top companies have played a very significant role in China's economic development.

Studying the top Chinese companies would reveal much useful information for people interested in the country's economy. For example in 2008, the state-owned companies have dominated the *Fortune*'s list, taking the top ten spots. Ranked first in sales is China Petroleum & Chemical, the biggest petrochemical and refining company in China, which is followed by PetroChina, the largest producer of crude oil and natural gas. Both companies have experienced significant revenue increases over the previous year, attributable to higher oil prices and China's growing demand for energy. Ranked third is China Mobile, the leading cell-phone operator, reflecting the country's immense growth in the wireless telecommunications market. The largest private company on *Fortune*'s list is computer maker Lenovo, ranked 13th.

Most companies on the list are in the heavy-industry sector, reflecting the frenzied development of the economy's infrastructure. The largest sector is steel production, followed by the petroleum and petrochemical industries. Other notable sectors include construction, mining, shipping/transportation, and manufacturing. In recent years, a rush of listings on the stock exchanges has added prominent newcomers to *Fortune*'s list of China's top 100 companies, among them several largest public offerings in the world, including: the China Life Insurance, the Industrial & Commercial Bank of China, and the Bank of China (Arora, 2007).

After the fantastic fireworks of the Beijing Olympic Games, the rest of the world are watching closely how China will proceed forward in the evolving global economy. Structural constraints, changing lending policies, environmental concerns, and a downturn in many sectors will likely limit growth. More significantly, since the country is highly open to exports and imports, a worldwide recession would further depress profit margins in China. However, with a huge and fast-growing domestic market, there are enough reasons to be cautiously optimistic about the country's long-term outlook. Consequently, China's top-tier companies may continually experience strong growth in the coming years, as accelerating industrialization and urbanization will lead to further expansion in private investment and domestic consumption over the long term. Although some companies may not eventually survive the race, others will likely adopt new management style, upgrade their technology, and emerge as globally competitive enterprises (Bailey and Song, 2005). Therefore, based on these observations, the editorial team is convinced that this guide to top Chinese companies will be a timely and useful tool for anyone studying China and the global economy.

The primary markets for *A Guide to the Top 100 Companies in China* are academic libraries of all sizes, research agencies and organizations with a focus on China and international business, and large to medium public libraries. The natural target audience includes undergraduates enrolled in colleges and universities, and we believe many graduate students in MBA programs and some high school students may also find the title useful for their study of Chinese and international business development. The book can be used not only by librarians searching for ready references on notable Chinese enterprises but also by individuals seeking to understand the *ins* and *outs* of the new Chinese economy over the last 30 years. In essence, *A Guide to the Top 100 Companies in China* will be a potential interest to anyone studying contemporary China and its huge market.

As a general reference guide to the Chinese economy, this title seeks to provide up-to-date and comprehensive coverage of the top Chinese enterprises. Companies selected in this Guide were based largely on their 2008 sales revenues. In compiling the list of companies, *Fortune* and *Standard & Poor's* lists, *Hurun* reports and other Chinese rankings are reviewed, and Chinese companies listed on the stock exchanges in Shanghai, Shenzhen, Hong Kong, Singapore, London, and New York are also examined. The geographic focus of the book is mainland China, although corporations from Hong Kong and Taiwan that conduct significant businesses in the People's Republic of China are included as well.

This reference book is the result of collaborative efforts across the globe. Over 40 scholars from the United States, mainland China, Hong Kong, the United Kingdom, Canada, France, Israel, Brazil, and Malaysia contributed to the collective undertaking. Depending on the importance and complexity of the topic, entries are roughly 1000–2000 words in length, briefly summarizing a company's historical development, main products and services, corporate structure, governance and leadership, business strategies, future development plans, as well as the key roles played in the Chinese and global economies. In addition, key business operations and drivers, competitive advantages and challenges, and major shareholders are included along with the most recent financial snapshot of the company in question, and references are also provided at the end of each entry.

A Guide to the Top 100 Companies in China is arranged in an alphabetical order by the English name of the included corporations. In addition to a keyword index and a list of abbreviations, a Chinese-to-English company name index is also provided for clarification and cross-reference purposes. It should be noted that all Chinese personal names in the book are listed following the East Asian custom, with family name first, followed by the given name (i.e., Deng Xiaoping). For typical Westerners, the romanization of Chinese words has generated many confusing variations in spelling over recent decades. This book follows the current common practice by listing all personal and place names in the standard Chinese *Pinyin* system, except for people from Hong Kong, Taiwan, and overseas, whose names are spelled following the traditional Wade-Giles system or their preferred Western names (e.g., Li Ka Shing). When a company uses an alternate spelling in their official English-language documents, we adopt the company's preferred spelling.

It is a daunting task to compile a comprehensive guide to the top enterprises in the world's most populous country while the nation is undergoing rapid and unprecedented economic development over the past three decades. The Information in this book is current as of press date. In consideration of the swift changes in China's economic landscapes, we will make efforts to revise the book in subsequent editions.

The publication of this book is the result of generous support of many people. We deeply appreciate the patience and good humor of our families, friends, and colleagues. We would like to thank all entry authors for their scholarly contributions, many of them are well-established academics in related fields. We are very grateful to Ms. Shalini, Editor at World Scientific Publishing Co., who is instrumental in reviewing our initial proposal and the publication of the book. We are also deeply indebted to the following individuals: Ms. Juliet Lee, Consulting Editor at World Scientific, for her professional guidance and support; Mr. Raguraman Gurusamy, Copyeditor at Mukesh Technologies, for his copyediting of the manuscript; and Miss Lei Guo, Student Assistant at Rollins China Center, for her work on the project web site. Finally, we would like to express our sincere appreciation to President Lewis Duncan, Provost Roger Casey, and Dean Laurie Joyner at Rollins, for their understanding of the essential relationship between teaching and scholarship.

Wenxian Zhang and Ilan Alon
Rollins College
Winter Park, Florida
USA

References

Alon, I and J McIntyre (eds) (2008). *The Globalization of Chinese Enterprises*. New York: Palgrave Macmillan.

Arora, R (2007). China's Top 100 Companies. *Fortune*, 28 August. http://money.cnn.com/magazines/fortune/fortune_archive/2007/09/03/100203550/index.htm. Retrieved on August 28, 2008.

Bailey, J and X Song (2005). Sizing up China's Corporate Elite. *BusinessWeek*, 29 July. http://www.businessweek.com/investor/content/jul2005/pi20050729_6371.htm. Retrieved on August 28, 2008.

财富 (中文版) 发布中国上市公司100强排行榜 (2008). *财富*, July [*Fortune* (Chinese Edition) Announces the Ranking of Top 100 Public Companies in China]. http://www.fortunechina.com/news/content/2008-07/11/content_8879.htm. Retrieved on August 28, 2008.

A Guide to the Top 100 Companies in China

Corporate Address and Contact Information

Air China Limited
Beijing International Post Office
PO Box 100071-666
Beijing 100071
People's Republic of China
Phone: (86)10-6459-5912
Fax: (86)10-6146-2538
http://www.airchina.com.cn/en/index.shtml

Air China Limited, also known as the China International Aviation Company (中国国际航空股份有限公司), is the second largest airline (after China Southern Airlines) in the People's Republic of China. The state-owned airline, which is headquartered in Beijing, is the 18th largest in the world and fourth largest in Asia, flying to 120 destinations. The predominate hubs for Air China are Beijing Capital, Shanghai Pudong, and Chengdu Shuangliu international airports.

Historical Development

Operations for the airline began on 1 July 1988, when the Civil Aviation Administration of China split into six separate entities — Air China, China Eastern, China Northern, China Southern, China Northwest, and China Southwest. Of the separate airlines, Air China was designated as the airline that would fly intercontinental flights. At the start of operations, the company had 6,000 employees and flew to 31 international and 30 domestic destinations. In 1989, the company entered an agreement with Lufthansa to form the Beijing Maintenance Aircraft Center, which served to maintain the Boeing aircraft that composed Air China's fleet.

In 1997, Air China reported sales of $1.38 billion, while operating numerous planes and 144 routes. Two years later, the company reported that it had flown 16 million passengers over the course of the year. In 2000, Air China partnered with the China National Aviation Company Group (CNACG) to establish a Hong Kong division. Soon thereafter, Air China experienced a period of rapid growth, and the company began to offer direct flights to both London and Hong Kong. In 2002, it was announced that the airline would further consolidate its operations with China Southwest Airlines. In 2004, the airline announced the absorption of Zhejiang Airlines. That same year, Air China was listed on the Hong Kong and London Stock Exchanges. In 2006, an agreement was announced in which Cathay Pacific would own 20% of Air China. In 20 years, the airline has grown substantially to become a leader in the growing Chinese aviation industry.

Corporate Structure and Leadership

The state-owned China National Aviation Holding Company operates Air China. The airline is led by a board of directors and a senior executive management team. Kong Dong is the chairman and a non-executive director and Cai Jianjiang serves as the president and CEO of the company. Cai is also the chairman of the strategy and investment committee, and a member of the aviation safety committee. A graduate of the China Civil Aviation Institute and the former general manager of Shenzhen Airlines Company Limited, Cai joined Air China in 2001, originally as head of the Shanghai branch. Besides Kong and Cai, the senior team also includes Fan Cheng (CFO, chief accountant, vice president and executive director), Sun Yude (vice president, chairman of supervisory committee and president of CNACG), Xu Chuanyu (chief pilot), and Zhang Lan (senior vice president). Air China's non-executive directors are composed of Wang Shixiang, Wang Yinxiang, Yao Weiting, Ma Xulun, Christopher Dale Pratt, Chen Nan Lok, Hu Hung Lick, Wu Zhipan, Zhang Ke, and Jia Kang. Supervisors for the company include Sun Yude, Liao Wei, Zhou Guoyou, Liu Feng, and Liu Guoqing. Altogether, the leadership team is known for its extensive experience and business acumen.

Air China is known for its multifaceted structure. The company has various branches, including Southwest, Zhejiang and Guizhou Provinces, Chongqing and Tianjin, and Inner Mongolia and Tibet Autonomous Regions. Air China also established a project and technology branch, headquartered in Beijing, with bases in various other locations. Flights around the world are controlled by an operating control center, which is in charge of managing the flight operations, creating operation manuals, aircraft performance and aircraft navigational materials, and other general operations. The company employees 2,875 pilots, who are known for adhering to strict safety standards. With 5,700 employees, one of the largest in the country, Air China's ground service department is highly revered for its work in the industry. As regard to the core corporate value, a special term, "Four Hearts", defines the philosophy of Air China's operations; the four services include _reassurance_, _satisfaction_, _easiness_, and _sensation_. Overall, the company implements a systematic management philosophy with a strong adherence to high safety and customer service standards. For all those reasons, Air China in recent years has been recognized with awards such as the International Civil Aviation Organizational Honorary Medal, the National Safe Production Advanced Collectivity, and the Safe Piloting Example Unit.

Main Routes and Services

As one of the largest airlines in the world, with Beijing as its main hub, Air China flies from China to Asia, the Middle East, Western Europe, and North America. Primary routes that the airline connects to include Shanghai Pudong, Chengdu Shuangliu, Chongqing Jiangbei, Dalian Zhoushuizi, Hangzhou Xiaoshan, Kunming Wujiaba, Nanning Wuxu, Xiamen Gaoqi international airports, Dubai, and Madrid Barajas Airports among others.

The airline is composed of four major components: the first is airline operation, which includes both the passenger and air cargo services; the second is engineering service, which oversees a multitude of areas including maintenance and repair; the third component is airport terminal service, which includes airport check-in, boarding, baggage, first-class, and other premium services; and the fourth segment focuses on many intangible areas such as airline catering and other features. In addition to its regular airline operations, the company also operates two subdivisions — Air China Cargo and Air China Business Jets. The maintenance standards are approved by the CAAC, FAA, and EASA. Licenced in

18 other countries, Air China's maintenance department has more than 9,000 engineers and technicians and owns nine major hangars where maintenance is performed.

Air China joined the Star Alliance in 2007, a frequent flyer program with other airlines such as United, Air Canada, and Turkish Airlines. In 2008, the company entered into numerous code-sharing agreements with various other airlines. The Star Alliance agreement expanded service for Air China customers to 897 destinations in 160 countries. The company also offers a frequent flyer program titled Phoenix Miles, which is the longest-running program of its kind in China, and millions of members take advantage of such services. In total, Air China owns 224 planes (composed of Boeing and Airbus) and operates 243 routes that cover 28 countries and districts. Of the routes, 69 are international, 6 are regional, and 168 are domestic, and the company offers online check-in options in 36 cities. Each week, the company flies over 6,000 flights that provide one million seats. Aircraft that Air China operates include the A330–200, B737–700, B757–200, B737–800, A319–100, and B737–600.

Challenges and Business Strategies

A primary challenge for Air China is the fragmentation of the market. Numerous competitors exist, particularly in the cargo segment, which results in a decline in market share for all when new competitors emerge. Additionally, many foreign airlines are eager to prosper in the growing Chinese market. China has liberalized aviation agreements that have enabled non-Chinese cargo shippers to attempt to gain significant market share. Furthermore, Air China and other Chinese airlines are greatly affected by the recent global economic slowdown. During poor economic times, all airlines experience the effects of market circumstances and require the infusion of capital from government and/or outside entities. A decline of international flights poses a significant challenge, yet Air China counters this by offering a multitude of services.

The business strategy of Air China is first to leverage its brand advantage. Specifically, Air China's brand is represented by its standards of high safety, strong customer service, and overall strength. The company utilizes cost-control methods to stay competitive, a thorough model of increased management efficiency versus effectiveness, and a very strict pilot-training program so that its safety record is maintained. To demonstrate the enormity of the company's dedication to training, the University of Air China will eventually serve as the airline's modern training base. The goal is to strategically market such strict training initiatives as a distinct competitive advantage.

The company also remains on the cutting edge with the latest in e-commerce technology and customer service. Above all, Air China relies on its strong history in the Chinese market to gain an advantage. The company presently has massive sales operations composed of 85 sales departments, 157 outlets, and 27,000 sales representatives, and will continue to emphasize its strong customer service strategy. Having over 2,000 key accounts currently, Air China is looking forward to pursuing large-scale growth in the coming years.

Michael A. Moodian, Margaret Minnis, and Yifang Zhang

References

Ahmed, AM, M Zairi, and KS Almarri (2006). SWOT analysis for Air China performance and its experience with quality. *Benchmarking: An International Journal* 13(1–2), 160–173.

Air China (2008). 2007 Annual Report. http://www.airchina.com.cn/AboutAirChina/AirChinaNews/InvestorRelations/AnnualInterimReport/images/2009/04/21/1A9C313DA4C475095F89EEB966300FE8.pdf. Retrieved on 14 May 2009.

Air China (2009). 2008 Annual Report. http://www.airchina.com.cn/en/ir/financial_information/images/2009/05/05/EF7E8EB938629C7A3B3B80BF5E5D1568.pdf. Retrieved on 14 May 2009.

Air China (2009). Company Profile. *http://www.airchina.com.cn/en/about_us/company_profile/company_profile.shtml*. Retrieved on 15 July 2009.

Denlinger, P (2004). Air China raises $1.07 billion in Hong Kong share pricing. *China Business Strategy*, 9 December. http://www.china-ready.com/news/Dec2004/AirChinaRaises107BillioninHongKongSharePricing120904.htm. Retrieved on 26 May 2009.

Kerr, J (2004). China confronts logistics challenges. *Logistics Management*, 1 May.

ALUMINUM CORPORATION OF CHINA

Corporate Address and Contact Information

Aluminum Corporation of China Limited (SEHK — 2600, NYSE — ACH, SSE — 601600)
No. 62 North Xizhimen Street
Haidian District
Beijing, People's Republic of China
Phone: (86)10-8229-8103
Fax: (86)10-8229-8158
http://www.chalco.com.cn

Aluminum Corporation of China Limited (中国铝业股份有限公司CHALCO) was established on 10 September 2001 as a joint stock limited company in the People's Republic of China. The group is the largest producer of alumina and primary aluminum in the PRC, and the third largest producer of alumina as well as the fourth largest producer of primary aluminum in the world. The group and its subsidiaries are engaged mainly in the exploration and production of bauxite, the production, sales and research of alumina, primary aluminum, and aluminum-fabricated products. Its operating entities include one bauxite branch, four integrated alumina and primary aluminum production plants, two alumina refineries, nine primary aluminum smelters, and one research institute.

Historical Background

Historically, the regulatory role of the non-ferrous metal industry and the supervision of the state-owned enterprises (SOEs) in this industry had been concurrently carried out by the China National Non-Ferrous Metals Industry Corporation. In order to separate the regulatory role from its supervisory function, the State Council dissolved the China National Non-Ferrous Metals Industry Corporation in April 1998, and subsequently established the State Non-Ferrous Metals Industry Bureau, and restructured all SOEs into three industrial groups: China Aluminum Corporation, China Copper, Lead, and Zinc Corporation, and China Rare Metals and Rare Earths Corporation in August 1999.

In July 2000, the State Council dissolved the three industrial groups and relinquished majority ownerships of the 28 SOEs in these industrial groups to local governments. The central government only retained 13 operating entities that included seven alumina and primary aluminum plants, one carbon plant, two metallurgical construction enterprises, one research institute, and one design institute. All these operating entities were subsequently transferred to a key SOE named Aluminum Corporation of China (CHINALCO), which was established in February 2001 under the direct control of the central government.

CHINALCO was again restructured in anticipation of an initial public offering in December 2001. According to a reorganization agreement, the major assets of CHINALCO, i.e. the alumina and primary aluminum operations, the Research Institute, mining operations, and mining rights of eight bauxite mines and other related assets and liabilities were transferred to its subsidiary Aluminum Corporation of China Limited. CHALCO was successfully listed on the Hong Kong Stock Exchange and the New York Stock Exchange on 11 and 12 December 2001, respectively, and after the listings, CHINALCO remains as the largest shareholder of CHALCO.

Corporate Structure and Leadership

CHALCO operates 12 branches throughout China and controls over numerous subsidiaries and associate companies. The branches are located in many provinces including Shandong, Henan, Guizhou, Shanxi, Guangxi, etc. The group has three main subsidiaries, i.e. China Aluminum International Trading (CHALCO Trading), Shandong Aluminum Company, and Aluminum and Power Company. CHALCO Trading imports aluminum-related materials for the group and exports all products of CHALCO worldwide. CHALCO employs about 94,300 people by 2008.

In March 2009, Xiong Weiping, aged 52 and current president of CHINALCO, replaced Xiao Yaqing as the executive director of CHALCO. After graduating from Central South University of Industry majoring in mining engineering, Xiong obtained a PhD in engineering and completed post-doctoral research in economics in Guanghua School of Management of Peking University. Recognized by the Ministry of Personnel of the PRC as one of the "Middle-Aged and Youth Experts with Special Contributions to the Nation", Xiong has an impressive record in academic achievement and extensive experience in economics, corporate management and metaliferous mining. He was formerly the general secretary of Hunan Youth Federation, and the president of Hunan Youth Union Committee, the vice-chancellor and dean of the Faculty of Management, professor, PhD advisor of Central South University of Industry, vice president of China Copper, Lead & Zinc Group Corporation, vice president of CHINALCO, executive director, senior vice president and president of CHALCO, and vice chairman and president of China National Travel Service (HK) Group Corporation.

Main Products and Services

CHALCO is a vertically integrated producer, operating across the aluminum value chain from bauxite mining, alumina refining, and smelting, to production of primary aluminum. As the largest integrated alumina and primary aluminum producer in China, CHALCO supplies alumina to its own four integrated plants and generates savings on transportation, warehousing, and related costs. In addition, CHALCO is able to assure its primary aluminum-smelting operations with a stable supply of alumina from its own alumina refineries. Its leading market position and vertical integrated operations generate a competitive advantage over its competitors.

The Company mainly operates in three business segments: the alumina business segment, the primary aluminum business segment, and corporate and other services segment.

Alumina business segment

This segment involves mining operations and purchasing of bauxite and other raw materials, refining bauxite into alumina, selling of alumina to the group's primary aluminum smelters in the primary aluminum segment, and marketing of the remaining alumina output to its external customers. This business segment also includes the production and sale of alumina hydrate, alumina chemicals and gallium. Alumina chemical products can be used in the production of chemical, pharmaceutical, ceramic, and construction materials. In the process of refining bauxite into alumina, the company also produces a by-product gallium, which is used in the electronics and telecommunications industries. CHALCO carries out production and trading of alumina products in Zunyi, Chongqing, and Guangxi within China as well as in Australia.

Primary aluminum business segment

This segment includes the production and sale of primary aluminum and related products. CHALCO manufactures primary aluminum ingots, other primary aluminum products and carbon products. It also produces specialty primary aluminum, such as electrical aluminum and aluminum alloys used for special industrial applications. Concurrently, CHALCO operates carbon plants to produce carbon products such as carbon anodes and cathodes that are used in its smelting operations. These carbon plants supply carbon products to the aluminum smelters and sell the surplus to other smelters. The company has its trading, production, and distribution of the primary aluminum products in Baotou, Fushun, Zunyi, and Lanzhou as well as in Shanxi Province.

Corporate and other services segment

This section includes operations of CHALCO headquarters, work conducted by its research institutes, and the provision of research and development services to third parties.

Challenges and Business Strategies

The domestic natural disasters of winter snowstorm and May earthquake caused substantial losses to the company in 2008. Together with the recent global financial tsunami, raw material price hikes, and sharply decreasing commodity prices posed unprecedented difficulties and challenges to CHALCO. Its total turnover in 2008 amounted to RMB 76,726 million, representing a YOY (year-over-year) decrease of 9.4%; and profit dropped to RMB 9.2 million, representing a substantial YOY decline of 99.91%. Looking forward, the company has to adopt effective measures to control costs and expenses to operate in an extremely turbulent economic environment. The group anticipates a reduction of its inventory and an increase of its revenue through an increase of its production output. It will further integrate its production, sales, and transportation functions according to a regional distribution arrangement that aims at maximizing selling prices and minimizing expenses through optimization of resources allocation. Since its procurement function fully leverages the advantages of centralized purchasing of raw materials, ancillary materials, and fuel and reduces logistics expenses, to reach to a reasonable inventory level, procurement practice will likely be consolidated based on a scientific procurement indicator.

CHALCO plans to implement a corresponding responsibility system on energy saving and emission reduction. Emphases will be exerted on close examinations of critical energy saving fields, and speeding up the progress of indicator optimization and the process of conformance to expected environmental standards. It will also seek to promote innovative energy-saving methods with new technologies and alternative energy in its production process.

CHALCO will continue focusing on resource protection and further strengthen its resource acquisition through various channels to enlarge its resource reserve. Meanwhile, the group will put more efforts in the management of investment and the construction of mines. It will also strive to improve its self-sufficiency ratio of bauxite supply while attempting a reduction of the cost of ores.

T.K.P. Leung

References

Aluminum Corporation of China Limited (2008). Interim Report. http://www.chalco.com.cn/zl/html/145/2008/20080908112706156472243/20080908112818078268527.pdf. Retrieved on 22 March 2009.

Aluminum Corporation of China Limited (2008). About CHALCO. http://www.chalco.com.cn/zl/web/column.jsp?ColumnID=130. Retrieved on 22 March 2009.

Aluminum Corporation of China Limited SWOT Analysis and Company Profile (2008). Datamonitor. Retrieved on 22 March 2009.

Aluminum in Asia-Pacific (2008). Datamonitor. Retrieved on 22 March 2009.

ANGANG STEEL

Corporate Address and Contact Information

Angang Steel Company Ltd.
Angang Industrial Zone
Tiexi District
Anshan, Liaoning Province 114021
People's Republic of China
Phone: (86)412-841-7273
Fax: (86)412-672-7772
http://www.ansteel.com.cn

The Angang Steel Company Ltd. (ANSTEEL 鞍钢股份有限公司) is located in Liaoyang, Liaoning Province, which is one of the oldest and continuously inhabited cities in northeast China, and an area rich in natural resources of iron, diamond, boron, petroleum, and natural gas. ANSTEEL engages in the production and sale of steel products primarily in the People's Republic of China, which include ferrous metal smelting and steel pressing and processing. The company offers hot-rolled sheets, cold-rolled sheets, galvanized steel sheets, color-coating plates, silicon steel, moderately thick plates, wire rods, and seamless steel pipes.

Historical Development

Established in 1992, Angang Steel Company Limited was formerly known as Angang New Steel Company Limited. ANSTEEL is controlled by the state-owned Anshan Iron and Steel Group, a holding company that traced its history back to 1948. Anshan Iron and Steel Group operates through some 30 subsidiaries (including Angang Steel), six large iron ore mines, four iron ore dressing, one iron-making, three steel-making, and more than a dozen steel-rolling plants. The framework for state ownership of steel plants was reaffirmed in the Chinese's Government's 10th Five-Year Plan for National Economic and Social Development, which specified that the state must hold a controlling stake in strategic enterprises of "pillar" industries that contribute to the national economy. On 8 May 1997, Anshan Iron and Steel Group consolidated its cold rolling, wire rod, and thick plate operations, and Angang New Steel Co. Ltd. was incorporated as a joint stock company within the Anshan Iron and Steel Group.

In December 2004, Angang New Steel Co. Ltd., listed on both the Hong Kong (HKG: 0347 — Ticker: ANGGY) and Shenzhen Stock Exchanges (000898) under the Anshan Iron and Steel Group (Angang), announced that the company planned to acquire a full ownership of the Angang Group New Iron and Steel Co. Ltd. (Angang Group Xingang), which is also controlled by Angang. In June of 2005, the combined firm proposed changing the corporate name from Angang New Steel Company Limited (ANSC) to Angang Steel Company Limited (ANSTEEL). In 2006, Angang Steel Company Limited purchased 100% equity of Angang Group New Iron and Steel Co. Ltd., and the company name was officially changed to Angang Steel Company Limited. The consolidated company produces products for both the foreign and domestic markets, and is primarily focused upon ferrous metal smelting and steel pressing and processing. In 2008, Angang announced that it would build a new steel plant in Fujian Province, PRC, which is expected to have a steel-making capacity of 10 million ton per annum.

Main Products, Corporate Structure, and Leadership

ANSTEEL is a specialized manufacturer of a wide variety of section steel products. The company prides itself on the high quality of its outputs, which include hot- and cold-rolled sheet stock, galvanized sheets, plate steel, medium thickness sheets, wire rods, seamless pipes, rails for light and heavy trains, spring steel bars, mid-steel bars, angles, channels, high-tensile steel-deformed bars, and elevator guide rails. These business-to-business products are primarily used in the PRC (about 84% domestic use) in industries such as automobile fabrication, plates for color-coating applications, construction, ship building, home electrical appliances, railway industries, and in the manufacture of pipelines.

With Angang Holding as the controlling shareholder, Angang Steel Company is a joint-stock enterprise with district property rights. Corporate officers for ANSTEEL include: Zhang Xiaogang (executive chairman and manager of Angang Group), Chen Ming (vice chairman, general manager, and executive director), Fu Wei (deputy general manager, senior engineer, and executive director), Fu Jihui (deputy secretary, senior accountant, and executive director), and Lin Daqing (deputy general manager).

The firm has seven subsidiary enterprises, including: metallurgy, machinery, chemical, engineering, technology, consultation, and maintenance. Outputs are in 22 product series with 112 different product specifications. The quality of its products has been recognized by ISO9001/9004/19011:2000 and ISO14001 certifications and quality accepted through examination by the Production Line Office of the State. Its primary SIC codes are 3312 (blast furnaces and steel mills) and 331111 (iron and steel mills). As of 2008, the company had 31,576 employees with 20,872 working in the steel-making plants, of which over 85 percent have technical secondary school diplomas or bachelor's degrees or higher. To improve the skill sets of its employees, the company has developed a training management system with almost 10,500 employees taking part through mid-2008. Each department has been charged with improving the overall quality of staff. This will be accomplished through master teaching apprentice programs.

Business Strategies

The company leans heavily on its quality management strategy. The performance excellence benchmark follows the tenants of W. Edwards Deming's continuous improvement model. A quality evaluation system has been implemented that focuses on the following indices: pass rate of outsourcing Class-A metallurgical materials, spot rate of steel products, rate of quality compliant from customers, and quality cost. The leadership team installed its quality management-benchmarking system along with the process improvement and checking analysis improvements system in 2008, and the campaign shows significant results to date. The company also developed and implemented a comprehensive and participatory management model, with all-member participation, focusing on continuing improvements.

In 2008, ANSTEEL focused its attention on marketing with two thrusts: specialized steel products and brand promotion. The firm is attempting to expand its sales channels through direct supply initiatives. There is some evidence that the strategy is working; as direct supply sales increased 3.89 percent in 2008. Specialized steel marketing initiates also appear to be working in the short run. First-half 2008 sales of specialized steel products accounted for 92.24% of the total sales volume of the company. Increases were seen in sales volumes of shipbuilding sheets (+25.54%), automotive sheets (52.64%), and home appliance sheets (27.58%) as compared with those of 2007.

ANSTEEL's Leadership is also looking for competitive advantages in the international steel products market. The company has adjusted its product mix for the international markets in response to anticipated customer needs. This strategic thrust enhanced its export coordination efforts and led to the exportation of 1.2 million ton of steel products, representing 15.63 percent of its total sales volume.

In line with the country's 11th Five-Year Plan, ANSTEEL has decreased its comprehensive energy-consumption rate, new water-consumption rate, and comprehensive energy-consumption rate when compared with 2007. The firm worked hard in the first half of 2008 to enhance its energy savings and emission reductions. These initiatives led to the best results in ANSTEEL's history in relation to utilization of blast furnace, coke, iron, and steel materials and consumption of energy and water — comprehensive energy-consumption rate (−2.17%,), new water-consumption rate (−10.56%), and comparable energy-consumption rate (−1.12%) when compared with those of the same period of 2007.

Challenges and Future Development Plans

A relatively small portion of ANSTEEL outputs finds its way into the export market. International customers include the automotive, construction, shipbuilding, railway, and pipeline construction industries. The worldwide recession affected the company in a variety of unfavorable ways: price increase in raw materials and fuels, constraints on transportation capacity, and natural disasters. Nonetheless, by adjusting its marketing strategy and optimizing production management, the company improved operation performance and achieved a record high for its output, sales revenue ($79.6 billion) and total profits of iron, steel and steel products ($12.06 billion) in 2008. As ANSTEEL imports some of its raw materials, equipment, spare parts, and materials, there does not appear to any significant foreign exchange risk. Its main competitors within the PRC are Baosteel, Handan Iron & Steel, and Wuhan Iron & Steel.

In 2008, ANSTEEL recorded sales of $79.6 billion, representing production of about 16 million tons of steel and 15 million tons of steel products. The company plans to utilize its competitive advantage in integrative production management and control to expedite progress in realized production output. Goals include optimizing management initiatives, rationalizing resource allocations, and maintaining effective coordination in production management, information exchange, and logistics, and transportation.

Quality benchmarking will continue to be implemented and enhanced leading to additional performance excellence. The firm intends to strengthen its investments in scientific research and development leading to technical innovations. ANSTEEL hopes to control raw material costs and establish a standard production cost management model in the future. The company has stated that it will initiate a comprehensive set of 36 energy-saving projects aimed at cost savings and emission reductions.

James P. Gilbert

References

Alon, I and JR McIntyre (eds.) (2008). *Globalization of Chinese Enterprises*. New York: Palgrave Macmillan.

Angang New Steel to buy parent assets (4 January 2005). XinhuaNet. www1.cei.gov.cn/ce/doc/ceni/200501042121.htm. Retrieved on 16 August 2009.

Angang New Steel to change name to Angang Steel Co Ltd. (27 June 2006). *Steel Guru*. www.steelguru.com/selectednews/index/2006/006/027/archives.html. Retrieved on 18 April 2009.

Angang Steel Company Limited (21 September 2008). *Interim Report 2008*. Financial Reports. angang.wspr.com.hk/index.php?SectionID=FinancialReports&PageID=2009&Language=eng. Retrieved on 24 January 2009.

Angang's listed arm to acquire another subsidiary of the group to integrate operations (31 December 2004). *China Business News* at High Beam Research. www.highbeam.com/doc/1G1-136213768.html. Retrieved on 16 August 2009.

Google Finance (2009). Angang Steel Company Limited. http://www.google.com/finance?q=Angang+Steel+Company+Limited. Retrieved on 14 April 2009.

ANYANG IRON & STEEL

Corporate Address and Contact Information

Anyang Iron & Steel Group Corporation
Meiyuanzhuang
Yindu District, Anyang
Henan Province 455004
People's Republic of China
Phone: (86)37-2312-2587
Fax: (86)37-2312-3096
www.angang.com.cn

After over 50 years of development, Anyang Iron & Steel Company (AISCO 安阳钢铁股份有限公司) — lately called *Angang* — has become one of the largest companies of China, and also an important base for the iron and steel industry in Henan Province, Central China. Since its foundation, AISCO, which is a state-controlled company, has maintained its profits in the past 27 years, and stands out among the 15 largest enterprises with the production capacity of five million tons of steel per annum.

Historical Development

Anyang Iron & Steel Company was founded in 1958. According to the International Iron and Steel Institute, AISCO ranks as the 12th largest Chinese company in the steel industry, and the 33rd largest in the same sector globally in 2007. In recent years, AISCO has won various awards, such as the National May 1st Labor Day Certificate, the Golden Horse Prize for Corporate Excellence, the National Outstanding Enterprise for its work policy, and the Enterprise for Outstanding Contributions to Henan Province.

AISCO's current leadership team include: Li Wenshan, chairman of the Board; Wang Ziliang, president and general manager, and Li Fuyong, deputy general manager. AISCO has more than 20,000 employees in 19 subsidiaries, and is engaged with steel production, mining, coking, and metallurgical construction.

AISCO controls current assets that overpass US$1.2 billion (10.13 billion yuan). Its main subsidiaries include: Anyang Steel Co. Ltd., Fuli Industry Co. Ltd., Automobile Transportation Co. Ltd., Wuyang Mining Co. Ltd., International Trading Co. Ltd., Metallurgical Design Co. Ltd., Henan Angang Building Co. Ltd., and Metallurgical Materials Co. Ltd.

Main Products and Services

The company is engaged in mining, coking, smelting, machinery, metallurgical construction, transportation, and trade. It is capable of providing more than 30 varieties of steel products and chemicals according to more than 2000 specifications, such as plates, steckel mill-rolled plates, high speed wire, reinforced bars, round steel, angle steel, channel steel, nodular cast iron pipes, and so forth. In 2007, AISCO produced nine million tons of steel, and produced ten million tons in 2008.

The company offers the following as main products: steel-making pig iron, foundry pig iron, carbon steel length reinforcement bars, round bars, medium channels and plates, heavy plates, sheets, seamless tubes and pipes, alloy steel (other than stainless), and cast iron pipes.

Anyang Iron & Steel Company is certified according to ISO9002 (1997) in quality management systems. The company has the following operations: blast furnaces — one 2.800 cu meters; steel-making plant — three basic oxygen converters one of which is 6 tons, the other 20 tons, and the last 100 tons; continuous casting machines — billets and double plates; slabs, including one SMS Demag for ultra-wide slabs (annual capacity 1.1 m tons); rolling mills of Morgan Construction for wire rods (550,000 tons); one medium plate (500,000 tons); a wide hot strip/sheet (3.5m tons); and seamless tube and pipe mills.

Challenges and Business Strategies

In March 2003, during the 10th Chinese Five-Year Plan (2001–2005), AISCO adopted a "three-stage" strategy that aimed to turn the company into a forward-looking iron and steel corporation with revenue of over RMB 30 billion within five years (2003–2008).

When it is carried out, "three one-thirds" formulates AISCO's product mix: with the first third be rounds, rod, and section covers; the second, plate and steckel mill-rolled plates; and finally, steel sheets. The plates-to-rolled steel ratio aims to be over 70 percent, and surcharge and technical content for the products also increase at leaps and bounds. As a result, the company's core competitive power has been greatly strengthened.

AISCO's major competitors in the greater China market include: Anshan Iron and Steel, located in Anshan; Baosteel, in Shanghai; and China Steel, located in Kaohsiung (Gaoxiong), Taiwan. While the company has both domestic and overseas product distributions, its major domestic market is China's central and southern regions. In 2008, AISCO received government approval for a 1.5 million-tone of cold-rolling mill. The company also reports investments for energy saving and emission reduction that surpasses RMB 2.1 billion.

In 2008, AISCO's annual income reached RMB 51 billion, the first year that it broke 50 billion yuan. The company reaped net profits of RMB 579.669 million in the first half of 2008, soaring 25.8% from a year before, thanks to hiking output and rising steel prices. AISCO gained operating revenue of RMB 20.068 billion, hiking 88.45% year after year. Its operating profits jumped 17.31% to RMB 794.783 million and total profits leaped 17.11% to RMB 796.4469 million. Basic earnings per share stood at CNY 0.25. However, the crises in the later half of 2008 changed this, and the net revenue declined almost 90 percent for the full year, due to weak demand and price decline. Therefore, in 2008 the operating income stood at 31.1 billion, 42.62% more than 2007, but net profits in CNY were only 0.12 billion, down 89.38% from 2007. The earnings per share were 91.38% less than the year before.

In light of the challenging business environment, several leading Chinese steel mills are set to cut production to cope with the pressure of weak demand, closing down their iron-smelting furnaces. The Shougang Group and three other big domestic iron and steel manufacturers slashed production by 20 percent in October 2008 amid slack domestic demand and dropping steel prices. Major regional steel makers such as Anyang Iron & Steel Group. Hebei Iron & Steel Group and Shandong Iron & Steel Group may have to follow the same route. However, given the huge growth potential of the Chinese market, in the coming years AISCO will still likely play an active and important role in the country's continuing economic reform.

Marco Antonio Tourinho Furtado and Tays Torres Ribeiro Chagas

References

Anyang Iron & Steel Group Co. (2009). Company profile. http://www.angang.com.cn/english/introduction.asp. Retrieved on 10 May 2009.

BusinessWeek (2008). Anyang Iron & Steel Inc. (600569: Shanghai Stock Exchange). http://investing.business-week.com/research/stocks/snapshot/snapshot.asp?capId=5497439. Retrieved on 18 December 2008.

China's steel prices plunge (13 October 2008). *China Daily*, http://www.chinadaily.com.cn/bizchina/2008-10/13/content_7100874.htm. Retrieved on 12 May 2009.

Hoover's (2008). Anyang Iron & Steel Group Co. http://www.hoovers.com/anyang-iron-&-steel/—ID__149791—/free-co-factsheet.xhtml. Retrieved on 6 December 2008.

Iron & Steel Works of the World Directory (2009). London: Metal Bulletin Directories.

BAIDU

Corporate Address and Contact Information

Baidu, Inc.
12th Floor Ideal International Plaza
58 West-North 4th Ring Road
Beijing 100080
People's Republic of China
Phone: (86)10-8262-1188
Fax: (86)10-8260-7007
http://www.baidu.com

The business revolution created by the Internet has spawned a set of small but rising in importance Chinese firms, working close to the global technology frontier and generating considerable interest. Baidu.com (百度) is perhaps the most important, as it operates in the space where profits seem the largest but also where the competition may be the strongest: paid search, with Google as the dominant player. Baidu's importance comes from its position of market share dominance in the world's largest Internet market, at least by number of users. The company has shown tenacity and innovation in its battle with Google for being the access point for the large and rapidly growing Internet audience in China.

At the same time, this is a very dynamic industry, always subject to rapid and unpredictable technological change. A position of strength today is of limited value in predicting sustainability over time.

Analysts of Chinese firms have been engaged in a significant debate over whether these firms are capable of competing with Western global firms. A group of pessimists argue that a combination of Chinese government involvement, a legacy of limited competition, disadvantages of size, organization, and technology, and innovation weaknesses make Chinese firms generally unable to hold their own against the formidable strengths of Western firms. By contrast, optimists cite the numerous Chinese success stories, especially those in high-tech industries. Baidu.com is one of the best examples of such a success, largely because it has been able to leverage its position as a Chinese firm and has adopted very competitive business strategies.

The Chinese Internet Market

Between June 2005 and December 2007, the number of Chinese web users doubled from 100 million to just over 200 million. In early 2008, China surpassed the United States with the largest number of Internet users. And by March 2009 that number had climbed to 316 million with more than 100 million, or one-third, accessing the Web via a cell phone. This figure represents about a 20% penetration rate of the potential Chinese Internet market, as compared to more than 70% rate in the United States China is likely to experience several more years of very rapid growth in Internet usage combined with higher spending rates by users as incomes in China continue to rise.

The growth of the Internet in a country long noted for control of access to information is quite amazing and reflects both the weakening of that control and the special value of the Internet to the Chinese. The Internet offers Chinese the opportunity to interact with each other in new and important ways, along with new forms of entertainment designed to appeal especially to those under 30. Because accessing the Internet is much more a cell phone experience in Chinese, social and interactive gaming via this connection, along with web-based value-added services (think text messaging), were popular in China before gaining importance in the West. Firms in the gaming space include NetEase and Shanda; those providing access to various services include KongZhong and Tom Online. Some of the firms in the social networking and video-sharing arena include Xiaonei.com, Tudou.com, and Wealink.com. Full purpose sites include Sina, Tencent, and Sohu. Other search engine firms are Sogou and Sousou. Aside from its rapid growth, Internet business in China has seen a considerable process of mergers and acquisitions since 2000, as larger firms have snapped up smaller ones to build a critical mass of services and users.

There are several negative features to the Chinese Internet, most importantly the continuing effort to control the content available to anyone accessing the Web from inside China. The Chinese government remains fearful of certain political content and sometimes uses the guise of controlling pornography to achieve this end. Known without affection inside China as the "Great Chinese Firewall", this set of restrictions even reaches so far as to undermine commercial activity such as eBay and its Chinese rival Alibaba. Coupled with the poor availability of broadband access, the Internet in China has several drawbacks that dampen the potential for this business in spite of the enormous potential.

Baidu's Operations and Business Model

Baidu was founded in 1999, shortly after Google, by a Chinese born but Silicon Valley-experienced executive, Li Yanhong (Robin). Li (born in 1968) remains the CEO and Chairman. His experience in the United States includes a master's degree in computer science and significant work in Internet companies. Baidu provides a full service, Chinese language search engine for accessing the Internet in China, along with an expanding array of other services to attract users. These include a collaboratively developed encyclopedia Baidu Baike (similar to Wikipedia, which is blocked in China) and an online community with query search. Perhaps the most important is an MP3 search service for finding music across the Web, though this capability has been criticized for providing pirated versions of music. Baidu also operates a search engine in Japan. The business model for Baidu is a combination of paid search advertising, similar to Google, and the sale of services and products over the Web. Advertisers are able to bid at auction for positions in Web pages generating search results for related products. By contrast, Google has advertisers bid an auction for the right to place ads next to search results.

Some measure of the size of the market for Baidu comes from advertising on the Web in China. One estimate puts such ad spending in China for 2009 at $1.7 billion, compared to $25.7 billion in the United States. Of the companies using search as a marketing tool in China and choosing more than one search engine, 86% use Baidu and 60% use Google. In response to Baidu, Google has adopted a more China-centered strategy with a more Chinese-looking site, hiring many more Chinese and developing strategic alliances with other Chinese Internet sites.

Baidu certainly benefits greatly from a "home court" advantage, especially its development from the outset in Chinese. But there has been a price to pay for its role as a Chinese firm. Baidu operates in the murky environment in China for intellectual property, which has led to several lawsuits by Western firms for supporting piracy. It has cooperated with the Chinese government in controlling news seen as unfavorable by the government, as has Google. And, Baidu has engaged in practices related to its paid search results that compromised the integrity of the information it provides. This has raised serious questions about the ability of the company to provide accurate and complete information.

Financial Data and Future Outlook

Baidu is somewhat unusual for a Chinese firm, as it is not only privately owned but publicly traded. Baidu has been very successful in raising capital outside of China. The initial public offering of Baidu stock was in August 2005 and the stock is trading on the NASDAQ exchange under the symbol BIDU. Nearly three-fourths of Baidu stock is owned by Western institutional investors and mutual funds. The company had a market capitalization in May 2009 of about $8 billion. This relatively high market capitalization rests on rapid growth in revenues and earnings and on a very high level of overall profitability. From 2006 to 2008, revenues grew from $107 million to $468 million; during the same period, net income grew from $38 million to $154 million. For 2008, this represents an extraordinary 31% return on revenue. In late 2008, the company had more than 6,000 employees.

Though Baidu, Inc. has some stains on its record and it benefits, perhaps unfairly, from the special aspects of the Chinese market, this company has a striking capacity to operate in one of the most competitive of all industries. It faces formidable competition, not only from many other Chinese firms but also from a firm that strikes fear in many companies, Google. The Internet business space remains in its infancy — less than 15 years have passed since e-business began. But Baidu is as well positioned as any Chinese firm to cope successfully with the changes to come.

Thomas D. Lairson

References

Baidu, Inc. (2009). Income statement. http://finance.yahoo.com/q/is?s=BIDU&annual. Retrieved on 26 May 2009.
Baidu.com, Inc. http://www.cnanalyst.com/baidu.html. Retrieved on 26 May 2009.

Barboza, D (2006). The rise of Baidu — that's Chinese for Google. *New York Times*, 5 August.

Chao, L and E Smith (2008). Google aims to crack China with music push. *Wall Street Journal*, 6 February, A1.

CNBC (2008). Baidu shares sink: Analyst cites Chinese TV report. 17 November. http://www.cnbc.com/id/27772580/site/14081545?__source=yahoo%7Cheadline%7Cquote%7Ctext%7C&par=yahoo. Retrieved on 26 May 2009.

The Economist (2008). The Internet in China: Alternative Reality. 31 January.

Fu, R (2009). China search engine report 2008: Advertisers and users behavior study. China Internet Watch, 7 March. http://www.chinainternetwatch.com/28/2008-china-search-engine-report. Retrieved on 25 May 2009.

Fu, R (2009). Update on the number of China Internet users. China Internet Watch, 14 April. http://www.chinainternetwatch.com/138/china-internet-users. Retrieved on 24 May 2009.

Gilboy, G (2004). The myth behind China's miracle. *Foreign Affairs*, 83(4) (July/August): 33–49.

Greising, D (2006). Gunning for Google. *Chicago Tribune Online*, 3 December. http://www.chicagotribune.com/business/chi-061203google-china-story,0,277335.story. Retrieved on 26 May 2009.

Hotchkiss, G (2007). Chinese eye tracking study: Google versus Baidu. 15 June. http://searchengineland.com/chinese-eye-tracking-study-baidu-vs-google-11477. Retrieved on 25 May 2009.

Naughton, B (2007). *The Chinese Economy*. Cambridge: MIT Press, pp. 349–374.

Segal, A (2002). *Digital Dragons*. Ithaca, NY: Cornell University Press.

Tschang, C (2009). Search engine squeeze? *BusinessWeek*, 12 January, p. 21.

BANK OF CHINA

Corporate Address and Contact Information

Bank of China Limited (SIC — 6021, NAICS — 522110)
1 Fuxingmen Nei Dajie
Beijing 100818
People's Republic of China
Phone: (86)10-6659-2638
Fax: (86)10-6659-4568
http://www.boc.cn
bocir@bank-of-china.com

The Bank of China Limited (BOC 中国银行股份有限公司) is the oldest bank in China and it ranks third among China's big four state-owned banks. With strong ties to the Chinese government, BOC has remained closely connected to China's financial history. It is China's flagship foreign exchange lender.

Historical Development

BOC was founded in 1912 when Dr. Sun Yatsen, president of the provisional government of the Republic of China, sanctioned the change of the existing Da Qing Bank in Shanghai into the Bank of China. BOC first served as the central bank until 1928 when it became the government-chartered international exchange bank. In 1949, it became the state-designated specialized foreign exchange bank.

Since its beginning, BOC has had international aspirations. BOC London Agency, the first overseas branch of Chinese banks, was established in 1929. BOC's global network grew gradually, with 34 overseas branches opening in the 1930s and 1940s. In 1949, BOC's operations split into two; one relocated with the Chinese Nationalist Party to Taiwan (later privatized in 1971), while the other stayed on the mainland as the BOC. Throughout the years, BOC contributed much to the recovery and development of the national economy, and it has since played an important and active role in the development of foreign trade.

With the opening up of the Chinese economy in the late 1970s, the Chinese financial sector underwent a few significant reforms. A major banking reform in 1994 transformed BOC from a specialized bank to a wholly state-owned commercial bank. BOC also played an important role in unifying the exchange rates, purchases and sales of foreign exchange, and incorporating foreign-funded enterprises into the foreign exchange sales system. That BOC later became one of the notes issuing banks in Hong Kong and Macau demonstrated its substantial financial strength, which helped stabilize the financial markets in Hong Kong and Macau before and after their handovers in 1997 and 1999, respectively.

The Asian Financial Crisis in 1997–1998 prompted BOC to recapitalize and restructure its banking system. In Hong Kong, it incorporated its wholly owned subsidiary specializing in investment banking, BOC International Holdings Ltd. This was the most internationalized investment bank established in Chinese banking history. In late 2001, BOC's Hong Kong operations were restructured again, merging 10 member banks of the former BOC Group, to incorporate the BOC (HK) Ltd., which later listed successfully on the Hong Kong Stock Exchange in July 2002.

In 2003, BOC was named one of the pilot banks for joint-stock reform. A year later, it was formally incorporated in Beijing as a state-controlled joint stock commercial bank. Two years later, in June 2006, BOC went public. It listed on the Hong Kong Stock Exchange and raised RMB 20 billion. The next month it listed on the Shanghai A-Stock Exchange. BOC stocks have been performing solidly since their IPOs.

Structure, Governance, and Leadership

BOC was among the first to be selected as a Shanghai-listed model company for corporate governance. Its organizational structure is headed by a Board of Directors with 15 members. The Board is assisted by a number of committees including asset-liability management and budget, business development and co-ordination, auditing, risk review, and remuneration. Xiao Gang has been BOC's chair since July 2004, and Li Lihui the vice-chair and president since August and July 2004, respectively. They bring with them many years of working experience in the banking industry, including the People's Bank of China for Xiao and the Industrial and Commercial Bank of China for Li. As of 24 May 2009, BOC has 249,278 employees.

Among BOC Group, members are BOC Hong Kong, BOCI International, and BOCG Insurance. Selected subsidiaries include BOC Group Insurance Company Ltd., BOC Aviation Private Ltd., BOC Hong Kong (Group) Ltd., BOCI-Prudential Asset Management Ltd., BOC Group Investment Ltd., and others.

Business Strengths and Ranking

BOC is engaged in banking and related financial services, primarily in China, Hong Kong and Macau. As of the end of 2008, BOC has 10,789 domestic and overseas branches, subsidiaries, and outlets, with a network in 29 countries and regions including Asia, Africa, America, and Europe. BOC's five principal lines of operations are: corporate banking, personal banking, treasury operations, investment banking, and insurance.

Since its founding, BOC has been known for business innovation and enhancement of product function and service quality in the domestic banking industry. BOC continues to bring in newer products and services and undergoes reforms as needed. It is the most internationalized commercial bank in China and among the first Chinese banks to recruit international experts. It is also one of the first to introduce business management concepts into its operations with a vision to become a premiere international bank. Its operations relating to international settlement, foreign exchange, and trade finance continue to be recognized by customers and peers.

BOC ranks favorably both domestically and internationally. Within China, BOC is the largest foreign-exchange bank and the second largest lender by assets. Internationally, BOC is the world's fourth largest bank by market capitalization (USD$96.2 billion). On *Fortune Global 500*, BOC moved up from rank 215 in 2007 to 187 in 2008; and on *Forbes Global 2000*, its rank moved from 56 in 2008 to 30 in 2009. It has also won numerous awards, including: Best Bank in China by *Euromoney*, Best Domestic Bank in China by *Euromoney* and the *Asset*, Best Trade Finance Bank in China and Best Foreign Exchange Bank in China by *Global Finance*, Best Local Trade Bank in China from *Trade Finance*, and one of the Top 10 Product Service Enterprises in China by the *Far Eastern Economic Review*.

Corporate Social Responsibility

BOC has demonstrated corporate social responsibility over the years. The 2008 earthquake in Sichuan brought upon emergency response mechanism by BOC. It opened a green channel for global donations with free remittance services for donors. Domestic and overseas BOC employees donated RMB 150 million toward disaster relief. BOC also pledged up to RMB 300 billion to support key enterprises, backbone industries, and major infrastructure projects in affected areas.

Additional areas in which BOC has played a supporting role include education and culture. BOC held about 60% of the student loan market in 2008 and ranked first among Chinese banks with RMB 10.88 billion of outstanding student loans. Among BOC's many contributions were RMB 10 million to the Tan Kan Kee Foundation for Science Awards, supporting funds for nearly 92,000 students to finish their studies during the 2008–2009 school year, a Poverty Relief and Education Charity Fund to promote education in remote and underdeveloped areas, and support for the Macau Academy Education Fund Society. BOC also formed a strategic alliance with the National Center for the Performing Arts to support two concerts and an art event. BOC Paris Branch sponsored the Treasures of Dunhuang exhibition held in Paris.

Challenges and Future Development Plans

A significant challenge faced by BOC remains the appreciation of RMB since the 2005 foreign exchange currency reform. The rising RMB has eroded foreign exchange assets. In response, BOC has been pushing RMB business development and reduce foreign bond investment. In concert with governmental efforts to internationalize RMB in global trading, BOC is gearing up to handle RMB-based cross-border trade settlements. It plans to use the clearing platform of BOC HK to facilitate RMB trade settlements there as well as among the ASEAN members. In addition, BOC is moving closer to an offshore RMB market in using RMB in global trading. These would help toward liberalizing the Chinese currency outside China, easing liquidity problems in the developed world, and shielding China's export-oriented economy from the impact of exchange rate fluctuations. Furthermore, BOC's newer RMB loans went mainly toward infrastructure projects involving railways, subways, and nuclear-power plants. Most significantly, BOC is the lead bank to provide the governments of Hong Kong, Macau, and Zhuhai a loan of RMB 22 billion for the construction of the main bridge linking the three cities. BOC is also lending support of RMB 9.3 billion to Taiwan enterprises active in high-technology manufacturing on the mainland.

Another major challenge is the global economic downturn of 2008. China's GDP growth slowed to 6.1% in the first quarter of 2009. Compared to foreign counterparts, China's banking sector still enjoys stable prospects. From 2007 to 2008, BOC's total assets have increased from RMB 5.99 trillion to RMB 6.96 trillion; total liabilities from RMB 5.54 trillion to RMB 6.46 trillion; shareholders' equity from RMB 454 billion to RMB 464 billion; and net income from RMB 56.2 billion to RMB 64.3 billion. However, due to BOC's exposure to overseas markets, it has suffered losses from its US sub-prime mortgage linked investments. Foreign currency assets that accounted for 35% of BOC's total assets in 2008 went down to 29% in the first quarter of 2009. For the same period, its net profit fell by 14.4% at RMB 18.57 billion (compared with RMB 21.7 billion a year earlier). Affected by the credit crunch, some initial foreign stake-holders sold their BOC holdings in early January 2009. BOC's chairman commented that there were many uncertainties and BOC felt the pressure. Correspondingly, BOC adjusted its assets-liabilities structure, reduced its foreign currency-dominated investment securities by 4.3%, and increased its RMB-dominated investments securities by 18.29%. In view of the government's latest macroeconomic policy, which includes a stimulus package in RMB 4 trillion to stimulate economic growth and an aggressively relaxed monetary policy to boost the economy, BOC has responded promptly by seizing related business opportunities.

BOC's main competitors include the Industrial and Commercial Bank of China, China Construction Bank, HSBC, and JP Morgan Chase among others. Historically speaking, BOC has always been on the top of most others international banks in China. Its international reputation has been further enhanced by achieving the "zero mistake and zero complaint" target as the sole official banking partner and major distribution channel for tickets and sale of licenced merchandise at the 2008 Beijing Olympics and Paralympics. BOC's future plans will include extending its international reach and improving its overseas business. It is looking toward further international expansion and becoming a global player. Already BOC became the first Chinese bank to join the TFFP (trade finance facilitation program) of the IADB (Inter-American Development Bank) in late 2008. As a participant, BOC will be able to expand its trading activities with Latin America and the Caribbean. Taking advantage of the global liquidity crisis, BOC has started offering residential mortgages in the mainstream UK mortgage market since May 2009.

Victoria Chu

References

Bank of China. *Business Week*. http://investing.businessweek.com/research/stocks/financials/financials.asp?ric=601988.SS. Retrieved on 11 June 2009.

Bank of China. *CSR 2008: Report of Bank of China Limited*. http://pic.bankofchina.com/bocappd/report/200905/P020090506420249785107.pdf. Retrieved on 11 June 2009.

Bank of China (2008). History of BOC. http://www.bank-of-china.com/en/aboutboc/ab1/200810/t20081027_8299.html. Retrieved on 13 June 2009.

Bank of China announces 2009 first quarter results profit attributable to shareholders reached RMB18.47 billion (28 April 2009). http://www.bank-of-china.com/en/bocinfo/bi1/200904/t20090428_673793.html. Retrieved on 9 June 2009.

Bank of China chairman lays out growth plan: Xiao addresses complex structure and jump in lending (28 May 2009). *The Wall Street Journal Asia*, p. 10.

Bank of China deal to keep bridge tolls down (15 April 2009). *South China Morning Post*, News, p. 3.

BOC eyes cross-border yuan trade settlements (15 April 2009). *South China Morning Post*, Business, p. 2.

BOC to begin UK mortgages (1 May 2009). *Financial Times Business*, LexisNexis Academic, 27 May 2009.

China moves closer to offshore yuan market (27 May 2009). *CE Inet Currency and Capital Markets*, Emerging Markets Information Services, 29 May 2009.

Chinese giant world No. 1 (15 April 2009). *The Australian*, Finance, p. 18.

Economist Intelligent Unit. *China: Monthly Report May 2009*, 27 May 2009.

Fortune Global 500 (21 July 2009). *Fortune*. http://money.cnn.com/magazines/fortune/global500/2008/full_list/101_200.html. Retrieved on 15 June 2009.

International Company Profiles: Bank of China Limited (24 May 2009). *Worldscope*, LexisNexis Academic, 27 May 2009.

The Global 2000 (8 April 2009). *Forbes*. http://www.forbes.com/lists/2009/18/global-09_The-Global-2000_Rank.html. Retrieved on 15 June 2009.

Toyoda, H (2008). First Chinese bank joins IADB trade programme. *Trade Finance*, 11(8): 24. EBSCOhost Business Source Complete, 29 May 2009.

Zhu, M (2009). Bank of China: What China's banks have learned from the crisis? *Euromoney* 40 (480), Banking 37. EBSCOhost Business Source Complete, 27 May 2009.

BANK OF COMMUNICATIONS

Corporate Address and Contact Information

Bank of Communications
188 Yincheng Zhong Road
Shanghai 200120
People's Republic of China
Phone: (86)-21-5876-6688
Fax: (86)-21-5879-8398
www.bankcomm.com

Having just celebrated its 100th anniversary in 2008, Bank of Communications (BOCOM 交通银行股份有限公司), now China's fifth largest, is the first internationally public share-holding bank with a longest historical standing in the Chinese banking sector. As a century-old bank, the development of BOCOM reflects the turbulent social history of the country in the last 100 years. In its early stage, BOCOM devoted itself to the promotion of the Chinese national economy, and in the last three decades, the bank served as a pioneer in China's financial reform. BOCOM is the first to launch the joint-stock system in the Chinese banking industry; the first to introduce competition into the banking sector; the first to bring in assets/liability ratio management to control risk; the first commercial bank to integrate banking, insurance, and securities in its business; the first to introduce overseas strategic investors; and the first among its peers to be listed in the Stock Exchange Market outside the mainland China.

Historical Development

BOCOM was initially founded on 4 March 1908, in the late Qing Dynasty, with the mission of regaining the licensing of railroads from overseas invaders and taking over the business of foreign remittance from foreign banks opened at that time in China. With its successful recapturing the right of way from Beijing and Wuhan late that year, the bank emerged onto the Chinese economic and financial stage. BOCOM opened its headquarters in Beijing, and soon started its branches in Tianjin, Shanghai, Wuhan, and

Guangzhou. The bank was the earliest in China's banking history to set up overseas branches in Hong Kong, Singapore, Rangoon, and an office in Saigon.

During the late Qing Dynasty, in terms of scale and position, BOCOM was next only to the Bank of Da Qing, then Chinese Central Bank, and was one of the note-issuing banks in the country. In the ensuing Warlord Era (1916–1928), BOCOM once again played the role of a national bank through note issue and national treasury co-management. In the Nationalists government, it was one of the four major banks as well as an important component of the financial system.

With the founding of People's Republic of China, Banks of Communications was restructured and re-opened on 1 November 1949. The bank was positioned as a financial institution with main business ranged from long-term credit loans to industrial, mining, communications, and transportation undertakings. But in 1952, the Ministry of Finance of the Chinese government took over the management of the bank, and in its foundation in 1954 the People's Construction Bank of China was established. Four years later, in 1958, Bank of Communications, except for its Hong Kong branch, stopped operation and was incorporated into People's Bank of China and People's Construction Bank of China, each taking over part of its business, thus resulted in the suspension of BOCOM.

With the economic reform starting from the 1980s, Shanghai municipal government proposed in 1984 to found a Shanghai-based comprehensive bank in order to regain its key position as an international financial center. The application was approved on 24 July 1986 and BOCOM resumed operation again on 1 April 1987. It was then China's first state-owned, joint-stock commercial bank. From 1987 to the end of 1993, BOCOM undertook a series of exploring and tentative measures in its management, which demonstrated successes as well as failures. Among them, the two-level corporate governance on a central and local basis was subsequently found a serious block to its further development at that time. On 8 January 1994, BOCOM underwent a round of restructuring, which turned the two-level corporate governance into a centralized system after the shareholders elected a new Board of Directors and a Board of Supervisors under the new articles of incorporation of the bank. This was a critical step and marked a new milestone in BOCOM's development.

Corporate Structure and Services

As a public company, BOCOM has the standard corporate governance structure in place with shareholders' general meeting, board of directors, board of supervisors, and senior management at the top. At present, Mr. Hu Huaibang serves as chairman of BOD, the directors of which come from different international countries and regions including the United Kingdom, the United States and Hong Kong SAR. Under the board of directors are five specialized committees, namely, the strategy committee, the audit committee, the risk management committee, the personnel and remuneration committee, and the social responsibility committee. The bank's senior management is headed by Mr. Li Jun (president), and the five specialized committees include the financial examination committee, the credit policy committee, the credit approving committee, the assets liabilities management committee, and the risk management committee. BOCOM aims to run a comprehensive bank with two systems, one being the traditional banking system by the bank itself, and the other being the non-banking financial service by those subsidiaries such as BOCOM Shroders Fund Management Co. Ltd., a joint venture with Shroders, established in August 2005, the acquired Hubei International Trust and Investment Co. Ltd., BOCOM Financial Leasing Company, and BOCOM International Holdings Limited in Hong Kong.

BOCOM's network includes 29 provincial branches and 2,625 outlets in 148 major cities all over China except for Tibet and Qinghai. Its overseas branches found locations in New York, Tokyo, Hong Kong, Singapore, Seoul, Macao, and Frankfurt as well as a representative office in London. In addition,

BOCOM has correspondent relations with over 1,000 banks in 125 countries or regions. At the end of 2008, the bank has 76,000 employees.

BOCOM provides diversified and comprehensive professional financial services in fields such as corporate banking, personal banking, international banking, and fee-based business. The bank focuses on mid- and high-end customers with high-value-added products or services such as its "OTO Fortune" and "BOCOM Fortune" brand. "OTO" stands for "one to one", and is an overall service system for its high-end customers who are qualified with at least RMB 500,000 (USD 73,529). BOCOM integrates its best resources to offer various individualized financial products or services by its CFA (*Chartered Financial Analyst*) sales representatives in service networks typically for OTO at exclusively favorable prices and service privileges, which includes financing packages, derivatives, comprehensive accounts, wealth management, financial planning, urgent assistance, and value-added services by its alliances. Other range of branded products are well represented by "FX Easy", "Man Jin Bao", "Win-To Fortune", "Pacific Card", "Nationwide Through", "Zhan Ye Tong", and "Fund Supermarket", which share a large market in the industry. The dual-currency credit card launched jointly with HSBC, known as "the Global Card for the Chinese", has 7.77 million cards in issue by 30 September 2008.

As of 31 December 2008, the bank's total asset was RMB 2.68 trillion (USD 394 billion), and its capital adequate ratio was 13.47%. Its ROAA and ROAE were 1.19% and 20.10%, respectively, and impaired loan ratio was 1.92%. The bank ranked 66th in the world in terms of total asset and 54th in terms of tier-1 capital.

Growth Strategies

Due to the undeveloped economic system in China, BOCOM was piled up with problems such as high ratio of non-performing loans, unreasonable capital structure, low capital adequacy ratio, etc. Consequently, as a part of deepening stockholding system reform, a trilogy of initiatives were launched since June 2004, which included the financial restructuring, introduction of strategic investors and listing in stock exchanges. The goal was to build the bank into a modern financial enterprise with sound corporate governance, adequate capital, tight internal control, safe operation, and admirable efficiency. The financial restructure began on 14 June 2004, when the bank took steps such as issuing subordinate debts, acquiring social insurance funds, and capital increment by the old shareholders, which in turn greatly improved its financial operations. BOCOM eventually shook off its huge non-performing assets, and the provision adequacy ratio as well the capital adequacy ratio were also enhanced. On 6 August 2004, new domestic and overseas strategic investors became significant stakeholders of the bank, among them was HSBC (Hong Kong and Shanghai Banking Corporation), which bought 19.9% of BOCOM shares. On 23 June 2005, BOCOM was listed on the Hong Kong Stock Exchange, being the first of the Chinese commercial banks on the stock exchange market outside the mainland. Two years later, on 15 May 2007, BOCOM was listed back on the Shanghai Stock Exchange, a returning to A-share market. As a market leader, BOCOM's experience in reform paves the way for the development of shareholding commercial banks in China.

Looking forward strategically, BOCOM aims at developing itself into a first-class public bank group focused on wealth management services. The so-called "four cabs" that drive the bank forward are its management orientation, business orientation, platform build-up, and the overseas strategy. Its management is oriented to construct the bank by specific standards of internationally classic public-shareholding banks. Based on the practices of advanced international banks, BOCOM has already devoted great efforts in building a procedural bank to optimize its business process. Major progress has been made in back-office centralization and organizational restructuring. Its business is targeted to become a best wealth management bank within three years. In order to build up an effective platform serving excellent wealth management, BOCOM intends to develop itself into a financial holding group with business in banking, securities, and insurance; and finally, its overseas extension would focus on Asian countries mainly.

Xiaorong Zhu

References

Bank of Communications (2008). Company profile. http://www.bankcomm.com/BankCommSite/en/invest_relation/more.jsp?type=companyintro&categoryPath=ROOT%3E%D3%A2%CE%C4%CD%F8%D5%BE%3EInvestor+Relations%3Eprofile. Retrieved on 3 May 2009.

王, 松奇 (2008). *中国商业银行竞争力报告*. 北京: 社会科学文献出版社 [Wang, S. *Annual Report on Competitiveness of China's Commercial Banks (2007)*. Beijing: Social Sciences Academic Press].

辛, 荣 (2008). 现代中资商业银行改革的先行探索. *新金融* 5, pp. 11–15 [Xin, R. A study on the pioneers of the modern Chinese commercial banking reform. *New Finance*].

中国建设银行研究部课题组 (2008). *中国商业银行发展报告*. 北京: 中国金融出版社 [Project Group of Research Department from Construction Bank of China, *China Commercial Bank Development Report*. Beijing: China Financial Press House].

BAOSTEEL

Corporate Address and Contact Information

Baoshan Iron & Steel Group Corporation (SIC — 3312, NAICS — 331111)
1813 Mudanjiang Road
Baoshan District
Shanghai, People's Republic of China
Phone: (86)21-2664-7000
Fax: (86)21-2664-6999
www.baosteel.com

Commonly known as Baosteel, Shanghai Baoshan Iron and Steel Group Corporation (上海宝山钢铁集团公司) is the largest iron and steel conglomerate in China. As a state-owned enterprise, it is operated under the auspices of the State-owned Assets Supervision & Administration Commission (SASAC) of the Chinese State Council. Ranked among the world's top 10 steel producers, the company has dominated the Chinese steel industry, contributing some 10 percent of the total domestic production. Over the past 30 years, Baosteel has been playing a very significant role in the country's economic development.

Historical Development

Two events taken place in late 1978 marked the beginning of China's reform era: the third plenum session of the 11th Congress of the Chinese Communist Party held in Beijing, and the start of construction of a new, large-scale integrated steel plant in the Baoshan District near Shanghai. After the official conclusion of the disastrous Cultural Revolution, the new Chinese leadership under pragmatic Deng Xiaoping realized the importance of steel production as an essential component of China's effort to modernize its industrial and economic infrastructure. Therefore, a plan was approved to construct one of the most modern steel plants of the time with advanced Japanese technology. Baoshan Iron and Steel was to be an exact copy of an existing plant in Kimitsu operated by the Nippon Steel.

Initially scheduled to be completed by 1982, a series of setbacks delayed the actual production to 1988. Soon after the facility was commissioned, however, it began to play a key role in China's total domestic steel output. A year later, Baoshan Iron and Steel became the primary supplier to the Shanghai Automotive Industry Group Corporation. During the early years of economic reform when China had not accumulated the significant foreign exchanges reserved it possesses today, Baosteel was regarded as a key component of a government plan for substitution of the nation's steel import, therefore received large state contracts throughout the 1990s. As the country's model steel enterprise, Baoshan Iron and Steel enjoyed a special status, which enabled the company to recruit among the best engineers and managers in China, and access to cutting-edge technology. In recent years, Baoshan Iron and Steel has also greatly benefited from the surge of Chinese economic expansion in which steel production could not keep up with the huge demand from the domestic market.

Corporate Structure and Leadership

Among the inaugural team was Xie Qihua, a 1968 Tsinghua University graduate who was recruited from the Shaanxi Steel Plant in 1978. Heading up the technical division, Xie rose through ranks to become the general manager in 1994. Under Xie, a domestic and international marketing arm, Baosteel Group International Trade Corporation was incorporated in 1996. This strategic move not only extended Baosteel's marketing network throughout China but also enabled the company to begin international expansion. Two years later Baosteel received authorization from the State Council to acquire the Shanghai Metallurgical Holding Group and Meishan Iron and Steel Company. As a result, the Shanghai Baosteel Group Corporation was formed to become China's leading integrated steelworks. The new conglomerate was the largest steel producer in the country with annual steel production of nearly 20 million tons. Throughout her tenure, Xie has successfully implemented the acquisition and merger as corporate strategy for expansion, and she has since been nicknamed as China's "Woman of Steel", "Steel Queen", and "Iron Lady". After her retirement in 2007, Xu Lejiang, an engineer who served as vice president since 1998, was appointed as chairman and CEO of Baosteel. With over 116,576 employees worldwide, the group is governed by a nine-member board of directors.

Shanghai Baosteel Group Corporation currently has more than two dozens of subsidiaries operating in China. Among them Shanghai Baoshan Iron and Steel Co. generates more than half of the group's total production. Other principal subsidiaries include: Baosteel Shanghai No. 1 Iron & Steel Co., which produces mainly premium stainless steel; Pudong Steel Corporation, a plate producer; No. 5 Steel Corporation, a specialty steel products producer; and Shanghai Meshan Co. and Ningbo Baoxin Stainless Steel Co. In addition, the group has established overseas operations, including: Baosteel America, Howa Trading (Japan), Baosteel Trading Europe GMBH (Germany), Baosteel Trading Co. (Brazil), Niagara Machinery Products (Canada), Baosteel Singapore Trading, and Baoyun Enterprise (Hong Kong).

Main Products and Services

Over recent years, Shanghai Baosteel has begun investing in developing new steel production technologies. Following its "premium products" strategy, Baosteel main products include carbon steel, stainless steel, and specially alloyed steel. By focusing on steel plate and steel tubing, Baosteel has built itself into a production center for automotive steel, oil and gas exploration steel, household appliance steel, transportation steel, electrical steel, boiler and pressure vessel steel, food and beverage packaging steel, metal product steel, special steel, and high-grade construction steel.

As a large conglomerate, besides its core business in the smelting and processing of iron and steel, Baosteel is also engaged in the production of electricity, coal, and industrial gases; the operations of port, storage, transportation, and other activities related to iron and steel; technology development, technology transfer, technical services, and technical management and consultation services; repair of automobiles; export of self-produced products and technology; import of auxiliary raw materials, instrument, meter, machinery, equipment, spare parts, and technology needed for its production and research.

Baosteel is one of the first metallurgic companies in China to obtain the ISO14001 certification, an international environmental management standard. Through implementation of quality management system in its manufacturing process, Baosteel's main products have been recognized by several international authoritative institutions, including the ISO9001 certification from BSI (British Standards Institution) and certification of QS9000 system by GM, Ford, and Chrysler, three most famous auto makers in the world. In addition to its Chinese seal of approval, Baosteel's products have also obtained recognition from special classification societies of America, Britain, France, Germany, Italy, Japan, and Norway. As a result, its steel products have been exported to over 40 countries and regions including Japan, South Korea, the United States, and the European Union.

Challenges and Business Strategies

With the continual economic reform, however, Baosteel in recently years found itself in competition with many new rivals, both foreign and domestic. Within China, Baosteel competes with Shanxi Taigang Stainless Steel, Angang New Steel, Wuhan Iron & Steel Processing, and Maanshan Iron & Steel among others; globally, Baosteel's main competitors include: Mittal Steel of the Netherlands, ThyssenKrupp of Germany, Nippon Steel of Japan, and POSCO of South Korea. When China was admitted to the World Trade Organization, the country's steel industry finally opened up for foreign competitions, which for the first time significantly threatened the Baosteel's dominance in Chinese domestic steel market. The Asian financial crisis of the late 1990s also proved to be a major challenge; when the regional economies collapsed, Baosteel's revenues also took nose dive. However, through successful mergers and acquisitions, Baosteel was able to remain profitable. Recognizing the importance of continual business expansion and diversification, Baosteel began to expand beyond steel production into other businesses such as trading, finance, engineering and technology, information technology, coal chemicals, steel product deep processing, comprehensive utilization, etc. In order to effectively compete in global market, Baosteel also formed a partnership alliance in 2001 with former domestic rivals in the Shougang Group and Wuhan Iron and Steel Group Corporation. Baosteel's globalization strategy includes a worldwide marketing network consisting of almost 20 trading companies at home and abroad. It also collaborates with international steel conglomerates, sets up strategic cooperation alliance with them to create synergy and realize common development.

To demonstrate its commitment to economic reform, Chinese government authorized the IPO of Baosteel on the Shanghai Stock Exchange in December 2000. Although the listing was restricted to domestic investors, it raised some RMB 7.7 billion, which became the country's largest ever public offering of that time. This strategic move not only had a major impact on Baosteel's corporate culture but also provided necessary capital for its investment on technology and future expansion. As of 31 December

2008, Shanghai Baosteel had total shareholders' equity of US$27.101 billion, the group's total assets were US$51.662 billion, annual revenue of $35.516 billion, and profits of US$2.313 billion.

In 2007, Baosteel Group was ranked number 307 of the *Fortune* Global 500 list with annual revenue of more than US$22.6 billions. In 2008, Baosteel's ranking jumped to 259 and then rose to 220 in 2009. The listing also marks for the sixth time that the group has been included among the global most respected companies by *Fortune*. Looking forward, Baosteel has drafted ambitious plans for expansion, currently constructing a state-of-the-art facility in Zhanjiang, Guangdong Province, at the cost of $10 billion. Expected to come into production by 2010, Baosteel will double its annual production capacity to 40 million tons, a lofty goal that will make Baosteel the top steel producer in the world.

Wenxian Zhang

References

Baoshan Iron & Steel Co. Ltd. (NBB: BAOS F). Mergent Online. Retrieved on 18 October 2008.

Baosteel Group Corporation (2007). *Annual Report.* http://tv.baosteel.com/web/group/pdf/ar2007e.pdf. Retrieved on 18 October 2008.

Baosteel Co. Ltd. (2006). Company profile. http://www.baosteel.com/plc_e/index.asp. Retrieved on 18 October 2008.

Cohen, M (2005). Shanghai Baosteel Group Corporation. In *International Directory of Company Histories*, Farmington Hills, MI: Gale (St. James Press), Vol. 71.

李, 春雷 (2002). *宝山: 宝钢 中国改革开放的经典之作*, 石家庄: 花山文艺出版社 [Li Chunlei, *Baoshan: Baosteel — Classic Achievement of Chinese Economic Reform*, Shijiazhuang: Huashan Wenyi Press].

BEIJING SHOUGANG

Corporate Address and Contact Information

Beijing Shougang Group Co. Ltd.
Shougang East Gate
Shijingshan District
Beijing, 100041
People's Republic of China
Tel: (86)10-8829-1114
http://www.shougang.com.cn/main.html

Beijing Shougang Group Co. (北京首钢集团) is one of the largest iron and steel manufacturers in China. The group primarily engaged in smelting, rolling, and processing of iron and steel products. It operates its businesses through metallurgy, chemical, construction materials, and electronics production. Its principal products are steel billets, steel materials, cold-rolled thin plates, chemical products, construction materials, and electronic products, among others. Shougang distributes its products in both domestic and overseas markets. As of 31 December 2008, the company had five subsidiaries and three affiliates, which involved in manufacture and sale of metallurgical products, chemicals, construction materials, and electronic products.

Corporate Development

Shougang Group traced its history back to 1919. However, by 1949, the company only had a total of 2.86 million tons in accumulated iron production. Since the founding of the People's Republic of China, the company had experienced a rapid growth. In 1958, through technology development, Shougang's steel operations went into operations. In 1964, Shougang built up China's first 30-ton oxygen top-blown converter. Adopting the coal blowing technology, Shougang No. 2 converter became the most advanced unit in China in the 1970s. After the economic reform was launched in 1979, Shougang transformed itself from a single-product (iron and steel manufacturing) company to a group corporation with businesses ranging from mechanical equipment manufacturing and electronics to mining, real estate, and foreign trade.

In recent years, competitions in the iron and steel manufacturing industry have become very intensive. Since 1998, Shougang has been implementing a series of measures to try to control costs and increase revenues. In 2007, its sales revenue, for its first time, surpassed 100 billion RMB, reached 109 billion, a 31% increase compared with that in 2006. Net profits amounted to 4.36 billion RMB, 60% increase. Steel production was 15.4 million tons, among which 7.13 tons are high-end products. Comparing with the figures in 2000, sales increased by 2.12 times, while net profits and steel production grew by 3.27 times and 91.2%, respectively. However, the group's non-steel businesses had experienced some losses since 2000. In 2004, Shougang turned around the situation and by 2007, net profits were 0.55 billion RMB. In 2008, its sales revenue amounted to 132 billion RMB, 15.59% increase with 4.49 billion RMB profits.

Shougang invested heavily in innovation and technology development. In 2007 alone, it applied for 52 patents. Shougang was also the first manufacturer to meet the technical requirement and receive the contract in the national West-East transportation of petro and natural gas project. In 2008, the company achieved 16 technical breakthroughs, successfully obtained 12 patents, established 12 new processing methods, and contributed to the development of two national standards. In 2009, Shougang plans to further improve its operation efficiency and expedite product structure adjustment. Based on the research on new processes and technologies, it intends to make progress in steel manufacturing and rapidly increase its product competitiveness. In addition, Shougang has become one of the top manufacturers in terms of energy saving and emission reduction in China. Since 2001, the company had been involving in 155 environmental protection projects with 1.2 billion RMB investments. Compared with figures of 2001, Shougang reduced emission of sulfur dioxide, dust, and smoke by 54.6%, 45.2%, and 45.6%, respectively, while comprehensive energy consumption per ton of steels decreased from 883.5 to 658 kg, and comprehensive water consumption per ton of steels dropped from 8.51 to 4.31 cubic meters.

In 2005, the Chinese State Council approved to move Shougang out of Beijing. The goal was to reduce pollution in Beijing area and build up a world-class iron and steel manufacturing base by integrating nearby iron and steel companies. The establishment of Shougang Group Company improved the iron and steel production deployment in Hebei Province and Beijing, and therefore contributed to the regional economic development.

Main Products and Services

Shougang has two kinds of products: steel and non-steel. Steel products cover deformed bar, high-strength inherent stress coil, mine high strength circular chain steel, cold forging steel and cold extruded steel, mild steel wire rods for wire drawing, welding electrodes, welding wire, carbon constructional quality steel, and general carbon steel. Non-steel products include pre-ERP (enterprise resource planning) information collection systems, telecom engineering and services, electric meters, gas meters, transmission systems, etc.

During the last three years, Shougang completed a round of restructuring in its manufacture deployment. Its investment in Tangshan had reached the original design targets and the group has grown to become one of the world-class iron and steel manufacturing companies in China. One of its subsidiaries, Shouqin, became a leading company in wide and heavy plate production. The company's cold-rolling products from factories in Shunyi have met the international requirements, and were exported to many developed countries.

To maintain technological advantages, Shougang signed a series of long-term contracts with top universities in China. According to the agreement, these universities would provide technical supports, research resources, and talents, while Shougang offers a platform for technology realization, financial support, and managerial practice.

Shougang partnered with 148 domestic as well as foreign companies and research institutes to conduct trainings, exchange technical information, and jointly develop new technologies and products. As technologies were continuously improved, the total number of employees decreased from 195,800 to 79,200, which created a favorable condition for its future development.

Challenges and Business Strategies

Because of tough competitions in the steel industry, Shougang strives to move gradually from low-end market segments to the high-end arena in both steel and non-steel products. As a strategic goal, according to its next five-year plan, Shougang seeks to improve its plate products in the field of car manufacturing and household appliance manufacturing. Besides the development in steel products, Shougang also tries to balance its product portfolio by investing in non-steel products. By 2010, sales in information technologies, automation, metallurgical equipment, car air conditioners, and large-scaled electric motors are expected to amount to 13.1 billion RMB, increasing by 1.47 times as compared with that of 2005. For its real estate businesses, the target figure is 1.22 billion RMB, while services in travel, education, medical care, training, and production coordination may contribute 7.7 billion RMB. Mining by 2010 is expected to increase to 19 million tons, which will include 6.2 million tons of coal and 4,000 tons in molybdenum concentrate, and sales revenues reaches 18 billion RMB.

As an established manufacturer in the steel and non-steel product development, Shougang has entered partnerships with NEC in large-scaled chip designing, manufacturing, and sealing, with Yaskawa in electric motor producing, and with Denso in the field of electric devices, all which have greatly enriched the company's technology pool and enhanced its management skills. Shougang also invested 10 million USD with its US, Japanese, and Australian partners in the research of melt-reduction technologies. Shougang cooperated with HYL to try to substitute natural gas with coke oven gas in direct reduced iron manufacturing. The company also established a joint venture with Castrip LLC from the United States, aiming to utilize high-speed continuous casting to produce thin steel strips.

In recent few years, Shougang has also made efforts to expand to many fields not closely related to its main businesses such as property management, tourism, hotel services, real estate, education and training, finance, medical equipment manufacturing and services, etc. Although enlarging product portfolio may reduce risks, stepping into areas that it could not benefit from its previous experiences, technologies, and resources and thus could not create synergies in-between may introduce another kinds of risks. Different businesses require different human capital as well as other resources. That will dilute the competitive advantages, which were achieved only by reaching a certain economic scale.

Dong Bian

References

Shougang Group Co. Ltd. (2009). Annual Report 2008. http://www.sggf.com.cn/asp-bin/news_images/483_1.rar. Retrieved on 18 June 2009.

高永生 (2009). 首建集团科技创新结硕果. *首钢日报* [Gao, Y. Scientific innovations yield results at Shougang Group. *Shougang Daily*.] http://www.sgdaily.com/Html/sgyw/2009-2/17/083440785.html. Retrieved on 29 June 2009.

柳翠云 (2009). 首钢明确科技创新工作重点. *首钢日报* [Liu, C. Shougang puts great emphasis on its technological innovations. *Shougang Daily*.] http://www.sgdaily.com/Html/sgyw/2009-5/27/084106828.html. Retrieved on 29 June 2009.

BEIQI FOTON MOTOR

Corporate Address and Contact Information

Beiqi Foton Motor Company Limited
Shayang Road
Shahe, Changping District
Beijing 102206
People's Republic of China
Phone: (86)10-8071-6459
Fax: (86)10-8071-6459
http://english.foton.com.cn/index.asp

Beiqi Foton Motor Company Limited (北汽福田汽车股份有限公司) is a commercial vehicle manufacturer ranked first in China for five consecutive years in total sales, and considered the top brand among the Chinese commercial vehicles. Established on 28 August 1996, Foton is headquartered in Changping District, Beijing. As a state-owned and listed holding company, Foton currently has 16 automobile assembly plants and many part and component divisions in eight provinces and municipalities across China, and over 29,000 employees, of which 2,582 are research and development personnel.

Historical Development

Foton was registered and established in Beijing in 1996. After passing the international certification of the ISO9001 quality system in 2000, Foton established a global customer service call center and began to offer 24-hour consulting service a year later. Foton established the largest heavy truck production base in Asia in 2004, namely, the Auman Truck Plant. Two years later, Foton's first passenger vehicle brand MP-X was launched. In 2008, Foton signed the global Letter of Intent on Cooperation with Daimler Corporation in Beijing, China.

Established in 2002, Foton Overseas Operations is responsible for the sales of Foton automobile in the global market. On 1 January 2008, it was renamed to Beijing Foton International Trade Co. Ltd. With 317 employees and after seven years of marketing accumulation and exploration, the company has exported products into more than 100 markets, which continuously ranks first in the export of Chinese commercial vehicles from 2004 to 2008. As a strategic goal, Foton strives to become a sustainable leader in the Chinese export market through internationalized plant construction, joint capital, cooperation, and other modes.

Corporate Structure, Products, and Services

Foton has three wholly owned subsidiaries: Beijing Foton International Trade, Inc., Changsha Foton Auto Technology Limited, and Zhucheng Foton Auto Sales Limited. In addition, Foton has established two joint ventures in which Foton holds more than 50% of equity, and owned minority interests in nine other firms. Xu Heyi, Chairman and CEO of Foton, is also the Chairman of Beijing Auto Industrial Corporation (BAIC) Holding Limited, the biggest shareholder of Foton. Before joining BAIC in 2002, Xu served in Beijing municipal government and had long experience in steel industry.

At present, Foton owns many brands covering passenger vehicles (MP-X, View, Sup, AUV, Saga, and Midi), light duty trucks (Aumark, Forland, Ollin, and Lovol), and medium-heavy-duty trucks (Shenzhou, Kunlun, Xiongshi, Qibing, and special-purpose truck). The accumulated sales of trucks have reached 2.4 million by 2008. In that year, 409,000 vehicles were sold and total revenue reached 4.4 billion dollars with a profit of 454 million dollars. The projected annual sales in 2010 will reach 800,000 to 1 million units, 20% of which will be sold overseas; and annual revenue will reach 10 billion US dollars.

Challenges and Business Strategies

As the leader of commercial vehicle manufacture in China, Foton has been trying to pursue a best-cost strategy while targeting the world market. Foton has become the second largest exporter of commercial vehicle in China. Until now, Foton has brought high-quality products and service to people in over 90 countries and districts all over the world. However, 2008 was a very volatile year for commercial vehicle producers. In light of the global slowdown, Foton focused on two initiatives; first, pursuing economic light truck market and second, stepping up the effort in new energy vehicle area. Among several notable progresses are: the joint venture with Cummings Engine; breakthrough in mid to heavy truck projects; and the establishment of Foton's Beijing New Energy Vehicle Design and Manufacturing Facility. To pursue the strategy of "organic growth, structure adjustment, and globalization", Foton invested 60 million dollars in R&D in 2008, accounts about 1.35% of the total sales, and a workforce of 2,500 people has been assembled to pursue new product development and technological innovation.

Overall, the company has formulated its growth strategies that include taking the commercial vehicle as the leading industry, while pursuing the management policies of high quality, low cost, and globalization. Simultaneously, Foton depends on its independent brands and innovation, creates the value with technology, captures the market by quality, and provides the products and service with high added value. However, the multiple brands marketing strategy may lead to a lack of synergies and spreading the resource to too many similar brands at same time. Furthermore, the global economic recession is having a negative impact of Foton's globalization strategy. On the other hand, the opportunity to pick up stressed assets from failing domestic and international competitor is growing and the potential in new energy vehicle market presents a promising picture for Foton. As part of Foton's globalization effort, the company is considering the possibility of acquiring GM's Opel unit in 2009.

Tom Tao

References

Beiqi Foton (2009). *Annual Report 2008.* http://www.foton.com.cn/tzzgx_db.php. Retrieved on 20 June 2009.

Beiqi Foton Motor Company Overview. *Hoovers.* http://www.hoovers.com/beiqi-foton-motor/—ID__150240—/free-co-factsheet.xhtml. Retrieved on 20 June 2009.

Beijing Foton Cummins Engine Company starts production of Cummins ISF light-duty engine (10 June 2009). *Forbes.* http://www.forbes.com/feeds/businesswire/2009/06/10/businesswire125537659.html. Retrieved on 20 June 2009.

China Automotive Yearbook (2005, 2006, and 2007). China automotive technology center. Tianjin: China.

Zhou, H (2008). Beiqi Foton debuts its first car. *China Daily.* 11 April. http://www2.chinadaily.com.cn/bizchina/2008-04/11/content_6610601.htm. Retrieved on 20 June 2009.

BENGANG STEEL PLATES

Corporate Address and Contact Information

Bengang Steel Plates Co. Ltd.
16 Renmin Road, Pingshan District
Benxi, Liaoning Province 117000
People's Republic of China
Phone: (86)414-7828734
Fax: (86)414-7824158
http://www.bxsteel.com

Bengang Steel Plates Co. Ltd. (本钢板材股份有限公司) is principally engaged in the smelting of steel and the rolling and processing of steel plates. The company primarily provides steel plates, steel billets, and other products. During the year ended 31 December 2008, Bengang produced approximately 7.43 million metric tons of iron, 7.4 million metric tons of steel and 6.66 million metric tons of hot-rolled steel plates. While exporting its products to overseas market, the company's major domestic markets include Northeastern China, Eastern China, and Northern China.

Corporate Development

Located in Benxi, Liaoning Province, Bengang Steel Plates Co. Ltd. traced its history back to 1905. On 15 July 1949, the company began to produce iron in Northeastern China under Communists' control, even before the People's Republic of China was established. Among its accomplishments, Bengang contributed irons and steels for the first cannon, first automobile and first satellite in the new republic. In 1994, Bengang was selected by the State Council as one of the first 100 companies for modern enterprise reform experiment. In 1996, Bengang was restructured into Benxi Iron and Steel Group Co. Ltd. and in 1997, the company was again designated by the State Council as one of the 120 key enterprises in China. During the same year Bengang Steel Plates Co. Ltd. was incorporated, which became a subsidiary of Bengang Steel Group Company, and was successfully listed on the Shenzhen Stock Exchange with 120 million A-Shares and 400 million B-Shares. As a large state-owned enterprise, Bengang had 61,897 employees, total assets of RMB 46.86 billion and net assets of 22.2 billion as of 2008.

As a publicly trade company, Bengang Steel Plates Co. Ltd. is governed by a Board of Directors. Yu Tianchen is the current chairman, who also serves as the chairman of Bengang Steel Group Company. Other members include Kang Wei (vice chairman and general manager), Zhang Jicheng (secretary), Zhang Guohua (deputy manager), Zhao Wei (director), Tian Binghu, Li Kai, and Wang Yiqiu (independent directors).

In addition to its core business in iron and steel production, Bengang also involves in the construction and services, mechanical and electrical manufacturing, power development, information industry, rail and highway transportation, communication, publishing, education and training, healthcare, logistics and trading, recycling, hotel, and tourism. Those operations have become an important part of Bengang in recent years. In 2007, the non-steel businesses generated RMB 5.84 billion in revenues.

Main Products and Services

Bengang Steel Plates Co. Ltd. engages in the smelting, metallurgy, processing, and distribution of steel and related products in the People's Republic of China. The company also engages in the production and processing of steel smelting, panel rolling, and other relevant products. Its products include molten steel, steel billets, hot plate, and scrap material. Altogether the company has developed over 110 series of products with 300 grades and about 1,000 specifications to meet different requirements of corporate clients. Among the recent products are X70 pipeline steel, automotive frame and girder steel, fine grain steel, hot-rolled high-strength steel, container steel, locomotive steel, and petroleum casingcoupling steel.

After years of development, Bengang has upgraded its production facilities to be a top steel manufacturer in China. The group currently has two mining operations and a dozen of furnaces of various capacities, and an annual production capability of over 10 million metric tons in iron, steel, and steel plates. The Bengang branded steel products have been widely used in the automobiles, electric appliances, machineries, tools and equipment, and military industry among others, and the company's customers include more than 100 key enterprises in China across 13 industries from auto and appliance industries to petroleum, petrochemical, transportation, sciences, and technological researches. In addition, the company has opened branch offices in Hong Kong, Korea, the United States, and European Union, and its steel products have been exported to more than 30 countries and regions around the world.

Challenges and Business Outlook

Within China, the major competitors of Bengang Steel Plates Co. Ltd. include Anyang Iron and Steel Inc., Maanshan Iron and Steel Company, Gansu Jiu Steel Group Hongxing Iron, Handan Iron and Steel Co. Ltd., Laiwu Steel Corporation, Hunan Valin Steel Company, Chongqing Iron and Steel Co. Ltd., Jinan Iron and Steel Co. Ltd., and Xinjiang Bayi Iron and Steel Co. Ltd. among others. In 2008, Bengang had total revenues of RMB 38.702 billion and gross profit of 3.652 billion. However, the company's net income was reduced substantially to RMB 165 million from 1.592 billion in 2007, due in large part to the sharp rise in cost of goods sold. The company was also negatively affected by the global economic recession in late 2008, and weak demands in the international steel market.

Despite the recent setback, Bengang is very ambitious about its future perspectives. As one of the key emerging powers in the 21st century, Chinese economy is expected to continue on the fast track of development in the foreseeable future. Consequently, demands for iron and steel products should remain relatively strong in the coming years, as the country is busy building up its modern industrial infrastructure. Under the framework of scientific development and guided by the principle of innovation, Bengang has formulated its development strategies of best qualities, value-added products, diversification, and globalization. The company aims to reach bold goals of 13.6 million metric tons in annual iron production, 14.6 million metric tons in steel, and 14.2 million metric tons in steel plates by the end of

2012. The grand expansion project will require a total investment of RMB 48.7 billion; and when completed, Bengang expects to reach annual revenue of RMB 100 billion and income of 12 billion.

Qun Du

References

Bengang to issue A-Shares (6 April 2006). *China Economic Review*. http://www.chinaeconomicreview.com/industry-focus/latest-news/article/2006-04-06/Bengang_to_issue_A-shares.html. Retrieved on 10 August 2009.

Google Finance (2009). Bengang Steel Plates Co. Ltd. http://www.google.com/finance?q=SHE:200761. Retrieved on 10 August 2009.

本溪钢铁(集团)有限责任公司 (2008). 本钢简介 [Brief introduction of Bengang Steel Group Company]. http://www.bxsteel.com/bgjj.html. Retrieved on 10 August 2009.

BYD

Corporate Address and Contact Information

BYD Company Limited Headquarters
3001 Hengping Road
Pingshan, Longgang
Shenzhen, Guangdong Province
People's Republic of China
Tel: (86)755-8988-8888
Fax: (86)755-8420-2222
www.byd.com.cn

Founded in 1995, the BYD Company (比亚迪股份有限公司), which stands for "Build Your Dreams" in English, is a fast growing hi-tech private company in IT and automobile industry in China. It makes 65% of the world's nickel-cadmium batteries and 30% of the world's lithium-ion mobile phone batteries. More notably, one of its subsidiaries, BYD Auto has ambitious plans for hybrid and electric automobiles, as a plug-in BYD electric hybrid sedan, F3DM, was launched in 2008, a year ahead of a similar car planned by Toyota. Warren Buffett, a world-renowned investor, bought a 10% share of BYD for $225 million in 2008.

Historical Development

Seeing that the battery industry has a promising future, Wang Chuanfu, a researcher at the General Research Institute for Nonferrous Metal, set up BYD Co. in 1995 with RMB 2.5 million (US$300,000) investment and 20 staff members in Shenzhen. At that time, the battery industry, especially the rechargeable battery industry, had been dominated by Japanese companies such as Sanyo and Toshiba for a long time, and there seemed to be little space for local startup companies such as BYD. However, Wang innovatively created a manufacturing line that can cut the cost down and maintain a high quality in the mean time. Thus, BYD's battery was soon accepted and became popular in the market.

Along the process, two major milestones were reached: first, in 2000, BYD was qualified as the first Chinese battery supplier for Motorola, and two years later it became the key rechargeable battery supplier to Nokia. Currently, BYD is estimated as the world's second largest maker of rechargeable batteries and the leader of Li-ion batteries, nickel cadmium (NiCd) batteries as well as nickel metal hydride (NiMH) batteries in the world. BYD's key customers include Nokia, Sony Ericsson, Motorola, Philips, TCL Communication, ZTE, Sony, and so on. The company was listed on the Hong Kong Stock Exchange on 31 July 2002.

More significantly, in 2003, BYD stepped into automobile industry by acquiring a bankrupt state-owned automaker, Shanxi Qianchuan Auto Company, with 269 million RMB, and BYD Auto was established. This acquisition has once regarded as an irrational diversification due to the target company's weakness in automobile technology, yet BYD presented outstanding performance in this new business and proved itself in the market. In 2005, after several years of efforts, BYD launched the first self-branded car, the F3, known for its high quality but low price. The F3 model had won 68 awards in China within a year, and by June 2006, BYD launched its first pure electric car, the F3e.

After establishing a good reputation in the rechargeable battery industry, BYD ventured into the mobile phone industry by offering electronics-manufacturing services (EMS) in 2003. BYD soon developed its handset components business by offering OEM (original equipment manufacture) as well as ODM (original design manufacture) to mobile phones manufacturers. In December 2007, BYD Electronics (BYDE) was spun off and listed on the Hong Kong Stock Exchange (0285 HK). BYDE mainly focuses on providing key mechanical components and assembly services for mobile phone companies. Amongst which, Nokia is its largest client, which accounted for 63% of BYD's sales in 2007.

Driving by an innovative spirit, and partly due to its strong battery technology independence, BYD has been developing new models of electric vehicles (EV), and has determined to become the leader in EV industry in the world. Now BYD Auto is one of the most famous domestic can makers and also the world leader in EV. Figure 1 clearly reflects BYD's remarkable success in batteries, electronic components, and auto business over the recent years.

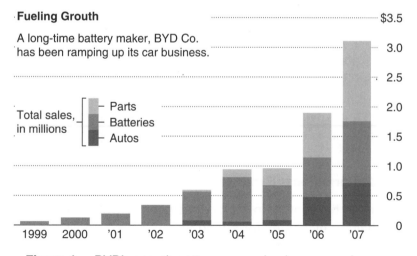

Figure 1. BYD's growth pattern across businesses and years.

Source: BYD Co.
Note: Converted from Chinese yuan at the current rate.

Corporate Structure and Leadership

Headquartered in Shenzhen, Guangdong Province, BYD has seven production bases in China, including three auto bases in Shenzhen, one auto base in Xi'an, one auto base in Beijing, and one auto base in Shanghai and Huizhou. BYD also has three overseas factories in IT business, located in India (Chennai), Hungary (Komaron), and Romania (Cluj-Napoca). In addition, BYD has established overseas branch offices in the United States, Europe, Japan, Korea, India, Taiwan, and Hong Kong. Up till 2009, the company has over 130,000 employees in total.

Wang Chuanfu, founder as well as BYD chairman, is the biggest shareholder, possessing 25.1% of BYD's total domestic shares and also 0.5% of its total H shares. Characterized with a strong visionary leadership, Wang was praised as "a combination of Thomas Edison and Jack Welch" by Berkshire Hathaway's Vice Chairman Munger. Under Wang's guidance, BYD has gained a leadership position in rechargeable battery and automobile markets around the world. With more than 3,000 members of R&D staff, BYD Auto has obtained more than 500 patents each year and is mastering the most advanced technology in EV in the world. In 2007, BYD ranked No. 81 in Top 100 Chinese Companies according *Forbes*, and among the top five automobile companies domestically.

Main Products and Services

BYD has three major business units, namely rechargeable batteries, handsets components, and automobile manufacturing. The rechargeable battery has two major types, which are Li-ion and nickel. Li-ion batteries are mainly used in mobile phones, laptops, digital cameras, and other consumer electronic products, while the nickel ones are used in power tools, cordless phones, and other types of electronic devices. From 2000, BYD began to supply its batteries to top phone manufacturers such as Motorola and Nokia, and after winning Motorola's Excellent Supplier Award in 2002, its customer base was further expanded to include other major mobile phone brands such as Sony-Ericsson, Philips, Bird, TCL, and Konka. In 2004, BYD was the top manufacturer of nickel batteries in the world and the second-biggest maker of Li-ion batteries. Due to its business relationship with those famous mobile phone manufacturers, in 2003, BYD entered the handsets components sector as an extension of its battery supply, which can be divided into four sub-sectors: casings, keypad, EMS, and other handset components including LCD screen and handset camera modules.

With a strong belief in its advanced rechargeable battery technology, BYD marched into the automobile business in 2003. Since then BYD Auto has been devoting much its attention to launch several successful models such as F3, F3R, F6, F8, and F0, from high-end cars to low-cost vehicles, covering standard cars, EV, HEV (hybrid electronic vehicle), as well as pure electric cars. With F3, BYD has successfully built its own brand and made a significant progress in the domestic automobile market. In 2008, BYD began to produce motors in Shenzhen with a total capacity of approximate 100,000 units per year.

Business Strategies and International Expansion

When Wang Chuanfu initiated his venture in battery business in 1995, the battery market was already dominated by Japanese battery magnates for a long time. Confronted with the challenges of technology monopoly and capital shortage, BYD adhered to low-cost strategy by cutting down production costs in every possible way. Moreover, BYD established strategic alliances with its suppliers, collaborating in the raw material R&D, which reduced the cost to a large extent, while still maintaining the quality of its products.

Since BYDE's listing on the Hong Kong Stock Exchange in 2007, a total of US$537 million was raised by this IPO, which not only provided necessary capital for enlarging its production capacity, but also enhanced the company's overseas acquisition, making international expansion as possible as it can, and important way to strengthening BYD's business relationship with key customers.

Having sophisticated battery technology and abundant crust design experiences, BYD built a smart connection between this two mature business areas and EV. Since the EV industry is still in its nascent stage in the world, BYD has followed a long-term strategy of combining its technical know-how in the rechargeable battery business with its automobile-manufacturing operation. Compared with other major EV automakers, BYD's technology independence not only reduces cooperative risks but also allows it to control battery costs. Globally, MidAmerican Energy's strategic investment in BYD plays an important role for BYD's international expansion. Buffet's investment in BYD based on its development of rechargeable batteries for EVs also enhances BYD's brand recognition around the world.

Challenges

Currently, Nokia and Motorola are core clients of BYD and BYDE, occupying more than 70% of its revenue in battery and handset component businesses. Such a high customer concentration is a double-edged sword. An over-reliance on these two mobile phone manufacturers posts serious potential risk for BYD. With more competitors emerging from this industry, BYD has to reduce its products' prices to generate more orders. What's worse, the company's products will be affected by the weak demand in 2009 due to the world financial crisis and economic recession.

Although BYD Auto may have become the first local manufacturer to launch an HEV, it will be difficult for the company to take full advantage of its first mover status. Chinese market is far from mature and lacking of infrastructure such as charging stations. This will deter customers from purchasing EVs. In addition, global competition for EV is heating up, as both domestic and international automakers such as Chery, Geely, Shanghai GM, ChangAn Motors, FAW, Toyota, GM, Honda, Nissan, Ford, and BMW are working hard on alternative-energy vehicles. Cooperation between battery makers and automakers have also been planned and announced: GM plans to partner with LG Chemical to build a battery production facility in the United States, Toyota will cooperate with Matsushita to set up a joint venture called the Panasonic EV Energy to produce NiMH battery. All of which will be significant threats to BYD Auto in the coming years.

In January 2009, believing that the automobile industry is an important pillar of the economy, the PRC government announced a package of policies to support the domestic automobile industry. BYD will certainly benefit a great deal from those favorable policies, especially the reduction in the purchase tax. What would be Wang's strategy to cope with the challenges and opportunities? When Buffett asked how BYD got so far ahead, Wang replied that the company was built on its technological know-how. Now what Wang needs to figure out is what kind of technological know-how will work out in the new arena of competition.

Jinghong Shao, Bing Ren, and Sunny Li Sun

References

BYD (2009). Annual Report. http://http://www.bydit.com/docc/investor/notify_show.asp?year=2008&sort=年度报告. Retrieved on 18 May 2009.

BYD. About Company. http://www.bydit.com/docc/about/company_p.asp. Retrieved on 18 May 2009.

Cazenove Asia (2009). BYD Company memo. Hong Kong & China Research, 20 February.

Gunther, M (2009). Warren Buffett takes charge. *Fortune*, 27 April, 44–50.

Morgan Stanley Report (2009). Huge valuation premium makes it be vulnerable to earnings miss. 31 March.

Shirouzu, N (2008). BYD to introduce China's first electric car. *Wall Street Journal*, 15 December. http://online.wsj.com/article/SB122928340145004821.html. Retrieved on 18 May 2009.

Shirouzu, N (2009). China puts its electric vehicles on center stage. *Wall Street Journal*, 23 April. http://online.wsj.com/article/SB124033688090439773.html. Retrieved on 18 May 2009.

Shirouzu, N (2009). Technology levels playing field in race to market electric car. *Wall Street Journal*, 12 January. http://online.wsj.com/article/SB123172034731572313.html. Retrieved on 18 May 2009.

Xia, R (2009). BYD (1211 HK), Automobiles and components: China, company report. Daiwa Institute of research, 6 March.

CHERY AUTOMOBILE

Corporate Address and Contact Information

Chery Automobile Co. Ltd.
8 Changchun Road
Economic & Technology Development District
Wuhu, Anhui Province 241006
People's Republic of China
Phone: (86)400-883-8888
Fax: (86)553-595-1289
www.chery.cn, www.cheryinternational.com

Chery Automobile Co. Ltd. (奇瑞汽车股份有限公司) is one of the most important of Chinese automobile manufacturers. Though it remains owned by the local government of Wuhu, and is by no means the very largest of China's car companies, Chery has been able to compete effectively in a very crowded domestic market and has established a significant position in international markets. This is rather remarkable for a firm founded in 1997 in a very poor province not known for economic innovation.

Historical Development

By Western standards, Chery is an unusual firm. It is the result of the hybrid nature of many Chinese businesses, combining government ownership and effective and competitive management. Quite simply, Chery exists because of the entrepreneurial efforts of government officials — known as the "Eight Guardians" — in a relatively small Chinese city looking to expand the economic base of their area and spurred on by the dramatic economic growth happening all around them. By the mid-1990s, economic reform had led to 15 years of rapid growth concentrated along the eastern coat of China. A second stage of growth extending these opportunities across the entire nation began in 1993. The Wuhu government, with support from the Anhui provincial government, was in the best position to define a new economic direction for the area and establish firms able to operate in the new market economy. The municipal officials purchased an automobile engine assembly line and engine technology from British Ford in 1996, attracted a number of entrepreneurial engineers from FAW-Volkswagen, and combined a set of auto parts companies already owned by the Wuhu government to establish the predecessor to Chery in 1997.

Skirting many of the laws and mandates of the central government, Chery moved quickly from engine production to produce its first car — the "Qi Rui" — in 2000. Unlicensed by the Chinese government and ordered to close, the firm negotiated with an existing state-owned Shanghai auto firm, SAIC (Shanghai Automotive Industry Corporation), to recapitalize and remain in business with the new name Chery. WTO entry for China in 2001 loosened regulations and by 2004, Chery had bought out SAIC.

The Chinese Automotive Industry

As with many businesses in China following the economic reform and opening to the world in 1978, the automobile business faced a large technology and managerial gap with world standards. Recognizing its bargaining power, the Chinese government decided to trade market access for technology and knowledge transfer via joint ventures between global firms and nascent Chinese firms. A system of joint venture firms followed as Volkswagen, General Motors, Jeep, Ford, Toyota, and Honda, among others, established production facilities in China. For example, FAW — First Auto Works — a Chinese firm dating to the 1950s, has joint venture relationships with Volkswagen, Toyota, and Mazda (owned by Ford) for the production and distribution of autos in China. Over time, the continuously improving technology and knowledge of auto production and management has been transferred to these joint venture firms. It was these new capabilities that Chery tapped into for its own development. But Chery was much more proactive than most other Chinese joint venture firms in working to capture and leverage its new technology and knowledge capabilities.

The Chinese auto industry is the most dynamic and complicated in the world. The growth rate of production is breathtaking. In 2000, and prior to WTO access, Chinese auto production was 2.1 million vehicles; in 2007, production was 8.9 million vehicles. Production more than quadrupled in only eight years, an astonishing feat. Perhaps even more remarkable is the remaining room for continued growth. Only 4% of Chinese own a car, whereas 60% of Europeans and 80% of Americans do so. Chinese production in 2007 grew by 22% over 2006, while world production grew by 5%. Approximately 42% of all growth in global auto production in 2007 came from China. However, the deepening global recession also affected China in 2008, when the growth rates of 20%+ slowed to near zero. By late 2008, Chinese auto firms were seeking government help in coping with falling demand. The rapid growth in Chinese auto production and use has also made an increasingly important contribution to an already serious problem of urban air pollution.

Production of cars and trucks in China takes place in two quite different types of firms. The first type is a Chinese firm directly connected to foreign auto firms through a joint venture and license that permits them to build a foreign-designed vehicle. There are eight major firms such as this. More than two-thirds of the vehicles produced in China are by Chinese firms using such a license. However, this proportion has been steadily declining in favor of the second type of producer, the Chinese independent firm that has developed its own brand. These firms number more than 100 and most are linked to local governments wanting to bolster the local economy and in a position to use local protectionist policies for this purpose. The result is a fragmented car market in which most independent firms operate at less than an efficient capacity. However, independent producers have expanded their minority position in the Chinese market, achieving almost 29% market share in 2007 up from only 18% in 2001. This situation creates a very competitive environment, with falling prices and significant losses by most independent firms. The autos produced by these independents usually sell for 30% less than similar joint venture brands. Virtually all commentators predict a consolidation in the industry, with many small and weak firms being absorbed by more competitive firms. Chinese autos have made significant strides in catching up to the global technology frontier but remain behind in important ways. For example, Chinese manufacturers have not adopted the practices of lean manufacturing very well, perhaps because of the advantages of low wages. However, as wages rise, these advantages decline and the incentives for lean production rise.

Chery as an Independent Automobile Firm

The President and CEO of Chery is Yin Tongyao, brought to the company from FAW in 1996. Chery is the largest of the independent auto firms in China, producing 489,000 vehicles in 2007. The second largest independent is Geely, located in Zhejiang Province, producing 220,000 vehicles in 2007. The market segment for Chery has traditionally been in the low-end, small, and inexpensive cars. However, it has recently expanded its product line considerably. Chery currently produces 12 models, ranging from subcompacts to sedans, SUVs, and vans. In addition, an all-electric car is in development. Along with Geely, it is a significant Chinese exporter of cars, mostly to Middle East nations, selling 120,000 units in 2007. Chery has followed a path of several Chinese firms, who quickly began exporting by selling products in parts of the world separated from competition by Western firms. Chery began exporting in 2001 and its sales are concentrated in Iran. Moreover, Chery has adopted an even more ambitious plan to establish assembly facilities and sales operations in as many as 50 countries and engage in a series of global strategic alliances. These relationships permit Chery to obtain knowledge and technology to stay abreast of global quality and innovation standards and develop knowledge of a variety of auto markets. The company has taken steps to enter the US auto market, though the timing of this is uncertain.

Probably a result of its independence, Chery has worked hard to develop its own capabilities as an auto producer. Chery has been aggressive in attracting talented engineers from other, usually joint venture, Chinese auto firms; but it has also been successful in bringing engineers from the United States, Japan, and South Korea. Combined with strategic alliances, Chery's efforts have been effective in capturing and applying knowledge. In a significant development, the company has been able to move from reverse engineering other company's designs to developing its own designs. Along the way, Chery has come to devote about 10% of sales to R&D, a very high figure for a developing nation firm. By contrast, the joint venture relationship between foreign firms and Chinese firms has not been as effective in leading to the development of design and other advanced capabilities. Other indicators of Chery's success come from important strides in adopting lean manufacturing and achieving the most advanced international certification for quality control. Chery may even be in a position to purchase the assets and brand of a Western auto firm during the economic crisis of 2009.

One of the most important issues in Chinese business involves the protection of intellectual property, with much criticism offered of Chinese firms for pilfering ideas and of the Chinese government for lax enforcement. Chery and the Chinese automotive industry, in general, have been associated with this problem. For several years, Chery was accused of copying the design of two GM-owned Daewoo autos without a license and without paying royalties. Chery has countered that it did have a license before GM's purchase of Daewoo. But Chery was able to hire several Daewoo engineers who brought complete car designs with them, designs used to produce both GM and Chery models. The GM lawsuit over this issue was settled in 2005.

Chery is positioned to become a very successful company. It has an entrepreneurial management, a strong set of knowledge, and technology capabilities, a very significant international presence and is located in the world's most dynamic automobile market.

Thomas D. Lairson

References

Aminpour, S and J Woetzel (2006). Applying lean manufacturing in China. *McKinsey Quarterly* (special edition).

Bradsher, K (2008). Increasingly, China's auto industry seeks a bailout. *New York Times*, 18 November.

Carmaking in China: Collision ahead (24 April 2008). *The Economist*.

Fairclough, G (2007). In China, Chery Automobile drives an industry shift. *Wall Street Journal Online*, 4 December. http://online.wsj.com/article/SB119671314593812115.html. Retrieved on May 22, 2009.

Fetscherin, M and M Sardy (2008). China shifts gear into the global auto market. In: Ilan Alon and John McIntyre (eds.), *Globalization of Chinese Enterprises*. New York: Palgrave Macmillan, pp. 181–193.

Gallagher, KS (2006). *China Shifts Gears*. Cambridge: MIT Press.

Heller, D and T Fujimoto (2004). Inter-firm learning in high-commitment and horizontal alliances: Findings from two cases in the world auto industry. *Annals of Business Administrative Science*, 3(3) (July): 35–52.

Gao, P (2008). Selling China's cars to the world: An interview with Chery's CEO. *McKinsey Quarterly* (May).

Mead, R and V Brajer (2006). Rise of the automobiles: The costs of increased NO_2 pollution in China's changing urban environment. *Journal of Contemporary China*, 15: 349–367.

Luo, J (2006). The Growth of Independent Chinese Automotive Companies. MIT International Motor Vehicle Program.

Sun, J (2006). China: The next global auto power? *Far Eastern Economic Review*, 169(2) (March): 39.

Zhao, Z *et al.* (2005). A dual networks perspective on inter-organizational transfer of R&D capabilities: International joint ventures in the Chinese automotive industry. *Journal of Management Studies*, 42(1) (January): 127–160.

CHINA AVIATION OIL (SINGAPORE)

Corporate Address and Contact Information

China Aviation Oil (Singapore) Corporation Ltd.
8 Temasek Blvd #31-02
Suntec Tower Three
Singapore 038988
Republic of Singapore
Phone: (65)6334-8979
Fax: (65)6333-5283
http://www.caosco.com/

China Aviation Oil (Singapore) Corporation Ltd. (中国航油(新加坡)股份有限公司) is the largest buyer of jet fuel in Asia. Its primary business is to obtain jet fuel from the international market for distribution to the civil aviation industry in China. Also known as CAO, the corporation engages in international trading of jet fuel and other oil products. In addition, the company has made investments in Shanghai Pudong International Airport Aviation Fuel Supply Company Ltd. and China National Aviation Fuel TSN-PEK (Tianjin-Beijing) Pipeline Transportation Corporation Ltd.

Corporate Development and Leadership

CAO was incorporated in Singapore in 1993, with China National Aviation Fuel Group Corporation (CNAF) as its biggest shareholder, which holds more than 51% of the total shares. CNAF is a state-owned company and the largest aviation transportation logistics service provider in the PRC. Established in China in 2002, CNAF provides fuel distribution, storage, and refueling service at major airports such as Shanghai and Beijing. As a subsidiary of CNAF, CAO was listed in the Singapore Exchange Securities Trading Limited, beginning 2001. In addition to CNAF, BP Investments Asia Limited, a subsidiary of BP, is another investor of CAO, holding 20% of the total issued shares.

CAO came into public attention in 2005 when it was embroiled with a trading scandal, involving its chief executive Chen Jiulin with losses running up to $550 million and the subsequent collapse of the company. Shortly after, Chen was arrested with the charge of insider trading, and was sentenced to 51-month imprisonment. CNAF has since came up with plans in an attempt to revive the company. Under the leadership of Chairman Wang Kai Yuen, who holds directorship positions in a number of public-listed companies in Singapore, CAO has put forth a set of well-defined controls and processes when it comes to corporate governance. In recent years, CAO established a special task force (STF) to take over the management, after the company experienced significant losses due to speculative options trading. With the mission of implementing decisions made by the Board of Directors and the senior officers, the STF successfully completed the debt and equity restructuring exercises in 2006.

For its recent efforts in business processes and operations, CAO received various awards. The company was recognized not only for its excellent performance during the Beijing Olympics but also for maintaining a consistently high standard of jet fuel quality and timely deliveries. In 2008, CAO was ranked 9th place by IE Singapore among the top 100 international corporations based on their revenues in Singapore operations; meanwhile, the *Yazhou Zhoukan* (*Asia Weekly*), a Chinese news publication in international affairs, also ranked CAO among the top 10 enterprises in Singapore, based on the revenues of Chinese enterprises.

Main Products and Services

CAO's core business is the procurement of jet fuel from overseas markets for distribution to the Chinese civil aviation industry. After the company completed its restructuring in 2006, the reestablishment and continuous growth of its jet fuel procurement business became the main focus of the corporation moving forward. CAO prides itself for its excellent customer service, as the company has many suppliers including trading houses, Chinese oil companies, refineries, and financial institutions that participate in open tenders. This unique tender model allows for efficiency and transparency, which in return helps to provide quality products.

Notable among the suppliers is Shanghai Pudong International Airport Aviation Fuel Supply Company Ltd. (SPIA), which was formed in 1997. CAO owns 33% stake in SPIA and is therefore the second largest shareholder. Currently serving more than 60 airlines, SPIA provides jet fuel procurement, distribution and storage services for all domestic and international airlines at the Pudong Airport, where International flights historically accounted for 75% to 85% of all scheduled flights.

In addition, another related operation is the China Aviation Oil Xinyuan Petrochemicals Co. Ltd. (Xinyuan), which was founded in 2004 in a joint set-up by CAO, Shenzhen Juzhengyuan Petrochemical Co. Ltd. (Juzhengyuan), and CNAF with a total registered capital of RMB 50 million. In 2007, CAO signed a share sale and purchase agreement to sell 41% of its 80% stake in Xinyuan to Juzhengyuan, for a total of RMB 20.5 million. Upon completion of the sale, CAO still holds 39%, whilst Juzhengyuan has 60% and CNAF only 1% stake in Xinyuan. Consequently, Xinyuan ceased to be a subsidiary but remains an associated company of CAO.

Corporate Operations and Growth Strategies

In 2008, CAO changed its business model from a solely jet fuel procurement company to jet fuel supply and trading, which significantly enhanced its capabilities in providing assured jet fuel supply. Through this strategic move, CAO hopes to expand its sources of jet fuel supply and improve its capabilities for long-term contracts, tenders, spot cargoes among others, hence ensuring continuous fuel supplies to the People's Republic of China.

It is noteworthy that despite the global economic slowdown, CAO performed by delivering impressive results during 2008. Although CAO is dependent on the volatile oil market, which experienced a rapid decrease in jet fuel prices in 2008, its supply and trading business were not seriously affected. Thus, profits were considered stable in 2008.

The company recorded a net profit of US$38.3 million, which reflects an increase of 14%, compared to 2007. The Olympics in 2008 also contributed to the overall demand of jet fuel and let to an increase of jet fuel supply of over 24%. The gross profit of jet fuel procurement in 2008 reached about US$22.5 million. CAO noted that the profit contribution of petrochemicals in 2008 was not so significant, due to its main focus on internal operational systems. However, it is expected that the petrochemical business will likely improve in 2009. Overall, the company's balance sheet remains strong and healthy, where net assets by the end of 2008 were at US$276 million and the cash reserve about US$153 million. In addition, the net asset value per share went from US$0.3716 in the year 2007 to US$0.3814 in 2008.

In light of the ongoing financial crisis, CAO expects air traffic volume to decrease in 2009. Nevertheless, the company expects China to remain one of the best spots in global economy with a projected GDP of 8%, and thus feels confident for its own future growth. Through strengthening its supply and shipping capabilities and value-added services, CAO still plans to implement its strategic goal of enhancing its value proposition in its share of PRC market. Oil markets, as usual, are expected to remain volatile in 2009, but that will not prevent CAO to expand to Asia-Pacific markets.

Industrial Risks and Challenges

Risk management is certainly one of the most important strategies for CAO, especially since its risk control and crisis prevention failed in 2005. Operating under corporate motto: "Effective Control, Timely Support and Balanced Growth", the company has continuously improved its risk management systems in 2008, a year that was very volatile in the world economy, triggered by the financial crisis. The price of crude oil rose steeply in 2008 from around US$90 to more than US$140 per barrel, and then followed by a sharp fall to US$35 per barrel by the end of 2008. This volatility reflects the very challenging environment for CAO's trading and risk management operations. In such an insecure environment, through an enterprise risk assessment CAO identified key risk indicators on a company-wide level and set up controls and mitigation plans accordingly. Furthermore, the company expects the market to stay volatile throughout 2009; CAO plans to stick to its risk management policies and procedures, and monitor closely risk factors such as the market, credit, and political and legal risks. Meanwhile CAO's major shareholders, CNAF and BP, pledge their supports for CAO to improve its system and processes and enhance its risk-management capabilities for a better common future. Facing the challenge of the financial crisis, CAO endeavors to create opportunities out of the current economic slowdown by seeking investments in synergetic oil-related assets and various segments complementing to the existing businesses. The future of CAO is yet to be seen.

Mareike Hoffschmidt-Fetscherin

References

China Aviation Oil (Singapore) Corporation Ltd (2009). *Annual Report*. http://cao.listedcompany.com/misc/ar2008.pdf. Retrieved on 6 June 2009.

China Aviation Oil (Singapore) Corporation Ltd (2007). *Corporate Profile*. http://www.caosco.com/profile.html. Retrieved on 6 June 2009.

Hoovers Company Records (2008). China Aviation Oil (Singapore) Corporation Ltd. http://www.hoovers.com/china-aviation-oil/—ID__138365—/free-co-profile.xhtml. Retrieved on 6 June 2009.

Jail term for China Aviation boss (26 March 2006). *BBC*, http://news.bbc.co.uk/1/hi/business/4827750.stm. Retrieved on 6 June 2009.

CHINA COAL ENERGY

Corporate Address and Contact Information

China Coal Energy Company Limited
1, Huangsi Street, Chaoyang District
Beijing 100120
People's Republic of China
Phone: (86)10-8225-6688
Fax: (86)10-8225-6484
http://www.chinacoalenergy.com
IRD@chinacoal.com

A joint stock company, China Coal Energy Company Limited (中国中煤能源股份有限公司) is the largest coal exporter and the largest independent coking enterprise in China. The company engages in the production, sale, and trading of coal in China, and involves in the production and sale of coke and coal-based chemicals. In addition, the company engages in the design, research and development, manufacture, marketing and sale, and after-sales services of coal-mining equipment; generation and sale of electric power; and production and sale of primary aluminum. Furthermore, it provides coalmine design services, and various transportation and agency services. China Coal Energy Company sells its products in mainland China, as well as exports to Korea, Japan, Taiwan, and rest of the Asia-Pacific region.

Corporate Development

Founded by China National Coal Group Corporation on 22 August 2006, China Coal Energy Company Limited was first listed on the Hong Kong Stock Exchange on 19 December 2006, and then finalized A-Share issue in February 2008. As one of the largest energy conglomerates, China Coal Energy Company integrates relevant engineering and technological service businesses comprising coal production and trading, coal chemical, coal-mining equipment manufacturing, power generation, and coal mine design, etc. China Coal Energy Company boasts abundant coal reserves that rank the second place in China and the fifth among all the listed coal enterprises in the world. The company is also the second largest coal enterprise and the largest manufacturer of coal-mining equipment in China, and its coal production reached 100.37 million tons in 2008.

China Coal Energy Company is governed by an eight-member Board of Directors, including five independent non-executive directors. Wang An is the current chairman, while Zhang Baoshan serves as vice chairman and Yang Lieke as president. The supervisory committee of China Coal Energy Company consists of three members. Moreover, China Coal Energy Company has established the following five committees under Board of Directors: strategy planning committee, audit committee, remuneration committee, nomination committee, and safety, health, and environmental committee. The committees operate in accordance with terms of reference established by the Board of Directors.

Despite its short history, China Coal Energy Company has distinguished itself with abundant resources, integrated business structure, advanced coal mining and washing technology, powerful network of marketing and customer services, a solid management team with rich operating experiences, and reputable product brands. The main subsidiaries of China Coal Energy Company include: China Coal Pingshuo Industry Coal Ltd. Co., Shanghai Datun Energy Resources Co. Ltd., China Coal and Coke Holdings Ltd., China National Coal Mining Equipment Co., China Coal Xian Engineering Design Co., China Coal Handan Design Engineering Co., China National Coal Development Co., China Coal Tendering Co., China National Coal Industry Qinhuangdao Imp. & Exp. Co., Shanghai China Coal East China Co., China Coal Energy Shandong Co., China National Coal Imp. & Exp. Tianjin Co., Huajin Coking Coal Co., China Coal Energy Heilongjiang Co., Zhongtian Synergetic Energy Co., China Coal Energy Company Limited Xinjiang, and Sunfield Resources Co.

Main Products and Services

Over recent years, China Coal Energy Company has developed the following products and services that are described in more details below, which include coking operations, coal-mining equipment manufacturing, coal mine design, and other operations such as consultations.

Coking operations

China Coal Energy Company operates one of China's largest coking businesses not affiliated with a steel maker. Its main products include coke and coal-based chemicals. In addition, the company provides export services to China's coke exporters who engage China Coal Energy Company as an export agent. In China, the direct export of coke products is subject to the export quota and permit system. When China Coal Group launched the first coking plant in May 2003, its coking operations focused on the sale of coke in the domestic market on a trading basis and the provision of export-related services. Since then China Coal Group has gradually increased its production by constructing new coking plants and upgrading existing facilities. China Coal Group has sold on average of one million tones of coke annually during recent years.

China Coal Energy Company's coke products mainly include metallurgical coke and foundry coke. It processes coking coal into coke in its five coking plants pursuant to specifications given by customers. The company also purchases and resells coke in the domestic and international markets. It produces coal-based chemicals in the coking plants and ancillary facilities. Its main chemicals products include coke oven gas, refined tar, benzene, technical and refined naphthalene, methanol, sulfur, and phenol. All the coke oven gas the company produces is used in power generation so as to increase the efficient use of resources and increase cost-efficient recycling. China Coal Energy Company, having been granted export quotas by the PRC, is one of the largest coke exporters in China. Through restructuring, the company has established comprehensive export and domestic trading operations, including the sales force, distribution network, customer relationships, and port facilities.

In 2008, the production of coke reached 3.67 million tons, representing an increase of 8.9% over 2007, of which equity production reached 2.83 million tons, representing an increase of 6.0% over 2007. Total coke sales amounted to 2.85 million tons, representing a decrease of 210,000 tons or 6.9% over 2007. Sales of self-produced coke amounted to 2.2 million tons and accounted for 77.2% of the total sales of coke, representing an increase of 3.0% over 2007.

Coal-mining equipment manufacturing

China Coal Energy Company is the largest coal-mining equipment manufacturer in the nation based on recent sales revenue, which focuses mainly on the production of mining and conveying equipment for longwall mining systems. In addition, China Coal Energy Company is one of the few mining equipment suppliers that are capable of providing comprehensive mining services, including design, production, installation, and testing services to underground mines within and outside China. China Coal Energy Company is also in the process of developing shortwall mining equipment. Its products include a complete set of equipment for underground mining systems, such as hydraulic roof supports, curved armored face conveyors, shearers, coal ploughs, stage loaders, breakers, and mining electric appliances.

In 2008, the total value of production of the company's coal-mining equipment operations amounted to RMB4.49 billion, representing an increase of RMB1.27 billion or 39.4% over 2007. The production volume of coal-mining equipment reached 213,000 tons, representing an increase of 5.4% over 2007, of which 15,205 units (sets) of major coal-mining equipment were produced. In 2008, the total value of newly signed contracts amounted to RMB5.2 billion, representing an increase of 67% over 2007.

Coalmine design and other operations

China Coal Energy Company is among the best coal mine design companies in China. In 2008, the company entered into 384 new contracts, including the contracts for prospecting design of coal mines, general contracting service, construction supervision, and rock soil projects with the total contract value of RMB1.02 billion. Therefore, the company had completed many medium and large projects both inside and outside of China. It is the principal designer of China's first 100 million-ton coalmine, Shendong Coal Mining Area. Responsible for designing about one-third of all underground coal mines in China, with production capacity of 10 million tons or above, the company has received more than 100 national and provincial awards in recognition of its outstanding mine design capability and service, among which four awards represented the highest national accolade, more than any of its competitors. China Coal Energy Company also engages in the businesses of primary aluminum production and sales, electric power generation, and coal transportation services.

Challenges and Business Strategies

With the rapid development of energy industry, China Coal Energy Company in recent years found itself face the following challenges: the need for a large transportation infrastructure due to the geographical distances between the locations of coal resources and major coal consumers; the continuous consolidation of the Chinese coal industry from numerous small mining operations utilizing outdated technologies to large coal-mining operations with advanced technologies; and increasingly stringent requirements for safe production and environmental protection.

Domestically, China Coal Energy Company competes with rival coke producers such as large steel makers who have their own coking plants, independent coking plants, and numerous coal producers that are equipped with coke production capabilities. China Coal Energy Company competes principally on the basis of quality, chemical characteristics of coke, transportation costs, and supply reliability and price. By having secure and stable raw material sources, China Coal Energy Company has a competitive advantage over other coal-mining companies in coking capacities. Due to its established sales and marketing network, as well as broad range of high-quality products, China Coal Energy Company is well positioned to compete with other coke producers in the country.

China Coal Energy Company dedicates significant resources to research and development. At present, the company has over 900 professionals engaged in the R&D of underground coal-mining equipment. Consequently, China Coal Energy Company was awarded five top prizes in China's coal industry, received patents for curved armored face conveyors, and developed a fully automated coal plough system and the first domestically manufactured 6.5-meter, heavy-duty hydraulic roof support and a complete equipment set of the super heavy-duty 3×700 KW armored-face conveyor. Recently the company's R&D unit was also selected to develop the equipment for a 6-million ton integrated mining face as part of a national research and development program.

China Coal Energy Company is increasing cooperation with companies outside of the country, having acquired the assets and technologies of an internationally renowned industrial chain manufacturing company based in the United Kingdom. In addition, China Coal Energy Company has recently worked with British and German businesses to produce gearbox electro-hydraulic control valve systems. The company also established a specialized research and development organization to centralize and coordinate research and development activities.

Despite the challenges, China Coal Energy Company is confident about its future in China. With increased transportation capacities, improved production technologies, increasing industry consolidation and more extensive usage, coal will maintain its strategic importance as the primary energy source and raw material in China. As a key energy-oriented enterprise, the company will seek to seize the market opportunity, rely on the science and technology progress, accelerate the pace of development, strive for steady growth of revenue and profit, and maximize long-term profits for shareholders in the coming years.

Hao Jiao

References

China Coal Energy Company Limited (2009). 2008 Annual report. http://www.chinacoalenergy.com/eng/UpLoadFolder/2009414203922634.pdf. Retrieved on 21 July 2009.

China Coal Energy Company Limited (2009). Company profile. http://www.chinacoalenergy.com/eng/gsgl.asp?nodeid=46. Retrieved on 21 July 2009.

China Coal Energy Company Limited (2007). The prospectus. http://www.chinacoalenergy.com/eng/UpLoadFolder/200741610135531.pdf. Retrieved on 21 July 2009.

CHINA COMMUNICATIONS CONSTRUCTION

Corporate Address and Contact Information

China Communications Construction Company Ltd.
85 Deshengmenwai Street
Xicheng District, Beijing
People's Republic of China
Phone: (86)10-8201-6655
Fax: (86)10-8201-6500
ir@ccccltd.cn
http://www.ccccltd.cn/ccccltd/main.php

China Communications Construction Company Ltd. (中国交通建设股份有限公司,CCCC), is the largest dredging, port construction, and design company in China. Headquartered in Beijing, it is also the third largest dredging company and the largest manufacturer of container cranes in the world. In 2008, *Fortune* ranked CCCC 426 in its *GLOBAL 500* list. For more than a century the company has been the most important transportation infrastructure provider in China. As a state-owned enterprise, CCCC operates under the principle of "honest service, high quality repayment, and constant surpassing" and the guideline of "scientific innovation, careful management, and win–win cooperation", and strives to build a bright future together with both local and international stakeholders. As of 31 December 2007, it has more than 82,000 employees and total assets of about RMB167 billion (USD 24.4 billion).

Historical Development

The origin of CCCC can be traced back to the late Qing Dynasty, when Emperor Guangxu ordered in 1905 the establishment of the Junpu (Military) Engineering Bureau. During the mid-20th century, four additional entities were founded, ranging from the First to the Fourth Port Construction Co. under China Communications. From thereon to the 1970s, a number of related companies on highway survey, design, and planning were also established. In 1979, the China Road and Bridge Corporation was founded in Beijing, and China Harbor Engineering Company Ltd. was formed the next year. In 1996, the China Harbor Engineering (Group) Corporation (CHEC) was established, which was followed by the China Road & Bridge Group (CRBC) in 1997. In order to better manage those operations, the Chinese Ministry of Communications set up two groups to consolidate state-owned assets of all related companies such as the four port construction companies, two highway engineering companies, and four highway planning institutes under the administration of these two corporate entities. In 2005, CHEC merged with CRBC to form the China Communications Construction Group. CCCC was established on 8 October 2006, and listed on the Hong Kong Stock Exchange in the same year.

Over the past 20 years, CCCC has actively participated in the growing global market. It is now a transnational company with growing presence in the markets of approximately 40 countries in Southeast Asia, the Middle East, Africa, and America. CCCC conducts its overseas construction and dredging operations primarily through two subsidiaries; China Harbor Engineering Company Limited and China Road and Bridge Company Limited. However, it maintains a centralized management system that coordinates the overseas operations.

Corporate Structure and Leadership

To meet the public listing requirement, CCCC is governed by a Board of Directors. Its inaugural board in 2006 consists of seven directors, including four independent non-executive directors, and with Zhou Jichang as the chairman. Born in 1950 and a 1977 Tongji University engineering graduate, Zhou started his career as a trainee with China Road and Bridge Corporation; from 1997 to 2005, he served as general manager of the company. Zhou believes both efforts and luck play important roles in achieving personal success. In line with the China Company Law, CCCC has established the Supervisory Committee that monitors its financial matters and supervises the actions of the board as well as senior management.

Main Products and Services

Figure 2 summarizes the four core businesses of CCCC and their related products and services.

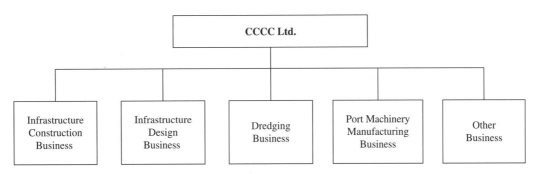

Figure 2. Core businesses of CCCC.

CCCC's infrastructure construction business includes port, road, bridge, and railway construction. In terms of total construction contracting revenues, CCCC is the largest port construction company and a leader in road and bridge construction in China. In 2006, the infrastructure construction business accounted for approximately 60% of the company's turnover.

Infrastructure design is another business sector of the company, which includes port, road, and bridge design. Constituted about 5% of the company's 2006 turnover, CCCC provides a complete range of design services, such as consulting, engineering survey, and feasibility studies that support its customers in the transportation infrastructure market both domestically and internationally.

CCCC is also actively conducting the dredging business that includes capital, maintenance, reclamation, and environmental protection dredging. The company has been involved in most of the major dredging and reclamation works along China's coastline and some international locations. The dredging business amounted approximately 10% of company turnover.

Accounted about 19% of company 2006 turnover, port machinery manufacturing is CCCC's second largest business segment, which includes container cranes, bulk material handling and heavy marine crane machinery, and large steel structures. By leveraging on CCCC's established platforms of the above four core businesses, the company also engages in road and bridge construction machinery manufacturing, logistics services, and trading of construction-related materials and equipment. CCCC's major customers are Chinese governmental agencies and other state-owned enterprises.

Challenges and Business Strategies

CCCC is a stated-owned entity entrusted to develop China's rapidly growing transportation infrastructure industry. The large Chinese internal market has enabled the company to develop integrated business, achieve economies of scale, and improve technological capabilities. As a result, these competitive strengths allow CCCC to realize synergies across its businesses to gain greater market share and to go global. As China's economy has grown significantly since its economic reforms in 1978, this requires more advanced transportation systems to move goods and people around and outside the country. The Chinese government in its 11th Five-Year Plan has earmarked a total amount of RMB 3.8 trillion for investment in transportation infrastructure. The macro fiscal and economic policies have given CCCC the leverage to grow and profit into future.

Nevertheless, the businesses of CCCC are subject to different risks. The global economic crisis in 2008 is expected to affect the company adversely as the construction activity has slowed down due to lower monetary liquidity. The company's operations are particularly susceptible to the policies set by the

Chinese government. In January 2009, the World Bank also barred one of its subsidiaries from World Bank-financed new projects for eight years, after an investigation showed "collusive practices" in the bidding for road-development work in the Philippines. Though the project is of no importance to CCCC, the success of its internationalization plans are yet to be evidenced.

Loi Teck Hui and Quek Kia Fatt

References

About company (2009). China Communications Construction Company Ltd. http://www.ccccltd.cn/ccccltd/main.php. Retrieved on 13 March 2009.

CCCC: Global Offering Prospectus (27 November 2006). http://www.ccccltd.com.cn/pdf/Global%20Offering.pdf. Retrieved on 19 March 2009.

China Communications Construction. *Wikipedia*. http://en.wikipedia.org/wiki/China_Communications_Construction. Retrieved on 15 March 2009.

GLOBAL 500: 426 — China Communications Construction (21 July 2008). *Fortune*. http://money.cnn.com/magazines/fortune/global500/2008/snapshots/11383.html. Retrieved on 17 March 2009.

Price Waterhouse Coopers (2007). Independent auditor's report: China Communications Construction Company Ltd. http://www.ccccltd.com.cn/pdf/080429/07auditor_E.pdf. Retrieved on 13 March 2009.

Sung, C. China Communications Construction denies Philippines wrongdoing (16 January 2009). *Bloomberg*. http://www.bloomberg.com/apps/news?pid=20601089&sid=aV3MkkQEvaq0&refer=china. Retrieved on 13 March 2009.

CHINA CONSTRUCTION BANK

Corporate Address and Contact Information

China Construction Bank Corp (SIC — 6022; NAIC — 522190)
No. 25, Finance Street
Xicheng District
Beijing, People's Republic of China
Phone: (86)10-6621-5533
Fax: (86)10-6621-8888
www.CCB.com

Originally known as the "People's Construction Bank of China", the China Construction Bank (中国建设银行CCB) is one of the biggest four banks in the People's Republic of China (PRC) and has been making significant contributions to Chinese economic development for more than half a century. Included among recent key projects financed by CCB are the Three Gorges Dam construction, Qinghai-Tibet Railways, and Shenzhou V Spacecraft.

Historical Development

Founded on 1 October 1954, the bank was a wholly state-owned bank under the direction of the Ministry of Finance of the PRC, in charge of administering and disbursing government funds for construction and infrastructure-related projects. For decades, the bank had played a key role in the planned economy of mainland China.

In 1979, the People's Construction Bank of China became a financial institution under the direction of the State Council and gradually assumed more commercial banking functions. In 1994, after the establishment of the China Development Bank, the People's Construction Bank of China became a full-service commercial bank, and two years later its name was changed to the "China Construction Bank". Since then, it has become a leading commercial bank in China, providing a comprehensive range of services. As the bellwether in China's financial reform, in late 2003, the State Council approved CCB's application to become a shareholding bank. On 17 September 2004, China Construction Bank was spun off into China Construction Bank Corporation and China Jianyin Investment Limited. After the separation, CCB took over all the commercial banking businesses and related assets and liabilities, including all deposits, loans, bank cards, clearing activities, and other businesses, and the related rights, ownership, and interests in intellectual property rights originally held by the bank. All CCB's other businesses, assets, and liabilities were transferred to Jianyin.

The year 2005 was an important milestone in the history of the bank. In March, CCB Chairman Zhang Enzhao resigned for "personal reasons". However, a lawsuit in the United States alleged that he received a bribe of $1 million from Alltel Information Services for securing a contract. Despite the negative publicity, on 17 June 2005, the Bank of America decided to acquire a nine-percent stake in China Construction Bank for US$3 billion, plus an option to purchase additional shares in the future to increase its ownership in CCB up to 19.9%. As the Bank of America was looking to greatly expand its Chinese business, which then had only branch offices in Hong Kong, Shanghai, and Guangzhou (Canton), this measure represented the US company's largest foray into China's fast growing banking sector. On 27 October 2005, China Construction Bank made an initial public offering on the Hong Kong Stock Exchange, and since February 2006 the share price has risen about 50 percent. In late 2007, CCB made China's second-largest initial public offering of 57.12 billion yuan ($7.6 billion) on the Shanghai Stock Exchange.

Corporate Structure and Services

China Construction Bank is engaged in the provision of corporate and personal banking services, conducting treasury operations and other banking businesses, and the provision of asset management and trustee services. Its core businesses are organized into four segments: corporate banking, personal banking, treasury business, and others. As of 31 December 2007, CCB had total assets of RMB 6,598,177 million and total deposits of RMB 5,340,316 million; and 2,729 self-service banking centers with 23,857 ATMs. CCB maintains its registered office in Beijing and its principal place of business in Hong Kong. By the end of 2007, CCB had total 13,448 branches throughout the People's Republic of China. Its overseas branches reached Hong Kong, Singapore, Frankfurt, Johannesburg, Tokyo, and Seoul. In addition, CCB has also established representative offices in London, New York, and Sydney.

As part of the shareholding restructuring, CCB was incorporated into a joint stock company with limited liability. This was followed by the establishment of a modern corporate governance framework, which defined the various authorities, and responsibilities of the shareholders' general meeting, the Board of Directors, the Board of Supervisors and the senior management. With nearly 300,000 employees, CCB is governed by the 17-member Board of Directors and the 7-member Board of Supervisors, all elected at shareholders' meetings. Its senior management team includes: Guo Shuqing (chairman), Zhang Jianguo (president), Xie Duyang (supervisor), and Pang Xiusheng (CFO). CCB's current subsidiaries include: China Construction Bank (Asia) Corporation Limited, CCB International Group Holdings Limited,

Jian Sing Development Company Limited, Sino-German Bausparkasse Co. (75%), CCB Financial Leasing Corporation Limited (75%), CCB Principal Asset Management Co. (65%), and QBE Hong Kong & Shanghai Insurance Company (25%).

CCB's main competitors within China are the other three large state-owned banks: Industrial and Commercial Bank of China, Bank of China, and Agricultural Bank of China. In addition, after the banking reform of the recent years, it also faces mounting competitions from market newcomers such as Shanghai Pudong Development Bank, Shenzhen Development Bank, and China Minsheng Bank among others.

Growth Strategies

Nevertheless, China Construction Bank is currently among the market leaders in China in a number of products and services, including infrastructure loans, residential mortgage, and bankcards. With the goal of becoming a world-class bank, CCB has a corporate strategy of focusing on its customers, products, and geographical regions. The bank has strived to strengthen its historically strong relationships with large corporate customers by focusing on leaders in strategic industries such as power, telecommunications, oil and gas, and infrastructure as well as major financial institutions and government agencies, and by developing relationships with small- and medium-enterprise customers. In the personal banking segment, CCB seeks to increase revenues from high-income retail customers while capitalizing on its cost efficiency and economy of scale to serve mass-market customers more efficiently. In terms of its services, CCB has developed both wholesale and retail products with a focus on fee-based businesses, including payment and settlement services, personal wealth management, and corporate treasury management. In light of high savings rates and a booming real estate market in China, CCB also endeavors to increase its personal-banking business with a focus on residential mortgages, diverse savings products, and an industry-leading credit card business. Its geographical focus is in the major cities of the more developed markets of the Yangtze River delta, Pearl River delta, and Bohai Rim regions. In addition, the company has an ambitious goal of growth in the capital cities of inland provinces in China. CCB has already built an extensive customer base and established relationships with many of the largest business groups and leading companies in industries that are strategically important to China's fast-growing economy.

During recent years, CCB has also expanded internationally. Notable among its efforts is that on 24 August 2006, CCB acquired the entire issued capital of Bank of America (Asia) Limited from Bank of America Corporation for a consideration of HK$9.71 billion, and renamed it to China Construction Bank (Asia) Corporation Limited; and on 29 December 2007, CCB invested RMB 3.38 billion and joined the force with Bank of America Corporation to establish CCB Financial Leasing Corporation Limited Co., holding a majority stake in the new company. CCB is also a member of the Global ATM Alliance, a joint venture of several major international banks that allows customers of the banks to use their ATM card or check card at another bank in the Global ATM Alliance with no fees when traveling internationally.

In 2007, *Fortune* magazine ranked CCB at 230 on its Global 500 List, which rose impressively from its previous position of 277. In 2008, the bank's ranking jumped to 181 and then leaped forward to 125 in 2009. Within the banking sector, CCB was ranked 21, with annual revenue of nearly $58 billion in 2008, an increase of 40% from 2007. CCB's annual profits also increased over 46%, reaching $13.328 billion in 2008. In light of the growing global influence of the Chinese economy, CCB will likely to play an increasingly important role in both domestic and world financial markets in the coming years.

Wenxian Zhang

References

China Construction Bank (2007). *Annual Report*. http://www.ccb.com/portal/uploadFiles/annualreport2007.1209119082546.pdf. Retrieved on 16 October 2008.

China Construction Bank (2007). Corporate Profile (中国建设银行). http://www.ccb.com/portal/en/home/index.html. Retrieved on 16 October 2008.

China Construction Bank (2004). Keep abreast with the world and strike brilliance: 50 years of glory of China Construction Bank. http://www.ccb.com/portal/en/today_ccb/second.jsp?column=ROOT%3E%D3%A2%CE%C4%CD%F8%D5%BE%3EToday%A1%AFs+CCB%3EAnniversary+Celebration&miniset_column=ROOT%3E%D3%A2%CE%C4%CD%F8%D5%BE%3EToday%A1%AFs+CCB. Retrieved on 16 October 2008.

China Construction Bank Corp (NBB: CICH F). Mergent Online. Retrieved on 16 October 2008.

CHINA COSCO

Corporate Address and Contact Information

China COSCO Holdings Company Limited (SEHK — 1919, SSE — 601919)
3rd Floor, No.1 Tongda Square
Tianjin Port Free Trade Zone
Tianjin, People's Republic of China
Phone: (86)22-6627-0898
Fax: (86)22-6627-0899
http://www.chinacosco.com

China COSCO Holdings Company Limited (中国远洋控股股份有限公司) was established on 3 March 2005 under the State-owned Assets Supervision and Administration Commission of the State Council of the People's Republic of China. It is the integrated platform of its parent company China Ocean Shipping (Group) Company. COSCO was listed on the Hong Kong Stock Exchange (H-share) in 2005 and the Shanghai Stock Exchange (A-share) in 2007. It is also one of the constituent stocks of the Shanghai Stock Exchange's SSE 50.

According to *Fortune* Global 500 rankings announced in July 2008, COSCO was ranked third in the global shipping industry based on revenues and profits, with an overall global ranking of 405. The company provides a wide range of services including container shipping, dry bulk shipping, logistics, terminals, and container leasing, covering the whole shipping value chain for both international and domestic customers through its subsidiaries. It has been successfully transformed into a global company with one of the most widely recognized and admired global brand names. It owns and operates a variety of merchant fleet of some 600 vessels with a total carrying capacity of up to 35 million DWT (deadweight tonnage), reaching an annual traffic volume of more than 300 million tons. In 2008, the group had an annual revenue increase of 16.6% (H-share) to CNY130.87 billion but a decrease of 40.1% in operating profit to CNY14.44 billion due to an extremely difficult global economic environment.

Historical Background

The predecessor of COSCO, i.e. China Ocean Shipping Company was founded in Beijing on 27 April 1961. Three years later, after securing a ship named *MV LI MING* through bank financing, the company quickly expanded its commerce by using the same business model, i.e. buying ships with bank loans, operating them under debts, returning loans with profits and accelerating development of routes. Its provision of wide range of shipping and logistics services contributed steadily to the healthy development of the Chinese economy, and by 1975 the company's fleet capacity exceeded 5 million DWT.

A major milestone in the company's history was reached on 26 September 1978, which marked the beginning of China's regular international container liner service. A containership by the name of *PING XIANG CHENG* from the company's Shanghai branch made a voyage from Shanghai with export containers to Sydney, Australia. On 18 April 1979, *MV LIU LIN HAI* launched her maiden voyage, sailing from Shanghai to Seattle, USA. This was the first merchant ship ever arrived in a US port after the normalization of diplomatic relations between China and the United States. From then on, the Sino-US maritime transportation service has flourished.

In 1978, COSCO reorganized its container business. A computer-aided operation center was established in Guangzhou in 1987, which marked the beginning of the automation era of COSCO. A British subsidiary was established in London in 1988, and China Ocean Shipping Company was renamed as China Ocean Shipping (Group) Company (COSCO) in 1992.

Corporate Structure and Leadership

Wei Jiafu, the Group's President and CEO, is a native of Jiangsu Province. Born in 1950, he received his master's degree in shipping management engineering from the Dalian Maritime University and then a doctorial degree in shipbuilding and marine architectural design from Tianjin University. Wei has served as the general manager of the Sino-Tanzania Marine Shipping Company, Tianjin Ocean Shipping Company, and the COSCO Bulk Carrier Company Limited. In 1998, he assumed the president responsibilities at COSCO; meantime, he also became the deputy committee secretary of COSCO's Chinese Communist Party (CCP).

Wei has extensive involvement with numerous Chinese and foreign associations. He was the president of the China Ship-Owners Association, deputy president of the China Enterprise Confederation and China Enterprise Directors Association. Among his other leadership positions include chairman of the China Ship-Owners Mutual Assurance Association, the deputy chairman of the China Merchants Bank, and a member of the State Steering Committee for Master's of Business Administration Education. Other executives of the company include: Chen Hongsheng (President), Zhang Fusheng (Vice Chairman), and Sun Yueying (Chief Financial Officer). COSCO employed approximately 34,300 people.

Main Products and Services

COSCO has six major business segments: container shipping and related business, dry bulk cargo shipping, integrated logistics services, container terminal, container leasing, and container manufacturing.

Container shipping and related business segment

The group operates its container shipping and related business through its wholly owned subsidiary, COSCO Container Lines Company (COSCON). As the largest liner carrier in China and a major liner in the world, COSCON operates 67 international routes, 11 international feeder service routes, 21 PRC coastal service routes, and 59 Pearl River Delta and Yangtze River feeder service routes as of 31 December 2008. The group's operating fleet included 141 container vessels with a total capacity of 496,317 TEUs. Its shipping activities classified by major operating routes include: Trans-Pacific routes,

Asia-Europe (including Mediterranean) route, Intra-Asia (including Australia) route, other international (including Trans-Atlantic) route, and PRC coastal route.

In response to the current global economic slowdown, COSCON employed a flexible approach to increase its revenues and to reduce its costs. The shipping volume of all major routes experienced a range of decline from 1.6 to 10.1%. However, COSCON quickly captured the market growth opportunity in the China and increased the shipping volume in the PRC coastal route by a handsome magnitude of 21.1%. As a result, the shipping and related business volume reached 5,792,593 TEUs, representing a slight increase of approximately 1.5% as compared to 2007. Nevertheless, its total revenues were slightly decreased by 4.3% to RMB 43,800 millions because of a substantial decrease of freight charges in all major routes especially in last quarter of 2008.

In order to cope with the arduous economic environment in 2008, COSCON implemented an effective cost control program. Its cost reduction strategy emphasized on increasing the number of vessels and reducing speed on 17 routes, and increased the cooperation among vessels and ports to reduce the operational time required at ports. As a result, the total fuel consumption was decreased by 3.9% and its capacity was increased by 14.7% as compared to 2007.

COSCON has an order book of a total of 59 self-owned and chartered-in vessels of various types, with a total capacity of 444,752 TEUs due to be delivered in five groups starting from 2009.

Dry bulk cargo shipping segment

With a dry bulk shipping volume of 293.1 million tons in 2008, this segment's revenue reached RMB 71.61 billion, representing an annual increase of 34.2%. As the largest dry bulk carrier in the world, COSCO owned 210 and chartered-in 233 vessels, with a total carrying capacity of 34.3 million DWT at the end of 2008. These vessels cover all categories of sizes, ranging from Capesize (over 100,000 DWT), Panamax (70-75,000 DWT), Handymax (52-58,000 DWT), and Handysize (15-35,000 DWT), enabling the company to transport domestic and international dry bulk cargo of all kinds. COSCO provides ocean-shipping services for grain, ore, coal, chemical fertilizer, steel, lumber, and agricultural products, and its service routes reach more than 1,000 ports in over 100 countries and regions.

Integrated logistics business segment

As a relatively small but high-growth segment of the group, the annual revenue of COSCO's project logistics, i.e. home appliance, automobile logistics, and chemical logistics, amounted to RMB 1.15 billion in 2008. By winning some major logistic projects, it had a substantial year-over-year (YOY) growth of 38.2%. Other businesses within this segment, i.e. shipping agency and freight forwarding business remained stable and were amounted to RMB 13.05 billion.

Container terminal segment

COSCO participates in this segment through one of its subsidiaries COSCO Pacific, which is the fifth largest terminal operator in the world with annual revenue of RMB 0.524 billion and a global market share of 5.5% in 2008. It has a total of 17 terminals in the Bohai Rim, Yangtze River Delta, Pearl River Delta, and Southeast coastal areas of China. It also has three terminals in locations outside China, namely COSCO-PSA Terminal in Singapore, Antwerp Terminal in Belgium and Suez Canal Terminal in Egypt. In addition, it has one investment terminal in Greece. These 21 terminals have 146 berths and a handling capacity of 45.88 million TEUs in 2008.

Container leasing, management, and sales business segment

COSCO involves in this segment through its subsidiary COSCO Pacific, which in turn, is being managed by one of COSCO Pacific's subsidiaries Florens Container Holding Limited. Florens remained as the second largest container leasing company and its container fleet reached 1,621,222 TEUs with a global market share of approximately 13.6%, and annual revenue of RMB 0.766 billion as of 2008.

Container-manufacturing segment

COSCO is engaged in this segment through the associated company of COSCO Pacific, i.e. China International Container (Group) Co. Ltd. (CIMC), in which COSCO Pacific holds 21.8% equity interest at the end of 2008. CIMC is the world's largest container manufacturer with more than 50% market share.

Challenges and Business Strategies

Looking forward, the group will face both challenges and opportunities. In 2009, international trade is likely to reduce substantially, and supply will almost certainly surpass demand for shipping and related services in the global shipping market. The main container route will continue to be adversely affected. The prospect of dry bulk shipping market remains dim. The markets of logistics and terminals will likely to experience negative impacts as well. However, market opportunities exist. In the short run, many governments are seeking to boost investment and consumption by launching stimulus economic policies, therefore the upstream and downstream of shipping industries will benefit from these policies and investments; in the long run, alliance and reliance among countries will be strengthened by the continuation of globalization, which will eventually lead to market growth in the world trade.

In response to the difficult international trading environment, effective strategies have to be implemented, which will include: reducing capacity in off-seasons, optimizing routes and networks, developing key accounts, and promoting high-profit cargo businesses. Specifically, COSCO needs to ensure a better match between the types of delivering cargoes and existing vessels in the dry bulk shipping area. In addition, better cooperation with strategic customers to anticipate future needs should be encouraged so as to strive for a healthy growth. Furthermore, the group aims to become an integrated logistics service provider with the highest profitability in China, focusing on providing high value-added service in the supply chain as well as shipping and international transport-related logistics services. COSCO will inevitably adjust its investments in new terminals and expand its existing terminals strategically. Finally, it will continue to reduce its container stocking by selling its containers and leasing them back for its daily leasing operations to other parties.

T. K. P. Leung

References

China COSCO Holdings Company Annual Report 2008.

China COSCO Holdings Company Limited (2008). About COSCO. http://www.cosco.com/en/about/index.jsp?leftnav=/1/1. Retrieved on 22 March 2009.

China COSCO Holdings Company Limited (2005). IPO Prospectus. http://www.hkexnews.hk/listedco/listconews/sehk/20050620/LTN20050620064.htm. Retrieved on 22 March 2009.

China COSCO was awarded 4th of 2007 rankings by *Marine Money* (11 July 2008). Your Industry News. http://www.yourindustrynews.com/blog/?p=1732. Retrieved on 22 March 2009.

Federal Maritime Commission (n.d.). China Ocean Shipping Company. http://www.fmc.gov/reading/ChinaOcean ShippingCompany.asp. Retrieved on 22 March 2009.

Global 500: Shipping Industries (21 July 2008). *Fortune*. http://money.cnn.com/magazines/fortune/global500/2008/industries/180/index.html. Retrieved on 22 March 2009.

Wei Jiafu (2009). In *Biographical Dictionary of New Chinese Entrepreneurs and Business Leaders*, W. Zhang and I. Alon (ed.), pp. 190–191, Cheltenham, UK: Edward Elgar.

CHINA EASTERN AIRLINES

Corporate Address and Contact Information

China Eastern Airlines Corporation Limited
2550 Hongqiao Road
Shanghai 200335
People's Republic of China
Phone: 86-21-95808
www.ce-air.com
IATA Code: MU
ICAO Code: CES
Ticket/Account Code: 781

Based in Shanghai, China Eastern Airlines Corporation Limited (中国东方航空股份有限公司) is a major Chinese airline operating international, regional, and domestic routes. Its main base is Shanghai Pudong International Airport, with a hub at Shanghai Hongqiao International Airport. China Eastern Airlines (CEA) currently does not belong to an airline alliance, but may be courted by Oneworld or SkyTeam. In July 2009, it merged with Shanghai Airlines, which is a member of Star Alliance. CEA maintains nine domestic branches and is the controlling shareholder of China Cargo Airlines.

CEA has been growing rapidly since it was established in 1988. In 1997, the company successfully completed its share reform and was listed on Shanghai (600115), Hong Kong (0670) and New York Security Exchanges (CAE). As of 2009, CEA operates over 80 international and regional routes and over 330 domestic routes, with connection to 110 cities in China and aboard. A worldwide network based in Shanghai covering China and connecting Japan, South Korea, Southeast Asia, Europe, America, Australia, Africa, and the Middle East has been formed, which provides smooth air travel for passengers at home and aboard. With the registered capital of RMB 2.558 billion and total assets of RMB 62.1 billion, CEA has about 50,000 employees and over 200 large to medium-sized modern jets, comprising mainly of A340-600, A340-300, A330, A320 series, B767, and B737 series.

Historical Development

CEA was officially established on 25 June 1988, based on the Huadong (East China) Branch of the Civil Aviation Administration of China (CAAC). In 1997, China Eastern took over money-losing China General Aviation and became the country's first airline to offer shares on the international market. A year later it founded China Cargo Airlines in a joint venture with COSCO. In March 2001, CEA completed the take over of Air Great Wall, and in 2002 China Yunnan Airlines and China Northwest Airlines merged into China Eastern.

CEA used to be owned by the Chinese government (61.64%), combined with both publicly held H-Shares (32.19%) and A-Shares (6.17%). On 9 November 2007, Singapore Airlines and Temasek Holdings (holding company which owns 55% of Singapore Airlines) reached an agreement to buy a combined 24% stake in CEA, in which Singapore Airlines would own 15.73% stake and Temasek Holdings 8.27% stake in the airline. Singapore Airlines' pending entry into the Chinese market prompted Hong Kong's Cathay Pacific Airlines to launch an attempt to block the deal by buying a significant stake in China Eastern and voting down the deal together with Air China (which already holds an 11% stake in China Eastern) at the shareholder's meeting in December 2007. However, on 24 September 2008, Cathay Pacific announced that it had abandoned such plans.

In January 2008, Air China's parent company, the China National Aviation Corporation, a state-owned corporation, announced that it would offer 32% more than Singapore Airlines for the 24% stake in China Eastern, potentially complicating the deal that Singapore Airlines and Temasek had proposed. In the end, minority shareholders declined the offer made by Singapore Airlines. With heavy loss in its revenue in 2008, CEA began to receive bailout funds from the Chinese government.

Corporate Structure and Main Services

CEA has a strong presence on routes in Asia, Europe, North America, and Australia. In December 2007, it began operation to New York's JFK airport from Shanghai, making it the longest non-stop route for the airline and the only Chinese airline that flies directly between Shanghai and New York's JFK.

CEA serves as a gateway to China. Key domestic routes from Shanghai include: Beijing (15 flights per day), Hong Kong (14 flights per day), Guangzhou (7 flights per day), Kunming (7 flights per day), Shenzhen (7 flights per day), Qingdao, Chengdu, Xian, Guilin, Haerbin, Shenyang, Changsha, Xiamen, Chongqing, Hainan Island, and other major destinations.

China Eastern Airlines has the following subsidiaries.

China Cargo Airlines

It is a wholly owned subsidiary of the company; it became independent in 2004, serving destinations in Japan, North America, and Europe.

China Eastern Airlines Jiangsu

Based in Nanjing, capital city of neighboring Jiangsu Province, it started operations in 1993 and operates services from Nanjing using aircraft from the parent company.

China Eastern Airlines Wuhan

Based in Wuhan, central China's Hubei Province, it started operations in 1986 and operates domestic scheduled services from Wuhan and international services to Thailand. In September 1997, the airline jointly founded the Xinxing (New Star) Alliance with five other provincial airlines.

China Eastern Airlines Yunnan

Based in Kunming in Southern China's Yunnan Province, it started operations in 1992 with domestic routes as well as tourist routes to Southeast Asia.

In May 2009, CEA opened an office in Taipei, Taiwan. As of June 2009, China Eastern Airlines had code share agreements with the following airlines: American Airlines, British Airways, Cathay Pacific, Japan Airlines, Qantas Airways, Aeroméxico, China Southern Airlines, Korean Air, Asiana Airlines, and Shanghai Airlines.

Business Strategies

CEA has been focusing on providing quality services for passengers and shippers. "Limited Routes, Unlimited Sincerity" and "Seamless Services" are CEA's customer service slogans. CEA's service covers ticket booking, check-in, transit, connecting flight, customs formality, and accommodation, etc. It provides nationwide, downtown check-in, and comprehensive cargo service that bring convenience to passengers and shippers.

CEA has fully implemented the brand-new development strategy of "Backbone-Network Operation Mode Centered in Shanghai". A backbone network that spreads from Shanghai, Xi'an and Kunming, supported by Beijing, Guangzhou, and Shenzhen and connected with Wuhan, Nanjing, Qingdao, Xiamen, and Hangzhou has been established. At the same time, CEA also implements the operation strategy of paying equal attention to both domestic and international markets.

CEA has been awarded twice the highest honor of flight safety in China's aviation industry, the Golden Eagle Cup. CEA's transportation and service have met the criteria of ISO9002 quality guarantee system, and have been awarded the "Five Star Diamond Award" by the American Hospitality Service Academy. For years, CEA has been making every effort to raise the technical skills of pilots and maintenance ability of the engineering staff. More than 500 pilots have been awarded the Safety Medal by the Civil Air Administration of China and 22 have been awarded the title of Meritorious Pilots.

Challenges

In 2008, CEA suffered a net loss of RMB 15.3 billion ($2.2 billion), due to falling passenger numbers, rising fuel costs and bad bets on fuel hedging contracts. The collapse in fuel costs has left CEA with a huge hole that only the government has been able to fill. Of all China's struggling airlines, China Eastern is in the worst shape, and the Chinese government had to inject RMB 7 billion ($1.02 billion) at the end of 2008 to help CEA to stay above the water. Without this bailout, it would probably have been forced to declare bankruptcy. CEA has said it would cut new plane deliveries to 13 in 2009, less than half of 29 originally planned.

In April 2009, CEA signed an all-around cooperation agreement with Bank of China, under which the latter will grant CEA a credit line of RMB 20 billion. In May 2009, CEA announced that it would sell two aircraft and lease them back to improve cash flows. It signed sales and leasing contracts with Bank of Communications Finance Leasing Co. Ltd. for two Airbus A340 jets, under such agreements, CEA will sell the two planes for their combined book value of about RMB 590 million ($86 million), and will pay about RMB 17 million each quarter to lease them back over the next five years. The Airline hoped that it would return to the black in 2009 due to a pick-up in the domestic air travel market.

CEA is also facing challenges in its management. According to a new government regulation released in early April 2009 that appears to apply to CEA, female middle or senior managers must be younger than 52 years old and male managers must be under 57. The new rule means 160 of the airline's 2,000 mid-level managers will be required to make way for younger staff. Another staff review in 2010 is expected to lead to the dismissal or transfer of many more current employees.

On 12 December 2008, Mr. Liu Shaoyong, former president of China Southern Airlines, took over the position of general manager and the board chairman of the CEA. CEA is the official partner of the 2010 Shanghai World Expo, which provides a great opportunity for it to recover and take off again.

Zhiqun Zhu

References

Anderlini, J, A Hill, and P Betts (2009). China Eastern seeks lift by dropping middle managers. *Financial Times*, 9 April, 18.

China Eastern (2006). About us. http://www.flychinaeastern.com/home.htm. Retrieved on 15 May 2009.

China Eastern Airlines releases 2008 annual results (28 April 2009). *China Hospitality News*. http://www.chinahospitalitynews.com/en/2009/04/28/11670-china-eastern-airlines-releases-2008-annual-results. Retrieved on 15 May 2009.

China Eastern Airlines gets 20 billion yuan credit line from Bank of China (28 April 2009). *Xinhua*. http://en.carnoc.com/list/10/10520.html. Retrieved on 15 May 2009.

Shen, S and E Klamann (2009). China Eastern to sell two aircraft to bolster Cash. *Reuters*. 4 May. http://www.reuters.com/article/rbssIndustryMaterialsUtilitiesNews/idUSSHA4113520090504. Retrieved on 15 May 2009.

CHINA INSURANCE INTERNATIONAL

Corporate Address and Contact Information

China Insurance International Holdings Company Limited
12/F Ming An Plaza
Phase II, 8 Sunning Road
Causeway Bay, Hong Kong
Phone: (852)2864-1999
Fax: (852)2866-2262
http://www.ciih.com
mail@ciih.com

China Insurance International Holdings Company Limited (CIIH 中保国际控股有限公司) is an insurance conglomerate incorporated and headquartered in Hong Kong. As an investment holding company listed on the Hong Kong Stock Exchange (966), CIIH underwrites reinsurance and direct life insurance products in the People's Republic of China, Hong Kong, Macau, Taiwan, Japan, Europe, and rest of Asia. It offers various life insurance products, including individual and group life insurance, health insurance, accident insurance, and annuity; and underwrites various property and casualty insurance, including motor insurance, liability insurance, credit insurance, guarantee insurance, and short-term accident and health insurance. The company also engages in assets management and insurance intermediaries and pensions businesses, as well as holds money market, fixed income, equity, and property investments. In addition, CIIH provides property damage, marine cargo, and hull and miscellaneous non-marine classes.

Corporate Development

Established and went public in 2000, CIIH was the first insurance-related company to become publicly listed in PRC. In the following year, CIIH opened its Shanghai Office and began to expand business nationwide in life, property and casualty insurance. Shortly after, CIIH issued 371 million new shares with net proceeds of HK$1.159 billion, and completed acquisition of Taiping Life Insurance Company Limited (TPL) and Taiping Insurance Company Limited (TPI).

Lin Fan, an insurance specialist with more than 28 years of experience, is the chairman of the company. The principal activity of CIIH is investment holding and its major operations are divided into four business lines carried out by different standalone subsidiaries. The four business lines are as follows: global reinsurance business, carried out by China International Reinsurance Company Limited (CIRe); direct life insurance business, carried out by TPL; direct property and casualty insurance business, carried out by TPI; and other businesses include asset management, reinsurance brokerage and pension management, carried out by separate subsidiaries.

In addition to CIRe, TPL, and TPI, CIIH has sole ownership of China Insurance Group Assets Management Ltd. (CIGAML) and Sino-Re Reinsurance Brokers Ltd. (Sino-Re), and holds majority equity interests in Ming An Insurance Hong Kong (51.34%) and Ming An Insurance China (51.34%). Besides its reinsurance, life, property, and casualty operations, CIIH also conducts the asset management business, which is operated by CIGAML and Taiping Asset Management Company Limited (TPAM). Incorporated in PRC and Hong Kong, respectively, CIGAML and TPAM are engaged in the provision of investment consultancy services to the CIIH Group in managing both its RMB and non-RMB investment portfolios. CIIH's insurance intermediary business is operated by Sino-Re. Incorporated in Hong Kong, Sino-Re mainly engages in broking services for reinsurance and insurance companies in Hong Kong, Macau, Singapore, and PRC. Finally, the company's pension-management business is operated by Taiping Pension Company Limited, which mainly provides various trustee and occupational annuity services in mainland China.

Main Products and Services

China Insurance International Holdings Company Limited mainly engages in the provision of global reinsurance, direct life, property, and casualty insurance businesses, which are outlined below.

Reinsurance business

China International Reinsurance Company Limited is wholly owned by CIIH and was incorporated in 1980. It mainly engages in the underwriting of all classes of global reinsurance business, except for casualty reinsurance business outside of Asia. CIRe's key markets are Hong Kong, China, Japan, other Asian countries or territories, Europe, and other parts of the world. CIRe is the largest professional reinsurance company incorporated in Hong Kong, and after almost three decades of development, the company had paid up capital of HK$1.60 billion as of 31 December 2008. CIRe holds A- rankings from A.M. Best, S&P, and Fitch, which are among the best ratings ever achieved for a PRC-affiliated company. CIRe's profit attributable to CIIH for the year ended 31 December 2008 was HK$51.85 million.

Life insurance business

The life insurance business is operated by TPL, which is 50.05% owned by CIIH and was incorporated in the PRC. Mainly engaged in the underwriting of direct life insurance policies in mainland China, TPL is CIIH's life insurance flagship and has a national license to issue domestic life insurance in the PRC. With paid up capital of RMB 2.33 billion, TPL's products are distributed through banks, individual agents, brokers and its direct marketing team. TPL has 33 main branches and more than 506 sub-branches and marketing centers in major cities throughout China. The company had 46,781 individual agents, and its market share in the Chinese life insurance market, measured by gross premiums written under PRC GAAP, was 2.6% for the year ending 31 December 2008. TPL is rated BBB+ by Fitch, and its profit attributable to CIIH in 2008 was HK$440.68 million. TPL also holds majority ownership in two subsidiaries: Taiping Pension Co. Ltd. (64.5%) and Taiping Asset Management Co. Ltd. (50.1%).

Property and casualty insurance business

The Taiping Insurance Company, which is 50.05% owned by CIIH and was incorporated in the PRC, has a national license to issue domestic property and casualty insurance. TPI's paid up capital is RMB 1.57 billion, and the company mainly engages in the underwriting of motor, marine, and non-marine, policies in mainland China. TPI has 27 main branches and more than 455 sub-branches and marketing centers in major cities in the PRC. The market share of TPI in the Chinese property and casualty insurance market, measured by gross premiums written under PRC GAAP was 1.7% in 2008. In addition, Ming An China is a property and casualty insurance company incorporated in the PRC with foreign capital, and received approval from China Insurance Regulatory Commission (CIRC) to be regulated as a domestic insurance company. With 18 main branches and 52 sub-branches in major cities, Ming An China is mainly engaged in underwriting motor, property, liability, and marine insurance in mainland China. Likewise, Ming An HK primarily engages in the property and casualty insurance business in Hong Kong, with paid up capital is HK$2.39 billion.

Business Strategies

Facing various challenges moving forward, CIIH has adopted different strategies in its major insurance operations. Specifically, in the reinsurance business, to manage the soft market cycle, CIRe focuses primarily on consolidating its current leading position while pursuing profitable growth opportunities. By being more selective in underwriting, the company seeks to maintain a strong domestic market position in Hong Kong, Macau, and mainland China. While strategically positioning itself in the growing Chinese market, CIRe endeavors to selectively expand into other Asian markets and develop treaty and facultative business in non-Asia markets. Moreover, to maximize core clients' business potential, CIRe also strives to maintain quality services and act as a leader and price setter in the core markets by focusing on profitability and cross-selling all reinsurance services (treaty and facultative, life and non-life, property, and casualty). The company believes the secrets for its business success are to control risk so as to comply with strict underwriting disciplines, invest prudently aiming at stable return and high liquidity, and make use of group assets management expertise to maximize the investment return.

The strategic focus of the Taiping Life Insurance Company is mainly on profitability to ensure that the corporate profit achieved is sustainable and that the earnings momentum is maintained. In order to achieve proper asset-liability matching on a highly consistent basis, TPL also pays great attentions to the professional investment management and underwriting disciplines. The company's business mix enhancement focuses on selling more high-value and high-quality products, such as regular premium products, through bank assurance, individual agency channels, and high-quality agency force. Likewise, the strategic focus of the Taiping Insurance Company is also on profitability. TPI has adopted strict underwriting policy with a focus on bottom-line results instead of solely on market share. The company seeks to strengthen its stand-alone capabilities in corporate governance, and maintain prudent reserving and high solvency margins guided by a conservative investment strategy.

Hao Jiao

References

China Insurance International Holdings Company Limited (2008). Annual report. http://www.ciih.com/pdf/2008916162646full_ar_eng.pdf. Retrieved on 21 July 2009.

China Insurance International Holdings Company Limited (2007). Brief introduction to the enterprise. http://www.ciih.com/eng/profile_overview.asp. Retrieved on 21 July 2009.

CHINA INTERNATIONAL MARINE CONTAINERS

Corporate Address and Contact Information

China International Marine Containers (Group) Co. Ltd.
2 Gangwan Avenue
Shekou Industrial Zone
Shenzhen, Guangduong Province 518067
People's Republic of China
Phone: (86)755-2669-1130
Fax: (86)755-2682-6579
http://www.cimc.com/DefaultE.asp

Also known as CIMC, China International Marine Containers (Group) Ltd. (中国国际海运集装箱(集团)股份有限公司), was founded in Shenzhen in January 1980, and was listed on the Shenzhen Stock Exchange in 1993. China Ocean Shipping Company (COSCO) and China Merchants Holdings are the two main shareholders of CIMC. In less than three decades, CIMC has grown to become a global leader in the transportation equipment manufacturing and services industry. Its product portfolio includes containers, trailers, tank equipment, and airport equipment. CIMC' total assets amount to RMB 34.558 billion in 2008. Net assets, annual sales and net profits reach RMB 13.417 billion, RMB 47.327 billion, and RMB 1.407 billion, respectively. CIMC has over 100 subsidiaries and 47,000 employees in China, North America, Europe, Asia, and Australia.

Historical Development

Established by China Merchants in 1980 along with its Denmark partner, CIMC was one of the four earliest container manufacturers in China. On 22 September 1982, the production line for the standard 20-foot containers was officially put into operation, and the business seemed to be on the right track. However, because of the low demand in the international marine transportation industry and cultural conflicts between partners, CIMC suffered consecutive losses from 1980 to 1986. Due to the unfavorable market conditions, CIMC's total number of employees decreased sharply from 330 to 59 by 1986. In that year, the company decided to switch from container manufacturing to steel frame production. After the Denmark investor decided to give up its right on the corporate management, China Merchants was put in charge of CIMC' operations. A year later, the marine container industry recovered. CIMC readjusted its investment strategies and went back to the container manufacturing. On 1 July 1987, COSCO invested in CIMC by holding 45% of the share, same as that of China Merchants, while the Denmark partner held the remaining 10%.

In 1991, CIMC produced around 140,000 containers and became a main player in the industry. At the same time, its other businesses such as airport boarding bridges grew rapidly. Although sales reached 0.2 billion RMB by 1991 and profits amounted to 43.45 million RMB, CIMC had to face challenges of industrial overcapacity and intensive competition caused by new rivals' advanced manufacturing technologies and heavy investments. During the next few years, CIMC decided to develop and deploy manufacturing bases in China, and acquired Dalian and Nantong Container Factories. Consequently, by the mid-1990s, CIMC had established manufacturing centers in the northern, southern, and eastern parts of China, which enables the company to act more quickly than its South Korean competitors.

From then on, CIMC was transformed from a single-product company to a multi-business corporation. In 1996, the company manufactured 199,000 containers, surpassing Hyundai and Jindo for the first time, and becoming the first in the dry cargo container-manufacturing industry segment. A year later, CIMC set its targets at the high-end market — reefer containers and special containers, accordingly two subsidiaries were established. In 1998, four reefer container and special container factories were acquired by CIMC and by 2002, the company had become the largest and all-typed container producer in the world. Sales revenue in 2007 reached 48.8 billion RMB and net profits 3.17 billion RMB. Although the economic downturn greatly influenced CIMC's operations in 2008, its industry leadership cannot be challenged at least for the next five years. CIMC sets up its goal to become a world-class enterprise by 2012 with net profits of 5 billion RMB and sales of 100 billion RMB.

Products and Services

The core business of CIMC is container manufacturing. The company owns and operates over 34 production bases throughout Southern Eastern and Northern China, distributed in 11 major cities along the coastline. CIMC is also the only supplier in China that can produce the whole series of containers, which include dry cargo, reefer, tank, and specials, all under CIMC' own intellectual property rights.

Besides its core business, CIMC also engages in vehicle business, marine fabrication, airport equipment, petrol chemical, beverages, and food equipment manufacturing. Since CIMC intended to produce first-class road transportation equipment and services in the global market, the vehicle business was one of the key areas that CIMC has invested heavily to expand its product portfolio, with 22 production bases established in China. Besides six regions in China, its products have been distributed in North America, Europe, and Asia, although most of its products are sold to the United States and Japan. CIMC is now one the largest special vehicle-manufacturing groups in the world, with over 200,000 units in annual vehicle production capacity.

In term of marine fabrication business, CIMC owns 29.90% of shares of Yantai Raffles Shipyard Limited, the biggest shareholder of the company. Raffles Shipyard is a leading specialist in offshore and marine fabrication. In addition to its advanced technologies and investments in the Mobile Offshore Drilling Rig and its matching ships, Raffles also has the second largest dry dock in Asia. The capacity of the enclosed, semi-submersible dry dock is 15,000 metric tons. Raffles' unit swing shore tackle crane and gantry crane can lift 2,000 metric tons and 20,000 metric tons of cargos, respectively.

CIMC's airport equipment business includes passenger boarding bridge, automatic air cargo-handling system, and automatic parking system. CIMC is the first manufacturer of ship boarding bridges in China, and its passenger boarding bridges are sold to over 10 markets such as North America, Europe, Africa, and Southeast Asia. The company can also produce passenger boarding bridges for A380 and B787. Recently, Charles de Gaulle International Airport in France purchased CIMC' passenger boarding bridges for these jumbo jets.

As regards to its petrol chemical, beverages, and food equipment business, CIMC seeks to become a leading special container manufacturer in the world. It has acquired Burg Industries B.V. of the Netherlands, which was one of the global suppliers of specialized static tanks. CIMC also holds Enric Energy Equipment, which is specialized in R&D, production, and sales of pressure container and compressor. These M&A activities have enriched CIMC's R&D capability, international market channels and global production. Consequently, CIMC has become a leading integrated and comprehensive business service provider and a key equipment manufacturer in the Chinese gas apparatus industry.

Strategies and Challenges

From a small container manufacturer in 1980, CIMC has grown to become the global leader in the industry in 29 years. The company's remarkable success can be attributed to the rapid development of the Chinese economy of the last three decades, its innovation management and rapid global expansion. CIMC invested heavily in innovation and global market development. From the very beginning, the top management of CIMC had realized the key for corporate growth was to explore new technologies and new markets.

Technologies are the core competence for a company in the container-manufacturing industry. CIMC invited many experts to help develop its technology as well as management innovation systems. Management process reengineering, R&D restructuring, technology information collection, development, and integration system designing all contribute enormously to the corporate growth. CIMC innovatively divided R&D into "platform R&D" and "tailored R&D": with cross-subsidiary teams are in charge of "platform R&D" to produce a kind of "all-can-use" technologies to sustain the whole corporate technology development, while each individual subsidiary will be responsible for "tailored R&D" to manufacture special products required by its customers.

New markets mean new development space. CIMC utilizes various ways to expand its business boundary. Merging and acquiring foreign as well as domestic players helped significantly in its market development. Manufacturing bases deploying, key management skills and technologies acquiring, global information system setting up and international market channel exploring pave a way for its internationalization.

Although CIMC has become the leader in the industry and seems not challengeable in the near future, the company still faces some difficulties. One of the challenges is that CIMC developed so rapidly in the last 29 years; heavy investment, large number of subsidiaries, and complicated corporate structure make it hard to cope with sudden economic changes such as the current financial crisis. Innovation and new market exploration can help to deal with industrial downturns; however, how to optimize its product portfolio so that it can be strong enough to beat competitions from new rivals, and how to enhance environmental situations and new technologies are among the serious questions CIMC has to answer in the near future. Another issue that CIMC has to handle is the succession. Current CEO, Mr. Mai Boliang, has a strong leadership role in the company, whom the whole corporate system operations reply on. So a key question is whether CIMC's success can be sustained after Mai's retirement in the coming years.

Dong Bian

References

Bian, D (2008). The emergence of a global leader: A working case study on CIMC. EM Lyon Business School.

CIMC (2009). Annual Report 2008. http://www.cimc.com/UpFiles/Report/1122.pdf. Retrieved on 29 June 2009.

Sun, LS and MJ Quan (2009). Mai Boliang. In *Biographical Dictionary of New Chinese Entrepreneurs and Business Leaders*. W Zhang and I Alon (eds.), pp. 116–118. Cheltenham, UK: Edward Elgar.

CHINA LIFE INSURANCE

Corporate Address and Contact Information

China Life Insurance (Group) Company Ltd. (SIC: 6311; NAICS: 524113)
16 Chaowai Ave.
Chaoyang District
Beijing, People's Republic of China
Phone: (86)10-8565-9999
Fax: (86)10-8525-2232
www.chinalife.com.cn

China Life Insurance (Group) Company Limited (China Life 中国人寿保险股份有限公司) is the world's biggest life insurer and the largest Chinese institutional investor. It dominates 44% of the Chinese domestic life insurance market. China Life has been ranked in "*Fortune 500*" for five consecutive years from 2004 to 2008, and it is the only insurer in China that has been ranked in the World Brand Lab's "2008 World's 500 Most Influential Brands". As the leader of the Chinese insurance industry, China Life not only actively involves in developing its core insurance business and its overseas business but also participates in professional training for insurance business.

Historical Development

China Life Insurance (Group) Company Limited is a state-owned (68%) life insurance company that was incorporated in 2003. In the same year, China Life issued shares on the New York Stock Exchange under the name "China Life Insurance Co. Ltd." and the symbol "LFC". It also issued H-Shares on the Hong Kong Stock Exchange under the name "China Life" and stock code "2328" in the same year. Three years later, in January 2007, China Life issued A-shares on the Shanghai Stock Exchange under the name "China Life" and stock code "601628". The gains from the stock markets allow China Life to pass AIG, ING Group NV, Allianz SE, and AXA to become the number one insurer in the world.

China Life Insurance (Group) Company Limited was originally incorporated by the People's insurance Company of China (PICC), PICC Life Insurance Company Ltd., and the former China Life Insurance Company. PICC was established in 1949 and it is the first insurance company in PRC established by the government. In 1996, PICC was incorporated and renamed as People's insurance (Group) Company of China. PICC Life Insurance Company Ltd. was one of the subsidiaries under PICC Group at that time. In 1999, PICC Group was incorporated again, and the name of PICC Life Insurance Company was changed into China Insurance Company. The financial reform in China enhances the formation of China Life Insurance (Group) Company Limited and generates opportunities for SOEs such as China Life to absorb investments from investors worldwide.

As the leading insurer in China, China Life has diversified its business from insurance to other financial and non-financial investments. It is also actively involved in educating and training professionals in insurance. China's insurers are tightly regulated, so there are limits on what they can invest in. For example, real estate investment is prohibited. To explore other opportunities and gain profits, China Life takes the advantage of its subsidiary — China Life Franklin Asset Management in Hong Kong to invest abroad to further reduce its risk in diversified investments. Due to the financial crisis from 2008, China Life slowed its investment expansion in the foreign market, starting by declining to bid for American International Assurance (AIA). The increasing uncertainty in the global financial market encourages China Life to focus on exploring and developing the Chinese domestic insurance market.

Over the years, China Life has developed a unique company culture, which aims at striving to construct and become a customer-oriented group that provides world-class international financial insurance products and services.

Corporate Structure and Leadership

China Life is the holding company of the following subsidiary companies (as shown in Figure 3): China Life Insurance Company Ltd., China Life Asset management Company Ltd., China Life Property & Casualty Insurance Company Ltd., China Life Pension Insurance Company Ltd., China Life Insurance (Overseas) Company Ltd., China Life Investment Holding Company Ltd., China Life Franklin Asset management Company Ltd., and China Life Education.

As the leading life insurer, China Life offers life insurance and annuity products to individuals, primarily though a distribution force comprised of approximately 716,000 exclusive agents operating in approximately 16,000 field offices throughout China. It also provides products and services through other agencies, banks, and organizations. All together, China Life had about 102 million individual and group life insurance policies, annuity contracts, and long-term health insurance policies at the end of 2008.

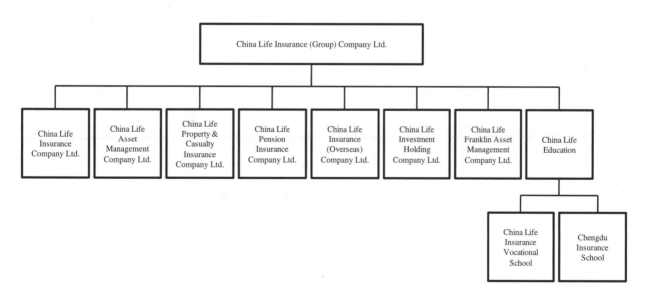

Figure 3. Corporate structure.

Source: Adapted from China Life company website http://www.chinalife.com.cn.

Main Products and Services

China Life Insurance (Group) Company Limited is the holding company of a chain of subsidiaries. It is mainly responsible for corporate strategy, asset management, structure construction, brand promotion, culture development, risk control, management supervision, and organization coordination. It provides various products and services to individuals and groups in China.

The company mainly operates in three segments: individual life insurance, group life insurance, and accident and health insurance. The individual life Insurance segment offers participating and nonparticipating life insurance and annuities to individuals, including long-term health and accident insurance products. The group life insurance segment provides participating and nonparticipating life insurance and annuities products to companies and institutions, including various long-term insurance products. The accident and health insurance segment provides short-term accident insurance and health insurance to individuals and groups.

Other than a provider for insurance products and services, China Life is also the largest institutional investor in China. By investing through its asset management subsidiaries, China Life successfully manages assets over RMB 100 billion. In November 2005, China Life Insurance Asset Management (Hong Kong) Company Limited, a subsidiary of China Life was incorporated in Hong Kong. Since then it has become an important subsidiary for China Life to operate its overseas business. Two years later, China Life Insurance Asset Management (Hong Kong) Company Limited was renamed as China Life Franklin Asset Management Company Limited after merging with a strategic investor in 2007. Under government regulations, China Life Franklin Asset Management Company Limited is allowed to engage in asset management and advising on securities in Hong Kong, which broadened the business scope of China Life.

Different from other insurers, China Life is one of the few companies that provides and develops education opportunities for professionals in insurance industry. The schools under China Life provide post-doctoral trainings and various vocational trainings related to insurance. By engaging in such educational activities, China Life is setting standards for China's fast-growing insurance industry.

Challenges and Business Strategies

Under the pressure of the global financial crisis from 2008, China Life is facing challenges in the global market despite of its government support. Doubts on capital adequacy of the insurers have led to a sell-off in leading insurers' shares over the world. China's financial markets were also stricken by the crisis. The Shanghai Composite Index was down 65% in 2008. Interest rates were falling, which adversely affected returns on fixed-income investments and leads to the lower yields in stock market, bond market, bank deposits, and mutual funds. Adding to the performance pressures was the 2008 earthquake in Sichuan province, which claimed 88,000 lives. It was one of the worst natural disasters in modern Chinese history. The catastrophe leads to tighter margins, which leads to the growing intensive competition in the life insurance industry in China.

Even though capital adequacy is not expected as a concern for China life because of its strong government background, it has suffered from the global economic and financial crisis. Just in the third quarter of 2008, China life's net profit fell more than 70%. For the whole year, China Life experienced a decrease of 45% (to RMB 21.3 billion) in net profit, and a fall of 61.4% in total investment return. However, the leaders of China Life still anticipate growth in the coming years. They claimed that since Chinese investors seek capital gains more than dividend income, there should be more speculation than long-term investment, which calls for comparable investment strategies, and will leads to potential opportunities for China Life.

In addition to the financial crisis, insurers such as China Life also face pressures from the tight regulations in China's financial markets. Even though after joining WTO, China has gradually loosen its regulation and opening its financial market to foreign investors, the process is still ongoing and not likely to be achieved in the short term. The undergoing reform in the financial markets challenges institutional investors such as China Life. While exploring for new opportunities, China Life needs to finds ways to integrate the world standards and compete with institutional investors from all over the world, who are apparently a lot more experienced in conducting global business. Where and how to invest is a question China Life needs to consider. For example, China Life is now experiencing difficulties in matching its assets with its liabilities. The bond market in China is still underdeveloped with limited measures in encouraging bond issuance, where long-term investment products are scarce. According to the China Life's company report, its asset allocation for 2008 was 58.6% in debt securities (52% in 2007), 13.3% in equities (23% in 2007), and about 21% in term deposits (20% in 2007).

Despite various challenges, China Life will continue its concentration on the domestic market and explore for international expansions when appropriate opportunities arise. Comparing with other countries and regions, China's insurance coverage is still low, only 10%. Thus, the domestic market has offered a great opportunity for insurers such as China Life to achieve substantial progress. With the continuous growth in the Chinese economy and income levels, the domestic demand for insurance products is expected to grow accordingly. Thus, in the future, China Life is expected to achieve continuous expansion through its insurance business in the coming years. In addition, with the reform of China's financial market, China Life is expected to gain more opportunities in managing its assets as well as its investments.

Hao Chen

References

China Life Insurance (Group) Company, Ltd. (2009). Company profile. http://www.chinalife.com.cn/001intro/index. html. Retrieved on 25 May 2009.

China Life Insurance (Group) Company, Ltd. (2009). Annual Report. http://secfilings.nyse.com/files.php?symbol= lfc&page=0&extras=0. Retrieved on 25 May 2009.

Deutsche Bank and CIRC (2009). Leading Life Insurers in China, 2008. *Market Share Reporter*, 2 September.

Forbes (2009). Forbes 2000 Company List. http://www.forbes.com/2009/04/08/worlds-largest-companies-business-global-09-global_land.html. Retrieved on 25 May 2009.

Mak, L (2009). Where to find China's assets. *Asian Investor*, March.

Sudip, R (2009). China Life toughs out volatile markets. *Euromoney*, 40 (480).

CHINA MENGNIU DAIRY

Corporate Address and Contact Information

Inner Mongolia Mengniu Dairy (Group) Company Limited (SIC-2-26, NAICS-311511)
Shengle Economic Development Zone
Hohhot City 011500
Inner Mongolia Autonomous Region
People's Republic of China
Phone: (86)47-1739-2222
http://mengniu.com.cn, http://mengniuir.com

Founded as a private company on 18 August 1999, the Inner Mongolia Mengniu Milk Industry Company Limited was renamed in 2003 as Inner Mongolia Mengniu Milk Industry (Group) Company Limited, which also came to be known as the Mengniu Group. The Mengniu Group is the principal operating subsidiary of the China Mengniu Dairy Company Limited (中国蒙牛乳业有限公司), which is an investment holding company. It was incorporated on 16 February 2004 in the Cayman Islands. In June 2004, it was listed on the Hong Kong Stock Exchange, the first Chinese dairy to list in Hong Kong. The Company's principal office is in Hong Kong, whereas the group is headquartered in Hohhot, Inner Mongolia Autonomous Region.

Corporate Development

This upstart company was founded by Niu Gensheng and nine former colleagues from the state-owned dairy, Inner Mongolia Yili Industrial Group Company Limited. They pooled their resources and built the company without any government subsidy, and then took an unconventional approach by investing firstly and substantially on marketing and brand building. The timing of this company coincided well with the growth of the Chinese economy. Continuous GDP growth, ongoing urbanization, improving living standards, increasing per-capita income, rising disposable income, and growing health consciousness among Chinese consumers have all helped to increase China's demand for quality dairy products. As per-capita consumption of milk is still relatively low among Chinese consumers, there is room for sustainable market growth. Despite the melamine incident in late 2008 that tainted the Chinese dairy industry, the market still grew by 7.5% in 2008, and it is one of the highest-growth subsectors of China's food industry.

As Mengniu's CEO and a founding member, Niu Gensheng has in-depth dairy industry experience. He worked for Yili for 17 years during which he served on its Board of Directors and as deputy chief executive in charge of production and operations. Niu has a college degree in administration and management, and holds a graduate degree in enterprise management. He is the current deputy chair of the Dairy Association of China, the China Dairy Industry Association, and the Second China National Committee of International Dairy Federation. A well-known entrepreneur, Niu has achieved celebrity status and is often seen on television discussing his business philosophy. The many recognitions he received, include but are not limited to, "CCTV People of the Year in Chinese Economy", "China's Most Influential Business Leaders", and "Outstanding Performers in China's Dairy Industry".

Niu is one among the five executive directors on the board of 10 directors. Mengniu's employee population has grown significantly over the years to 23,500 in 2008. In 2005, the Mengniu Commercial Study College was set up as an internal training center to develop and provide staff training programs.

Mengniu produces, markets, and distributes dairy products in China, including Hong Kong and Macau. It also exports to Singapore, the Philippines, and Malaysia. Mengniu operates through three segments — liquid milk products, ice creams, and other dairy products. Within each segment, there is a diverse range of dairy products and different brands. For example, within liquid milk, Mengniu's major revenue generator (90% in 2008), there is its core product UHT (Ultra High Temperature) milk, over 20 varieties of milk beverages, and over 40 varieties of flavored yogurt. In the ice-cream segment, there are over 100 flavors and different brands. Other dairy products include different kinds of milk powder and milk tablets. Mengniu also engages in the packaging of dairy products, the cultivating and selling of cattle embryos.

Business Strategies and Drivers

Mengniu's major competitors in China are Shanghai Bright Dairy & Food Company Limited and Inner Mongolia Yili Industrial Group Company Limited. Since its founding, Mengniu has been ascending steadily, and it has become one of the three leading dairies in China. A combination of leadership with extensive dairy industry experience and practical business approaches has helped bring success within its short history.

Niu and his colleagues believe strongly in business branding and marketing. Even at the beginning, they started by investing millions of RMB to brand building prior to establishing their manufacturing facilities. As the company grows, they continue to pounce on unique marketing opportunities, promotional and advertising campaigns to further enhance brand and product awareness. Most notably, Mengniu became the official provider of dairy products for China's first astronaut, Yang Liwei, who touched down on Inner Mongolian grasslands in October 2003. Over the years, Mengniu has worked with domestic and international partners on such efforts. These partners include Hunan TV, Shandong TV, Disney Hong Kong, and the National Basketball Association (NBA). Mengniu has become a model for a new breed of Chinese company.

Mengniu is the core brand of the group. *Meng* refers to Inner Mongolia and *niu* to cows. Mengniu prides its products as natural, pure, good quality, fresh, healthy, and trendy. This brand has become one of the leading national consumer brands with a solid customer base. Mengniu's goals are to nurture a strong Chinese dairy industry, to be the brand that makes the nation and its people proud, and also to become one of the leading dairy players in the global market. Mengniu is China's second largest dairy company and among the world's largest emerging dairy markets. It is the national bestseller of liquid milk. Mengniu's revenue went from RMB 37.3 million in 1999 (August to December) to RMB 21.32 billion in 2007, and it became the first Chinese dairy to post revenues in excess of RMB 2 billion. Its EBITDA increased from RMB 610 million in 2004 to RMB 1.67 billion in 2007. The number of production plants increased up from 11 in 2004 to 23 in 2008, and its annual production capacity increased from 50,000 tons in 2000 to 5.5 million tons during the first six months of 2008.

In addition to solid branding and successful marketing strategies proven by numerous national awards received, product development is another important key driver. Mengniu continues to optimize product mix, diverse product portfolio, improve existing products, and develop new products to suit different market segments. It has received many certifications and product awards. A few foreign companies have been involved in joint-venture developmental efforts. Strategic business alliances include Groupe Danone, Arla Foods, Disney Hong Kong, NBA, Starbucks, and KFC.

Mengniu continues to emphasize research and development. In late 2004, it established the Mengniu–Australia International Ranch to promote the application of scientific knowledge and techniques to grass planting, dairy cow breeding, rearing and milking, and to improve quality and quantity of dairy supply. Home to 10,000 Australian-bred cows, this ranch is said to resemble a bovine spa with milking robots, music, foam mats, automatic cow grooming brush, and other comfort measures. In 2007, Mengniu opened a research institute in Helingeer with other renowned institutes including Cambridge University and the Chinese Academy of Sciences. Mengniu participates in both national and international industry exchanges, setting up workshops overseas and hosting international dairy events.

Mengniu has also presented itself as a socially and environmentally responsible enterprise. Among its charitable activities, it donated RMB 12 million in funds and milk to help fight SARS in 2003. In 2006, it launched a yearlong milk sponsorship program covering 500 schools in impoverished areas. Responding to the "three agricultures" policy, it continues to encourage dairy farmers to pursue technical advancements in raising livestock and optimization of the production processes. In addition, Mengniu helped complete the construction of China's first methane power plant in Helingeer in 2007. In early 2008, it spent over RMB 10 million to help victims of the snowstorms in southern China, and then later that year another RMB 12 million to help victims of the Sichuan earthquake.

Major Challenge

China's quality watchdog, the General Administration of Quality Supervision, Inspection and Quarantine (AQSIQ) conducted nationwide tests in September 2008 on infant formulae, and 22 companies, including Mengniu, were implicated with adding the industrial chemical melamine. Thousands of infants were sickened and six deaths were reported. This public health incident blighted the entire Chinese dairy industry. Milk export to overseas market plunged 91.8% in October. Mengniu's infant milk powder and liquid milk samples were found to be tainted. This crisis hampered Mengniu's financials, brand reputation, and consumer confidence. Mengniu conducted a massive product recall and disposal. Its stock was suspended from trade for a week, falling to a historic low of HKD 6.03 on 27 October 2008 (compare with a historic high of HKD 26.10 on 16 May 2008). As a result, the company decided not to pay a final dividend for 2008.

Mengniu's liquid milk segment accounted for 90% of its total revenue, and it holds 41% of the Chinese liquid milk market. This crisis brought about its first ever loss in revenue, RMB 948.6 million (compared with a profit of RMB 935.6 million in 2007). In addition, Mengniu was dealt a further blow in early 2009 by an incident involving the unapproved addictive osteoblast milk protein (OMP) used in its Milk Deluxe series. AQSIQ assessed its safety and deemed it not harmful. However, since Mengniu's import procedure was not legal, it ordered Mengniu to stop adding OMP.

Mengniu's damage-control measures included written apologies to consumers, cash contribution to a medical compensation fund for melamine victims, major investment to upgrade its quality control system, and increased advertising and promotional activities to regain consumer confidence. Rebuilding reputation and brand image would take time. By April 2009, CEO Niu reported that sales had recovered to 80% of pre-scandal levels.

The melamine and OMP incidents prompted the passing of a new Food Safety Law with a special focus on food addictives by the National People's Congress on 28 February 2009. This should help with building trust regarding food and beverage products produced on the mainland.

Victoria Chu

References

China Mengniu Dairy Company Limited. Company overview. http://mengniuir.com/about.htm. Retrieved on 15 April 2009.

China Mengniu Dairy Company Limited. *Annual Report 2008*. http://www.mengniuir.com/admin/attach/20090429d_e.pdf. Retrieved on 20 June 2009.

China's free range cash cow: Upstart Mengniu Dairy isn't tethered to the state. It's thriving — and the shareholders are contented (24 October 2005). *Business Week*. http://www.businessweek.com/magazine/content/05_43/b3956083.htm. Retrieved on 30 April 2009.

Datamonitor Industry Profiles: Dairy in China (16 December 2008). *Datamonitor*, Emerging Markets Information Services. Retrieved on 23 April 2009.

Mengniu begins the long journey back (13 December 2008). *South China Morning Post*, Emerging Markets Information Services. [23 April 2009].

Mengniu pays for scandal with 948.6m yuan loss (17 April 2009). *South China Morning Post*, Emerging Markets Information Services. [23 April 2009].

Milk scandal devastates export market (7 December 2008). *Shanghai Daily*, Emerging Markets Information Services [23 April 2009].

CHINA MERCHANTS BANK

Corporate Address and Contact Information

China Merchants Bank Co. Ltd.
7088 Shennan Boulevard
Futian District, Shenzhen
Guangdong Province 518040
People's Republic of China
Phone: (86)755-8319-8888
Fax: (86)755-8319-5109
www.cmbchina.com
cmb@cmbchina.com

China Merchants Bank (CMB 招商银行股份有限公司) is the first share-holding commercial bank in China that is wholly owned and controlled by corporate legal entities. CMB mainly focuses on the Chinese domestic market. It is the first commercial bank introducing Internet banking, e-mail, and mobile telephone-based online payment platform and solution in China. The company ranked first in "The Best Banking Institution in China" and third in "The Best Banking Institution in Asia" in the selection of "Asia's Best Companies for 2008" organized by *Euromoney*. Over the past 20 years, CMB has been playing a vital role in the country's economic development.

Historical Development

Until 1979, The People's Bank of China was the only bank in charge of a large number of issues, such as the conduct of monetary policy, exchange policy, foreign reserve management, deposit-taking, commercial-lending activities, and the financing of development projects. The introduction of a two-tier banking system in 1979 was the first milestone in the modernization of the Chinese banking system. China Merchants Bank is one of the second-tier banks established after the commencement of Chinese banking system reform.

China Merchants Bank was established on 8 April 1987 as a small regional bank located in Shekou, Shenzhen. However, CBM has transitioned itself from a regional bank into a national commercial bank with certain scale and influence. With headquarters located in Shenzhen, Guangdong Province, the bank has been building up its business network and, penetrated into cities around the country. As of December 2008, the company had 44 branches in 30 major cities in China. After developing the domestic business, the bank aimed on expanding the business overseas. CMB has established correspondent relationship with 1,756 overseas financial institutions in 93 countries and regions. On 8 October 2008, New York Branch of CMB officially commenced operation. It was the first time that a Chinese bank was approved by the Federal Reserve to establish a branch in the United States since the enactment of the Foreign Bank Supervision Enhancement Act of 1991 in the United States.

Since its inception, CMB underwent substantial capital investment three times. The bank launched IPO with the issuance of 1.5 billion common shares in March 2002, was successfully listed on the Shanghai Stock Exchange on 9 April 2002. In September 2006, the bank was also listed on the Hong Kong Stock Exchange.

Main Product and Services

CMB is a pioneer in the use of technical innovation and IT as a competitive tool in the rapidly evolving Chinese banking sector. CMB provides commercial and retail banking services in China. The bank operates in the following segments: corporate banking, retail banking, treasury business, and others.

The corporate banking segment provides financial services to corporations and institutions such as lending and deposit-taking activities, project and structured finance products, syndicated loans, cash management, investment advice, and other investment services. Retail banking includes provision of financial services to retail customers. Treasury business segment covers interbank and capital market activities and proprietary trading. Its other segment comprises the equity investments.

China Merchants Bank remains the leading position in the domestic bankcard arena. CMB uses an IT-driven strategy to introduce an "All-in-one card", which integrates a suite of financial products to drive its personal banking business. The "All-in-one card", which was launched in July 1995, was rewarded as a milestone invention of personal banking in the industry. As of December 2008, the accumulated issuing volume of the card has exceeded 33 million, while the deposit per card goes beyond RMB 4500.

In September 1999, China Merchants Bank first launched on-line banking service platform "All-in-one net", which was once again in the leading place both in terms of technical capacity and business volume. This service was chosen by many leading enterprises and e-commerce websites as either the main or exclusive on-line settlement provider. In 2 June 2003, as the representative product of Chinese e-commerce and on-line banking, "All-in-one net" was granted "Nomination Award" by International Computer World Honors Program (CHP).

China Merchants Bank is the first of the kind in developing a series of e-banking distribution channel, such as on-line banking, phone banking, mobile banking, and self-service banking, etc. to offer its clients with "triple-A" financial services. Acting upon the principle of Market Segmentation, China merchants bank, expect for its efforts to provide quality services to the general public, it goes ahead further to develop "one-to-one" tailor made services to its affluent clients with its ever-improving professional and individualized service quality. In August 2004, the bank created another top-performing service in the country by establishing a "Customer Satisfaction Index System" to achieve a sustainable competitive advantage of management and service quality.

Growth Strategies

China Merchants Bank has generally been adhering to the "technology-oriented" development strategy. CMB has undertaken a number of measures that combined market explorations and innovations in respect of products and services, which enables the bank to perform well above its competitors. The bank has also been constantly adjusting itself in an effort to meet the ever-changing demands of the market as well as its clients. By enacting the substantial advantages of the unified electronic platform, the bank has launched a series of industry leading financial products and services, and also successfully built up some well-known brand names such as "All-in-one card", "All-in-one net", "Sunflower", "Go Fortune", "China Merchants Bank Credit Card", and "Wealth Management Account" which has been widely accepted by the society as an IT-driven commercial bank.

In recent years, the bank also pursed a number of business expansion and diversification strategy. In June 2006, China Merchants Bank entered into an agreement to acquire certain equity interests in China Merchants Fund Management Co. Ltd. In 2007, the CMB was approved to establish a wholly owned finance leasing company and to acquire 33.4% equity interest in China Merchants Fund Management Co. Ltd. so as to become its largest shareholder.

In 2008, the CMB advanced important steps toward globalized and comprehensive operations. The New York Branch was opened for business on Wall Street, which was the first branch that a Chinese bank was approved to establish in the United States. The bank successfully took over Wing Lung Bank, a bank with 75 years' history that ranked fourth among Hong Kong's local banks. It was so far the biggest acquisition of controlling equity interests in a bank in mainland China and was the biggest acquisition of the kind in recent years in Hong Kong. Other growth initiatives and major activities included the successful subscription for shares in Taizhou Commercial Bank, the successful issuance of the first tranche of asset-backed securities, the commencement of the business operation of CMB Financial Leasing Company Limited, the steady progress of the acquisition of equity interests in CIGNA & CMC Life Insurance Company and in the Trust & Investment Corporation of the Tibet Autonomous Region.

China Merchants Bank is well recognized by its clients and the general public as a bank of innovation, for the quality service, and for the advanced technologies. It not only results in a reform and development of Chinese banking industry but also allows the bank to achieve excellent business performance. As per the annual report of 2008, the accumulated taxable profit was above to 26 billion Yuan. The major operating indicators such as profit per capita, return on equity ranked the top among domestic commercial banks. In the recent years, China Merchants Bank won rewards and recognition granted by a number of domestic and overseas press organizations as "The Best Domestic Commercial Bank in China", "The most respectable Enterprises in China", and one of "the Top 10 Public Companies in China", respectively.

Mohammad Faisal Ahammad

References

China Merchant Bank (2008). *Annual Report.* http://file.cmbchina.com/cmbir/781cd545-d7d5-44ba-9048-100b41ca1058.pdf. Retrieved on 23 May 2009.

China Merchant Bank (2007). *Annual Report.* http://file.cmbchina.com/cmbir/20080611/c43784fa-4cc0-4ee9-a13b-e28623c57e56.pdf. Retrieved on 23 May 2009.

China Merchant Bank (2006). *Annual Report.* http://file.cmbchina.com/cmbir/20080611/89846bf8-192a-467c-a48e-f031f173c8d7.pdf. Retrieved on 23 May 2009.

CHINA MINMETALS

Corporate Address and Contact Information

China Minmetals Corporation
5 Sanlihe Road
Haidian District
Beijing 100044
People's Republic of China
Phone: (86)10-6849-5888
Fax: (86)10-6833-5570
http://www.minmetals.com
support@minmetals.com.cn

China Minmetals Corporation (中国五矿集团公司) is one of the largest metals and minerals trading companies in the world, and the largest iron and steel trader in China. The company exports coke, coal, and ferroalloys; imports iron ore, steel scraps, and slabs and billets; and sells about 20 million tons of steel products annually. It has domestic iron ore-mining operations and helps steel producers abroad with facility construction and equipment supply. Other subsidiaries deal in financial services, real estate development, and transportation logistics. China Minmetals' sales network stretches through Africa, the Americas, Asia, Australia, and Europe. It operates more than 100 offices in China and more than 40 companies abroad.

Historical Development

China Minerals Corp., one of the predecessors of China Minmetals Corporation, was established in 1950 soon after the formation of the People's Republic of China. Its primary business was steel and raw materials distribution. However, in the early 1980s, the company began diversifying away from its core business into engineering and hotels while also establishing many wholly owned subsidiaries, partnerships, and alliances in coastal cities and in China's new special economic zones.

In the late 1980s, in accordance with China government policy, the company became financially independent and, for the first time, took responsibility for profits and losses. By 1997, the company was ready to list on the Shanghai Stock Exchange as China Minmetals Group, eventually changing to its current name, China Minmetals Corporation, in 2004.

Today, Minmetals has evolved from a pure import and export company into a fully integrated global enterprise with substantial resources in both downstream and upstream industries. It is now one of the largest metals and minerals trading companies in the world and the largest iron and steel trader in China. The core business involves trading, investing in, and operating businesses in steel and other metal products. Minmetals operates 24 mines and owns large-scale reserves of iron ore, coking coal, ferberite, and bauxite. Its non-ferrous product interests include copper, aluminum, tungsten, tin, antimony, lead, zinc, and nickel.

Minmetals is also involved in diversified activities such as electrical products, real estate development, financial services, marine shipping, mining, and other non-related activities.

Corporate Structure and Services

China Minmetals Corporation is a state-owned enterprise based in Beijing. It has five major business units comprising iron and steel, non-ferrous metals, finance, real estate, and logistics.

As a parent organization, Minmetals seeks synergy across all businesses through provision of a wide-range of services including finance and logistics. It operates more than 100 subsidiaries and offices in 25 Chinese provinces and regions, together with almost 200 wholly owned or joint venture investments. Minmetals also holds controlling interests in 18 listed companies in China and operates more than 40 companies abroad.

Minmetals interest in the financial sector includes a joint venture with the French insurance giant AXA, which makes it the first insurance company to become a Qualified Domestic Institutional Investor (QDII) in China. Minmetals' property interests include development of residential and industrial real estate, commercial real estate, building and installment, and mining construction. The group also has majority shareholdings in Beijing Shangri-la Hotel and minority holdings in other hotels and office blocks.

Minmetals' logistics division has evolved into a major business in its own right, comprising 49 domestic subsidiaries and providing a fully integrated service that includes freight forwarding, marine shipping, cargo space chartering, insurance, storage, and freight transportation. Minmetals currently ranks number three among all shipping companies in the country.

Financial Performance

In the later part of 2008, all of Minmetals' five key businesses were adversely affected by the global financial crisis and higher costs of imported alumina. In spite of this, Minmetals reported a growth in business and profits for the 10th consecutive year. While operating revenue rose to RMB 180.9 billion (USD 25.7 billion), up 15.9%, and sales revenue reached RMB $27.7 billion (USD 4.1 million), up 28%, profit remained relatively flat at RMB 7.1 billion (USD 1.04 billion), increasing by only 4.4%.

According to Zhou Zhongshu, President of China Minmetals, the group's consistent record of growth was difficult to maintain in 2008 against a backdrop of severe natural disasters and the international financial crisis. In 2008, ferrous and non-ferrous metals businesses accounted for 79.5% of total group profits while the contributions of property and financial services businesses continued to increase. In 2005, Minmetals implemented a five-year plan with the objective to double business revenue to RMB 200 billion and profits to RMB 6 billion. These targets were achieved during 2008, more than one year ahead of schedule.

Key Challenges and Business Strategies

In the past 20 years, national economic growth has been the major driver of China Minmetals Corporation's expansion. The new century saw the Chinese government introduce plans for rationalization of the steel industry. This, together with the competitive pressures arising from international expansion, has been the main catalyst for recent organizational change.

Moving forward, Minmetals faces a number of challenges at both macro and industry levels. In the near-term, government policy is expected to change rapidly in response to global and domestic economic circumstances. The government will also play a key role in determining mergers and acquisitions related to the Steel Industry Plan. As one of the nation's 39 key enterprises related to national economic security, Minmetals will be called upon to show leadership in implementing macroeconomic policy changes and, thereby, safe-guarding China's national interests.

Cyclical fluctuations in the price of, and demand for, raw materials will be a continuing challenge in the metals business while ongoing international examination of China's exchange rate will increase the complexity of Minmetals' strategic decision making.

Overseas expansion is a key plank in Minmetals' strategic plans for its core metal business. Reserves of iron ore, chromium, copper, gold, and molybdenum are being expanded through resources integration and a series of international acquisitions. While consolidating existing markets in Europe, Japan, Australia, and South America, the group is also opening up new markets in Southeast Asia, India, and Russia.

Supply chain control through reverse integration is a primary strategic focus as the company invests in mine development, smelting, processing, and manufacture. Where acquisition is not a viable option, Minmetals seeks to establish strategic alliances and long-term supply agreements.

In the financial business, strong international competition within the domestic market underscores the importance of operational change and internationalization. Minmetals has signaled its intention to develop upstream businesses including leasing, insurance, futures, and other securities business.

Minmetals' interests in the property sector have been focused in residential property, tourism, and commercial real estate, with recent expansion realized through acquisition of property-related businesses both in China and abroad. In the future, the group will also pursue major industrial real estate projects.

Minmetals' logistics operations provide a strategic opportunity to the group both as a competitive advantage to its own operations and as a key business unit. Minmetals will seek to grow this business through further expansion of services and introduction of modern logistics systems.

Future Outlook

Minmetals acknowledges that its international competitiveness is underpinned by the quality of its human capital. Management skills in China are at a premium, yet the skills and innovative capabilities for high-level decision making are critical to Minmetals' success. Technology upgrades and the capabilities to optimize its value are accorded a high priority throughout the group.

China Minmetals Corporation has the financial strength, the market position, and the government support to work through the current macroeconomic turbulence and become an even stronger global player in mining and metals production. Its future is heavily dependent on its ability to control its supply channels through shrewd acquisitions and alliances, a competency that the group appears to be confirming as we enter the new decade.

Lin Song and Terence R. Egan

References

China Minmetals Corporation. About Minmetals. http://www.minmetals.com/english/introduction.jsp. Retrieved on 20 May 2009.

China Minmetals profits hit US$932m (23 January 2008). Xinhua News Agency http://www.china.org.cn/business/2008-01/23/content_1240429.htm. Retrieved on 25 February 2009.

China Minmetals reports growth for 9th straight year (12 February 2009). http://news.xinhuanet.com/english/2009-02/12/content_10808294.htm. Retrieved on 25 February 2009.

Chaney, J (2009). China's Minmetals warns of '08 profit decline (6 March). Reuters http://www.reuters.com/article/rbssIndustryMaterialsUtilitiesNews/idUSHKG25324820090307. Retrieved on 15 March 2009.

Hemerling, M, DC Michael, and H Michaelis (2006). *China's Global Challengers: The Strategic Implications of Chinese Outbound M&A*. Boston Consulting Group. http://www.bcg.com/impact_expertise/publications/files/Chinas_Global_Challengers_May06.pdf. Retrieved on 20 May 2009.

Litvak, IA (2005). *China Minmetals Corporation and Noranda, Inc.* Richard Ivey School of Business, University of Western Ontario.

CHINA MINSHENG BANKING

Corporate Address and Contact Information

China Minshen Banking Corp. Ltd.
2 Fuxingmennei Street
Xicheng District
Beijing 100031
People's Republic of China
Phone: (86)10-5856-0088
www.cmbc.com.cn

China Minsheng Banking Corporation Ltd. (CMBC中国民生银行股份有限公司), founded on 12 January 1996, is one of the young but dynamic and innovative commercial banks in China. CMBC is the country's first national, non state-owned joint-stock bank as well as the first of its kind listed in the Chinese Stock Exchange Market. The bank is probably one of the safest bets with its non-performing loan ratio being 1.2 % in 2008, in sharp contrast with China's other four state-owned commercial banks. Distinguishing from other banks in China, CMBC has established standardized operation under modern corporate system, clear market positioning to small- and medium-sized corporate customers and its advanced IT system, all contribute to the bank's quick growth in its short history.

Historical Development

In 1995, China National Federation of Industry and Commerce was reported to facilitate the founding of China Minsheng Bank, which was finally established on 12 January 1996 in Beijing. Being a joint-stock bank run exactly under of the Company Law and the Commercial Bank Law of China, CMBC was to function as a model of a formal business system for the Chinese banking sector. In addition, the bank also aimed to provide more financial supports to those private businesses in its business growth. Therefore, from the very beginning, CMBC oriented its target market to be non-state-owned, hi-tech, small- and medium-sized businesses. However, the bank experienced very poor operation results in the first three years. The non-performing loan ratio by the end of 1999 reached 8.72%, and the loss for ROE was about 40%.

To turn around the undesirable situation, in April 2000, CMBC changed its leadership team, with the new one headed by Dong Wenbiao, who was well known for his initiative and outstanding track record. Under the new leadership, CMBC soon recovered from the decline and doubled its total assets and loans within a year. By the end of that year, the bank successfully launched its A-share IPO on the Shanghai Stock Exchange. By 2004, CMBC's total assets came to RMB 445.4 billion (USD 65.5 billion), the total loan amount to RMB 253.5 billion (USD 37.3 billion), and the capital adequacy rate 8.59%, which means the bank has overcome the initial survival crisis.

On 8 November 2004, CMBC successfully issued subordinated bonds of RMB 5.8 billion (USD 853 million), which was the first in China to do so by private placement in the national inter-bank bond market. On 26 October 2005, the bank, among others, was the first again to accomplish the share-trading reform, which provided a successful model for the share-trading reform in the Chinese capital market. From 2005, CMBC entered a stage of adjustment and enhancement. In February 2007, CMBC initiated the Five-Year Development Program (2007–2011), which outlines an ambitious goal for CMBC to become an international financial holding group with commercial bank business as its core activities to offer holistic financial products or services to its customers by the end of program period.

Since its listing, CMBC has conducted a series of innovations both on business and management, such as the "integrated" scientific platform, two-rate performance appraisal mechanism, three-card program, independent appraisal system, eight basic management systems, business model of centralized processing, and the reform of divisional system. Up to 30 June 2008, CMBC had total assets of RMB 1,062.2 billion (USD 156 billion), net profit of RMB 6.046 billion (USD 889 million), total deposits of RMB 760.404 billion (USD 111.8 billion), total loans (including discount) of RMB 612.051 billion (USD 90 billion), and non-performing loan ratio of 1.2%, maintaining a leading position in China in many of its business sectors. In addition, the bank is also on the acquisitions trail to expend into overseas markets. On 3 March 2008, CMBC took over US-based UCBH (United Commercial Bank Holdings) with 10% stake.

Corporate Structure and Services

Till March 2009, CMBC has 26 branches in mainland China, one directly governed branch, and one representative office in Hong Kong, totaling 348 establishments.

As a public company, CMBC has a standardized corporate governance structure, with six committees (strategic development, risk management, audit, related party transaction control, nomination, and remuneration evaluation) under the Board of Directors, and two committees (supervision and nomination) under the Board of Supervisors. CMBC seeks to run the bank under the framework of real corporate governance from the initial founding, and its practices often take great significances to the reform of the other Chinese banks. The innovativeness on its corporate governance is embodied by its appointment of the independent directors and its internationalized way to disclose the information. CMBC was the first bank to engage international auditors to do auditing, the transparency and specialization of which further enhances its level on the corporate governance.

The present chairman of BOD is Mr. Dong Wenbiao, the former president of the bank. Born in 1957, Don once worked as a deputy dean of Henan Institute of Financial Management, and later was appointed as the managing director of Zhengzhou Branch, Bank of Communications and chairman as well as president of Haitong Securities Co. Ltd. His outstanding performances in each of these positions made him a legendary figure in the industry. Included among the top management team are Hong Qi, President; Wu Touhong, CFO; Liang Yutang, Shao Ping, and Zhao Pinzhang, VPs; and Mao Xiaofeng, Secretary.

CMBC provides personal, corporate, and e-banking services, including personal savings, loans, debit cards, financial planning, international personal financing, and corporate deposits, bills, trading, asset management, wealth management, settlement, financial leasing, and intermediate. Among them, the most successful includes business finance, which is a division engaged in the loans to small- and medium-sized businesses. CMBC has increased such loans by RMB 13 billion (USD 1.9 billion) in 2008, ranked second in all Chinese banks. In addition, CMBC has also been successful in trade finance and automobile finance.

CMBC underwent a structural reform in 2008–2009, as a result four product divisions as well as six sector divisions were built. The four product divisions are business finance department, trade finance department, investment banking department, and financial marketing department. The six sector divisions include property finance department, energy finance department, traffic finance department, metallurgy finance department, credit card center, and private banking department. The restructuring proves to be a great success, as financial statistics show that by June of 2008, the division departments contribute to more than 50% of the whole profits earned by the bank, and the net non-interest income from the divisions accounts for 74% of the total net non-interest income.

Growth Strategies

In the recent years, CMBC kept an average assets increasing rate of about 25% and the growth rate of net profits 40%. The bank has changed its strategies from serving big corporate customers to critical big ones but largely on small- and medium-sized businesses, from only low risk-taking products to mid-level ones, from earnings mainly by interest margins to diversified incomes, and from product selling only to customer relations management as well as the provision of holistic financial services to customers. The new business tactics involve the promotion of credit cards, personal loans, financing, trade finance, and enlargement of personal and intermediary service percentage to the total income as well as diversification and intensification of the management style and business model. Looking forward, CMBC will continue to modulate the makeup of its customers, the structure of assets, and the composition of revenue. It is hoped that after another five-year development, the bank will realize its expectations that 40% of the income comes from large corporate customers, 30% from small- and medium-sized ones, and 30% from retailing. Finally, the financial services to those small-sized businesses would still be its primary focus.

For its outstanding performance, CMBC was ranked 18th of the "Top 100 Most Dynamic Chinese Enterprises" in 2004; listed 22nd among the Top 500 Chinese Enterprises in IT Competitiveness in 2005; awarded the "Best Online Bank 2005"; and ranked first among the "Top 100 Listed Private Enterprises 2006" in terms of market value and social contribution. In addition, CMBC was named the "Best Trade Finance Bank"; received the "Award for Excellent Innovations in China's Banking Industry" and the "Best Personal Wealth Management Brand" in 2007; and the "4th Gold Round Table Award for the Board of Directors of Chinese Listed Companies" in 2008.

CMBC is also getting international acceptance. It was ranked 28th in terms of total assets among the 200 Asian banks by *the Banker* in 2005, listed 7th in the "2006 Top 10 Chinese Enterprises" by *Forbes*, and was one of the "Top 50 Largest Listed Enterprises in Asia Pacific Region" by *Forbes* again in 2007. Furthermore, the bank was ranked second in terms of comprehensive competitiveness in *The Report on the Competitiveness of China's Commercial Banks 2008*, and ranked first in terms of corporate governance and process-oriented bank.

Xiaorong Zhu

References

China Minshen Banking Corp. Ltd. (2009). Company profile. http://www.cmbc.com.cn/en/about/jianjie.shtml. Retrieved on 30 April 2009.

王，松奇 (2008). *中国商业银行竞争力报告*. 北京：社会科学文献出版社 [Wang, S. *Annual Report on Competitiveness of China's Commercial Banks (2007)*. Beijing: Social Sciences Academic Press].

中国建设银行研究部课题组 (2008). *中国商业银行发展报告*. 北京：中国金融出版社 [Project Group of Research Department from Construction Bank of China, *China Commercial Bank Development Report*. Beijing: China Financial Press House].

CHINA MOBILE COMMUNICATIONS

Corporate Address and Contact Information

China Mobile Communications Corporation
No. 29, Financial Street
Xicheng District
Beijing 100032
People's Republic of China
http://www.chinamobile.com/en/mainland/index.html

China Mobile Limited
60/F, The Center
99 Queen's Road Central
Hong Kong, SAR

People's Republic of China
Phone: (85)2-3121-8888
Fax: (85)2-2511-9092
http://www.chinamobileltd.com

Over the decade since its creation in 2000, China Mobile Communications Corporation (China Mobile 中国移动有限公司) has become the largest wireless telecommunications provider in the world. Through its wholly owned subsidiary, China Mobile (HK) Group Limited, the company is the majority shareholder of China Mobile Limited, which is publicly traded on the Hong Kong and New York Stock Exchanges. As of mid-2009, China Mobile held the largest market capitalization of all overseas-traded Chinese companies and all Asian telecommunications carriers. The company has been listed in the *Fortune* Global 500 for several years, and was ranked at number 148 in 2008, having climbed 32 places from its 2007 ranking. Additionally, in September 2008, China Mobile became the first company from mainland China to be named to the *Dow Jones* Sustainability Index, a reference standard for socially responsible investing.

Historical Development

China Mobile emerged from the breakup of the state-controlled monopoly that was China Telecom back in the mid-1990s. By 1998, China Telecom was facing significant pressure from the central government that desperately needed to foster competition in domestic industries as China made its bid to join the World Trade Organization (WTO). The monopolistic company and its close partnership with the Ministry of Posts and Telecommunications (MPT) were both forced into reforms over the subsequent two years. The MPT was merged into the Ministry of Information Industry (MII), which was given less direct control, but more regulatory oversight over the telecom industry. Beginning in 1999, China Telecom was divided along its lines of service: fixed-line, mobile, paging, and satellite communications.

Officially launched in April 2000, China Mobile grew rapidly, and by year's end served almost 80% of China's wireless market. The company's major competitor was China United Telecommunications Corporation (China Unicom), to which China's central government (side-stepping the MPT monopoly) had years earlier granted a license to provide mobile telecom service. Unicom's initial focus was paging, having been sold China Telecom's paging network as part of the ongoing restructuring. However, with the financial market backing their successful public offering (IPO), Unicom was beginning to emerge as a solid rival to China Mobile, in a regulatory environment that was increasingly supportive of balanced competition.

China Mobile's own IPO on the Hong Kong Stock Exchange and New York Stock Exchange, back in 1997 under the name China Telecom (HK) Limited, had been quite successful in its own right, raising US$4.2 billion. This allowed the company to grow by acquisition of a number of provincial mobile carriers, such as Jiangsu Mobile, Fujian Mobile, and Hainan Mobile even before officially adopting the China Mobile moniker in 2000. A US$2.5 billion capital infusion, in the form of a share-purchase agreement with European Vodaphone Group Plc., paved the way for the further acquisition of regional mobile networks. The company also began issuing corporate bonds in 2001, which were enthusiastically received by the commercial markets.

By 2003, China already had around 200 million mobile subscribers, accounting for 20% of the global user base. This number has since grown tremendously, as regulators have pushed for broader mobile penetration, spurring further price competition among the major players in the market. By mid-2008, China was closing in on 600 million mobile users, more than the combined populations of the United States and Japan. China Mobile's share of the market has declined to roughly two-thirds, largely as a result of industry regulation and restructuring that has boosted some of the smaller players. A major industry overhaul, implemented in October 2008, established three major integrated companies in the Chinese telecom industry: China Mobile, China Unicom, and China Telecom (the dominant fixed-line provider that had retained the original company name). By way of a complex series of acquisitions of smaller operators, and the transfer of some holdings, each of these three companies was equipped to compete in the mobile, fixed-line, and broadband segments of the market.

Corporate Structure and Leadership

China Mobile Limited is lead by a team of 13 executive and non-executive directors, with Mr. Wang Jianzhou at the helm as chairman and CEO since November 2004. Wang is a senior engineer (professor level) with roughly 30 years of experience in the telecom industry, including leadership roles within the corporate structure of competitor China Unicom, as well as within the MPT and MII. He holds a doctoral degree in business administration from Hong Kong Polytechnic University.

The publicly traded China Mobile Limited serves a holding company for the 32 operating subsidiary companies that make up China Mobile Group, one in each of the PRC's 31 provinces and the special administrative region (SAR) of Hong Kong. The largest shareholder of the company is China Mobile (Hong Kong) Group Limited, which owns roughly 75% of the company's shares, with the remaining 25% held by public investors. In total, the company had 138,368 employees at the end of 2008. The company has been making efforts to streamline and standardize management of the many subsidiary companies under a project called "One China Mobile". The goal is to leverage a centralized, computerized management system to enhance both management efficiency and effectiveness.

2008 was a challenging year for the company's leadership, with the company having to deal with natural disasters in the form of earthquakes and flooding, and the massive service interruptions that ensued, plus having to deliver on the commitments made as major communications partner to the 2008 Beijing Olympic Games. By all accounts, the company delivered on all fronts, earning significant praise from adversely impacted communities and the International Olympic Committee alike. In addition, the company was ranked among the top globally performing companies on the *FT Global 500* (fifth place), *Forbes Global 2000* (78th place), and the *Info Tech 100* (seventh place). Moody's Investors Service and Standard and Poor's awarded credit ratings of A1/Stable and A+/Stable respectively, identical to the ratings for China's sovereign debt. The company finished 2008 with RMB 112.8 billion in net profit, representing a 27.4% net profit margin.

Main Products and Services

China Mobile provides customers with mobile telecommunications services that range broadly from local, long distance, and international voice service, to value added data services including broadband multimedia services and customizable information services. The company is constantly innovating to develop products and applications targeted at stratified market segments, as a means of driving higher average revenues per user (ARPU). As mobile handsets, with value-added multimedia applications, become an integral part of Chinese daily life, the company envisions the convergence of voice, data, and video, on a platform that meets the communications, education, and entertainment demands of individuals, families, and corporations.

The company's total subscriber base was listed officially at over 457 million users, and was increasing at over 7 million per month at the end of 2008. The same year saw total operating revenues of RMB 412.3 billion, up 15.5% from 2007 revenues, with value-added services (VAS) accounting for 27.5% of

2008 revenues. The most popular of the company's VAS offerings were Color Ringtone service (where customers can create or select custom ringtones to greet incoming callers), internal and third-party wireless applications (WAP) and mobile messaging services (MMS), which allow users to send multimedia messages, rather than simple text messages. These three services experienced 21.9%, 42.9%, and 83.7% growth respectively during 2008, demonstrating the company's ability to capitalize on the rapidly growing adoption of these technologies. Additionally, the company is seeing expanding adoption of its mobile music and mobile paper content (digitized printed media). The company's multimedia instant messaging service, "Fetion" grew to second place in mainland China's IM market with 147 million total subscribers.

Challenges and Business Strategies

While holding the dominant position in China's huge wireless market with over 65% market share, China Mobile still faces significant challenges. Government policies to stimulate demand and competition in the mobile telecom industry have had a mixed effect on the company. The lower mobile tariffs had aided the rapid growth of the subscriber base, but smaller competitors have been allowed to offer prices 10–20% below those of China Mobile in certain markets. Across the industry, new users have been courted with promotional rates and subsidized handsets, both of which erode revenues. These competitive forces are most keenly felt in large cities where the market is mature and approaching saturation.

In response, the company leadership has sought to expand rapidly in underserved rural areas, where market penetration is very low, taking advantage of their solid financial foundation and huge economies of scale in infrastructure development. The company's 2009 budget included RMB 32 billion of capital expenditures on current technology deployment, 70% of which is earmarked for rural development.

Another major area of challenge comes from the next generation of technology. China's telecom industry regulators decided to license not one, but three, third-generation (3G) technologies for the China market. As part of their efforts to foster competition and technology development, China Mobile was granted the license to develop and deploy the least mature of these technologies, called TD-SCDMA, a home-grown evolution of a failed competitor for European 3G adoption. While the central government is offering the company significant support in the development and evolution of the new standard, the limited availability of applications on that platform may prove a deterrent to some potential high-end users. Here the company will use its strength to its advantage. In early 2009, the company announced that it would buy a minority stake in Far EasTone, a Taiwanese company, and enter into a strategic cooperation agreement aimed at enhancing the value chain and vendor support for TD-SCDMA. Such strategic investments also extend the global footprint of China Mobile, and add value for roaming customers who travel beyond the mainland provinces and Hong Kong.

Mr. Wang and the leadership team at China Mobile hope to harness the company's world-class innovation and execution capability to overcome these challenges and thereby remain the dominant force in Chinese telecommunications, well into the future.

Keith L. Whittingham

References

And then there were three (23 January 2003). *Economist*. http://www.economist.com. Retrieved on 20 May 2009.

China Mobile Communication Corporation (2009). About CMCC. http://www.chinamobile.com/en/mainland/about/index.html. Retrieved on 28 May 2009.

China Mobile Limited (2009). *Annual Report 2008*. http://www.chinamobileltd.com/ir.php?menu=3. Retrieved on 28 May 2009.

Industry Shakeup Creates 3 Telecom Giants (25 May 2008). *China Daily*. http://www2.chinadaily.com.cn/china/2008-05/25/content_6709799.htm. Retrieved on 20 May 2009.

McCully, AD (2003). China Telecom. In *International Directory of Company Histories*. Farmington Hills MI: Gale (St. James Press), Vol. 50.

Meng, C (2009). Going across the strait — Strategic investment in FET. *Bank of America/Merrill Lynch Research Report*, 29 April. http://www.ml.com. Retrieved on 18 May 2009.

Rewired (29 May 2008). *Economist*. http://www.economist.com. Retrieved on 8 May 2009.

CHINA NATIONAL OFFSHORE OIL

Corporate Address & Contact Information

China National Offshore Oil Corporation
25 Chaoyangmenbei Avenue
Dongcheng District
Beijing 100010
People's Republic of China
Phone: (86)10-8452-1604
Fax: (86)10-6460-2503
www.cnooc.com.cn, www.cnoocltd.com

Best known by its acronym, CNOOC, the China National Offshore Oil Corporation (中国海洋石油总公司) is a state-owned enterprise designed as a vehicle to engage in the international energy trade. CNOOC operates internationally through its subsidiaries, such as the publicly listed and traded CNOOC Ltd. (中国海洋石油有限公司), which CNOOC controls with a 64% stake.

Historical Development

CNOOC was formed in 1982 for the express purpose of establishing an international energy multinational capable of dealing with the pre-existing global giants on a competitive basis. At its inception, the company was the sole Chinese corporation permitted to deal with energy trading internationally, and as such enjoyed an initial period of growth greatly bolstered by its monopoly-in-fact status.

CNOOC took a portion of its operations and assets public with the establishment and listing of CNOOC Limited in August 1999. CNOOC Limited was initially incorporated in Hong Kong and was listed on both the New York Stock Exchange (code: CEO) and the Stock Exchange of Hong Kong Limited (code: 0883) in February of 2001, rapidly becoming a constituent stock of the Hang Seng Index in July of 2001.

Corporate Leadership

In 1982, China's Deputy Minister of the Ministry of Petroleum Industry, Qin Wencai, was appointed as the first president of CNOOC. An accomplished politician as well as businessman, Qin was involved in the drafting of China's *Regulations of the People's Republic of China Concerning the Exploitation of*

Offshore Petroleum Resources in Cooperation with Overseas Partners, and can claim major responsibility for establishing many of the foundational advantages that CNOOC continues to enjoy to this day. The second president, Zhong Yiming, focused on establishing operations both with and without foreign partnerships while investing in major research into downstream petrochemical projects. Growth was continued in a similar manner by the third president, Wang Yan. The fourth president, Wei Liucheng, set the stage for CNOOC to catapult itself into mainstream global awareness. He developed the financial and capital side of the organization, taking the company public on both the Hong Kong and New York Stock Exchanges.

The current president and CEO of both China National Offshore Oil Co. (CNOOC) and CNOOC Ltd., Fu Chengyu, has led one of China's most important industries into an era of growth and prosperity, exploding onto the international stage with bold plans and dynamic new approaches to the energy industry. Fu received his B.S. in petroleum engineering from the Northeast Petroleum Institute in China and his master's degree in petroleum engineering from the University of Southern California. He has more than 30 years of experience in China's petroleum industry. Fu first joined CNOOC in 1982 and has since held executive leadership positions throughout the corporation and its subsidiaries. In October of 2003, he was appointed as President of CNOOC and as both Chairman of the Board and CEO of the company.

His term of leadership has been highlighted by bold moves and aggressive undertakings in the international arena. 2005 saw CNOOC make a cash offer for American oil company Unocal. While political pressures prevented the deal from coming to fruition, it was a landmark event in which CNOOC, under Fu's leadership, leapt out and announced its intent to compete globally, on even terms, with all the major global oil players. The proposed deal highlighted both the financial strength and the long-term, international strategic outlook of Fu and CNOOC. The deal illustrates the corporate commitment to growth through acquisition of key business units and a demonstrated willingness to pursue sophisticated global financial transactions. At the same time, the total compensation for the Fu and his top five executives together is less than five million dollars — quite remarkable for a team producing operating margins in excess of 40% for four of the last five years.

Main Products and Services

The scope of CNOOC activities, including the parent company and its numerous subsidiaries, is tremendous and places it squarely among the global energy giants of our time. CNOOC's core energy activities can be divided into six business sectors: first, oil and gas exploration; second, technical services; third, chemical and fertilizer production and refining; fourth, natural gas and power generation; fifth, financial services; and finally, logistic service and new energy development. Focusing on its primary energy industry activities, the CNOOC group is China's largest producer of offshore crude oil and natural gas and one of the largest independent oil and gas exploration and production companies in the world.

Being a true international energy multinational, CNOOC is not only engaged in the production, synthesis, and trade of raw and refined energy products but also deeply engaged in the corollary activities of energy production — chemical production, materials production, mining and mineral acquisition, refining, and metallurgy, to name just a few — not to mention engaging in all the research, development, and logistic activities necessary to support its continued involvement in such large scale industry. While CNOOC holds itself out as being mainly engaged in oil and natural gas exploration, development, production, and sales, it would be a grave mistake to examine CNOOC as anything other than a modern multinational: that is to say, CNOOC is engaged in the business of doing business.

Challenges and Business Strategies

CEO Fu's long-term strategies and international outlook seem to have paid off. October of 2007 has seen CNOOC make its debut in the Fortune 500 top enterprises in the world at number 469 and among the 50 companies with the fastest growing operating income, CNOOC ranks number 10. Concurrently, CNOOC is the fastest growing oil company in sales in the entire world. CNOOC is currently in the process of developing itself into a fully integrated energy company. Toward that end, CNOOC has the leading position in liquid natural gas sector in China and is expanding its market shares by focusing on downstream products such as urea, heavy bitumen, and fuel oil. CNOOC expects its current plan of adding to reserves, bringing new projects online (13 in 2008, 10 expected in 2009), and hitting a production target of 225–231 MMBOE (Million Barrels of Oil Equivalent) will put it on the path to achieve 6–10% average annual production growth through 2015.

Nonetheless, both Fu and CNOOC, under his direction, face rapidly increasing market competition from both domestic and international energy players as China continues to make progress on its WTO commitments. CNOOC is, at its heart, a state-owned company; it paid 60% of its 2007 total profit to the state in taxes. At the same time, CNOOC no longer holds an exclusive monopoly over the right to do business with foreign oil interests and other Chinese oil companies will no doubt continue to make inroads into CNOOC's monopoly. Both PetroChina and Sinochem are aggressively pursuing international assets and partnerships. Moreover, excessive state control has also hurt CNOOC's bottom line (albeit hurting its domestic competitors as well). Although CNOOC has been profitable for eight years and the recipient of numerous awards for business leadership in China, state price controls limited the price CNOOC could charge for oil during periods of intense price skyrocketing. CNOOC, while still performing admirably, largely missed out on the astounding record profits earned by foreign oil companies during the same time period.

Michael J. Miske

References

CNOOC Ltd. (2009). 2008 Annual Report. http://www.cnoocltd.com/encnoocltd/tzzgx/dqbd/nianbao/images/2009410578.pdf. Retrieved on 19 August 2009.

CNOOC makes debut in Fortune 500 (9 October 2007). CNOOC press release, www.cnooc.com.cn/yyww/xwygg/246712.shtml. Retrieved on 19 August 2009.

Good, A (2009). China oil & gas industry update. *Morningstar*, 11 March. http://quicktake.morningstar.com/Stocknet/san.aspx?id=295290. Retrieved on 19 August 2009.

Good, A (2009). New developments for the Chinese oil and gas sector. *Morningstar*, 15 June. http://quicktake.morningstar.com/Stocknet/san.aspx?id=283418. Retrieved on 19 August 2009.

Miske, M (2009). Fu Chengyu. In *Biographical Dictionary of New Chinese Entrepreneurs and Business Leaders*. W Zhang and A Alon (eds.), pp. 39–40. Northampton, MA: Edward Elgar Publishing.

Powell, B (2005). Uncharted waters. *Time Magazine*, 11 July. http://www.time.com/time/magazine/article/0,9171,1081438,00.html. Retrieved on 19 August 2009.

CHINA PACIFIC INSURANCE

Corporate Address and Contact Information

China Pacific Insurance (Group) Company Ltd. (SIC: 6311/6321/6331; NAICS: 524113/524114/524126)
190 Yincheng Zhong Road
Shanghai, People's Republic of China
Phone: (86)21-5877-6688
Fax: (86)21-6887-0922
www.cpic.com.cn
service@cpic.com.cn

China Pacific Insurance (Group) Company Ltd. (中国太平洋保险(集团)股份有限公司), or CPIC Group, is the second largest property insurer (after People's Insurance Company of China) and the third largest life insurance company (after China Life Insurance and Ping An Insurance) in PRC. It provides integrated insurance services, including life insurance, property insurance, and reinsurance, through its subsidiaries. CPIC is focusing on developing high-quality insurance products and services to utilize its competitive advantage in the Chinese insurance industry.

Historical Development

China Pacific Insurance (Group) Company Ltd. (CPIC) was established on the basis of China Pacific Insurance Company Ltd., which was founded in 1991 by the Insurance Division of the Shanghai branch of the Bank of Communications. It is headquartered in Shanghai, with registered capital at RMB 7.7 billion. In 2007, CPIC issued A-shares on the Shanghai Stock Exchange under the name "CPIC" and stock code "601601". At the first trading day, its share price raised 70% to its IPO price, signaling the high expectation of the investors. CPIC has been planning to issue H-shares on the Hong Kong Stock Exchange since 2001. To prepare for the listing, the CPIC has been streamlining its subsidiary structure, concentrating ownership. However, it is still not clear when the CPIC H-shares will be publicly traded.

Over the years, CPIC has achieved continuous growth in its business throughout the country. In 2007, the company recorded premium income of RMB 742 billion, a 32.5% increase than that of the year before. It has also received many honors and grown to become the third in the life insurance industry in mainland China. Together with China Life and Ping An, CPIC is an important leg of the tripod that represents the Chinese insurance industry. According to the Chinese consumers' satisfaction survey, which was conducted by the China Quality Association together with China Consumer Association and China Enterprises Research Center of Tsinghua University in 2003 and 2005, CPIC ranked the first in the overall satisfaction evaluation. Its customers' service line was also ranked among the Top 10 Satisfactory Brands of Call Centers in China as reviewed by the market information center of *People's Daily* in 2005, and as "the best customer service center in finance industry" sponsored by *Financial News* in 2008. By providing online services, CPIC achieved substantial growth. In 2008, it was ranked 48th among China's Top 500 Enterprises and 2nd among China's Top 500 Enterprises in the Service Industry, as well as in China's comprehensive insurance industry by the China Enterprises Confederation and China Entrepreneur Association.

CPIC has also made substantial progress in the property insurance business by providing various products to national events such as the 2008 Olympics, the Eastern Asian Games, etc. From 2002 to

2008, it ranked first for seven consecutive years in the survey on service quality of insurance industry sponsored by the China Association for Quality Promotion, an authoritative service quality supervision organization in China. In addition, CPIC is solely or jointly involved in the launching insurance, returning insurance, and the third-party liability insurance of 22 satellites home and abroad, reaching its services to diverse industry to satisfy the needs of different organizations and individuals.

While focusing on its financial development, CPIC has dedicated itself to charity activities in fulfilling its duty as a corporate citizen. It has taken an active role in helping the orphans, the disabled, and other people in flood-stricken areas since its establishment. In 2004, it donated RMB 6.27 million worth's life accident insurance and accident medical care insurance to the Chinese sports team attending 2004 Athens Paralympics Games.

Corporate Structure

China Pacific Insurance (Group) Company Ltd. is the holding company of the following subsidiary companies (as shown in Figure 4): China Pacific Life Insurance Company Ltd., China Pacific Property Insurance Company Ltd., Pacific Asset Management Company Ltd., China Pacific Insurance (HK) Company Ltd., and Pacific-Antai Life Insurance Company Ltd.

CPIC has approximately 185,000 insurance agents for insurance products and approximately 18,400 employees for related direct sales and marketing activities. It also has a large number of brokers, agents, and other intermediaries for promoting CPIC insurance products. Nationwide, CPIC has over 5,000 branches and marketing outlets, providing a wide range of risk prevention solutions, financial advices, and asset management to both individual and institutional clients.

Main Products and Services

CPIC is the holding and investment company whose subsidiaries are involved in various insurance businesses. Its main product and services concentrate on the insurance-related areas, each subsidiary takes responsibility of a particular area. Currently, CPIC has about 150 insurance products covering life, annuity, health, property, etc.

China Pacific Life Insurance Company Ltd. (CPIC Life) was incorporated in 2001 in Shanghai. It is a nationwide shareholder-owned commercial life insurance company, offering customers a variety

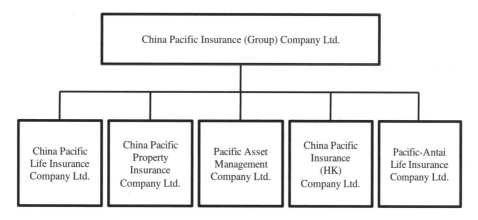

Figure 4.   Corporate structure.

Source: Adapted from CPIC company website http://www.cpic.com.cn.

of life products. Its predecessor is the life division of CPIC. CPIC Life provides over 100 products and services to its customers, including life, annuity, health, and accident life insurance, through its branches and distribution units across the country, as well as its subsidiaries and representative offices in Hong Kong, London, and New York. CPIC Life is also striving to improve its emergency assistance system and its call center service over the years. In 2008, the premium income of China Pacific Life Insurance reached RMB 66.09 billion, with a 9% market share in the Chinese life insurance market.

China Pacific Property Insurance Company Ltd. (CPIC Property) is responsible for the property and casualty insurance. It offers a variety of property insurance, short-term health insurance, and accident insurance. Its products and services cover industries such as electricity, automobile, machinery, chemistry, electronics, water conservancy, construction, bridges, roads, space and aviation marine, and high-tech. CPIC Property has established business ties with both domestic and international insurers, re-insurers and related institutions, and strived to provide quality risk-management services for its clients. Despite the 2008 global financial crisis, it generated a total premium of RMB 27.88 billion with an 18.7% increase comparing to 2007, helping CPIC achieve an 11.4% property insurance market share in China in 2008.

China Pacific Assets Management Company (CPIC Asset management) Ltd. was founded in 2006. Its business includes self-owned capital and premiums, entrusted capital management, capital management-related consulting services, and other asset management-related business. By the end of 2008, its net profit reaches RMB 18 million. CPIC Asset management has established complete mechanism for entrusted capital management. It has opened separate accounts for different entrusted capital, aiming to prevent moral risks.

China Pacific Insurance (HK) Company Ltd. (CPIC HK) was formed in 1994 in Hong Kong. It engages in general insurance business and other customer-tailored insurance, and provides services to individuals and organizations in Hong Kong and Macao. In 2008, CPIC HK achieved a premium of HKD 171 million, outperforming its competitors in Hong Kong.

Other than providing insurance products and services, CPIC also provides postdoctoral training since 2004. By cooperating with the post-doctoral research program of Fudan University, CPIC has jointly admitted post-doctorates to help develop innovative insurance products and services.

Challenges and Business Strategies

With the increasing competition and uncertainty in the financial market worldwide, CPIC aims at strengthening its position in the Chinese domestic market. It plans to spend RMB 498 million to increase its stake in Changjiang Pension Insurance Company to 51.75%. If approved by the regulatory authority, it will be the first major merger and acquisition transaction between two Chinese domestic insurers, which will likely help CPIC in exceeding its rival Ping An Insurance in pension insurance market in China.

After decades of development, CIPC has become one of the most renowned insurance companies in China. CIPC pays much attention to the construction of its brand image and online services. It also focuses on improving the hotline system and the emergency assistance service. By and large, CPIC has been working toward its goal of becoming the leading financial group with international competitiveness focusing on Chinese domestic insurance business. In the future, CPIC is planning to develop further by emphasizing more on internationalization and diversification to enhance its innovation ability and support its transformation into a competitive player in the global financial market.

Hao Chen

References

China Pacific Insurance (Group) Co. Ltd. (2009). Company profile. https://www.cpic.com.cn/cpic/en/about/index.jsp. Retrieved on [25 may 2009].

Datamonitor (2004). Non-life insurance industry profile: China. www.datamonitor.com. Retrieved on 25 May 2009.

Datamonitor (2004). Life insurance & pensions industry profile: China. www.datamonitor.com. Retrieved on 25 May 2009.

Hogue, RD (1999). The Chinese insurance market. *Insurance Advocate*, 110(23).

CHINA PETROLEUM AND CHEMICAL

Corporate Address and Contact Information

China Petroleum & Chemical Corporation
6A Huixindong Street
Chaoyang District
Beijing 100029
People's Republic of China
Phone: (86)10-6499-0060
Fax: (86)10-6499-0022
http://www.sinopec.com/

China Petroleum and Chemical Corporation (中国石油化工股份有限公司) is a vertically integrated energy and chemical company. As China's largest producer and supplier of refined oil products and major petrochemical products, the company is engaged in all aspects of operations relating to oil and natural gas that include exploration, production, refining, marketing, and distribution. Operated primarily in China, it is headquartered in Beijing and employs more than 334,000 people.

Historical Development

China Petroleum and Chemical Corporation (Sinopec) was established in 2000 when its parent company, China Petrochemical Corporation (Sinopec Group), reorganized its assets into one company. As a result, Sinopec Group, a state-owned company, holds a stake of 75.8% in the company.

After laying its first oil pipeline in Southern China in 2000, Sinopec issued 2.8 billion domestic A-Shares in China in 2001, and consequently became the first Chinese company to be listed on four stock exchanges around the world, including the Hong Kong Stock Exchange, the New York Stock Exchange, the London Stock Exchange, and the Shanghai Stock Exchange. In the same year, the company acquired the National Star Petroleum from its parent company, China Petrochemical Corporation; later that year, Sinopec also joined the force with the Sinopec Shanghai Petrochemical Corporation (SPC), and British Petroleum (BP) to form a new joint venture, Shanghai Secco Petrochemical Company. In 2002, in an effort to further consolidate its operations, the company agreed to exchange certain water plants, geophysical assets, and inspection and maintenance service for some petrol stations, oil depot assets, and interests owned by Sinopec Group.

In 2004, the company announced plans to work with BP on the construction of an acetic acid project in Beijing. During the same year, Sinopec further acquired chemical assets, catalyst assets, and service stations from Sinopec Group and sold down-hole operation assets as a swap. In 2005, the company entered into an agreement to purchase catalyst assets from Shanghai Petrochemical, and established Sinopec Corporation Gas Company in Beijing. Later in 2005, the company began to construct a refining project with a refining capacity of 10 million tons per annum. In addition, Sinopec established BP YPC Acetyls Company in Nanjing, a joint venture with BP, to manufacture acetic acid.

In 2006, the company discovered the Puguang Gas Field in the Northeast region of Sichuan Province, which turns out to be the largest and richest gas field ever discovered in China, with the aggregate proved recoverable reserves estimated at 251.1 billion cubic meters. In the same year, the company formed a strategic alliance with McDonald's, which enabled the fast food giant to establish drive-thru restaurants in Sinopec's gas stations. Meanwhile Sinopec launched another project in Tianjin with one million tons per annum ethylene and associated facilities, and acquired the oil production assets of the Shengli Petroleum Administration Bureau from Sinopec Group.

Sinopec speeded up its expansion drive in 2007. After entering into an agreement with China Resources to acquire 20 oil and gas stations, petroleum product, and refined oil business in Hong Kong, it signed a memorandum of understanding (MOU) to take a minority stake in the Orinoco projects in Venezuela, and partnered with CNOOC (*China National Offshore Oil Corporation*) and the Guangdong provincial government to form a joint venture, Guangdong Natural Gas Pipeline. During the same year, Sinopec formed a joint venture with DuPont to produce ethylene vinyl acetate (EVA) in China, signed a contract with Iran to develop its Yadavaran oil field, and Sinopec SenMei (Fujian) Petroleum Company (SSPC), a joint venture of Sinopec, Exxon Mobil, and Saudi Armco Sino Company, was also launched. In addition, Sinopec and Chinese automaker Chery reached a full-range strategic partnership agreement, in which both companies would combine efforts to develop green-energy vehicles.

Sinopec has further strengthened its strategic partnership with international firms over recent years. In 2008, it reached an agreement with BP to set up an acetic acid factory in Southwestern China, and received approval from the Chinese government for a $900 million joint chemical Verbund facility with BASF (Badische Anilin und Soda Fabrik) in Nanjing. Sinopec also signed a joint venture (JV) agreement with Mitsubishi to manufacture and sell chemical products in China, and planned to invest up to $4.5 billion to establish a refining factory in Khanh Hoa, Vietnam along with Petrolimexis, the largest Vietnamese state-owned petroleum-trading company. Within China, Sinopec signed an agreement with the local government to jointly construct China's single integrated refining and petrochemical complex in Zhejiang Province, which upon completion would carry a processing capacity of approximately 300,000 barrels per day. In strategic cooperation with the Shanghai municipal government, the company also planned to build a refining and petrochemical complex in Shanghai to increase fuel supply to the metropolis.

Corporate Structure and Financial Data

Sinopec primarily operates through five principal business segments: exploration and production, refining, marketing and distribution, chemicals, and the corporate and others segment. Its subsidiaries include 13 oilfields, regional companies, gas, pipeline and storage facilities, 26 refineries and petrochemical operations, 19 oil products and sale operations scattered around the country, eight subsidiaries and joint ventures, six research institutions, and four other related businesses.

For 2008, Sinopec's total asset reached 752.235 billion RMB, with total revenue of 1452.1 billion RMB and a total profit of 24.226 billion RMB. In 2008, Sinopec's net profit fell 47%, the first such decline in seven years. However, Sinopec expects its first quarter earnings to rise more than 50% in 2009, as oil costs drop and domestic fuel prices climb. Unlike its bigger rival PetroChina Co., which is keeping its capital budget flat and slashing output, Sinopec plans to increase capital spending and production, as the company has announced to increase its capital expenditures by 4.2% to RMB 111.8 billion, of which 55 billion will be spent on developing oil and gas fields and building gas pipelines in China. In 2009, Sinopec plans to refine 184 million metric tons of crude oil, up 8.9% from last year, and produce 1.4% more crude oil, or 42.4 million tons, and 20% more natural gas, or 10 billion cubic feet. Output of fuel, mainly gasoline and diesel, is forecasted to rise 8.6% to 115 million tons.

Main Products, Services, and Growth Strategies

As a leading producer and marketer of oil and petrochemical products in China, Sinopec's principal operations include exploration, development, production, and marketing of crude oil and natural gas, oil refining and marketing, and production and sales of petrochemicals, chemical fibers, chemical fertilizers, and other chemicals. The company also engages in storage and pipeline transportation of crude oil and natural gas, import and export of crude oil, natural gas, refined oil products, petrochemicals, chemicals, and other related commodities. The company operates through more than 80 subsidiaries and branches mainly located in China.

The exploration and production segment of Sinopec explores and develops oil fields, produces crude oil and natural gas, and sells products to the refining segment of the company. Most of its oil and gas reserves are located in the eastern, western, and southern parts of China, covering 26 provinces. At the end of 2007, Sinopec had proved oil and gas reserves of 4,079 million barrels of oil equivalent (MMBOE); and in the fiscal year 2007, the company produced 291.7 million barrels of crude oil and 282.6 billion cubic feet (BCF) of natural gas.

Sinopec's refining business segment processes and purifies crude oil, which is sourced from both its own exploration and production segment and external suppliers and manufacturers, and sells petroleum products. Sinopec is the largest refiner of petroleum in China based on crude oil throughput. The company's major oil products include gasoline, kerosene, diesel, lube oil, chemical light feedstock, fuel oil, solvent oil, petroleum wax, asphalt, petroleum coke, liquefied petroleum gas (LPG), propylene, and benzene products for refining. The company has 30 branches (subsidiaries), mainly located in China's southeast coastal regions, middle, and lower reaches of Yangtze River and in Northern China. By the end of 2007, the company's total processing capacity reached 190 million tons per annum.

The marketing and distribution segments own and operate oil depots and service stations across the country, and distribute and sell refined petroleum products (mainly gasoline and diesel) in China through wholesale and retail sales networks. At the end of 2007, the company owned 29,062 retail stations, among which 657 sites are under franchise agreement.

The company's chemicals segment manufactures and markets petrochemical products, derivative petrochemical products, and other chemical products mainly to external customers. As the largest producer and distributor of petrochemicals in China, Sinopec produces and distributes a range of petrochemical products, including intermediates, synthetic resin, synthetic fiber monomers and polymers, and chemical fertilizer. At the end of 2007, the company had 10 ethylene plants (including two joint venture companies), 24 synthetic resin plants, 13 producers of synthetic fiber monomers and polymers, eight synthetic fiber plants, five synthetic rubber plants, and six urea plants. The corporate and others segment consists principally of trading activities of the import and export subsidiaries and the company's research and development activities.

William X. Wei

References

China Petroleum & Chemical Corporation Company Profile. http://english.sinopec.com. Retrieved on 26 April 2009.

China Petroleum & Chemical Corporation (2009). *Annual Report*. http://english.sinopec.com/download_center/reports/2008/20090330/download/AnnualReport2008.pdf. Retrieved on 26 April 2009.

Datamonitor (2008). *China Petroleum & Chemical Corporation Company Profile*. http://reports.manta.com/datamonitor/summary/0289-17385_ITM. Retrieved on 26 April 2009.

Poon, A (2009). Sinopec's earnings decrease by 47%. *Wall Street Journal* (30 March). http://online.wsj.com/article/SB123835907162166979.html. Retrieved on 26 April 2009.

CHINA RAILWAY ENGINEERING

Corporate Address and Contact Information

China Railway Group Limited
1 Xinghuo Road
Fengtai District
Beijing 100070
People's Republic of China
Phone: (86)010-5184-5717
http://www.crec.cn
ir@crec.cn

China Railway Group Limited (CREC 中国中铁股份有限公司) is a state-owned enterprise, subject to operational oversight by the government of People's Republic of China. Headquartered in Beijing, it is listed on both the Shanghai (SSE: 601390) and Hong Kong (SEHK: 390) Stock Exchanges. CREC was founded in 2007 as a joint stock company after its controlling shareholder, the large construction group China Railway Engineering Corporation (CRECG中国铁路工程总公司). CREC is the largest multi-functional integrated construction group in the PRC and Asia, and the third largest construction contractor in the world with 284,000 employees. The company offers a full range of construction-related services, including infrastructure construction, building construction, surveying, design, consulting services, engineering equipment, component manufacturing, properties development, and mining. China Railway Group consists of 46 subsidiary companies, which include 28 fully owned companies, 15 holding subsidiaries, four branch companies, and three joint ventures.

Historical Development

The history of CREC can be traced back to the 1950s when the Construction Bureau and the Design Bureau of the Ministry of Railways were established. The birth of CREC took place in June 1989, when the ministry of railways dissolved the General Bureau of Capital Construction and established CRECG, which then was disjoined from the Ministry and handed over to the central government in September 2000. CRECG itself was placed under the auspices of the State-owned Assets Supervision and Administration Commission (SASAC) of the State Council, and was the first pilot enterprise developed under the new system. Then, CREC was established as a joint stock company with limited liability, when its shareholder CRECG undertook major reorganization in 2007. The registered capital consisted of RMB 12.8 billion, which is fully held by CRECG.

The historical development of CREC involved many plans, where scientific research played a major role, especially during the Eighth Five-Year Plan (1991–1995), where a major breakthrough was the Nanning-Kunming railway, a project characterized by complicated geological and tough topographic conditions. The company reached many milestones and accomplished a series of significant scientific and technological achievements in design and construction technology such as the large-span bridge with high-pier, tunneling in high ground stress, high gas broken stratum, and expansive soil roadbed. Later, during the Ninth Five-Year Plan (1996–2000), the company built the super-long tunnel, the large-span bridge structures and railway speed upgrading projects. More recently, during the Tenth Five-Year Plan (2001–2005), CREC developed the Chinese-styled "ballastless" track technology and the 900-ton bridge girder erection machine, which helped to meet technological challenges. To undertake such major projects, CREC always extended its research continually and enhanced its knowledge on the construction of roadbed, bridge, track laying, and tunnel in plateau permafrost regions. As a result, CREC received many awards for its excellence and high-quality works and was recognized by the Ministry of Railways.

Corporate Structure and Leadership

CREC consists of 31 companies, including large construction enterprises, R&D companies, as well as investment companies. Next to the main corporate headquarters in Beijing, CREC has four other regional centers and 17 branches. With 284,000 employees, the group is presented in over 1,000 cities. The workforce includes roughly 106,378 technical specialists concentrating on construction, 456 professional and executive engineers, as well as 9,934 staff members.

China Railway operates with its corporate motto of "strive to challenge limits and achieve excellence". It has participated in the construction of all domestic major railway lines and constructed, rebuilt, and extended a total length of above 50,000 km, accounting for more than two-thirds of total operating length of railway lines constructed in the PRC. Under the leadership of its Chairman Shi Dahua, who emphasizes that the company is dedicated to "the causes of serving the nation and vitalizing the commerce", China Railway strives to build the domestic infrastructure and extend opportunities of mobility for generations to come.

CREC's corporate structure was established in accordance to the PRC's Company Law, Securities Law, the listing rules, and other relevant regulations. The governance includes the Board of Directors, the board committee, and senior management. The company's board includes nine directors, of which three are executive directors, five independent non-executives, and one non-executive. The board committee consists of the following groups: audit committee, remuneration committee, strategy committee, nomination committee, and safety, health, and environmental protection committee, with the supervisory committee and the president and other senior management in charge of key operations.

Main Products and Services

As the biggest railway construction contractor in mainland China, CREC has built all major railway lines, such as Chengdu-Kunming Railway, Qinghai-Tibet Railway, which is considered the highest railway line in the world, and Datong-Qinhuangdao Railway, the longest heavy-duty railway line in China. The total line length constructed by CREC adds up to 50,000 km. Moreover, the company has constructed railway bridges crossing the Yangtze River or the Yellow River, exceeding more than 2700 km, railway tunnels more than 2800 km, 3400 kilometers expressways, and 566 km metropolitan railways. CREC has its primary operations in the following sectors: transportation (40.7%), highway construction (24.2%), municipal building (23.2%), engineering machinery (2.2%), biology medical (2.1%), real estate development (1.9%), and others (4.8%).

The company further constructed major railway stations such as the Nanjing Railway Station and the Beijing Railway Station, and other electrified railway lines of more than 22,660 km in length, which represents approximately 95% of the total operating electrified railway lines in the PRC. Even though railway construction is the core business of CREC, the company also constructs signaling and communication systems for railway use. Moreover, CREC has been involved in more than 230 overseas projects including railway, expressway, bridge, tunnel, building construction, dredging, airport, and municipal work projects in more than 55 other countries and regions globally since the 1970s.

Growth Strategies

Over the years, China Railway has won more than 200 national supreme prizes in the fields of engineering, construction, research, and design. In 2006, it was recognized as the third largest construction company in the world and ranked 654th on 2008 *Forbes* Global 2000 list. Moreover, CREC was ranked 342nd in *Fortune* Global 500 companies and listed 417th in World's Most Influential Brands and ranked 13th in China's Top 500 Enterprises. While making significant contributions to China's infrastructure construction and economic development, CREC has established many new records in the history of bridge and tunnel construction and electrified railway lines in the PRC, Asia as well as around the world. With its mission of "stick to scientific development, build up a harmonious corporation, and create enterprise value", China Railway has sought to make even more impressive progress in recent years. This becomes evident in its most current annual report. In 2008, CREC's revenue was RMB 93 billion, reflecting a growth of 26.6%, compared to 2007. The profit for the period was RMB 2.181 billion, representing a growth of 167.6%. The profit of equity holders of CREC was RMB 1.906 billion, representing an increase of 190.1%. In addition, the value of new contracts increased by 119.2% up to RMB 179.8 billion, including significant projects, such as the Beijing-Shanghai High-Speed Railway.

CREC has reached a very dominant market share in China. The company's continual growth in revenues, profits, and contracts has further strengthened its position as the largest railway construction enterprise. The future will bring many promising projects, not only in railway construction, but also in various sectors such as construction of highways, bridges, tunnels, and municipal works. Moreover, based on the strong foundation of its infrastructure and overseas business, the company further expanded into property development (China Railway Real Estate), mining, and other relevant businesses. In 2008, the total developed site area averaged 9.24 million square meters. In addition, CREC has founded international joint ventures, such as in Mongolia, in order to invest in the development of overseas mining.

CREC has also improved its corporate governance structure and enhanced the operating efficiency as well as controlled production cost. Clearly, CREC will maintain sustainable growth, considering the demand for new and better infrastructure in China. This in return will trigger demand and generate for more market opportunities for the company. CREC's primary goal is to improve development strategies, make room for more business opportunities, and enhance its brand recognition. Another goal is to aggressively expand its market share in the survey, design and consulting services, and engineering equipment and component manufacturing businesses, as well as to further strengthen its property development business. Finally, CREC will adhere to the strategy of international expedition, and strive to develop its global business, increase and improve the proportion of its overseas operation.

Environment and Industry Challenges

As a large construction company, CREC naturally faces many issues in the area of environmental protection. In various projects, the company had to pay great attentions to the impacts of its construction on environmental situations. The Qinghai-Tibet Railway construction was one such example, where CREC confronted three problems during the early construction period: frozen earth, fragile ecological system, frigid weather, and lack of oxygen. Those challenges require various adjustments, such as production safety, higher project quality, and better environmental protection.

With that comes the industry challenge, where serious environmental issues require technological development and inventions to reduce various risks associated with the construction process. CREC has put great efforts into research and scientific development, and environmental protection is a priority for CREC. In the case of the Qinghai-Tibet Railway construction, CREC has sought permanent solutions for the protection of the ecological environment along railway lines. It also looked out for wild-life protection and wetland and water resource protection.

Dedicated to environmental protection, the company has introduced and implemented into its operation the Environmental Management System (EMS) certified with ISO14001. CREC's approach is to regularly improve its environmental performance and, ultimately, to minimize or even prevent any environmental impacts of its operations, activities, products, and services in the long run. The company plans to identify materials, processes, products, and wastes that cause or may cause pollution, and will implement measures to avoid, reduce, or control pollution where technically and economically viable. Furthermore, CREC will comply with applicable environmental laws, regulations, codes of practice, and other requirements that relate to the environmental aspects to which the company subscribes.

Mareike Hoffschmidt-Fetscherin

References

China Railway announces H shares 2008 interim results, net profit soared 190% (2 September 2008). http://www.todayir.com/webcasting/china_railway_08ir/press.pdf. Retrieved on 1 June 2009.

China Railway Group Limited (2008). Interim results presentation. http://www.crec.cn/c_admin/images/20081217121051.pdf. Retrieved on 1 June 2009.

China Railway Group Limited (2008). History, reorganization and corporate structure. https://www.guococap.com/marketSensor/IPO_Prospectuses/00390/E115.pdf. Retrieved on 1 June 2009.

CHINA RESOURCES NATIONAL

Corporate Address and Contact Information

China Resources (Holdings) Co. Ltd.
Floor 49, CRC Building
26 Harbor Road
Wanchai, Hong Kong
Phone: (852)2879-7888
Fax: (852)2827-5774
http://www.crc.com.hk/scripts/engindex.asp
crc@crc.com.hk

Based in Hong Kong, China Resources National Corporation (华润创业有限公司) is one of the leading conglomerates operating both in Hong Kong and in the mainland China with 300,000 employees. China Resources' products and services touch every facet of people's lives in the greater China region, as its core businesses cover retail, power, breweries, real estate, food, medicine, textiles, chemical products, gas, compressor, etc. Among its subsidiaries, China Resources Vanguard Co. Ltd. (CR Vanguard) is the largest supermarket chain in Hong Kong and the mainland China; China Resources Snow Breweries Limited (CR Snow Breweries) is one of the premier companies in China's brewing industry; China Resources Power Holdings Co. Ltd. (CR Power, HK836) is one of the most rapidly developed enterprises among all of Hong Kong's listed power companies; and China Resources Land Limited (CR Land, HK 1109) is a nationwide property development company with a total asset of over RMB 10 billion (USD 1.4 billion), while the total net asset tops over RMB 4 billion (USD 0.7 billion). China Resources has played an important role in China's economic development in the past and will likely to do so in the future.

Historical Development

The history of China Resources can be traced back to as early as 1938 during the Sino-Japanese war in China. In order to unite the liberal democrats from both Hong Kong and overseas to support the war efforts, Zhou Enlai, the then one of the key leaders from the Chinese Communist Party and later the premier of the country, asked Yang Lian'An to establish Liow & Company in Hong Kong, which later grew to become today's China Resources.

In 1948, Liow & Company was renamed to China Resources, which means "the great land of China, endowed with abundant natural resources". From 1952 until the mid-1980s, China Resources has been the sole agent of the country's import and export trading companies in Hong Kong, Macao, and Southeast Asia, serving as the first bridge for the trade between China and the world. In 1983, after relocating its headquarters into the newly built China Resources Building in Hong Kong, the company was restructured and incorporated as China Resources (Holdings) Co. Ltd. (CRH).

In 1992, China Resources injected assets into the listed company Daly Wing and renamed it to China Resources Enterprise, which became the first listed company of China Resources, and marked the beginning of China Resources' expansion using the capital market. Since then the company' assets and operation drives have been switched into high gear and as a result, its leading position in the main business sectors has been further consolidated. By 2008, China Resources' total assets reached more than HKD 300 billion.

Corporate Structure, Main Products, and Services

Song Lin, a graduate in engineering of Tongji University who joined the company since 1985, is the chairman of China Resources (Holdings) Co. Ltd., while Qiao Shibo serves as president, who graduated from Jilin University and once worked as the director of the Ministry of Foreign Trade and Economic Cooperation.

China Resources' businesses can be classified into the following groups.

Commodity manufacture and distribution

China Resources Holdings operates primarily in the industries closely related to people's daily life. Among its affiliates, the profit centers that engaged in commodity manufacture and distribution are the largest business units, which include the following: China Resources Snow Breweries Limited, jointly founded by CR Enterprise and SAB Miller; Ng Fung Hong Limited, an integrated food enterprise; China Resources Textile (Holdings) Limited, one of the China's leading textile manufacturers and distributors with a comprehensive import, export, and sales network with customers worldwide; Teck Soon Hong Ltd., specializing in processing natural spices, synthesized spices, essences, and sesame oil; China Resources Microelectronics (Holdings) Ltd., mainly engaged in high-tech microelectronics on business investment, development, and operation management; China Resources Chemicals Holdings Ltd., engaged in the investment, development, operation, and management of chemical packaging materials plants, and producing and distributing many kinds of high-quality chemical products; China Resources Cement Holdings Limited; and China Resources (Shenyang) Sanyo Compressor Co. Ltd.

The profit centers engaged in distribution business include: China Resources Retail (Group) Co. Ltd., one of the leading retail groups in Hong Kong, which operates Chinese Arts & Crafts and CR Care; China Resources Vanguard Co. Ltd., a flagship business operating a supermarket network under CR Enterprise, and one of the largest supermarket chains in Hong Kong and the mainland China, managing approximately 476 stores in Hong Kong, Guangdong, Zhejiang, Jiangsu, Tianjin, and Beijing; China Resources Logistics (Holdings) Limited, focused on warehousing and distribution services.

Real estate business

China Resources' real estate business mainly covers the areas in China's mainland and Hong Kong, and Thailand, operating the civilian residential development, commercial real estate development, property management, construction and supply of building materials, and other diverse real estate businesses. Up to now, the profit centers engaged in the real estate and related industries include: China Resources Land Limited; Thailand All Seasons Property Co. Ltd., and China Resources Property Ltd.

Infrastructure and utilities

Aimed at diversifying investment risks and sustaining stable long-term returns, China Resources Holdings started to invest in large infrastructure and utilities in the 1980s by cooperating with other Hong Kong consortiums. Today, China Resources has shifted its focus onto the public utilities more closely related to the people's livelihood, mainly electricity and gas. The profit centers engaged in infrastructure and public utilities include: China Resources Power Holdings Ltd., China Resources Gas (Group) Limited, and China Resources Development and Investment Co. Ltd.

Pharmaceutical production and distribution

Entrusted by the State-owned Assets Supervision and Administration Commission (SASAC) of the State Council, China Resources Holdings has undertaken the important task of establishing the platform of pharmaceutical industry, which is supported by central state-owned enterprises, among them China Worldbest Group Co. Ltd. (CWGC) and 999 Group Co. Ltd. As one of China's largest pharmaceutical enterprises, CWGC's total sales revenue and export volume rank among the top in the national pharmaceutical industry, while 999 Group is one of the China's largest integrative pharmaceutical companies. In addition, China Resources holds 29.625% equities of Shandong Dong-E E-Jiao Ltd., being the single largest shareholder of the A-Share listed company in China.

Corporate Culture, Strategies, and Challenges

Dedicated to the promotion of the mutual progress of the industry and society, China Resources seeks to fulfill its corporate responsibilities, despite many ups and downs in its development. Under the guiding principles of "Honesty and Credibility First" and "Human-oriented", China Resources strives to manage all its enterprises and staff with high moral standards, aiming to fulfill its commitment of creating a better life in an open and human-oriented manner.

Since late 2008, many industries in China have been severely affected by the economic slowdowns triggered by the global financial crisis. In light of such economic pressure, China Resources endeavors to carry out its differentiated competition strategies as well as nationwide development strategy, while continuing to enhance the productivity of its property value chain and maintain a competitive and leading position throughout the country.

Different from the focused strategy, China Resources is extending its business to the widest possibility of its touch, from natural resources to energy development and supply, property development, manufacturing and distribution of food, pharmacy, and beer, and so on. By its economy of scale and scope of business, it is utilizing its core resources to every possible opportunity to gain profits. Even under the severe world financial crisis, in the first quarter of 2009, the company had achieved a 30% rise of turnover and a 57% rise of its net profit.

Following the national development strategies of "Revitalize Northeast China", "China Western Development" and "Rise of Central China", China Resources is moving north and west from the south and east China's coastal areas: the company is making large-scale investments in China's central, western, and northern provinces such as Anhui, Hunan, Hubei, Sichuan, and Ningxia. One of its newest and largest investments was announced on 25 May 2009, when China Resources entered a strategic cooperation agreement with Ningxia Hui Autonomous Region and its capital city, Yinchuan, on a broad investment deal of over RMB 10 billion (USD 1.4 billion) in the next few years, which ranges from the chained supermarket development, gas and electricity supply, to property development, and the manufacturing and distribution of food, pharmacy, and beers.

Xueyuan (Adrian) Liu and Xue Tang

References

BusinessWeek (2009). China Resources (Holdings) Co. http://investing.businessweek.com/research/stocks/private/snapshot.asp?privcapId=20822913. Retrieved on 9 June 2009.

China Resources (Holdings) Co. (2009). About us. http://www.crc.com.hk/scripts/eng2007/about.asp. Retrieved on 9 June 2009.

华润集团一季度营业额同比增长30% (12 may 2009). [China Resources first quarter revenue increase 30%]. SASAC. http://www.sasac.gov.cn/n1180/n1226/n2410/n314259/n315149/6383900.html. Retrieved on 12 May 2009.

Hoovers (2009). China Resources (Holdings) Co. Ltd. http://www.hoovers.com/china-resources-(holdings)/—ID__157520—/free-co-profile.xhtml. Retrieved on 9 June 2009.

Kwok, J (2009). CRP headquarters to get HK$600m 'green' makeover. *China Daily* (HK Edition), 6 June. http://www.chinadaily.com.cn/hkedition/2009-06/06/content_8255392.htm#. Retrieved on 9 June 2009.

Woetzel, J (2008). Reassessing China's state-owned enterprises. *The McKinsey Quarterly*, July.

CHINA SHENHUA ENERGY

Corporate Address and Contact Information

China Shenhua Energy Company Limited (SEHK — 1088, SSE — 601088)
4th Floor, Zhouji Tower
6 Ande Road, Dongcheng District
Beijing, People's Republic of China
Phone: (86)10-5813-3355
Fax: (86)10-8488-2107
http://www.csec.com/

China Shenhua Energy Company Limited (中国神华能源股份有限公司CSEC) is a leading integrated, coal-based energy company. Ranked 336 in *Forbes* 2000 and was the 11th largest company in PRC in 2008, CSEC is engaged in the production and sales of coal, power generation, and heat supply in the PRC. Its coal business involves coal mining and processing, sales and marketing, and coal transportation through its exclusive port and railway facilities.

Historical Background

In 1985, a company named Huaneng Refined Coal Company started its coal production and railway operations at the Shendong Mines that were scattered around the border of the Inner Mongolia Autonomous Region and Shaanxi Province. In 1995, with government investment of RMB 2.58 billion, the company was renamed the Shenhua Group and was approved by the State Council to become a state-owned enterprise. In 1999, the group expanded its business to power generation by merging with Guohua Power, and by 2002, Shenhua finished the integration of its coal production, rail, and port network after putting its Huanghua Port into operation.

On 8 November 2004, China *Shenhua* Energy Company Limited was established as a joint stock limited company and a subsidiary of the Shenhua Group. Prior to the reorganization, the Shenhua Group engaged in the operation of coalmines, power plants, and research activities. The restructuring of the Shenhua Group led to a transfer of its core business operations that included coal production, transportation and sales, power generation, mining rights, other related assets and liabilities to China Shenhua Energy Company. After this reshuffle, CSEC entered into a series of agreements with the Shenhua Group and its subsidiaries to supply them with products and services.

CSEC is the largest coal producer in China and is the second largest listed coal company in the world, right after the Peabody Energy Corporation traded on the New York Stock Exchange. CSEC is listed on both the Hong Kong (H-Shares) and Shanghai Stock Exchanges (SSE). In addition to its inclusion in the SSE Composite Index of top 50 public companies, in December 2007, CSEC became a Hang Seng Index Constituent Stock.

Corporate Structure and Leadership

After its restructuring, the former senior management of the Shenhua Group was appointed to oversee the operations of CSEC, and Chen Biting became the chairman of the inaugural Board of Directors, who had also served as CSEC executive director since November 2004. Chen had led the Board and the management to expand CSEC core businesses. Prior to joining the Shenhua Group in November 2000, Chen was the vice governor of Jiangsu Province. After his retirement in late 2008, Dr. Zhang Xiwu was appointed as chairman and executive director of CSEC. Zhang, aged 50, had previously served as the general manager and had held numerous executive positions within the Shenhua Group. Receiving both his master's (1997) and PhD degree (2003) from Liaoning University of Engineering and Technology, Zhang was the deputy chief of the Bureau of Coal Industry of Jilin Province prior to joining the Shenhua Group in August 1995.

CSEC had a total number of 58,827 employees as of 31 December 2008, with a significant number of those involving in its operation and maintenance function. It has also improved its corporate governance by establishing standardized structure in strict compliance with relevant laws and regulatory requirements of the PRC. As a result, it won the "2006 Best Corporate Governance in Asia" award issued by *Finance Asia*.

Main Products and Services

The company's operations are divided into four business sectors: coal, railway, port, and power segment.

Coal segment

CSEC is the largest coal producer in China and currently operates a total of four mine groups, namely Shendong Mines, Wanli Mines, Zhunge'er Mines, and Shengli Mines in China. At the end of 2008, the company sold 232.7 tons coal, accounting for 8.6% of the total national production of 2.70 billion tons. As of 31 December 2007, the company had a marketable coal reserve of 7.320 billion tons based on JORC (Australasian Joint Ore Reserves Committee) standard, with resource reserve of 18.024 billion tons. It is estimated that the coal reserves can be mined for around 46 years.

CSEC sells its coal to external customers including domestic and export sales, and to its internal power segment. The company attempts to increase its coal output by 15 million tons annually within the next five years, which will make the company the world's biggest coal producer.

Railway segment

CSEC currently owns and operates five railways, including Shenshuo Railway, Shuohuang Railway, Dazhun Railway, Baoshen Railway, and Huangwan Railway, with an aggregate length of approximately 1,367 km. The Shenshuo and Shuohuang Railways are the country's two major railways for the coal transportation from the western regions to eastern China. The company transports its coal mainly through its own railways. Meantime, part of the coal is transported through state-owned railways.

The company self-owned integrated transport system creates a unique competitive advantage over other domestic coal producers, as it ensures CSEC to deliver a stable supply of coal products to different geographical areas in China. Moreover, the company can transport coal to ports and sell products to all markets in the country as well as other overseas markets. By reducing the transportation cost per ton, CSEC's railway system has improved its operational efficiency, and hence decreased the total coal transportation cost. In 2008, the total turnover of coal transportation by the group was 123.3 billion ton km, of which 81.4% was pipelined through self-owned railways and the remaining 18.6% was channeled through state-owned railways.

Port segment

CSEC owns and operates Huanghua Port and Shenhua Tianjin Coal Dock. They have become the major transportation hubs for the coal sales to domestic coastal markets and overseas markets, of which

Huanghua Port is the second largest port for seaborne coal in China. CSEC transported 101.1 million tons or 72.5% of its seaborne coal through its self-owned ports, and the remaining 38.3 million tons or 27.5% through third-party ports such as Qinhuangdao Port, Tianjin Port, and others with an aggregate seaborne coal sale of 139.4 million tons in 2008.

Power segment

As of 31 December 2008, CSEC controlled and operated 14 coal-fired power plants with a total installed capacity of 18,001 MW (Megawatts). It also operated some wind power and gas-fired power generation business. The company has attached great importance to the environmental protection and the application of advanced technology to power generation. Desulfurization devices have been installed in 87% of the generating units and achieved the highest cleaning standard within the country by the end of 2007. The company has also committed to the development of clean coal-fired operations. Electrostatic precipitators have been established in 82.5% of the coal-fired units and have reached a total overall de-dusting efficiency of over 99% by the end of 2007. In addition, the company initiated green energy projects and commenced wind power business in Zhuhai, and its installed capacity reached 16 MW in 2008.

In 2007, coal consumption for the power segment of the company was 34.1 million tons, of which 89.7% or 30.60 million tons were inter-segment sales provided by the coal segment of CSEC. The company also operates a gas-fired power plant, Yuyao Power, alongside the coal-fired power generation plants. CSEC's gross power generation was 79.74 billion kWh and total power dispatched was 74.35 billion kWh in 2007.

Challenges and Business Strategies

With regards to the energy crisis of recent years, the Chinese government may implement a macroeconomic control policy to prevent rapid price increase and to ensure a steady and rapid development of the economy. Despite growing concerns for a global slowdown or recession, China's economy may still achieve continuous growth, which would likely enhance the demand for energy-related products such as coal, and would certainly be helpful for the development of coal and power industry. In light of this positive outlook, it is expected that the tight supply of coal will continue. In particular, the tight supply of thermal coal may be worsened during the peak consumption seasons. The potential reform of resource tax and other policy-driven cost may affect cost control of CSEC. Recently, the government's temporary price capping policy has curbed further increase of coal spot price.

In the long run, the reform of domestic coal market will continue. Under the national industrial guidelines of "preferring large enterprises to small enterprises", large-scale coal producers such as CSEC would have more room for development. To further coordinate the linkage among production, transportation, and distribution, CSEC will seek to optimize the efficiency of the transportation system and enhance transportation capacity of existing railway and ports. To this end, and together with other related measures, the company will enhance the transportation capacity of Shenshuo–Shuohuang Railways by putting trains with 10,000 tons loading capacity into use. In addition, CSEC is also conducting preparation work of sub-line railway and continues to carry out the inward channel-broadening project to Huanghua Port so as to improve port transportation capacity. To enhance operation management, CSEC aims to impose tight control on costs and budget expenses. It also attempts to reduce the non-productive expenditure by strengthening cost accounting and makes efforts to overcome the cost pressures brought by rising price and policy-driven expenses.

T. K. P. Leung

References

EconomyWatch (2008). China Shenhua Energy. http://www.economywatch.com/companies/forbes-list/china/china-shenhua-energy.html. Retrieved on 22 March 2009.

The Global 2000 (2008). *Forbes* http://www.forbes.com/lists/2008/18/biz_2000global08_The-Global-2000-China_10Rank.html. Retrieved on 22 March 2009.

刘黎 (2008). 五大电力集团拟推动煤电路港一体化. 新华网, 27 September [Liu, Li. Five large power groups plan to integrate coal, electricity, rail and port systems. Xinhua Net] http://www.cns.hk:89/cj/cyzh/news/2008/09-27/1396544.shtml. Retrieved on 22 March 2009.

CHINA SHIPPING CONTAINER LINES

Corporate Address and Contact Information

China Shipping Container Lines Company Limited
(Shanghai A-Share: 601866: Hong Kong H-Share: 2866)
27th Story, 450 Fushan Road
Pudong District, Shanghai
People's Republic of China
Phone: (86)21-6596-6105
Fax: (86)21-6596-6498
www.cscl.com.cn

China Shipping Container Lines Company Limited (CSCL中海集运) ranks eighth in the global container shipping industry. CSCL is the second largest container shipping company in China, only after China Ocean Shipping (Group) Company (COSCO) Container Lines. With nearly 40% market share of domestic container shipping business, CSCL is a subsidiary of China Shipping (中国海运), a well-known shipping company operated under the state-owned Assets Supervision & Administration Commission (SASAC) of the Chinese State Council.

Historical Development

Although in the past 30 years, some Chinese local governments have owned small shipping operations, the country's shipping industry has been mainly monopolized by three large stated-owned companies, China COSCO, Sinotrans, and China Shipping. Before China joined the WTO, the nation's business leaders realized that its shipping industry would have to face fierce competition in the global container shipping market, since the well-established international shipping companies have already been operating with a large number of vessels and worldwide service. Therefore, China's Shipping companies were reorganized to improve business efficiency, shipping coverage, and global competitiveness, and as a result, CSCL was found in Shanghai in 1997, focusing mainly on the container shipping services.

Since its founding, CSCL has been playing a very significant role in the fast-growing Chinese international trade. CSCL has many branch operations not only in China but also in most important port cities of developed countries. Since China joined the WTO in 2001, the company's container shipping business has experienced remarkable expansion, growing bigger and stronger, much in step with the country's overall economy. According to Drewry's *2006/2007 Annual Report*, global containerized cargo volume grew from 1980 through 2005 at 9.8% per year, and TEU (Twenty-Foot Equivalent Units) growth rates was nearly two times higher than the world GDP growth rate. Comparing the performance among the top 30 lines, CSCL's global market shares rose impressively from 1.67% to 3.80% between 2000 and 2006, which represented an increase of 126%, second only to CMA-CGM Group of France, as indicated by *BRS Alphaliner Report* in 2006. In terms of its shipping TEU statistics, CSCL was ranked 10th in the global container shipping industry in 2004; by 2007, CSCL quickly climbed to the sixth place. During the global economic recession, according to the Deutsche Bank Research in 2008, the container shipping business would face a turbulent time in 2009, followed by a modest recovery by 2010. As China is increasingly becoming the world factory for many consumed goods, Asia will likely dominate the global market, which will present a good opportunity for CSCL's further expansion.

With strong support from the Chinese government, CSCL has grown very quickly and acquired some terminals and container business assets. CSCL first went public in June 2004, issuing 2.42 billion H-shares on the Hong Kong Stock Exchange, which raised about HK $7.5 billion to expand its container shipping lines. In December 2007, CSCL had another IPO on the Shanghai Stock Exchange, raising additional RMB 15.8 billion for buying 12 new large container vessels and acquiring some terminal assets of China Shipping.

Corporate Structure and Leadership

In terms of corporate ownership, China Shipping holds 58.97% of CSCL, while the rest of shares have been issued to the public. CSCL is directly managed by China Shipping, which appoints most of its managers and board members. CSCL's chairman and CEO also hold high-level executive positions in China Shipping.

Much of CSCL's recent success was due to the leadership of its former Chinaman Li Kelin, who was also the CEO of China Shipping until his retirement. He was credited for leading CSCL to the international shipping market and its successful IPO in Hong Kong. Li Shaode, current board chairman, also serves as the CEO of China Shipping, who is a professional with more than 40 years of experience in international shipping business. Another veteran among the corporate leadership team is CEO Huang Xiaowen, who was the former CEO of Wuzhou Shipping Company, one of CSCL's subsidiaries in Southern China. Aiming to build a top shipping company with low-operating cost, together they have expanded CSCL's shipping outreach around the globe, steadily raised the capital from the financial markets and increased vessel capacities.

Despite its short history and government control background, CSCL has evolved into a truly international company. As container shipping is a worldwide business, CSCL is more globally positioned than most of the Chinese state-owned companies. It has more than 50 routine lines focusing on intra-Asia, trans-Pacific, and Europe-Asia routes; in addition, CSCL has also added some new lines from China to Middle East and Africa. Currently, CSCL has over 150 agencies in countries around the world, all are managed by regional managers in their port locations, and many foreign offices have recruited local directors or managers.

Main Products and Services

A new comer in the global container shipping market, CSCL has grown tremendously over the last decade, as the Chinese economy is booming as a "global factory" and its container shipping demand has increased much faster than the rest of world. In recent years, China's export-oriented manufacture economy has dramatically changed the country's maritime logistic chain and international trade. According to the *Shipping Statistics and Market Overview* (2008), Shanghai, Hong Kong, Shenzhen, and Qingdao ports were listed on the 2007 Global Top Ten Container Ports, which all enjoyed an annual TEU-growth rate over 25% from 1997 to 2006.

China Shipping, CSCL's corporate owner, is a diversified service company engaging primarily in shipping and modern logistics businesses. It also serves as an independent ship agency, providing a wide range of services in freight forwarding, ship repair, terminal operation, container business, trade, finance, real estate, IT, and contract employment. CSCL has 148 high-speed container vessels with a capacity of 466,550 TEU (AXS-Alphaliner, 25 April 2009). The company mainly engages in international container shipping, although CSCL also maintains a small chart vessel operation and global line Asia Mediterranean American Express (AMAX) service.

Over the years, CSCL has owned and operated difference types of container vessels. More than 70 of its container vessels have a capability over 4,000 TEU and with an average age of 4.2 years; those vessels account for 81% of the whole operating capacity. In the past five years, CSCL has added about 40 large, new vessels, among them the current eight biggest ships are made by Samsung Heavy Industry Co., which each can carry more than 9,572 TEU containers, and another eight 13,300 TEU container vessels are also on order from Samsung. Comparing with its oceangoing ships, CSCL's domestic container vessels are small and average around 10 years old, which are used mainly for transferring containers from inland river ports to the nearby seaside international ports. A subsidiary based in Shanghai, Puhai operates in the Yangtze River delta region, transferring containers from river ports to the Shanghai Yangshan deep-water port; another subsidiary operating in the Pearl River delta region, Wuzhou Shipping carries containers to Hong Kong and Shenzhen ports, so that larger corporate fleets can ship them around the world.

The logistics of container shipping typically flow from shipper, subcontractor, container terminal, and ocean shipping to container terminal, subcontractor, and consignee. By cooperating with companies from other countries, CSCL strives to update its shipping service model from the port-to-port to door-to-door. With more than 100 branches in nearly 140 countries, CSCL aims to serve its customers with better quality and localized support. The company has recruited local employees to help enhance its service and marketing. Since its shipping price is much lower when the vessels return to China, CSCL has cooperated with some Chinese companies in import business, such as transporting recycled papers and material from developed countries to China.

Challenges and Business Strategies

International container shipping market is a very competitive business. CSCL competes domestically with COSCO, and globally with Maersk Lines and Mediterranean Shipping Company (MSC), both are the market leaders in the global container shipping industry. Currently, alliances and vessel-sharing agreements are the preferred option in global shipping; and there are three major alliances, which are the New World Alliance (APL, Mitsui O.S.K. Lines, and Hyundai Merchant Marine), the Grand Alliance (NYK Line, Orient Overseas Container Line, and Hapag Lloyd), and CYHK (COSCO, "K" Line, Yang Ming Line, and Hanjin Shipping). Since 2000, mergers and acquisitions have increased in the global shipping industry, among them: CMA-CGM took over Delmas in 2005 and Maersk acquired P&O Nedlloyd in 2006. Since large European shipping companies have a long history in the global shipping field, they generally have more experience in worldwide shipping operations with excellent management and loyal customers in many countries. For example, Maersk's core competence is its economy of scale and synergies, global service coverage, and networking, as it has four times larger TEU capacities than CSCL. Competitors' business scale, scope, and quality of service have become the model for CSCL to strike to achieve, and its approach is through cooperation with big players as well as support from the Chinese government. Thus far, CSCL has cooperated with the third liner, CMA-CGM Group and other major liners while independently operating its global network.

A relatively new company with little more than 10 years in existence, CSCL focuses mainly on China's booming international trade business. Its strategy is to rely on the parent company to expand its business both horizontally and vertically. By investing in container business, CSCL seeks to optimize its supplying chain and reduce operational risks. Another major initiative is to reduce the cost of average TEU-mile by building eight 13,300 TEU Very Large Container Ships (VLCS); when delivered, they will likely increase CSCL's shipping capacity and further connect Chinese main ports to American and European markets. Since CSCL has invested in Yangshan pier and domestic shipping business on the Yangtze River, the port city has become the strategic focus point of CSCL's master plan in future growth. Furthermore, since the Chinese government has invested billions of capital on the railway construction, inland railway system will be upgraded in the next five years. By cooperating with China Railway and other transport companies, CSCL has also begun to integrate the inland railway transportation into its worldwide services.

Because of the strict regulations implemented by the International Maritime Organization for safety and environmental protection, the crude oil price has been climbing steadily in recent years. Despite the current correction, the shipping costs are expected to rise in the long run. To cope with the global financial crisis and the industry recession cycle, CSCL takes measures to reduce its voyage and internal operating costs. Convinced that it could balance its shipping business in the volatile global market, CSCL have recently opened some new lines in the emerging markets of African and Mid-Eastern regions. With backing from the Chinese government, CSCL still plans to buy more vessels during the down cycle, and is optimistic that its business will grow very quickly after 2010.

Zicheng Li

References

Annual Report: Container Market Review and Forecast 2006/2007. London: Drewry Publishing.

China Shipping Container Lines Company Limited (2008). *Annual Report*. http://www.cscl.com.cn/imgs/prospectus/08040202cn.pdf. Retrieved on 5 January 2009.

Liner Market Shares 2008. AXS-Alphaliner. http://www.axs-alphaliner.com/top100/index.php. Retrieved on 25 April 2009.

Prospects for the Container Shipping Industry, IQCP Container Terminal Business 2009. Hamburg: Deutsche Bank Research, 8 December 2008.

Salles, BR (2006). *Liner Shipping Report*. http://www.brs-paris.com/newsletters/liner_studies/no29/BRS-rep-0601.pdf. Retrieved on 2 February 2009.

Shipping Statistics and Market Overview (2008). Institute of Shipping Economics & Logistics. Germany: Bremen.

Voorde, E and T Vanelslander (2009). *Market Power and Vertical and Horizontal Integration in the Maritime Shipping and Port Industry*. OECD/ITF Joint Transport Research Centre Discussion Papers, OECD Publishing.

CHINA SOUTHERN AIRLINES

Corporate Address and Contact Information

China Southern Airlines Company Limited
278 Jichang Road
Guangzhou, Guangdong Province 510405
People's Republic of China
Phone: (86)20-8613-0870
Fax: (86)20-8613-0873
http://www.csair.com/en/index.asp

Headquartered in Guangzhou, Guangdong Province, China Southern Airlines Company (CSA 中国南方航空股份有限公司) is an air transportation provider, with most of its operations occurring in China. CSA, together with its subsidiaries, offers domestic and international passenger, cargo, and mail airline services. In 2007, CSA's revenues were approximately $6.7 billion with a workforce of approximately 45,470 people. The company also provides freight and logistics services, air catering services, pilot-training services, aircraft and engine repair and maintenance services, flight simulation services, and airport ground services, as well as the selling of duty-free goods in flights. In addition, it offers financial and property management services. As of 31 December 2008, China Southern Airlines operated a fleet of 348 aircrafts, reaching 905 destinations and connecting a multitude of countries, regions, and cities worldwide.

Historical Development

China Southern Airlines was established in 1995. In 1997, it was listed on both the New York and Hong Kong Stock Exchanges, and in 2000, the company bought Zhongyuan Airlines. It undertook an interest transfer and capital injection agreement in 2002 with China State Post Bureau, Shanghai Municipal Post Office, Post Office of the Inner Mongolian Autonomous Region, and China Philately. Out of this agreement, CSA contributed $18.12 million in cash to purchase a 49% interest in China Postal Airlines. The company was placed on the Shanghai Stock Exchange in 2003. During the same year, CSA also purchased China Northern Airlines and China Xinjiang Airlines. The company became part of the SkyTeam Alliance in 2004, a mileage program that allows customers of one airline use their frequent flyer points with other airlines within the program. In 2005, the company also became part of a flyer loyalty program that was affiliated with China Airlines based in Taiwan.

CSA provides airline services in the commercial sector, as well as air cargo and mail operations. In February 2006, the company opened the Ho Chi Minh City Branch of the Sky Pearl Club in Vietnam, and in June, CSA entered the Global Airline Alliance Adherence Agreement (GAAAA) with the SkyTeam. As of December 2008, CSA had 348 aircraft, mostly composed of Boeing 737s as well as the 747, 757, and 777 models, and the Airbus 300, 320, and 330 series. In 2008, CSA also became a substantially large buyer of Boeing's B787-8 Dreamliner aircraft. The average age of the company's aircrafts at the end of 2008 was 6.3 years.

China Southern Airlines is the first airline in China to own and operate its own terminals — Terminal One at Beijing Capital International Airport, Terminal One at Xi'an Xianyang International Airport, and Terminal Three at Urumqi Diwobao International Airport. CSA attaches key importance to its branded products strategy, offering a host of reliable and convenient on-time services. The airline currently has the largest frequent flyer program in China — The Sky Pearl Club — with more than 4.2 million members, enjoying numerous opportunities for free flights and flight upgrades.

Corporate Structure and Leadership

China Southern Airlines Company Limited operates as a subsidiary of China Southern Air Holding Company. Main individuals within this organizational structure include directors, supervisors, joint company secretaries, and internal auditors. As of April 2009, the company's executive directors included Si Xianmin, Li Wenxin, Wang Quanhua, Liu Baoheng, Tan Wangeng, Xu Jiebo, and Chen Zhenyou. Wang Zhi, Sui Guangjun, Gong Huazhang, and Lam Kwong Yu composed the independent non-executive directors. Si Xianmin, Chairman of the Board, received his MBA from the School of Economics of Tsinghua University. He is also a political science specialist who began his career with civil aviation in 1975 and once held the position of director of the political division of the Henan Branch of CSA.

The president of the company is Tan Wangeng, who also serves as a director. He holds a master's degree in economics and is a graduate of Sun Yatsen University, where he majored in regional economics. Prior to joining CSA, Tan served as the head of the infrastructure department and director of human resources for Beijing Aircraft Maintenance and Engineering Corporation from 1990 to 1996. From 2006 to 2009, he was the executive vice president of CSA. The company has a supervisory committee, which consists of five members. Its main role is to oversee CSA's senior management, which includes the board, executive officers, and other members of the management team. Their role is also to ensure that everyone is representing the company's best interests and complying with the law in all business endeavors.

China Southern Airlines has 13 branches located throughout China, including: Beijing, Dalian, Guangxi, Hainan, Henan, Hubei, Hunan, Heilongjiang, Jilin, Northern, Shenzhen, Xinjiang, and Zhuhai Helicopter Company. The airline conducts a portion of its operations through five subsidiaries, namely Xiamen Airlines, Shantou Airlines, Zhuhai Airlines, Guizhou Airlines, and Chongqing Airlines. During 2008, the airline's subsidiaries carried 14.27 million passengers and accounted for 25% and 22% of the CSA's passengers carried and passenger revenue, respectively. In addition, the company operates two bases in Shanghai and Xian and 18 domestic sales and ticket offices situated throughout China, including Chendu, Hangzhou, Nanjing, and Taibei.

Main Routes and Services

As China's largest airline, China Southern Airlines has 54 international offices located in major metropolitan markets around the world, including: Amsterdam, Dubai, Lagos, Los Angeles, Paris, Singapore, Seoul, Sharjah, Sydney, Tokyo, New York, London, Vancouver, Dibai, and Brisbane. In 2007, over three million safe flight hours were achieved by CSA. Consequently, the company received the Three-Star Safety Award from the Civil Aviation Administration of China (CAAC), which was a highly regarded recognition for safe flight operations in the aviation industry in China. In 2008, with more than five million safe flight hours, China Southern Airlines was presented the Five-Star Flight Safety Award by the CAAC — the current most prestigious award for safe flight operations in the Chinese aviation industry, becoming the only Chinese carrier maintaining the longest safety record and occupying a leading position in the international aviation industry.

The company also provides air cargo and mail services. Such operations are integrated with its airline-related businesses, including aircraft and engine maintenance, flight simulation, and air-catering operations. During 2008, the company operated 653 routes, of which 522 were domestic, 103 were international, and 28 were regional. Its route network covers commercial centers and booming economic regions in mainland China. The airline is the first Chinese carrier to introduce its own computer reservation system and Internet e-ticketing, and the first to introduce its own revenue management, system operations control, finance management, human resources, cargo, and office automation systems. CSA has established a mammoth cargo station ranked first in mainland China and the third largest in the world.

Although CSA's operations focus primarily on the domestic market, the company operates regional routes, and international flights. Its regional operations include flights between destinations in China and Hong Kong, Macau, and Taiwan. The company's international operations include scheduled services to the cities in Australia, Belgium, France, India, Iran, Japan, Kazakhstan, Korea, Kyrgyzstan, Nepal, the Netherlands, Nigeria, Pakistan, Russia, Saudi Arabia, Tajikistan, the United Arab Emirates, the United States, and Southeast Asian destinations.

In recent years, CSA has been seeking to expand its international market in developing countries. Plans to launch 10 new international routes were declared in February 2007, which included Dubai, Luanda, New Delhi, Phuket, Sendai, Sapporo, Siem Reap, Vientiane, and Yangon. A new code-share union with Pakistan International Airlines was made public in March 2007, and an affiliation with Continental Airlines began in June 2007. This partnership encompassed admittance to the airport lounge, widespread code sharing services, and frequent flyer capabilities. In 2008, the company acquired 26% interest in China Southern West Australian Flying College. China Southern Airlines, with more than 3,300 comprehensively trained and experienced pilots, owns and operates its own independent pilot-training centers for pilots and flight attendants.

Challenges and Business Strategies

Major competitors of CSA include AMR Corporation, China Airlines, Cathay Pacific Airways Limited, Singapore Airlines Limited, and Air China Limited. As China's leading airlines for several consecutive years, CSA carried nearly 57 million passengers in 2007, being ranked first in Asia and fourth globally. Currently, CSA is among the world's top 10 commercial airlines. In 2008, facing the global economic recession, the airline received governmental support that included injection of capital and taxation exemption.

Despite government support, the airline still faces many challenges in the years ahead, such as the growth of the airline industry within the Chinese market by foreign companies. The global economy will always have a major impact on CSA's international flight attendance, as the recent decline of the demand for international flights has presented a great challenge. To cope, CSA continuously works to improve its operational effectiveness and customer services, and begins to offer more upscale service elements, which include sophisticated check-in service assistance and mobile marketing, thus creating a more streamlined experience for customers. Competitive pricing has been and will continue to be an advantage for CSA, as it is making a constant effort to illuminate its successes to maintain high stature. In 2008, *Global Traveler*, a well-respected magazine, named CSA "The Best Airline of China", and a popular and well-renowned financial website awarded the airline the honor of "Best Listed Company of Investor Relations" in the same year.

Safety will always be an area to improve upon in order for CSA to stay successful long term. The airline will continue to accelerate the process of building its safety management system, and in turn, strengthening the culture of safety. Despite the recent economic slowdown, the company is confident of its future business growth, and the primary business strategy is to constantly leverage its standing as the number one airline in China.

Michael A. Moodian, Margaret Minnis, and Yifang Zhang

References

China Southern Airlines (2009). *2008 Annual Report.* http://www.csair.com/en/investor/other/20090424_out_en.pdf. Retrieved on 7 July 2009.

China Southern Airlines (2008). *2007 Annual Report.* http://www.csair.com/en/investor/other/E1010725.pdf. Retrieved on 7 July 2009.

China Southern Airlines Co. Ltd. (2008). *Euromonitor International: Local Company Profile.*

Datamonitor (2008). Airlines in China, Industry Profile.

LexisNexis (2009). China Southern Airlines Co. Ltd.

CHINA TELECOM

Corporate Address and Contact Information

China Telecom Corporation Limited
31 Jinrong Street
Xicheng District
Beijing 100032
People's Republic of China
Phone: (86)10-6642-8166
Fax: (86)10-6601-0728
http://www.chinatelecom-h.com/eng/global/home.htm
ir@chinatelecom.com.cn

China Telecom Corporation Limited (China Telecom 中国电信股份有限公司) is the largest fixed-line telecommunications provider in China, with over 200 million fixed-line (also called wireline) subscribers, as of the end of 2008. While still largely owned by the central government of the PRC, China Telecom offered for sale a 20-percent stake of the company in a 2002 initial public offering, an aggressive move in a financial market that was then very sceptical of telecoms. In addition to the wireline customer base, China Telecom also services some 44 million broadband subscribers and another 28 million recently added mobile subscribers, the results of a complex mix of corporate strategy and bold industry restructuring.

Historical Development

Born out of the breakup of the service operations of China's Ministry of Post and Telecommunications (MPT) in the 1990s, China Telecom Corporation Limited was given the mandate to provide fixed line service to 21 southern and eastern provinces in the PRC, including the port city of Shanghai. A corporate counterpart, China Network Communications Corporation (China Netcom) provided service to the 10 northern provinces of China, and the city of Beijing. This breakup was an early step, under the leadership of Wu Jichuan, the then Post and Telecommunications Minister, to transform the Chinese telecom monopoly into a globally competitive, market-oriented industry, using "managed competition". The intent was to drive Chinese telecommunications, via a short-cut route, to the levels of competition, innovation, efficiency, and market penetration achieved over a much longer period in the free-market economies of the United States, Europe, and Asia, while maintaining considerable state ownership and control.

From the start of its "independent" operations, the road was anticipated to be difficult. Globally, wireline telecom providers had begun to face revenue erosion, through declines in both subscriber count and average revenue per user (ARPU), due to wireless competition. This was particularly true in the developing world, where wireline penetration was incomplete, and where wireless deployment was considerably more cost-effective. Even though the underserved Chinese wireline market was vast by global standards, the China Telecom leadership was acutely aware that their future success would not be found in delivering more of the same standard wireline voice service.

China Telecom, therefore, aggressively pursued a number of strategies to offer new services to old and new markets. These included the acquisition of rights to deploy the Personal Handyphone System (PHS), called Xiao Ling Tong or "Little Smart". This technology, originated in Japan and enhanced for the Chinese market by entrepreneur Wu Ying, is essentially a long-range cordless phone technology, which allows wireline service providers the opportunity to push broadband content to portable handsets within a limited area (typically within a city). PHS effectively gave China Telecom an entrée into the mobile communications market.

Another market of interest to China Telecom was the growing number of US firms entering China to conduct operations. Seizing upon this trend, China Telecom developed a series of offerings to provide end-to-end communications solutions to foreign firms operating in China. In 2002, the company became the first Chinese telecom firm to establish a US headquarters, with the opening of their office in the Washington, DC area. Business communication services continue to be a major product segment for China Telecom even today.

The development of the wireless market in China has significantly impacted the landscape of the entire telecommunications industry over the past decade, catalyzed possibly by China's long-awaited decision regarding the competing standards for third generation (3G) wireless communications. This culminated in a major industry overhaul, implemented by regulators in late 2008, which consolidated the industry into three major players, each with capabilities in the wireline, wireless, and broadband spaces. China Telecom, along with rivals China Mobile, the largest wireless provider in the world, and China Unicom, a long-time competitor from the MPT days, are now in a pitched battle for dominance of the largest telecom market on the planet.

Corporate Structure and Leadership

China Telecom utilizes the approach of business process re-engineering as a critical component of management innovation. To better respond to market dynamics, the company has adopted a new organizational structure with complementary "front-end" and "back-end" units. The "front-end" is the customer-facing portion of the business, comprised of a product management structure that feeds the three major market segments: large enterprises, business subscribers, and public (household/individual) subscribers. These, in turn, connect with the end user through account managers, community managers, rural contract agents, and the customer service structure.

The "front-end" is supported by a "back-end" structure, which consists of the network resources, including construction, operations and maintenance, and process development functions. These feed into the network infrastructure that serves the "front-end" customer through internal service agreements.

China Telecom is led by a highly experienced team of directors and senior executives, led by Chairman and CEO Wang Xiaochu. Mr. Wang brings to China Telecom almost 30 years of management experience in the telecom industry, including having served as Chairman and CEO of China Mobile (Hong Kong) Limited. He led the development of China Telecom's network management systems along with numerous other IT projects. He is supported by a team of seven executive directors and six non-executive directors, all of whom bring substantial corporate leadership experience, many with regional or national telecom providers.

Main Products and Services

China Telecom provides a full menu of telecommunications services to wireline and mobile customers in the PRC, in both the business and personal arenas. In addition to traditional voice service, which has seen significant declines in recent years, customers also are offered data and broadband multimedia services. With the recently acquired CDMA (code-division multiple-access) mobile network, these advanced services are available to both wired and wireless users. Increasingly, these services are offered in bundles designed for business or household applications.

In the government and business sector, voice, data, and broadband access are integrated through the company's BizNavigator service. This is accompanied by office administration and information management services developed for industry-specific applications, such as hotels, academic campuses, and hospitals.

Household customers, in addition to the discrete voice, data, and broadband access services, can select the company's OneHome integrated service bundle. Additional value-added information service offerings, including entertainment and wealth management, are available to differentiated segments of the household market.

Challenges and Business Strategies

While China Telecom is secure as the nation's largest wireline telecom provider, the global shift toward mobile communications places the company at a significant disadvantage compared to its largest domestic rivals. In addition to customers foregoing the physical limitations of wireline communication service in favor of the flexibility of mobile service, the company's newly acquired mobile business is running a distant third behind the incumbent wireless providers, China Mobile and China Unicom. The PRC, with a population of 1.3 billion, had over 580 million mobile phone subscribers by the middle of 2008, almost triple the number of China Telecom's wireline subscriber base. The Chinese telecom industry restructuring of 2008 attempted to create an element of competitive balance among the three major players.

China Telecom must find a way to challenge the dominance of China Mobile, which served almost 400 million mobile users by mid-2008. To do this, China Telecom was allowed, as part of the industry re-shuffle, to purchase one of the two wireless networks from intermediate rival China Unicom. This left China Unicom with roughly 125 million mobile users and gave China Telecom potentially 43 million mobile customers; however, many of these may have been induced to remain with China Unicom because, by the end of 2008, China Telecom listed only 28 million mobile users. With mobile use on the rise, and wireline declining, Wang and his team face the task of growing their mobile business at a tremendous rate, while maintaining the loyalty of their current business and household customers.

In 2008 and 2009, the company's efforts were focused around a number of critical business strategies, aimed at enhancing its competitive position. These included an integrated development strategy aimed to retaining wireline voice customers in the government, enterprise, and household sectors, aggressive development of information application services, and the rapid scaling of the wireless CDMA customer base.

As traditional wireline revenues from voice calls have declined, the company has shifted resources to develop and support new services. Wireline subscribers declined overall from 220 million to 208 million during 2008, a decline of 5.6%. This shows accelerating decline, when compared with the drop of 1.1% observed during the previous year. Corresponding declines were measured in voice service usage in the local, domestic long distance, and international long distance service areas. Wireline broadband subscribers, on the other hand, have shown an increase in number at a 25% annual rate in recent years. In 2008, the percentage of wireline revenue from non-voice services rose from 37% to 46%. This is, in part, due to heavy promotion of bundled services. Revenues from BizNavigator services in 2008 were up roughly 11% from the previous year. The subscriber base in this sector of the market increased 34% in the same period. The popular OneHome residential package was adopted by over 20% of China Telecom's household customers in 2008 due to special pricing and incentives. OneHome subscribers more than doubled in number in 2008, increasing to almost 24 million from less than 11 million the previous year.

The company's information services offerings, with a focus on business traveling and information search services saw revenues increase by 44.6% in 2008 over the prior year, to RMB 4.8 million. Additionally, IT services and applications for government and business customers, generated revenues of RMB 3.5 million in 2008, an increase of 83.8% over 2007 sales. These latter services highlighted such features as video applications and network management services. The rapid scale development and deployment of these services required the company to build broad cross-functional teams and to standardize many operational platforms across the company. This enhanced internal capability translated into better customer service capacity, and may help position China Telecom for higher customer retention.

The integration of the acquired CDMA wireless business poses a unique challenge. The company has adopted the strategies of targeting the mid-to-high end of the market and rapid development of economies of scale. The first step has been to transition as many of the incumbent's customers as possible, and to streamline operations and processes. Additionally, the company must migrate its legacy PHS mobile users to the new technology with minimal attrition. Solidifying this customer base has required significant handset subsidies to reduce barriers for customers, along with the associated earnings losses. Here the company has adopted the concept of the Internet handset, and promoted their broadband household and business offerings as a differentiation strategy aimed at achieving high average revenues per user. As third generation (3G) mobile technologies are rolled out across China, the company hopes to be positioned in the minds of consumers as a leading provider of the end-to-end mobile Internet experience.

In 2008, China Telecom Corporation Limited was ranked number 288 on the *Fortune* Global 500 list with annual revenue in excess of US$27.8 billions. This was a decline of 13 places from the number 275 spot the previous year, even though revenues grew by roughly US$3 billion. With its commitment to strategies of growth and change, China Telecom is well positioned to hold on to its place among the largest telecommunications providers in the world.

Keith L. Whittingham

References

Cao, D (2009). Wu Ying. In *Biographical Dictionary of New Chinese Entrepreneurs and Business Leaders*. W Zhang and I Alon (eds.), pp. 201–202. Cheltenham, UK: Edward Elgar.

China Telecom Corporation Limited (2009). Business overview. http://www.chinatelecom-h.com/eng/global/home.htm. Retrieved on 26 May 2009.

Dialing the markets (17 October 2002). *Economist*. http://www.economist.com. Retrieved on 8 May 2009.

Global 500 2008: Annual ranking of the world's largest companies. *Fortune*. http://money.cnn.com/magazines/fortune/global500/2008/index.html. Retrieved on 27 May 2009.

Industry Shakeup Creates 3 Telecom Giants (25 May 2008). *China Daily*. http://www2.chinadaily.com.cn/china/2008-05/25/content_6709799.htm. Retrieved on 20 May 2009.

McCully, AD (2003). China Telecom. In *International Directory of Company Histories.* Farmington Hills, MI: Gale (St. James Press), Vol. 50.

Rewired (29 May 2008). *Economist.* http://www.economist.com. Retrieved on 8 May 2009.

CHINA UNICOM

Corporate Address and Contact Information

China Unicom (Hong Kong) Limited
75th Floor, The Center
99 Queen's Road Central
Hong Kong
Phone: (852)2126-2018
http://www.chinaunicom.com.hk/en/aboutus/about_info.html

Commonly known as China Unicom, China United Network Communications Group (中国联通股份有限公司) is a full-service telecommunications provider serving all of the PRC, and is firmly in position as the second largest mobile provider in the country, after China Mobile. Through a complex shareholder structure, the group owns 57.3% of the publicly traded China Unicom (Hong Kong) Limited, which is listed on the New York Stock Exchange (Symbol: CHU) and the Hong Kong Stock Exchange (Code: 0762). The public company, in turn, is sole owner of three operating subsidiaries, China United Network Communications Corporation Limited, China Netcom Group Corporation (Hong Kong) Limited, and China Unicom International Limited (as of March 2009). In 2008, the group as a whole earned RMB 14.3 billion in profit, on revenues of RMB 148 billion (after exclusions and adjustments).

Historical Development

China Unicom was created in 1994, and gained prominence as China engaged in the process of joining the World Trade Organization (WTO). The PRC was being urged to demonstrate the openness of its industries to competition, domestic and foreign. As the world was in the midst of a major "high-tech boom", brought about by the explosion of Internet traffic, a lot of attention was brought to bear on the PRC's telecommunications industry, which then effectively operated as a government-directed monopoly. The China Telecommunications Corporation (China Telecom) controlled virtually all fixed-wire, mobile, paging, and satellite communications, under close regulation of the Ministry of Posts and Telecommunications (MPT). Both MPT and China Telecom were able to effectively thwart the competitive advances of China Unicom.

Beginning in 1998, the central government took steps to reshape the Chinese telecom industry into a more efficient, customer-focused one, an effort that continues to this day. This initially involved weakening the protective oversight that MPT offered China Telecom. The postal services were made independent, and the remainder of MPT was merged into the Ministry of Information Industry (MII). The following year saw the dismantling of China Telecom into separate businesses, based on services offered. The mobile business was spun off and launched publicly, and eventually became what is China Mobile today. The satellite business was separated to form independent company ChinaSat. China Telecom's paging business was offered to China Unicom, an acquisition that resulted in the company developing an 80% share of the country's paging market.

On the strength of the success of the acquired paging business, China Unicom went to the public financial markets in June 2000 and held a successful initial public offering (IPO) that raised almost US$7 billion on the Hong Kong and New York Stock Exchanges. To lend the company competitive strength, MII allowed China Unicom to offer mobile prices on its GSM (Global System for Mobile) network at up to 20% lower, in some cases, than the dominant China Mobile. The financial market success and improved competitive positioning allowed China Unicom to expand it mobile offerings in 2002, as it first commenced operations using the CDMA (code-division multiple access) wireless technology. In 2002, China Unicom became the first telecom company from mainland China to offer mobile services outside of the mainland when the company deployed a CDMA network to offer roaming services to its traveling customers. This was followed the next year by service expansion into Vietnam.

By the end of 2007, China Unicom had over 120 million subscribers on its GSM network, and almost 42 million subscribers on its CDMA network, in addition to a number of business customers leasing fixed lines for broadband services. Like the rest of the industry, and observers around the world, the company waited for the PRC central government to make a decision on licenses for the third generation (3G) of wireless technology. But the MII had another move to make first, one that would change the shape of China Unicom, and indeed of the entire industry. The regulator had long been hinting at another phase of its major restructuring of the country's telecom industry. In May 2008, it was announced that China Unicom was to sell its CDMA networks and business to China Telecom, strengthening Telecom's ability to compete in the mobile arena. Additionally, Unicom was to acquire China Netcom, a largely fixed-line provider with strength in China's Northern provinces, enhancing Unicom's competitiveness in the wireline world.

Corporate Leadership

China Unicom is led by a team of eleven directors and seven senior vice presidents. Of the directors, seven are non-executive and four are executive, including the Chairman and CEO, Chang Xiaobing. Mr. Chang holds a doctor's degree in business administration from the Hong Kong Polytechnic University (2005), and is a seasoned executive with over 27 years experience in China's telecom industry, at operational, managerial, and executive levels. He previously served in the MPT at the provincial level, and later in a senior departmental leadership role in the MII. Chang rose to serve as director of the Telecommunications Administration in the MII from 2000 to 2004, during which time he served as a vice president of China Telecom. In this role, Chang directed China Telecom's entrance into the North American telecom market in 2002, with the establishment of the company's US headquarters in Washington DC, a first for a Chinese telecom company. In November 2004, he was appointed to his current role at China Unicom.

Main Product and Service Offerings

China Unicom utilizes its expansive mobile and fixed-line networks to deliver a broad range of services to its customers. These services include basic voice services to local, long distance, and international destinations, as well as value-added services (VAS) such as data and broadband multimedia transmissions, which include everything from paging to high-resolution video content.

With the sale of wireless CDMA operations to China Telecom completed in October 2008, China Unicom has consolidated its mobile offerings around its GSM network, which supports both voice communications and GPRS (general packet radio service) data communications. Among the VAS offered to mobile customers are SMS (short message service), MMS (multimedia message service), and Color Ring Back service (by which users can select or create custom ringing tones to replace the standard tones that callers hear when waiting for the user to answer). VAS revenue increased over 20% in 2008, to almost RMB 16.3 billion, and made up almost a quarter of all mobile revenues. GRPS access has been extended to all 31 provinces and regions in the PRC, and the company continues to introduce new applications such as mobile stock quote and trading which debuted in 2008. By the end of that year, the company had established international agreements supporting roaming GSM customers from 69 countries and allowing PRC users to roam in 27 countries.

The company offers Internet access and applications to both fixed-line and mobile customers, through its China 169 service, via DSL, fiber, WLAN, and GPRS connections. Residential customers can access this service through the Family Gateway, a home network solution that supports multiple hardware formats. Household users can also subscribe to the CU Max broadband portal, offering multimedia content and applications, for entertainment and education, from a variety of vendors across the entire PRC. Government and business customers make use of China Unicom's Internet Data Center (IDC) platform, that offers high-bandwidth hosting and IP (Internet protocol) services, security services (including firewall, data storage, and network-monitoring services), and other value-added services.

Challenges and Business Strategies

As competition intensifies in the Chinese telecom market, China Unicom faces a number of pressures. GSM users grew 10.6% during 2008, from 120.6 million to 133.4 million, but this growth rate was down from the 12.7% observed in the prior 12-month period. Average revenue per user (ARPU) also declined to a monthly value of RMB 42.3 in 2008, down 7.4% year-over-year. Much of this decline was due to tariff adjustments on mobile services made by the central government to stimulate demand. This is further compounded by the generous handset subsidies offered to entice new customers, creating further downward pressure on profits.

Significant issues also face the fixed-line side of the business. This market sector in China has been eroding as government mandated tariffs make mobile communications more cost effective than fixed-line. China Unicom's fixed-line subscriber base declined during the course of 2008 from 110.8 million users to 100.1 million, almost a 10% drop. Infrastructure expansion is also more costly for fixed-line than for wireless. However, as the major competitors move toward bundled wired and wireless services, this market cannot be ignored. The merger with China Netcom gave the company a substantial wired network presence in the 10 Northern provinces; but competition with the fixed-line network of China Telecom will require significant capital expenditure in the wired sector, a move that will certainly appear risky to investors.

Against these challenges, Mr. Chang and his team must build synergies within their organization. While building scale at a managed rate in the fixed-line business, particularly in the southern provinces, the company must aggressively deepen the penetration of their bundled services (fixed-line and wireless) and their value-added services. More content-rich broadband services are planned, in order to secure more high-end subscribers and increase ARPU results. One area advantage for China Unicom is in third generation (3G) wireless technology. The government has granted the company a license to develop and deploy the WCDMA (wideband-CDMA) 3G standard. This standard, which has been broadly adopted in Europe, is relatively well developed compared to the competing standards that the company's major competitors in China will deploy. The development of value-added application should thus be accelerated. If China Unicom can take great advantage of their effective 3G head start, the company should be able to offset their fixed-line limitations and compete effectively for a bigger share of the largest telecom market in the world.

Keith L. Whittingham

References

And then there were three (23 January 2003). *Economist*. http://www.economist.com. Retrieved on 20 May 2009.

China Unicom (Hong Kong) Limited (2009). About us. http://www.chinaunicom.com.hk/en/home/default.html. Retrieved on 30 May 2009.

China Unicom (Hong Kong) Limited (2009). *Annual Report 2008*. http://www.chinaunicom.com.hk/en/investor/ir_report.html. Retrieved on 30 May 2009.

Industry shakeup creates 3 telecom giants (25 May 2008). *China Daily*. http://www.chinadaily.com.cn/china/2008-05/25/content_6709799.htm. Retrieved on 20 May 2009.

McCully, AD (2003). China Telecom. In *International Directory of Company Histories*. Farmington Hills, MI: Gale (St. James Press), Vol. 50.

Meng, C and C Fan (2008). Acquisition of parent's fixed line in Southern China. *Bank of America/Merrill Lynch Research Report*, 17 December. http://www.ml.com. Retrieved on 18 May 2009.

Rewired (29 May 2008). *Economist*, http://www.economist.com. Retrieved on 8 May 2009.

Zhang, W (2009). Chang Xiaobing. In *Biographical Dictionary of New Chinese Entrepreneurs and Business Leaders*. W Zhang and I Alon (eds.), pp. 10–11, Cheltenham, UK: Edward Elgar.

CHINA VANKE

Corporate Address and Contact Information

China Vanke Company Limited
Vanke Architecture Research Centre
63 Meilin Road
Futian District, Shenzhen
Guangdong Province 518083
People's Republic of China
Phone: (86)755-2560-6666
Fax: (86)755-2553-1696
http://www.vanke.com/main/

Established in 1984, and commonly known as Vanke, China Vanke Company Limited (万科企业股份有限公司) is the largest residential real estate developer in mainland China, which develops, manages, and sells property and provides investment and consulting services. Widely viewed as possessing one of the country's most recognizable brands, the company focuses on urban residential development and management across all regions of China. The company is headquartered in Shenzhen, Guangdong and its parent company is China Resources. China Vanke was listed on the Shenzhen Stock Exchange in 1991.

Historical Development

A large part of Vanke's success can be attributed to major reformations taking place in China over the course of the past two decades. Until the early 1980s, all property in China was owned, developed, and allocated by the state. Following the economic reforms in the same decade, Chinese citizens gained the ability to purchase partial or full ownership rights to the apartments and homes they lived in. With the liberation of the housing market and the country's embracing of free enterprise, millions of migrant workers relocated to factories in special economic zones (SEZs) and large urban coastal cities. Consequently, demand for new residential real estate has continued to grow over the past quarter century, resulting in China possessing the most dynamic housing market in the world. In 2007 alone, the country added 5.5 million new housing units, nearly four times what the United States built and more than one-quarter of all new housing stock in the world. Vanke has been able to benefit tremendously from the growth in China's housing market; during the year ending 31 December 2008, the company sold approximately 5.57 million square meters of properties, and reached total revenue of RMB 18.449 billion and a net income of 1.756 billion.

Vanke's principal activities include the development, management and sale of properties, with a strong focus on helping the country's emerging middle class become *yezhu* (homeowners). Its high-rise apartment towers, single-story suburban developments, and luxury-gated communities can be found in 20 cities across the Pearl River Delta, the Yangtze River Delta, and the Bohai Rim Region.

Corporate Structure and Leadership

Wang Shi, founder and chairman of China Vanke, is often viewed as the epitome of China's new entrepreneur. Known as China's "Donald Trump" and once a poor migrant and a former People's Liberation Army soldier, Wang founded and managed Vanke's predecessor company in 1984, a subsidiary of a state-owned enterprise that traded home appliances and electronics. The company was renamed to Vanke four years later and experimented with many different types of businesses from fertilizer and food processing to media and real estate development. In 1988, Wang transformed the business into a public shareholding company, and in the mid-1990s, a market downturn forced the company to abandon all businesses but one: housing development. Since 1993, Vanke has set the development of residential property as its core business, and has continued to successfully grow the business through an aggressive series of acquisitions. Today, it is recognized as one of the "International Best Small Companies" by *Forbes*, in addition to recently being recognized as a "Best Citizen Enterprise in China".

Challenges and Business Strategies

Since its inception, one of Vanke's primary competitive advantages has been its ability to build and sustain a strong brand image through its Western-style marketing. Through branding the company's developments not as simply a "place to live" but rather an opportunity for the Chinese to buy into and "climb the ladder rungs" to higher status, security, and style, Vanke continues to drive this strong paradigm change in the mind of the Chinese homeowner through extremely effective marketing, utilizing the successful marketing slogan "live your dreams". As such, the company promotes the freedom to choose where and how to live, in addition to the opportunity to accumulate wealth.

Throughout the years, the company has sought to be seen as a "role model" for an industry that has often had a corrupt past and riddles with business fraud. In 1988, the company adopted a "no bribery" rule as part of its core principles when the company went public. In a country where all land continues to be owned by the state (often creating challenges for developers such as Vanke), the company has sought to be seen as a highly ethical and transparent company. As such, Vanke's Western-style ethics have also been a vital part of the firm's marketing efforts and have resulted in a strong natural appeal to China's middle class, serving as a strong differentiator and competitive advantage for the company.

In addition to utilizing its strong branding to differentiate itself from its competition, Vanke has also sought to differentiate itself through its product offerings. Unlike most developers, Vanke manages the properties it builds, which removes an incentive to cut corners on construction and reinforce the company's focus on quality. Vanke's property management segment accounts for approximately 1% of its total revenues, and in 2008, the company announced a joint venture with CB Richard Ellis to provide management at its high-end properties.

In 2007, the company began to offer fully decorated units. As most housing units in China are sold as empty shells (with the buyer having to provide plumbing, doors, and flooring after purchase), Vanke began to utilize this product offering as a way to not only differentiate itself but also be seen as a more "environmentally friendly" company. Vanke estimates that it will be able to reduce construction waste by two tons per household by doing all finishing work prior to the consumer purchasing the home. The company's goal is to furnish 90% of all homes that it sells by 2010, which will also serve to reduce the large amount of construction waste. In addition, Vanke is also the first Chinese company to move into prefabricated housing. Seen as a bold move in a country where labor is abundant and continues to remain relatively inexpensive, Wang sees this as an important initiative in that it will allow for a more consistent standard of quality in his housing. It also fits with the company's mission to be more environmentally friendly as the company seeks to cater to a market that has a growing ecological awareness.

Vanke utilizes a conservative approach in regards to its project resources, choosing not to secure resources needed to develop and sustain projects beyond a two-year period. As a result, the company often maintains a lower inventory amount versus that of its competitors; however, this strategic approach prevents the company from tying up capital and lowering capital turnover efficiency, and ultimately allows for increased flexibility.

A challenging economic environment in 2009 has resulted in the company having an increased focus on organizational efficiencies. As such, the company has radically cut back on office construction and has turned toward more affordable, lower-priced housing developments, manufactured under government contract. Plans are currently under way to build housing for the millions left homeless after the 2008 earthquake hit China's southwest Sichuan Province, with Vanke estimating that it would invest $14.6 million in post-quake rebuilding. In the coming years, it is projected that the company will concentrate its resources through limiting new housing developments mainly to Shenzhen, Beijing, and Shanghai. In addition, the company will continue to focus on growth through acquisitions. In 2007 alone, Vanke purchased 13 companies either directly or through stock purchases. As of 2009, the company has approximately 180 subsidiaries, most of which are property development companies.

Matt Amick

References

Balfour, F and A Pasternack (2008). China Vanke Company, Ltd. *Architectural Record*. April.

Building a green reputation (31 March 2009). *The New Zealand Herald.*

China Vanke (2009). 2008 Annual Report. http://www.vanke.com/Article2.aspx?id=63078. Retrieved on 15 May 2009.

China Vanke Co. Ltd. *Hoovers,* http://www.hoovers.com/china-vanke/—ID__159878—/free-co-factsheet.xhtml. Retrieved on 24 June 2009.

Larmer, B (2008). Building wonderland. *The New York Times,* 6 April. http://www.nytimes.com/2008/04/06/realestate/keymagazine/406china-t.html. Retrieved on 24 June 2009.

Mo, X (2009). Wang Shi. In *Biographical Dictionary of New Chinese Entrepreneurs and Business Leaders.* W Zhang and I Alon (eds.), pp. 178–180, Cheltenham, UK: Edward Elgar.

Vanke's real estate sales fall sharply (10 September 2008). *The International Herald Tribune.*

CITIC, CITIC PACIFIC, AND CHINA CITIC BANK

Corporate Address and Contact Information

CITIC
Capital Mansion, 6 Xinyuan Nanlu
Chaoyang District, Beijing 10000
People's Republic of China
Phone: (010)6466-0088
Fax: (010)6466-1186
http://www.citic.com/

CITIC Pacific
32nd Floor, CITIC Tower
1 Tim Mei Avenue Central
Hong Kong
Phone: (852)2820-2111
Fax: (852)2877-2771
http://www.citicpacific.com

China CITIC Bank
C Block, Fuhua Mansion, No. 8
Chaoyangmenbei Dajie
Dongcheng District, Beijing 100027
People's Republic of China
Phone: (010)6554-1658
Fax: (010)6554-1671
http://bank.ecitic.com

CITIC Group (中国中信集团公司), formerly known as China International Trust and Investment Corporation, is a state-owned investment firm. In line with the needs to reform Chinese economy, Rong Yiren established the company in 1979 with the approval of Deng Xiaoping, the former Chairman of Chinese Communist Party. CITIC now has 44 subsidiaries with operations in countries such as the United States, Australia, Canada, and Japan. Aimed to attract foreign capital and to introduce advanced technologies and scientific practices into China, CITIC has registered net assets worth of approximately USD 14.96 billion at the end of 2007, and about 68,000 employees.

CITIC Pacific (中信泰富) and China CITIC Bank (中信银行) are two major subsidiaries of CITIC. Headquartered in Hong Kong, the establishment of CITIC Pacific can be traced back to 1985, which was listed on the Hong Kong Stock Exchange in 2007. Established in 1987 and as China's seventh-largest lender in terms of total assets, China CITIC Bank was listed on both the Shanghai and Hong Kong Stock

Exchanges in 2007. The company is a comprehensive commercial bank with extensive local network across the nation, and branch offices in more than 70 countries around the world.

Historical Development

During its formation period (1979–1984), CITIC focused primarily on utilizing the foreign capital for the development of China's domestic economy, and undertook many projects through using a variety of financing methods and new technologies and practices. Under the leadership of Rong, who defined the CITIC's corporate guiding principles as "law-abiding, upright and honest, practical and realistic, innovative, modest and prudent, working as a team, industrious and self-motivated, and vigorous and efficient in implementing", CITIC experienced a period of rapid growth in 1985–1988, during which time the company initiated organizational reforms, established subsidiaries for local and international operations, and diversified its businesses to become a conglomerate. From 1989 to1992, CITIC undertook another major reorganization with a main focus of strengthening management, improving economic returns, capturing business opportunities, pursuing healthy growth, and developing long-term strategic plans. Since 1993, after Rong assumed vice president of the People's Republic of China, CITIC has been trying to stabilize its operations. New corporate leadership team was established and the company reexamined its core operations and moved toward lead management and more stringent macro policies control. In order to develop the China CITIC Bank, CITIC has, in recent years, resorted to tapping into its own resources by means of, for instance, capital increases via bond issuance. As a socially responsible corporation, CITIC spent nearly RMB 200 million in 2007 to assist rebuilding of Shenzha town (Tibet) and initiatives such as rural education (Yunnan, Tibet, Guizhou, etc.), national afforestation program (Hubei), poverty eradication, cultural developments, etc.

Since its founding, CITIC Pacific has over the years pursued various expansion plans so as to position the company as a major player in mainland China for its core businesses. Like many other large corporations around the world, CITIC Pacific is not free from corporate mishaps because of vulnerable corporate governance. In late 2008, it became a victim of the global financial market turmoil, when unauthorized bets on the foreign currency market by its two senior executives brought to company exchange losses of nearly HK$2 billion. In the midst of corporate chaos, the management of CITIC Pacific is reorganized in order to meet stakeholders' expectations.

China CITIC Bank was formed in 1987, following a proposal from Rong Yiren in 1984 to the leaders of Chinese Communist Party that CITIC needed a bank, under its flagship, that would handle and manage its massive foreign exchange transactions. With the backing of the State Council and the Chinese Central Bank, China CITIC Bank was registered as a state-owned composite bank. In 2006, the bank formed strategic alliances with Spain's Banco Bilbao Vizcaya Argentaria (BBVA), a multinational Spanish banking group. In recent years, in light of China's entry into WTO and its fast-growing banking sector, China CITIC Bank has been aggressively seeking new ways to improve its core businesses and foster sustainable corporate growth over long run.

Corporate Structure and Leadership

As with all other public companies, CITIC is governed by a Board of Directors. Its fate is closely associated with its founder, Rong Yiren (1916–2005). Graduated from St John's University, Shanghai, Rong was one of the few capitalists who stayed in mainland China after 1949 when the Nationalists were defeated by the Communists. Although Rong was obliged to preside over the nationalization of all of his family assets in 1956, his fortunes changed for better when Deng Xiaoping took over from Mao Zedong as the new leader of China. In 1979, Rong formed CITIC to pioneer the reforms in the financial sector, with an ambitious goal of developing international business and attracting foreign investment and technology to China. During the 1990s, CITIC aggressively expanded its businesses. It has since established a strong presence in Hong Kong, where Rong's son, Larry Rong, was the chairman of CITIC Pacific until recently, when he resigned due to huge speculative losses suffered by the company during the global financial crisis.

In 2006, Kong Dan succeeded Wang Jun as the Chairman of CITIC Group. Born in 1947, Kong, who was president of China Construction Bank, is also the chairman of China CITIC Bank. In 2009, Chang Zhenming was appointed the chairman of CITIC Pacific, who has served as the vice chairman and president of CITIC group and has over 20 years of experience in banking, finance, and securities business.

Main Products and Services

CITIC mainly engages in the provision of financial and banking services, which include securities business, insurance, investment, trusts business, funds, futures, banking, etc. The total assets, revenues, and net profits of its finance subsidiaries accounted for about 78% of CITIC Group statistics in 2006, although non-financial businesses have been growing in importance. That segment of businesses include real estate, civil infrastructure, engineering project contracting, resources and energy, manufacturing, IT services, etc., which contributed about 10% of the total assets, 52% of total revenues, and 40% of total net profits of the CITIC Group in 2006.

The core businesses of CITIC Pacific are steel manufacturing, developing and investing property, power generation, aviation, distribution of motor vehicles, and consumer products throughout China. Other non-core businesses include investment management and financial advisory. China CITIC Bank is a commercial bank offering broad range of retail and corporate banking products and services, which include credit card, loan, deposit accounts, electronic transfer, foreign exchange management, etc. As a wholly owned subsidiary of CITIC, China CITIC Bank has a total asset of RMB 576 billion (USD 71 billion). As of 2006, China CITIC Bank had a non-performing loan (NPL) ratio of 2.5% (RMB 11.1 billion). The bank's capital adequacy ratio is 9.1%.

Challenges and Business Strategies

As noted above, historical review suggests that the Rong family has played a crucial role in shaping the course of the CITIC Group over the past 30 years. Nevertheless, CITIC Group has since been striving to stabilize and consolidate its diverse business operations, as the top management is constantly seeking innovative technologies and practices to sustain the corporate growth and long-term profitability. Despite the current global financial crisis, both the financial and non-financial businesses of CITIC are expected to benefit continuously from the rapid development of the Chinese economy. With the new management team installed recently, it is yet to be seen how CITIC leaders will tackle many strategic issues such as growing competitions from both local and international firms, corporate governance reform, scientific management, and the challenge of globalization.

Loi Teck Hui and Quek Kia Fatt

References

China CITIC Bank. http://bank.ecitic.com/investorrelation/index_en.html. Retrieved on 12 April 2009.

CITIC, *Wikipedia.* http://en.wikipedia.org/wiki/CITIC. Retrieved on 10 April 2009.

CITIC Pacific. http://www.citicpacific.com. Retrieved on 11 April 2009.

CITIC Pacific Chairman Resigns in Management Reshuffle, *Xinhuanet,* 8 April 2009 http://news.xinhuanet.com/english/2009-04/08/content_11151795.htm. Retrieved on 11 April 2009.

Leung, A and R Wong. CITIC Pacific warns potential $2 billion forex losses (20 October 2008). *Reuters.* http://www.reuters.com/article/forexNews/idUSTRE49J5NI20081020. Retrieved on 7 April 2009.

PricewaterhouseCoopers, *CITIC Pacific's 2007 Annual Report.* http://www.citicpacific.com. Retrieved on 9 April 2009.

RSM China, *CITIC Group's 2007 Annual Report.* http://www.citic.com/wps/portal. Retrieved on 9 April 2009.

中信泰富 (CITIC Pacific). http://baike.baidu.com/view/494202.htm. Retrieved on 11 April 2009.

DAQIN RAILWAY

Corporate Address and Contact Information

Daqin Railway Company Limited (SIC-4011, NAICS-482111)
14 Zhanbei Road
Datong
Shanxi Province 037005
People's Republic of China
Phone: (86)352-712-1248
Fax: (86)352-712-1990
http://daqintielu.com/

The company name Daqin Railway (short for Daqin Railway Company Limited, 大秦铁路股份有限公司) is derived from the two terminal cities on the Daqin railway line, namely Datong in Shanxi and Qinhuangdao in Hebei by the Bohai Sea. China's main coal artery runs between these two cities. Datong is also known as China's capital of coal, and Qinhuangdao is China's largest coal exporting port where coal is shipped to South China and abroad to Taiwan, Japan, and South Korea.

Daqin Railway is a rail transportation company engaged in the business of line-haul operating railroads. It provides freight transportation primarily for coal and secondarily for other cargo including: coke, cement, non-ferrous ore, iron and steel, timber, and ferrous minerals. It is China's first railway with heavy-loaded trains designed exclusively for the transportation of coal. It has remained China's principal coal carrier and the largest coal transportation enterprise.

Historical Development

Coal is used mainly in power generation and steel-manufacturing companies. Coal supports about two-thirds of China's electricity needs. As China's GDP continued to grow rapidly during the past decade, the expanding economy needed much energy and power generation. As the most energy-efficient transportation model on land, rail has always been China's primary mode of moving raw materials. However, existing rail network capacity remains inadequate for transporting enough coal. The only two railways connecting coalfields to seaports are the Daqin line from west to east, and the Shuohuang line from north to south. Congestion on the railway network has become a transportation bottleneck that leads to delays in delivering the needed raw material, and hence a major impediment to not only the development of the coal industry but also the roaring economy's domestic energy needs.

The length of China's railway in operation increased only from 73,000 km in 2003 to 78,000 km in 2007; whereas the freight traffic increased from 1.72 trillion ton-km in 2003 to 2.38 trillion ton-km in 2007.

According to the Ministry of Railway (MOR), the railway system was only able to meet about 35% of rail freight demand. Realizing the worsening railway problem, the Chinese government increased spending to expand the railway network. The government is also bringing in more deregulation and private investment into the formerly highly regulated rail sector. The current Five Year Plan (FYP) (2006–2010) calls for an extension to 100,000 km by 2010 and to 120,000 km by 2020. This FYP allots RMB 1.25 trillion on railway infrastructure construction, more than four times under the previous FYP. In late 2008, under revised guidelines, the government planned to invest RMB 2 trillion over the next three to five years. The MOR's goal is to meet 90% of rail freight demand when the rail reform is complete.

In concert with the government's railway development effort, Daqin Railway was established on 28 October 2004, primarily as a freight rail company to transport coal. Its inaugural freight service took place in early March 2006. A 204-box train loaded with 20,000 tons of coal, driven by five sets of China-made Shaoshan electrified engines, left Hudong station in Shanxi and arrived at Qinhuangdao port about 10 hours later. MOR officials remarked that this journey was a great breakthrough in China's heavy-loading freight transport in the railway sector.

Main Products and Services

Primarily a transportation company offering freight services of coal to electricity generation and steel-manufacturing industries, Daqin Railway also engages in the manufacture, installation, repair, and maintenance of railway transportation equipment, facilities, and its accessories. It also undertakes railway construction projects, organizes and manages engineering survey, design, and construction, provides loading and unloading of goods and warehousing services, and sells and stores related raw materials and spare parts needed. In addition, the company provides locomotive towing, truck repair, ticketing, and other related services.

Daqin Railway runs three main railway lines, namely Daqin (Datong-Qinhuangdao), Jingbao (Beijing-Baotou), and North Tongpu (Datong-Taiyuan). It has four branch lines, including Kouquan, Yungang, Ningke, and Pingshuo. These lines also link up with four regional lines, which are Shenshuo, Dazhun, Ningjing, and Jigang. Daqin Railway's total length of rail measures 3,185.87 km, with 1,157.3 km in operation. Daqin line itself is 653 km in length, based on coal transportation tracks laid in north China between 1985 and 1992. Daqin Railway's trains operate on electrified double track heavy haul railway, and are designed to carry an annual capacity of 100 million tons of coal. The largest unit can carry up to 20,000 tons.

Exceeding expectations, Daqin Railway's freight volumes went from 150 million tons in 2004 to 350 million tons in 2008. It is predicted to reach 400 million tons by 2010 and meet its transportation bottleneck. In addition, Daqin Railway purchased assets from Fengshada and North Tongpu lines in early 2005, and started a passenger train business that yields about 4.2% of its total revenue.

Corporate Structure and Leadership

Although Daqin Railway is a state-owned enterprise, it is not run by the MOR. It was originally sponsored by the Beijing Railway Bureau, a major shareholder (72.94%). These shares went to the Taiyuan Railway Bureau (TRB) under China's railway reform in March 2005. Additional shareholders include: China Huaneng Group, Datang International Power Generation Co. Ltd., China Coal energy Group Corporation, Qinhuangdao Port Group Co. Ltd., China Life Insurance Co. Ltd., New China Life Insurance Co. Ltd., Tonfang Investment Ltd., Datong Coal Mine Group Co. Ltd., China Railway Construction Investment Co. Ltd., and others. Its starting capital was RMB 10 billion.

Daqin Railway has a total of 40,388 employees as of the third quarter of 2008. Its corporate structure with a Board of Directors is headed by Guan Bolin who succeeded Wang Baoguo as general manager on 30 December 2008. Guan has had years of experience working in the railway industry. Before becoming the general manager of Daqin Railway, he was the secretary of TRB's Business Management Association. Prior to that, he held positions including party secretary at Datong Railway's branch office at Chawu Power Supply Section, department head of the Party's Datong branch office, division head of the Datong Section of Datong Railway, and department head of Passenger Transportation within the TRB.

Growth Strategies

Daqin Railway became the first domestically listed railway company to trade A-shares in 2006. Its IPO was listed on the Shanghai Stock Exchange on 1 August 2006. Issuing stock as a way of raising cash, Daqin Railway raised RMB 15 billion by issuing 3.03 billion shares at RMB 4.95 per share. Proceeds of the share sale were used for railway construction, capacity expansion, and new equipment. The China International Capital Corporation Ltd., an investment bank partly owned by Morgan Stanley, underwrote this share sale. This move marks a significant step in the reform of the railway investment in China. Daqin Railway remains China's largest listed train company. On *Forbes Global 2000*, Daqin Railway ranked 1209 in 2007, 1114 in 2008, and 948 in 2009. Among *China's Top 500 Tax-Paying Enterprises*, it ranked 79 in 2005, 61 in 2006, and 57 in 2007. Historic stock prices range approximately from RMB 5.54 in 2006 to 27.1 in 2008.

In Fall 2008, China Securities Regulatory Commission approved Daqin Railway to issue RMB 13.5 billion corporate bonds. This would raise funds for purchasing wagons and large locomotives to expand the fleet and to reduce borrowing costs. Daqin Railway planned to buy 3,000 open-goods wagons for RMB 1.65 billion, 360 electric locomotives for RMB 15.61 billion, and use the remaining funds to replenish its working capital.

In addition, Qinhuangdao Port received approval for a multi-billion RMB expansion project in 2005 to support Daqin Railway. Construction also began at Caofeidian Port on Bohai Bay to handle surplus from Daqin Railway. There is also a Daqin Railway Special Line project in Jinxi Steel in RMB 400 million, which could process annually 6 million tons of coke from Taiyuan and 3 million tons of iron ore at Caofeidian Port.

Business Challenges

Daqin Railway's main competitors within China include China Railway Tielong Container Logistics Company Limited, Inner Mongolia Yitai Coal Company Limited, and China Shenhua Energy Company Limited. Daqin Railway has been able to increase revenues year after year. The company's total revenue grew from RMB 12.71 billion in 2006 to 16.07 billion in 2007, and to 20.23 billion in January 2008. It has been most impressive in reducing the percentage of sales devoted to cost of goods sold. For the first three quarters of 2008, it reported a net profit of RMB 5.59 billion or RMB 0.43 per share on an operating revenue of RMB 17.70 billion, against a net profit of RMB 4.66 billion or RMB 0.36 per share on an operating revenue of RMB 15.23 billion for the same period in 2007.

Due to the global financial crisis started in 2008, there has been earnings decline in energy, industries, and materials. The Chinese economy has slowed down and reduced fuel demand accordingly. Daqin Railway's stock started dipping in mid/late 2008 after rapid rises especially in 2007. A US Bancorp analyst commented that companies in certain areas including railway infrastructure, electrical equipment, health care, food and beverage, and retail industries may be among the best performers in 2009. As of

March 2009, Daqin Railway remains an outperforming stock on the Shanghai Stock Exchange, and it was also added to Goldman Sachs' Asia-Pacific Conviction Buy List.

Victoria Chu

References

Daqin Railway Co. Ltd. (NBB: DAQI F). *Mergent Online*. Retrieved on 16 March 2009.

Daqin Railway Co. Ltd. reports earnings results for the third quarter and first nine months of 2008 (29 October 2008). *Business Week*. http://investing.businessweek.com/research/stocks/snapshot/snapshot.asp?capId=28009454. Retrieved on [15 April 2009].

Datamonitor (2008). Daqin Railway Co. Ltd. Company Profile.

Emerging Markets Information Services (2009). Daqin Railway Co. Ltd.

The Global 2000 (8 April 2009). *Forbes*. http://www.forbes.com/lists/2009/18/global-09_The-Global-2000_Company_6.html. Retrieved on 15 April 2009.

Ho, CK (2009). Daqin Railway added to Goldman Sachs Conviction Buy List (24 March). *Bloomberg*. http://www.bloomberg.com/apps/news?pid=newsarchive&sid=aQk1nlMEloJY. Retrieved on 15 April 2009.

Shanghai Securities News (31 December 2008). http://www.cnstock.com/paper_new/html/2008-12/31/content_66804694.htm. Retrieved on 15 April 2009.

DATANG INTERNATIONAL POWER GENERATION

Corporate Address and Contact Information

Datang International Power Generation Co. Ltd.
8/F, 482 Guanganmennei Ave.
Xuanwu District
Beijing 100053
People's Republic of China
Phone: (86)10-8358-1901
Fax: (86)10-8358-1911
http://www.dtpower.com

Commonly known as Datang International Power or Datang Power, Datang International Power Generation Co. Ltd. (大唐国际发电股份有限公司) is a state-owned power-producing corporation in mainland China. As one of the five largest power-producers in the country, Datang holds a premier position in Northern China. Datang Power develops and operates power plants, along with the sale of electricity in China. The company also sells thermal power, besides undertaking the maintenance and repair of power equipment and offering other power-related technical services.

Corporate Development

Datang Power, formerly known as Beijing Datang Power Generation Co. Ltd., was incorporated on 13 December 1994 as a joint stock limited company. The company was registered with the Chinese State Administration for Industry and Commerce. Datang Power was listed on both the Hong Kong and London

Stock Exchanges on 21 March 1997. On 13 May 1998, it was converted to a Sino-foreign joint stock limited company; and in 2001, the company obtained approval for its American Depository Receipts to be traded on the OTC Exchange in the United States. On 15 March 2004, it was renamed as Datang International Power Generation Co. Ltd. The total installed capacity of the company was 15,410 megawatts (MW) as of 30 June 2006. The registered capital of Datang Power was about 5.163 billion RMB, with the total assets of the company and its subsidiaries around 73.486 billion RMB.

The management board of Datang Power consists of 15 directors: two of them are executive directors, eight are non-executive directors, and five are independent non-executive directors. Zhang Yi and Yang Hongming are the executive directors of the company. Zhai Ruoyu, Hu Shengmu, Fang Qinghai, Liu Haixia, Guan Tiangang, Su Tiegang, Ye Yonghui, and Tong Yunshang are the non-executive directors. Xie Songlin, Xu Daping, Yu Changchun, Liu Chaoan, and Xia Qing are the independent non-executive directors. Zhai Ruoyu is the chairman of the company, while Zhang Yi is the president of Datang Power.

Main Products and Services

Datang Power is primarily engaged in the development and operation of power plants. As one of the largest independent power producers in the People's Republic of China, the company sells the self-produced electricity within the country, and undertakes repair and maintenance of all kinds of power equipment. Moreover, the company provides technical and consulting services in all power-related matters.

Currently, Datang Power is managing 18 power companies as its subsidiaries and four power plants. They are Douhe Power Plant, Gaojing Thermal Power Plant, Zhangjiakou Power Plant, Xiahuayuan Power Plant, Panshan Power Company, Huaze Hydropower Company, Yungang Thermal Power Company, Tuoketuo Power Company, Tangshan Thermal Power Company, Shentou Power Company, Liancheng Power Company, Wangtan Power Company, Nalan Hydropower Company, Chaozhou Power Company, Honghe Power Company, Ningde Power Company, Wushashan Power Project, and Lixianjiang Hydropower Company.

Douhe Power generated 10,546,000 Mega Watt hours (MWh) in 2006 on a gross basis. Gaojing Thermal Power generated 3,463,000 MWh. Zhangjiakou Power generated 14,202,000 MWh. Xiahuayuan Power generated 2,443,000 MWh. Datang Panshan Power generated 7,011,000 MWh. Datang Huaze Hydropower achieved a gross generation of 30,900 MWh in 2006. Datang Yungang Thermal Power generated 2,997,000 MWh. Datang Tuoketuo Power generated 21,407,000 MWh. Datang Tangshan Thermal Power achieved a gross generation of 4,776,000 MWh in 2006. Datang Shentou Power generated 5,703,000 MWh. Datang Liancheng Power generated 3,483,000 MWh in 2006. On a combined basis, the company achieved a gross power generation of 93,459,000 MWh on an installed capacity of 19,430 MW in 2006. On-grid power generation amounted to 87,902,000 MWh.

Challenges and Business Strategies

In 2008, due to global financial crisis, the demand for electricity slowed down, and the speed of electric power production growth fell. Compared to the previous year, the installed capacity of power plants in the country rose by 10.34% in 2008; electricity consumption rose by 5.25%, and electric power production rose by about 5.18% (Annual report 2008). During 2008, total power generation of the company and its subsidiaries amounted to 126.689 billion kWh (kilowatt hours), representing an increase of 7.12% as compared to the previous year, while in 2007 the growth rate had been 26.56% (Annual Report 2007, 2008). At the same time, electricity coal price continued to rise while quality worsened, which to certain extent hurt the profits of electric power production.

In spite of challenges mentioned above, there are still growth opportunities. As China enters the 11th five-year development period, the company anticipates the power demand to be robust in the coming years and expects the demand growth to remain at about 10% per annum. China had been concentrating on energy conservation along with reduction in consumption; at the same time, the country strives to maintain a sustainable development. Datang has been servicing the regions with the most robust growth potential. For example, Datang Power had been supplying power to the Beijing-Tianjin-Tangshan or BTT area, a region with a strong economic growth. The operating power plants of the company are located in this service area and are connected to the BTT Power Grid. Datang Power is also servicing the eastern coastal provinces and other regions such as Yunnan, Chongqing, and Shanxi. Looking ahead, Datang Power believes that the major developments in the Tianjin Binhai New District, as well as the construction of the heavy chemical industry zone of Bohai Rim in Tangshan region would spur strong demand for electricity. The growth from this region is expected to be above 12% per annum in the coming years. On the other hand, the growth of new installed capacities in the BTT Power Grid is likely to be marginally lower than the demand growth during the next few years. This could put pressure on the power grid. However, the company plans to compensate this by enhancing the utilization hours of the regional power generation.

Besides maintaining a geographical proximity to the growth regions the company services, Datang has strategized its competitive advantage by maintaining stable production growth, strictly reducing its production cost, installing additional capacities, participating in the technology innovations, being proactive in environment protection, and taking measures to control the prices of coal inputs. For example, the company has invested Shanxi Tashan Coal Mine, which starts to show the coal production capabilities; it also diversifies its coal purchases to international markets to gain competitive cost of coal.

Under those business initiatives, Datang Power has been witnessing a steady growth. For the year ended 31 December 2008, the company reported operating revenue of 36,836 million RMB, an increase of 12.43% from the previous year. However, net profit declined to 761 million RMB in 2008, from 3,564 million RMB in 2007. According to Datang Chairman Zhai Ruoyu, natural disasters in China in 2008 and the higher demand for power due to the Beijing Olympic Games put pressure on the power generation capacity of the company. Thermal coal prices remained at high levels, affecting profitability. Still, the company had been able to generate profits in 2008 due to stringent cost control measures and pruning of unnecessary expenses.

In 2008, Datang Power obtained approval for 16 projects based on coal-fired power, hydropower, nuclear power, and wind power. The company received another approval for phase one of two-unit coalmine with a production facility of 10 million tons of coal per annum. In 2009, Datang Power expects further progress in its installed capacity and power production, despite the slowdown in the Chinese economy. Still, the electricity demand definitely dropped in early 2009. During the first quarter ended 31 March 2009, Datang Power and its subsidiaries were able to generate about 27.8 billion kWh of power, and sold to the tune of 26.1 billion kWh. This was a decline of 5% from the first quarter of 2008. The possible decline in power demand, high coal prices, and low tariff barriers could influence the profitability in a negative fashion. In spite of these difficulties, Datang Power is planning to strengthen its operation management and expand its financing channels to improve the profitability in the near future.

Amir Shoham and Hui He

References

Datang International Power Generation Co. Ltd. *2007 Annual Report* (English). Mergent Online. Retrieved on 3 May 2009.

Datang International Power Generation Co. Ltd. *2008 Annual Report* (Chinese). Mergent Online. Retrieved on 3 May 2009.

Datang International Power Generation Co. Ltd (NBB: DIPG F). Mergent Online. Retrieved on 3 May 2009.

Datang International Power Generation Co. Ltd. Company profile. http://www.dtpower.com/en/profile/pro_stru.jsp. Retrieved on 19 May 2009.

Datang Power announces 2008 annual results (31 March 2009). PRNewswire-Asia. http://news.prnewswire.com/DisplayReleaseContent.aspx?ACCT=104&STORY=/www/story/03-31-2009/0004997387&EDATE=. Retrieved on 19 May 2009.

DIGITAL CHINA

Corporate Address and Contact Information

Digital China Holdings Limited
Suite 2008, 20/F, Devon House
Taikoo Place, 979 King's Road
Quarry Bay, Hong Kong
Phone: (852)3416-8000
Fax: (852)2805-5991
www.digitalchina.com.hk

Spun off from the former Legend Group (renamed to Lenovo since 2003) in 2000, Digital China Holding Ltd. (神州数码控股有限公司) is a leading information technology company in the People's Republic of China. As a major IT service provider in the country, the company has held the top position in IT product distribution for many years. Digital China has been focusing on transforming itself into the most comprehensive IT solution provider for customers across China.

Corporate Development

Digital China is a combination of the former Legend Technology Limited, Legend Advanced Systems Limited, and Legend Networks Limited. After its incorporation, Digital China was listed on the Hong Kong Stock Exchange on 1 June 2001. At the same year, it was named by the International Data Corporation (IDC) as China's largest distributor of IT products, largest provider of systems integration services, and one of the top three networking products vendors in China.

Over the past eight years, Digital China has sought to build its competitive advantage in the IT distribution sector. It has systematically established regional centers in 19 major cities in Great China, including recently Changsha, Xinjiang, and Harbin in 2007. Digital China distributes products and offers services through a network of more than 9,000 distributors and agents throughout the country. It also has formed strategic partnership with over 100 leading IT vendors worldwide. In addition, three instant technology logistics centers in Beijing, Shanghai, and Guangzhou have been built to ensure that it can provide the best and most convenient IT services to the users in China.

With its dominant position in IT distribution sector, Digital China also cultivates into other sectors, especially the high-marginal IT service sector. During the process, Digital China relied on various ways to sharpen its competitive advantage in IT service industry, including: setting up a joint-venture, Digital

China Management System Limited, to tap into China's ERP (Enterprise Resource Planning) market in November 2001; acquiring SicTech NorthNet Co. Ltd. (renamed to Digital China SicTech Co. Ltd.), to develop China's e-government market in 2002; setting up joint-venture, Digital China System Access Holding Limited (DCSA), to provide international services to China's financial sector in July 2005; and establishing Beijing Si-Tech Information Technology Co. Ltd., to enhance the Group's ability in providing customized solutions for the telecommunications sector, etc.

With more than 4,100 software talents, and the establishment of two IT service centers in Xi'an and Chengdu, Digital China is accelerating its growth in IT service sector. According to an analysis report provided by IDC in April 2008, the group is a firm leader in the government and banking sub-sectors. The effective cultivation of core capabilities in three key areas, namely software development in R&D bases, application software standardization, and products support, outsourcing, and maintenance services (PSOM) has played an extremely important role in the attainment of overall profitability for the service business.

Main Services and Competitive Advantage

After years of sequential development, Digital China has mainly focused on eight major business segments in the China market: IT planning, IT process outsourcing, application development, application integration, hardware infrastructure services, maintenance, hardware installation, distribution, and retail. A full range of IT services are available to industry clients, large enterprises, small- and mid-sized enterprises (SMEs), and individual consumers.

The competitive advantages of Digital China are outlined below. First, the company knows the market it operates. Legend, from which Digital China was spun off, was one of the first-batch of enterprises born in the 1980s when China underwent the modern economic reform. Because of its close association with Lenovo, Digital China focuses on the China market and always stays at the forefront of the market. Second, Digital China introduces the best. It sources from around the globe and brings only the best products that meet the need of customers in China. Third, it adds value. Digital China offers value-added services to suppliers or resellers to effectively manage their business. Overall, Digital China offers a total package. It provides customer-centered solutions and IT strategies, based on modern IT infrastructure to satisfy the application demands of Chinese users ranging from individuals to large-scale industrial enterprises.

Digital China's distribution segment, together with the systems integration service, has grown steadily over the years. More importantly, the IT service segment began to generate positive profit in 2007 after years of negative results, and it has systematically increased in the previous two years.

Corporate Structure and Leadership

GUO Wei is the current president and CEO of Digital China, a position he holds since 2000. A senior engineer and a member of the Legend group since 1988, he was appointed in 1997 as executive director and senior vice president of Legend Group, he also served as the general manger of Legend Technology Limited and Legend Advanced Systems Limited.

As of 31 March 2008, the Board of Digital China was comprised of ten directors, including two executive directors, four non-executive directors, and four independent non-executive directors. The management team mainly includes Guo Wei (Chairman and Chief Executive Officer), Lin Yang (President), He Jun (CFO), Mao Xiangqian (Senior Vice President), Yan Guorong (Senior Vice President), and Chen Yong (Senior Vice President).

Lenovo Holdings Limited remains Digital China's biggest shareholder, once accounting for 49.16% of its common share. However, in 2007, Digital China was engaged in a significant capital restructure since its incorporation. During the process, Lenovo Holdings Limited transferred part of its shares to some new investors. The final shareholder structure in November 2007 included: Lenovo Holding Limited, 16.23%; Hony Capital controlled by Lenovo Holdings, 8.03%; SAIF Partners, 18.35%; IDG VC, 3.44%; KIL, 10.47%; and the public shareholders, 43.26%. After the restructuring, Digital China enjoys the benefits of a more balanced shareholding structure and improved corporate governance standards.

In March 2009, Digital China announced another round of restructuring plan, in which the company would be split from originally three divisions (the Enterprise Client Division, the SMEs Division, and the Individuals Division) into six business units to deal with business clients, individual users, supply chain services, systems technology, software services, and integrated services. The former enterprise-targeted IT services division would be split into strategic divisions for software services and integrated services. The new systems technology business unit would provide product support solutions and value-added services for enterprise-level clients. The former SMEs and individual user-targeted volume sales division would be divided into strategic divisions dealing with business, consumer, and supply chain service operations.

Challenges and Strategies

Despite the world financial crisis, according to the latest *Springboard Research*, the IT market in China will not be affected severely, mainly due to the central government's economic stimulus plan and the increasing environmental protection investment.

However, Digital China is still facing tough challenges from other firms, both foreign and domestic. In the IT service sector, its competitors include IBM, HP, and other local companies such as Kingdee and Ufida. In IT products distribution sector, the international distribution enterprises have already set foot in China to compete with Digital China, such as Ingram Micro, and the home appliance retailers in China also encroach the market share, such as Gome in China. At the same time, the excess of the IT products put additional pressures on the decreasing sheer profit.

To grasp the opportunities and overcome the tough competitions, Digital China has set up its future growth strategies: the company will continually focus on the business model transformation, namely, a comprehensive strategic shift to the customer-focused and service-oriented approach, a stronger focus on customer requirements from different market segments and implementation of a comprehensive strategic setup in the service business. Digital China will further expand into high-marginal business segments and accelerate its sales to guarantee a better-than-market top-line growth by initiating different management mechanism. In addition, the company will further strengthen the rigid risk-management mechanism to guarantee a healthy business environment.

In 2008, Digital China was ranked first in the "China Business Technology Top 100" by *Information Weekly*. In the first three quarters of 2008/2009 financial year (by the end of 2008), Digital China has earned a revenue of HK$32.249 billion, a net profit increase of 22.11% compared to last fiscal year. The company's IT service has contributed HK$4.103 billion in revenue, an annual increase of 33.44%. With its excellent management in place and continuous transformation, Digital China is to play a more significant role in the IT industry in China in the coming years.

Xueyuan (Adrian) Liu and Yinhua Shu

References

Digital China (2008), Annual report 2007/2008. http://www.digitalchina.com/Functions/DocumentDownload.aspx?Code=FR200804011&SeqNo=25. Retrieved on 22 May 2009.

Digital China (2009). Company profile. http://www.digitalchina.com.hk/aboutus/companyprofile.aspx. Retrieved on 22 May 2009.

DONGFANG ELECTRIC

Corporate Address and Contact Information

Dongfang Electric Corporation (SHA: 600875)
333 Shuhan Road
Jinniu District
Chengdu, Sichuan Province
People's Republic of China
Phone: (86)28-8758-3603
Fax: (86)28-8758-3551
http://www.dongfang.com

Dongfang Electric Corporation Limited (东方电气股份有限公司, shortened as Dongfang Electric) is located in Sichuan Province, and was formerly known as Dongfang Electric Company Limited. Established in 1984, it is one of the largest enterprises in China engaging in the manufacturing of generating equipment and the contracts of generating station projects. Listed among the 225 largest international contractors, Dongfang Electric has been designated by the Chinese central government as one of the key state-owned enterprises relating to national security and economic vitality.

Historical Development

Deyang Hydroelectric Equipment Factory, the first subsidiary enterprise of Dongfang Electric, was established in 1958, which later changed its name to Dongfang Electric Machinery Co. Ltd. At that time, the factory was the state-planned electric power equipment-manufacturing base. For a very long time, the factory's production of electric generating sets was limited to below 200,000 kW, and in 1966, both the Dongfang Steam Turbine Factory and Dongfang Boiler Factory were launched.

From the 1970s, Dongfang Electric Machinery Co., together with the two other factories, joined forces to start the research and development of larger electric generating sets. In 1981, the 170,000 kW electric-generating set designed completely by Dongfang factories was installed in the Gezhouba project on the Yangtze River. This 11.3-meter diameter generating set remains to be the largest Kaplan turbine set in the world today, marking a major milestone in the history of Kaplan turbine. After 11 years of efforts, Dongfang's first 300,000 kW thermal power-generating units were introduced in 1983, and based on the core group of Dongfang factories, Dongfang Electric Company Limited was established in the following year.

During the massive Three Gorges Project, after a joint effort in the development of a 700,000 kW hydroelectric generating unit with a foreign company for the left bank of the Yangtze River, Dongfang

Electric invested more than 20 million RMB into its second stage of innovation, and successfully developed a more superior generating unit model for the right bank project, which let the company won the bidding, thus marked the end of the history of China's dependence on foreign techniques for the design and manufacturing of large hydro generators.

In the field of thermal power, Dongfang Electric researched and independently developed a series of innovative products, which it possesses intellectual properties, such as the 600,000 kW Subcritical Pressure Orimusion Oil Fuel Boiler. In the field of nuclear power, during the nineth Five-Year Plan Period (1997–2002), Dongfang Electric manufactured 2 one-million KW nuclear power units for Ling Ao Phase I nuclear project through collaboration with Framatom and Alstom, and it successively tackled a number of key technical problems and completed quite a few localization projects. For its outstanding performance, Dongfang Electric received a National Key Science and Technology project prize. During the 10th Five-Year Plan Period (2002–2007), Dongfang Electric operated at a surplus of 2.3 billion RMB, a sharp contrast to a loss of 5 billion at the end of the previous Five-Year plan. At the end of 2006, Dongfang Electric set a new record of its annual production capability at 2992.5 MW, which placed it the first in the world for three consecutive years.

After the 10th Five-Year Plan, Dongfang Electric won over several important contracts and orders for the Ling Ao Phase II Nuclear Power Plant in Guangdong Province by cooperating with a multinational company. Currently, Dongfang Electric holds a leading place with regard to nuclear power equipment manufacturing, and the corporation has been reorganized into a group that owns 65 subsidiary companies, taking up a key position among the three major national electric power generator-manufacturing bases in China.

Main Products and Services

Dongfang Electric mainly engages in the design, production, and sale of power-generating equipment and large and medium AC and DC motors and special motors. Other activities include maintenance of machinery and technology improvement. As one of the key bases for the domestic production of comprehensive technological equipment in China, Dongfang's technology center has a first-class, integrated technology developing capacity in the Chinese generating equipment manufacture industry; and its leading status as a national enterprise technology center has been confirmed by several national economic and trade agencies during recent years.

Dongfang Electric conducts its core business in the fields of the manufacturing of equipments for large hydropower stations, thermal power stations, and nuclear power stations as well as contracting of generating station projects, including the complete set of design, manufacture, supply, or technical service of the generating equipment, and the service for turnkey project of generating station. The corporation has received the certificate of "First-Class General Contract Qualification for the Construction of Power Station" issued by the Ministry of Construction as well as the other certificates of general contract qualifications in the fields of irrigation works and hydropower, electric installation, power transmission, and environmental protection projects.

Dongfang Electric has an annual capacity of 10,000 MW in generating equipment manufacture; it is capable of producing large thermal power-generating units of 300 MW and 600 MW, and water turbine generator sets of 400 MW and 550 MW in batch quantity. The company has also reached a capability of batch producing extra-large water turbine generator sets of 700 MW; at the same time, it can also produce the nuclear power units of 1000 MW.

Dongfang Electric has generally contracted more than 60 large and medium generating station projects within China and abroad, which add up to an impressive sum of RMB 29 billion. The completed and ongoing projects include: Shengli Generating Station, Shouyangshan Generating Station, Tuoketuo Generating Factory, Bengal Great Harbor Generating Station, Alake Generating Station in Iran, Baluota Hydropower Station in Pakistan, etc. Dongfang-brand products have been exported to more than 20 countries and regions, while its contract services reach over 10 countries around the world.

At present, Dongfang Electric occupies more than 30% of the domestic main engine market of large thermal power stations, and up to 40% of hydropower market. The total foreign contracting sum of the corporation is 2.95 billion dollars, which contributes about 0.7 billion dollars of foreign currency to its corporate bottom line.

Challenges and Corporate Strategies

Dongfang Electric has more than 10 subsidiaries under the corporation, a few subsidiaries under the joint stock company, and one subsidiary under its Dongfang investment management company.

Since the corporation is based mainly in Sichuan Province, Dongfang Electric was seriously affected during the disastrous earthquake in May 2008. Dongfang Steam Turbine Co. Ltd. is located in Mianzhu City, one of the regions worst hit by the earthquake, and its production equipment was seriously damaged and staff injured during the catastrophe. However, as the leading electric corporation in the nation, Dongfang Electric quickly bounced back under a massive government stimulus plan of RMB 4,000 billion after the earthquake. On 24 May 2008, Dongfang won a RMB 4.5 billion order from China Huaneng Group, the biggest electric power group in China. It was a strong and effective support to the re-construction of Dongfang Electric.

Dongfang Electric enjoyed the second half of 2008, as the price for iron and steel continuously fell, the production cost was reduced and profit soared. For the third quarter of 2008, Dongfang Electric's total revenue was more than 7 billion RMB, with the net income reaching 320 million RMB. All things considered, the prospect of Dongfang Electric is quite bright, and stronger performance ahead is expected.

Wei Qian

References

Dongfang Electric Corporation. Company Profile. http://www.dongfang.com.cn. Retrieved on 27 April 2009.

Dongfang Electric Corporation Limited. Third Quarter 2008 Report, http://irm.p5w.net/finalpage/2008-10-28/45710034.PDF. Retrieved on 27 April 2009.

Dongfang Electric Corporation Limited (2009). Google Finance, http://www.google.com/finance?q=SHA:600875. Retrieved on 27 April 2009.

黄全权 (2008). 遭受地震"重创"的东方电气集团获得45亿元订单支持 (24 May), *新华网* [Huang, Q. Dongfang Electric Group won RMB 4.5 billion contract after suffering heavy damage from earthquake. *Xinhua News*].

梁小琴 (2007). 东方电气集团公司自主创新求发展纪实 (15 June). *人民日报* [Liang, X. The development and innovations of Dongfang Electric Group (15 June), *People's Daily*].

朱嘉蒂 (2008). 东方电气 (1072.HK) 跌 8%; 旗下生产受地震打击 (20 May), 道琼斯通讯社 [Zhu, J. Dongfang Electric fell 8%; Production facilities damaged by earthquake (20 May 2008). *Dow Jones*].

邹陈东，李雁争 (2007). 东方电气集团: 从"中国制造"到"中国创造" (31 July), *上海证券报* [Zou, C and Li, Y. Dongfang Electric: From made in China to created in China (31 July 2007). *Shanghai Security News*].

DONGFENG MOTOR

Corporate Address and Contact Information

Dongfeng Motor Corporation (SIC — 3711; NAIC — 336111)
29 Baiye Road
Wuhan, Hubei 442000
People's Republic of China
Phone: (86)719-8226-962
Fax: (86) 719-8226-845
www.dfmc.com.cn/main.aspx

Dongfeng Motor Corporation (DFMC, 东风汽车集团股份有限公司), one of the "Big Three" Chinese automakers, is recognized as the leader of the booming automobile industry in central China. This government-owned company, located in Hubei Province, is mainly engaged in the production of passenger vehicles, commercial vehicles, engines, auto parts and components, and equipment and it captures more than 50% of the medium truck market and nearly 35% of the heavy truck market within China. Over the past few years, DFMC has concentrated on the development of various partnerships with foreign automakers and the development of its own brand in an effort to eventually establish itself as an international automotive competitor.

Historical Development

Founded in 1969, as the Second Automobile Works Co., DFMC emerged at the behest of Mao Zedong's "Third Front" strategy to support the development of heavy industry and economic growth. The company was intentionally located in Hubei Province, far inland, in order to protect it from potential foreign attacks as envisioned by Mao. Through over 40 years of development, a set of R&D and manufacturing facilities has been established, as well as an extensive distribution and after-sales network which unfolds a business display footed in Hubei while radiating the entire nation simultaneously.

The development course of DFMC has consisted of four major stages. From its foundation in 1969 until the beginning of the reform era in 1978, the company underwent a phase coined as "Hard Work and Carrying Out". This period consisted mainly of manufacturing and production of various automobiles, and the firm put a 2.5-ton cross-country cruiser and a 5-ton civil vehicle into production. Following years of retrenchment under Mao Zedong's direction, Deng Xiaoping initiated an era of reform beginning in 1978 aimed at reviving the Chinese economy through heavy industry and technology. This precipitated the second stage of DFMC's development, which was characterized by an increase in development and refulgence, ranged from 1978–1993. It was within this phase that DFMC built into a yearly capacity of 100,000 vehicles and embarked on the light car business, overcoming the economic stagnation. The third phase occurred from 1994 to 1999 and was termed as "Reform and Adjustment". In 1998, DFMC stated a loss of RMB 540 million at the first mergence of financial statements, and an annual loss of RMB 396 million. Consequently, the firm implemented an important reform system in 1999. This internal restructuring allowed DFMC to enter its fourth stage (2000–present) on the rise, as production and sales broke 220,000 vehicles and total profit rose to RMB 1.38 billion, wholly making up the deficit experienced in 1998. One year later, the company's main business indexes surpassed historic records, and by 2003,

DFMC was launching joint ventures with international automakers and establishing its dominance within the Chinese market.

Since DFMC emphasized becoming an industry leader, its performance has gradually improved. In the years of 2004 through 2007, the company's sales were up from 523,000 vehicles in 2004, to 729,000 (2005), 932,000 (2006), and 1,137,000 vehicles in 2007, respectively. In 2007 alone, DFMC had a sales income of RMB 164.8 billion, and a market share of 12.94%. Consequently, DFMC ranks 20th in the top 500 Chinese enterprises and 5th in the top 500 Chinese manufacturers. In hopes of becoming an international competitor, the firm made an Initial Public Offering in December 2005, yet remains 70% owned by China's central government. Furthermore, it continues to establish joint ventures with foreign automakers, striving to learn their technologies and develop self-innovative capabilities to launch its own brand of commercial vehicles within the international market.

Main Products and Services

In recent years, DFMC has heavily invested in developing an independent model to sell it in the domestic and global market. As noted above, in 2007, DFMC sold 1.137 million vehicles, where cars accounted for 45% of sales, medium and heavy trucks represented more than 30%. Its domestic market share of medium- and heavy-duty commercial vehicles and medium-duty buses ranked first within the industry, while the light-duty commercial vehicles and SUVs secured second, and passenger cars third as DFMC captured 12.94% of the total domestic market share. Besides its core business of passenger and commercial vehicles, DFMC has developed an auto parts and components business as well. Having set aside more than $28 million to invest in an auto part reproduction plant to develop a system that recycles waste and old parts into new parts, DFMC has joined with several companies within the industry to assist in power train control, hybrid electric vehicle technologies, and body electronics. This supplemental business has allowed the company to establish differentiated advantages over its competitors, thereby assisting it in the process of emerging as a global competitor.

Corporate Structure and Leadership

Under the leadership of CEO and Chairman of the Board Xu Ping, DFMC's main businesses include passenger vehicles, commercial vehicles, engines, auto parts and components, and equipment. DFMC's major business facilities are located in Shiyan, Xiangfan, Wuhan, and Guangzhou, with several other production facilities located across Mainland China. By placing an emphasis on scientific development and a renewed dedication to technological innovation through in-house R&D, the firm has experienced a significant growth in business over recent years.

Aligned with the trend of the development of the world auto industry, DFMC has defined its position and set a goal to emerge as a centennial company capable of sustained growth, an internationalized company that is world-oriented, and an open company capable of independent development. With its passenger vehicle business booming, the construction of an independent model underway, and the efficient and aggressive implementation of reforms, DFMC appears to be on a fast-growth track to achieving both its domestic and its international objectives.

In addition to having developed superior technologies within the domestic market, DFMC has established more joint ventures than any other Chinese auto manufacturers. Its partnerships with PSA

Peugeot Citroen of France, Nissan, and Honda of Japan, Kia of South Korea, and Cummins of the United States have not only boosted sales but also permitted DFMC to develop new innovative capabilities to aid in the process of becoming a global competitor.

Growth Strategies

As one of the three leading automobile manufacturers in China, DFMC has maintained a fast yet steady pace of development and has demonstrated a strong commitment to technological innovation and industrial leadership. With the goal of selling two million vehicles by 2010, DFMC plans to further optimize its operations by establishing an independent brand and through sustainable improvements in cost-effective body electronics and hybrid electronic vehicle solutions that will be deployed in its next-generation system designs. Additionally, through the establishment of joint ventures with renowned brands, DFMC is striving to support the synchronous growth of its vehicles in a growing market characterized by an increasing Chinese middle class.

As part of its goal to become the industry's technological leader, DFMC plans to establish a joint venture with Freescale Semiconductor to produce an automotive electronics lab that will develop silicon, software and hardware platforms, and system-level solutions to be used in the next generation of DFMC's vehicles for the Chinese and export markets. These firms will develop key automotive applications, underlying software and hardware platforms, modeling tools, demonstration panels, in-vehicle networking solutions, and low-end body control modules. Through the production of these innovative technologies, DFMC plans to launch its own brand of commercial vehicles that will be sold over the global market.

Upon perfecting its technological capabilities, DFMC will implement a dual-brand strategy with Nissan for light commercial vehicles, where Nissan-branded LCVs will be targeted at the premium market and DFMC-branded vehicles will target the broader market. Additionally, DFMC has been viewed as a potential buyer of GM in an effort to grasp an opportunity of acquiring overseas assets. DFMC will continue to seek good performance in partnerships while pursuing rapid growth to maintain its swift and steady rise in business, and it will continue to promote its R&D competence to boost in-house innovation and ultimately establish itself as a global auto conglomerate.

Current Environment and Industry Challenges

With the continual economic reform, DFMC has encountered many new competitors within the Chinese automobile industry. The emergence of new, independent automakers has fulfilled the growing need for lower-cost cars without JV alliances. As a result, those firms are likely to achieve superior growth rates in terms of car production, as they seek export sales more aggressively. Within China, DFMC competes with Chery Automobile, Geely Auto, Shanghai Automotive, and China First Automotive, among others; globally, they encounter firms such as Toyota, Ford, and Volkswagen.

Unstable political and economic environments and a declining US automotive industry provide significant challenges for DFMC as well the international market. Let alone the current financial crisis and the uncertainty of the exchange rate. In an environment where regional inequality, unemployment, and the pressure to cut prices increase, the rising cost of raw materials has resulted in conflicts between economic and corporate priorities. Additionally, the burgeoning number of vehicles is straining the nation's air quality and road infrastructure, resulting in stricter policies toward energy and emissions efficiency within China.

As the global auto industry struggles during the financial crisis, key export markets are beginning to crumble, resulting in the development of a stagnant market. In 2008, after six years of growth over 20%,

Chinese automakers reported a sales growth of 6.7%, which is the lowest in 10 years. With price liberalization and tax controls common, high-end manufacturers are beginning to experience a severe decline in sales. Consequently, while the Chinese automakers seek lower taxes on new cars, reduced fuel prices, and increased grants for R&D, the government has issued an economic stimulus package aimed at reviving China's pillar industries. Within the auto industry, the nation's leaders have created tax incentives for consumers and strict controls to prevent overproduction, while additionally investing in alternative-fuel vehicles and research for the introduction of self-branded automobiles. Through initially reviving the domestic market, the government hopes to support its automobile companies in penetrating the global market. Based on this outlook, DFMC will likely continue to play a leading role in the fast-growing domestic market and become a significant player of the global auto industry in the coming years.

Marc Fetscherin

References

Dongfeng Motor Corporation (2007). Corporate profile. http://www.dfmc.com.cn/info/introduce_en.aspx. Retrieved on 16 April 2009.

Dongfeng Motor Corporation (2007). Hoovers Company Records www.hoovers.com. Retrieved on 16 April 2009.

Ni, J (2005). *Automotive Management Briefing: Development of China's Automotive Industry*, S.M. Wu Manufacturing Research Center, University of Michigan. http://www.cargroup.org/mbs2005/documents/JunNiChinaAutomotiveTraverseCity.pdf. Retrieved on 16 April 2009.

Wong, K. Carmakers brace for industry revamp in economic uncertainty (9 March 2009). *South China Morning Post*, p. 2, Business.

FOSUN INTERNATIONAL

Corporate Address and Contact Information

Fosun International
No. 2, East Fuxing Road
Shanghai 200010
People's Republic of China
Phone: (86)21-6332-5858
Fax: (86)21-6332-5028
www.fosun.com

Since the permission for private sector companies to exist in China after 1978, a number of highly successful, innovative, and unique companies have come into existence. Many of them were the results of a combination of change, unique individuals spotting an opportunity, and government relaxation of specific areas of control. Fosun typifies all three of these.

As of 2009, Fosun International (复星国际有限公司), the holding company of Fosun, has become the largest private sector conglomerate in the People's Republic of China. It has come a long way from the year when it was founded in 1992 on borrowed capital of US$4,500, by four ex-graduates of Fudan University, Shanghai. Central to its establishment, and growth over the last two decades, has been the personality of one of its founders, and its current Chairman, Guo Guangchang.

Corporate Leadership

Born in 1967, in Zhejiang, the highly entrepreneurial province on the coast around Shanghai, Guo was from a humble farming background, but what might loosely be called "positive discriminatory" educational policies toward the end of the Cultural Revolution in 1976, and at the beginning of the reform and opening up period from 1978 onwards meant that he attended decent middle and high schools, and was able to study philosophy at Fudan University, one of China's elite schools. One story states that Guo resigned from Fudan University where he was a postgraduate in 1992 in anger over being criticized for undertaking an unofficial survey. With three other colleagues, Liang Xinjun, Wang Qunbin, and Fan Wei, he established Guangxin Technology Development Company, specializing in the production of medication for Hepatitis A, of which there is a very high incidence in China. Fosun Pharmaceutical Company was set up in 1994, directly derived from this. One of the striking features of Fosun is the stability of its main management. Apart from Guo, Liang still serves as CEO and vice chairman of the main holding company board, Wang is president, and Fan Wei serves as executive director.

Guo has been by way and afar the highest profile of Fosun's directors. Membership of the 10th National People's Congress (NPC), the 3000 strong Chinese advisory body to the government serving as a de facto parliament, shows that Guo has, unlike many other leading entrepreneurs, not neglected keeping an eye on the political functions of businessmen, even in the ostensibly more liberal environment of 21st century China. The company website also proudly declares that Fosun is one of China's top corporate payers of tax. Guo's personal wealth put him as the second richest person in China according to *Forbes* annual "China Rich List", in 2002, with wealth of USD 3.6 billion, and the third richest in 2007, with an increase to USD 4.85 billion. This made him the richest man in Shanghai.

Company Structure and Core Competences

Along with a focus on the personality and drive of the leading director and founder, Fosun shares one other characteristic with Chinese non-state enterprises — its diverse operations, and complex structure. Fosun likes to declare in public statements that it resembles the operations of Hutchinson Whampoa, Li Kai Shing's main business vehicle in Hong Kong SAR. Like Hutchinson, it has divisions in the mainland into several different and sometimes contradictory, areas of business. These mainly divide into: pharmacy (with a stake in Sinopharm), property (through, among others, Forte), steel (with partial ownership of several coastal iron and steel plants, such as Nanjing), mining (Hainan Mining and Huxiao), and retail (for instance, in Yong'an Insurance). The company has come some way from focusing purely on pharmaceuticals (something that Li Kai Shing, through part ownership of the chain of chemists in Hong Kong and the Mainland Watson, and interests in traditional Chinese medicine also does). Its interests embrace steel, property, financial services, chemicals, retailing, even genetic engineering. This begs the question how on earth does it manage to co-ordinate and structure all of these diverse interests. On the holding companies website, it describes its three key assets as: "the capability to explore and capture China's high growth investment opportunities, the capability to continuously improve management efficiency and the capability to optimize financing from multiple sources." That does not help much, however, in understanding what its core values and business principles are. These come across more as very astute, and highly opportunistic.

In terms of company structure, this is at least a little more straightforward. Fosun International is 78% owned by Fosun Holdings, and 22% by public shareholders. This was as a result of its initial public offering on 16 July 2007 on the main market in Hong Kong SAR, where it became the sixth most over-subscribed mainland Chinese company to list till then, and managed to attract support from high profile subscribers ranging from Li Kai Shing, to Robert Kwok, AIG, and the Government Investment Corporate from Singapore. The listing raised USD 1.5 billion. Beneath Fosun International is Fosun Group. Under this is ranged the five main areas of operation listed above, with the partial holdings in a range of other companies.

Financially, at least according to date from various sources, the company is sound. In 2002, it had a turnover across all its operations of USD 1 billion, and paid USD 10 million in taxes, with 4,000 employees. In 2008, this had increased to turnover of USD 5.9 billion, and profits of USD 1 billion, with tax of USD 40 million. It had been the largest non-state payer of taxes from 2004 onwards. Its profit growth from 2007 to 2008 was a phenomenal (215%), with a profit margin of 17%. All this tells us clearly is that Fosun was not into low margin return business.

Future Growth Strategy

Fosun's diverse portfolio means that, much like Hutchinson Whampoa, its key expertise is in efficient management, profit maximization, and flexibility in reacting to market conditions. Guo himself in a statement about the company on the Fosun website states that the priorities for the company remain focusing on the sustained urbanization of China, looking at consumption and investment patterns, and "supplying consumers across the world". This final ambition highlights one area where Fosun has been very low profile. Despite its company name containing the word "international", and its listing on Hong Kong, Fosun is very much dedicated to the Chinese domestic market. Its international operations at most are simply those of export. The economic downturn from 2008 onwards, with the disappearance of foreign markets, and the increased need for a strong domestic Chinese consumer response, only underlined how necessary a refocus on the internal market was for decent growth. A clue to the company's future direction can be seen in the major investment of USD 55 million in Tianjin Iron and Steel in 2008. This confirmed a pattern for the company of looking largely at resource opportunities in coastal provinces.

In choosing to focus so sharply on the internal Chinese market, perhaps Fosun is right. However diverse its interests within China, at least it seems, at least from its profitability, to know its strengths. However, like many major non-state entities, it suffers from the over-reliance on the drive and push of one leading figure. Guo will at some point need to think about who succeeds him, and how the company survives in the coming decades. As of 2009, however, Fosun is doing fine.

Kerry Brown

References

Fosun International (2008). Overview of Fosun. http://www.fosun-international.com/en/company/index2.asp. Retrieved on 10 June 2009.

Fosun International invests USD 3.8 billion into Tianjin Iron and Steel (16 June 2008). *China Mining.* http://www.chinamining.org/News/2008-06-16/1213628509d14615.html. Retrieved on 10 June 2009.

IW profile of Fosun International (2009). *Industry Week.* http://www.industryweek.com/research/iw1000/2008/iw1000Company.asp?Input=712. Retrieved on 10 June 2009.

The 400 China Richest: Guo Guangchang (1 November 2007). *Forbes.* http://www.forbes.com/lists/2007/74/biz_07china_Guo-Guangchang_CYTD.html. Retrieved on 10 June 2009.

FOXCONN INTERNATIONAL

Corporate Address and Contact Information

Foxconn International Holdings Ltd.
2, 2nd Donghuan Road
10th Yousong Industrial District
Longhua Baoan, Shenzhen
Guangdong Province
People's Republic of China
http://www.fih-foxconn.com

Foxconn International Holdings Limited (富士康国际控股有限公司, hereafter Foxconn) is an investment holding company established in 2001. The company went public in Hong Kong in 2005, but its Taiwan-based parent Hon Hai Precision Industry Company Limited retained 72% of its shares. Hon Hai, founded by Terry Gou in 1974, began to invest heavily in China in the late 1980s, ahead of rival Taiwanese firms. Foxconn today, with its vertically integrated units strategically located across China, is the flagship in Gou's manufacturing empire.

Corporate Development

Foxconn holds several top records: China's largest exporter since 2002, the world's largest manufacturer of mobile phones since 2005, and an underdog that overtook the industry leaders by growing its revenues more than 10 times in five years. In spite of these achievements, hardly anyone outside Foxconn's industry has heard of its name because it is a "stealth manufacturer" that makes confidentiality of its operations a policy to its customers who are not eager for consumers to know the real identity of the manufacturers of their brand name products. The unique role played by electronic manufacturing service (EMS) providers has many analysts confused. Foxconn is not in the "Goods Sector"; in fact, it defines itself as "a service company rather than a manufacturing concern".

The success of this reticent giant can be attributed to company founder Terry Gou's understanding of the dynamics of the industry in which it competes. A prescient move that led the company to start producing connectors in 1981 prepared it to slowly work its way up the component chain to modules, circuit boards, and eventually into computer enclosures, before expanding laterally into computers, communications, and consumer electronics (3C). Always making the right calls, Gou is unapologetic about his autocratic leadership style, defending it as essential when decisions must be made under immense time pressure.

Growth Strategies

The 3C industry has compressed product life cycles and frequent innovations cause prices to slide soon after product launch. Sellers of these products (i.e., Foxconn's customers) can only reap big profits if they achieve time to market, time to volume, and time to revenue. As such, Foxconn builds its deployment strategy on three principles: product development at co-located sites, production on three continents, and global fulfillment and logistic support.

To speed up time to market, Foxconn establishes R&D facilities near its most important customers. Product designers and engineers work together to get the new design ready for mass production in timely manner. To achieve time to volume, Foxconn can ramp up production simultaneously in its factories on three continents. Production interruptions can be minimized because Foxconn manufactures many of the components to be used in the assembly. Vertical integration affords Foxconn not only a procurement advantage but also a cost advantage because the higher-margin component business can subsidize the low-margin assembly work and it allows Foxconn to quote 10–20% less than its competitors while generating more profits. Strong cash flow enables Foxconn to make strategic acquisitions, such as those in Finland and Mexico in 2003. With these acquisitions, Foxconn can produce in proximity to its major customers virtually everywhere in the world rather than being confined to China, home to 80% of its production capacity. Production close to final market facilitates fulfillment, which in turn helps customers achieve time to revenues. Business expands; with increased scale, Foxconn resorts to forward pricing to further undercut its rivals.

Foxconn prides its competence to consistently deliver speed, quality, engineering services, flexibility, and cost savings on its "e-CMMS" (e-enabled Components, Module, Move, and Service) model. Rivals who scoffed at the model before rushed to copy it around the globe as Foxconn overtook them one by one. This development, while vindicating Gou's ideas, creates more competition for his business. Until recently, Foxconn was able to carve a niche in the cutthroat EMS business with its unique vertical product integration model (i.e., extending from upstream to downstream) and lateral expansion of product lines. However, even as Foxconn's margins remained ahead of rivals, they had shrunk considerably in recent years. When Gou reminded his deputies to suppress the temptation of growth and be wary of which industry they entered, his exhortation actually acknowledged the necessities for Foxconn to seek new growth opportunities.

Business Challenges

The most pressing challenge for Foxconn Holdings is increased competition in a shrinking market. Flextronics may pose some threats to Foxconn after acquiring Solectron, but the real challenge will come from Chinese rivals that are increasingly aggressive in bargaining for outsourcing work. These entrants will keep pressure on margins, no matter how efficient Foxconn becomes. BYD, an upstart nicknamed "Little Foxconn", is one of the most formidable rivals. The two were embroiled in acrimonious legal disputes between 2006 and 2008. The spats were eventually settled out of court, but they were portrayed very differently in the media in mainland China and Taiwan, headquarters of Foxconn's parent. While Taiwanese media generally reported the disputes as industrial espionage and theft of trade secrets, their mainland counterpart portrayed them as vicious attempts by Foxconn to nip BYD in its bud as the two companies increasingly went after an overlapping set of customers in a dwindling pool.

Focusing on a set of elite customers and developing strategic relationship with them used to fuel Foxconn's growth, but it came at a cost. Foxconn not only gave up developing its own brands to avoid competing with its customers but also turned down certain orders, such as production of "shan zhai ji" (literally translated as bandit phones or low-end knockoffs that cater to local needs), a fast growing segment in China. However, in spite of such goodwill, customers treat Foxconn primarily as a means to achieving greater flexibility and reducing risk in volatile markets. When market demand keeps shrinking with no upswing in sight, these customers not only decelerate outsourcing but also reclaim production by moving it in house.

Future Development Plans

Reduced orders and unrelenting cost pressures imposed by customers force Foxconn to seek new growth opportunities fast. For new customers, Foxconn will start to look inward. Instead of using China solely as an export platform, it will target Chinese brands requiring manufacturing services. In this sense, investments made in the interior since 2008 are not merely cost-cutting measures but redeployment of production capacities to get ready for these business opportunities. In terms of new product, Foxconn aims to leverage its hardware expertise and extend into software. Gou predicted in 2007 that the future technology competition would not be about hardware but software. In early 2009, about 10,000 software specialists were recruited as the company prepared to enter the contract software business. Foxconn may even trump Indian firms that currently dominate this business because it can offer a package of hardware and software; its massive hardware manufacturing will also offer software a development and test ground.

Foxconn also intends to take on more design-intensive orders. To strengthen its design capabilities, Foxconn has been actively acquiring smaller rivals. However, the time pressure that prompts Foxconn to use acquisitions as a substitute for R&D also makes it difficult for new units to assimilate smoothly. Furthermore, even as new blood gets infused into the company, Gou remains indispensable. This is evident when he returned from his retirement to retake the helm in 2008 amid falling business orders and stock prices. For a founder who preaches "the important thing in any organization is leadership, not management" and his practical involvement integral to Foxconn's phenomenal success, his succession arrangement raises concerns.

Finally, an ambitious endeavor — Yungning Project — was initiated in 2008 to build a successor team. "Yungning" (永营) can be literally translated as "forever operate." Foxconn's long-term vision is to transform itself from an industrial conglomerate into a technological powerhouse and eventually an integrated device manufacturer in five to ten years. This may explain why Foxconn is adamant that it will not trim R&D expenses in this recessionary climate: Gou firmly believes that whoever owns the technology will emerge as the leader when the economy picks up again.

Carmencita Cheung

References

Berg, D and NG Einspruch (2008). Economic sector analysis of China's 100 largest companies. In *The Proceedings of the 2008 International Conference on Service Systems and Service Management*. pp.1–3. Melbourne.

张戌谊, 张殿文 (2001). 宏海如何争霸全球? *e 天下杂志* [Chang, HI and TW Chang. How will Hon Hai grow it global market share? *TechVantage Magazine*], August. http://www.techvantage.com.tw/content/008/008070.asp. Retrieved on 8 June 2009.

Dean, J (2007). The Forbidden City of Terry Gou. *The Wall Street Journal*, 11 August 2007.

熊毅晰 (2009). 郭台铭 痛定思痛, 加入山寨大军. *天下杂志* [Hsiung, IH. Collecting his thoughts, Terry Gou joins the Army of Shan Zhai Ji. *CommonWealth Magazine* (Chinese edition)], Issue No. 421, May 2009.

Hsiung, J (2006). Terry Gou reveals the Hon Hai philosophy. *CommonWealth Magazine*, Issue No. 349, 21 June 2006.

Normile, D (2004). Why is Hon Hai so shy? *Electronic Business*, 1 April 2004.

Pick, A (2006). Foxconn's strategic coup: How does Terry Guo build success? *iSuppli Corp. White Paper*, July 2006. http://www.emsnow.com/newsarchives/archivedetails.cfm?ID=13980. Retrieved on 8 June 2009.

GOME ELECTRICAL APPLIANCES

Corporate Address and Contact Information

GOME Electrical Appliances Holdings Ltd.
18/F, Block B, Eagle Plaza

26 Xiaoyun Road
Chao Yang District
Beijing 100016
People's Republic of China
Phone: (86-10)5928-8915
Fax: (86-10)5928-8925
http://www.gome.com.hk/eng/index.asp

Like the Best Buy in the United States, GOME Electrical Appliances Holding Ltd. (国美电器控股有限公司) is the largest and most influential enterprise in the electrical appliance retail industry in China. Founded in 1987 by a legendary young man named Huang Guangyu, and after 22-year ups and downs, GOME has successfully expanded into most of the major cities in China and gained consumer recognitions around the country. Currently, the company has a 10% market share in the retailing market of the electrical appliances in China. Nicknamed "price butcher", Huang and GOME have brought many cost-effective electrical appliances with good quality to Chinese people and therefore played a significant role in the economic development of China over the last two decades.

Historical Development

Huang's business story is a typical Chinese rags-to-riches story. He was born in Shantou, a coastal city in Guangdong province in southern China. At the age of 16, Huang quitted high school and went to do business in Mongolia with his elder brother Huang Junqing. A year later, the brothers decided to switch from clothing to consumer electronics, because they had the vision that an increase of income would go along with an increasing demand for household appliances. With only RMB 5000 (approximately US$500 at that time) as their initial investment and more importantly, their indefatigable strive, the young and entrepreneurial Huang brothers started their business from a roadside stall at Beijing in 1987 selling radios and gadgets purchased from factories nearby their hometown in Southern China. Just in a few years time, household appliances and consumer electronics rose to the top of the shopping list for many Chinese families, and the Huang brothers' business took off.

After the initial success, in 1993, the Huang brothers separated their business into two parts: the younger brother, Huang Guangyu, continued the retail business of household appliances by establishing the retail store chain GOME, which marked a significant milestone in the development of its chain store network; while the elder brother, Huang Junqin, founded Towercrest Group (新恒基集团) and tried to get a stake in the booming real estate market.

By 1999, GOME took the first step outside Beijing and established its first retail outlet in Tianjin. Since then, the group has been expanding rapidly into other major cities in China and gained wider recognition of the Chinese consumers. In July 2004, the group obtained a listing status in Hong Kong through an asset injection of a 65% stake in GOME Appliance Co. Ltd. into a Hong Kong-listed company. In August 2004, the listed entity officially adopted the name GOME Electrical Appliances Holding Ltd.

Since its establishment in 1987, GOME has persistently pursued the corporate philosophy of "Business Opportunities for Mutual Prosperity". With aggressive development in the retail business of electrical appliances and consumer electronic products in mainland China, the group has become the largest and most influential retailer in the industry. In 2004, it was selected as one of the "Key and Strategically Important Enterprises" in China by the Ministry of Commerce.

At the beginning of 2005, the group announced the Four Year Growth Initiative spanning 2005–2008. Under such a plan, the group aimed to enlarge its network coverage and to raise its national market share to 10–15% by the end of 2008. In 2006, the group set up a strategic alliance with Warburg Pincus, and merged with China Paradise. In 2007, the group acquired Dazhong Electronics. In August 2007, GOME announced to extend its business into clothing stores and real estate business. By 2008, the GOME's total store count reached 859 stores, and achieved a record of sales revenue of approximately RMB 45.9 billion.

Huang Guangyu, the founder of the group, was the chairman of the board of seven directors until his resignation in 2009, after he was detained by the Ministry of Public Security in November 2008 for alleged inside trading. In GOME's administrative system, the members of decision-making level are appointed by the board, especially by Huang directly. Only in this way, can Huang's orders be implemented efficiently in over 30 strategic regions.

Business Strategies

From the very beginning, GOME faced enormous obstacles to grow its business. In the early 1990s, people used to buy electrical appliances in the state-owned shopping centers and they would rather pay more money in the state-owned stores than to buy the cheaper ones from GOME. Besides, many of the electrical appliances in GOME's shopping centers were imported, normally with a price tag of RMB 10,000 (USD 1500) or more. That was much too expensive compared with people's income at that time. So GOME modified its strategy by pushing the domestic electrical appliances to build up price competitive advantage with good quality, and as a result, GOME's sales increased dramatically. In order to further reduce the price, GOME overleapt the brokers and negotiated with the manufacturers directly. After the two rounds of restructuring on products adjustment and channel rebuilding, GOME laid a good foundation for its future development. By 1999, GOME took the first step outside Beijing and established its first retail outlet in Tianjin and started an interlinking business strategy all over China. Ten years later, 859 stores belong to the listed company and the total stores network spanned across 182 cities.

Currently, GOME has developed a successful business strategy with three important features: low price, quick turnover, and good service. GOME's core strategy is lower price every day, sometimes just a couple of yuan lower than their competitors'. Apart from low-price strategy, GOME promises customers with free delivery and free maintenance. Under the slogan "service is the king", the company has established a "rainbow service" system to meet the diverse needs of customers.

If GOME is described as a sports car, LENQ are the four engines: L means "low-price strategy", which is GOME's key competitive strategy. Through channel rebuilding GOME can get appliances at a lower price from manufacturers than its competitors, and therefore its retail price is always a little bit lower; E means "excellent services", as GOME strives to provide its customers highly satisfactory services; N means "new", as GOME always pushes itself to be more innovative and innovation on business model, product structure, operation, marketing, service, and management has helped build up GOME's valuable advantages; and Q means "quick". Information is the foundation and assurance for business success. The one who can quickly acquire the latest and most useful information will be the winner in the end, and GOME is making every effort to be that winner.

Challenges and Future Development Plans

With the continuous economic reform, GOME in recent years found itself in competition with many rivals, both foreign and domestic. Within China, its main competitor is Suning, the second largest retailer of electrical appliances. In the world market, GOME's main competitors include Wal-Mart and Metro Group. Apart from the challenges from retail industry, the current global financial crisis is another tough challenge

GOME has to face. The Chinese government encourages appliances retailers to sell appliances to the countryside and GOME is one of the appliances retailers that successfully obtained the license. When fully implemented, this initiative will contribute positively to both revenue and profit of GOME operation in the coming years.

Facing with the ongoing economic slowdown, GOME has to modify its ambitious expanding strategy. According to the 2008 annual report released on 27 April 2009, GOME will seek to optimize its existing stores' earnings to increase the profit per store. In order to achieve the target goal, GOME plans to shut down 100 stores with low profits, while at the same time, to open 100 new stores with higher profit margins to maintain the total number of stores. Whereas Suning Appliance, GOME's top competitor and the second largest electrical appliances retailer in China, may look this as a golden opportunity to expand and occupy the market share, it will still likely meet tough competition from GOME in the near future.

Electrical appliance retail business has three obvious features and trends: cooperation and scale, capital operation, and M&A. GOME's financial system can be summarized by the following three major sources: banks, capital markets, and industry diversity. The company's powerful financial system helps bring GOME ample cash flow and support its fast expansion. Another appealing development plan GOME envisioned is to integrate manufacturers upstream to strengthen its low price strategy. At the same time, GOME is trying to explore the market overseas, and the very initial step is to set up retail stores in Hong Kong in near future.

Xueyuan (Adrian) Liu and Zhiwei Yang

References

陈茜 (2008). 国美2011年欲将市场占有率超过20%. *财经*, 18 April [Chen, Q. GOME plans to increase its market share to over 20% by 2011. *Caijing*]. http://www.cheaa.com/News/HangYe/2008/4/188734125523.html. Retrieved on 18 April 2008.

陈小秋 (2008). 国美发布07全年业绩，市场占有率冲20%. *21世纪经济报道*, 17 April [Chen, X. GOME issued 07 report, aimed a market share of 20%. *21st Century Economic Report*]. http://xiazai.zol.com.cn/article_topic/89/894948.html. Retrieved on 17 April 2008.

Lattermann, C (2009). Huang Guangyu. In: W Zhang and I Alon (eds.). *Biographical Dictionary of New Chinese Entrepreneurs and Business Leaders.* Cheltenham, UK: Edward Elgar, pp. 58–59.

岳伟 (2009). 业绩大幅落后苏宁，国美今年拿掉100家弱势门店. *每日经济新闻*, 30 April [Yue, W. Trailing behind Suning, GOME plans to close 100 weak stores this year. *Daily Economic News*] http://stock.hexun.com/2009-04-30/117253942.html. Retrieved on 30 April 2009.

赵建华，王澄明 (2005). *国美商业帝国*，广西师范大学出版社 [Zhao J and C Wang. *GOME Business Empire*. Guilin: Guangxi Normal University Press].

GREAT WALL TECHNOLOGY

Corporate Address and Contact Information

Great Wall Technology Co. Ltd.
2 Keyuan Road
Technology & Industry Park
Nanshan District

Shenzhen 518057
People's Republic of China
Phone: (86)755-2672-8686
Fax: (86)755-2650-4493
http://www.greatwalltech.com

In 1985, the first Chinese computer — Great Wall 0520CH — was independently designed and manufactured by Chinese engineers. From that modest beginning the national computer industry was born, in which Great Wall has been playing a significant role for more than 20 years. Great Wall Technology is a state-owned and public-traded corporation with a large production capacity of all core computer parts.

Historical Development

Great Wall Technology Company Limited (长城科技股份有限公司) was established by China Great Wall Computer Group Company (Great Wall Group) on 20 March 1998. The company was based in Shenzhen, China with a registered capital of RMB 744 million, and was listed on the Hong Kong Stock Exchange on 5 August 1999. The company was classified as an "Information Technology Stock" by the Hong Kong Hang Seng Index Services in May 2000, and its registered capital has since grown to RMB 1.2 billion.

On 2 August 2005, the State-owned Assets Supervision and Administration Commission (SASAC) of the State Council has announced a plan to restructure six enterprises including China Electronics Corporation (CEC), under which the Great Wall Group would be consolidated. As a result of the Restructuring, Great Wall Group became a wholly owned subsidiary of CEC, which in turn became the controlling shareholder of Great Wall Technology through its ownership of 62.11% shares of the company. CEC is an enterprise directly administered by SASAC. It primarily engages in the design and manufacturing of integrated circuits, software and integrated system services and research, development and manufacturing of other communication products. The business of Great Wall Technology and its subsidiaries covers computer components, computer manufacturing, GSM/CDMA mobile phone production, software and system integration, and broadband network services.

Great Wall Technology directly holds significant interests in China Great Wall Computer Shenzhen Co. Ltd. (Great Wall Computer), Shenzhen Kaifa Technology Co. Ltd. (Great Wall Kaifa), Shenzhen Kaifa Magnetics Recording Co. Ltd. (Kaifa Magnetics), Shenzhen ExcelStor Technology Limited (ExcelStor Technology), ExcelStor Great Wall Technology Limited (ExcelStor Great Wall), Great Wall Computer Software and Systems Incorporation Limited (GWCSS), and Great Wall Broadband Network Service Co. Ltd. (Great Wall Broadband). In 2007, Great Wall's annual revenue surpassed RMB 23.8 billion, and its export sales ranked third among the top 100 enterprises of the Chinese electronic and information industry.

With the purchase of the largest monitor manufacturer in the world, Admiral Overseas Corporation (AOC), and armed with a desire to cross-holding shares with multinational companies, Great Wall marched onto the global market. For years, Great Wall Technology has been in close cooperation with some of the well-known global companies such as IBM, Hitachi, Elcoteq, Kingston, Seagate, Western Digital, *Hitachi Global Storage Technologies*, Komag, Samsung, Maxtor, etc. Benefiting from all those collaborative experiences, Great Wall Technology now holds the world's leading manufacture technology, while successfully implemented the advanced management system in its operation and trained groups of R&D, manufacture, and management teams.

Main Products and Services

Great Wall Technology and its subsidiaries engage mainly in the following major fields: computer components, computer manufacturing, GSM, CDMA mobile phones, software and system integration, and broadband networks and value-added services. As the first PC manufacturer in China, Great Wall Computer produces computer systems and related peripherals, computer core parts, broadband network, and digital products such as desktops, notebooks, monitors, power supplies, severs, printers, and consumable electronics. In addition, the company also provides technical support, and its power supply for computers has 30% market shares of the OEM market, holding the top spot in China.

At present, Kaifa is the second largest manufacturer of its core product HSA (Head Stack Assembly) in the world, occupying over 10% of the global market share. Its meter products sell well in Europe and Asia, with an accumulated export volume exceeding 20 million meters and making three records among the enterprises in Shenzhen. As the largest remote control meters developer and manufacturer in China, Kaifa was among the first group to be granted qualifications and licenses for FCR (Fiscal Cash Register) manufacturing. With an annual capacity of 700 thousand units, Kaifa also has the largest FCR R&D and manufacturing facilities in China.

Corporate Structure and Leadership

The China Great Wall Computer Group Corporation holds 62% shares of the Great Wall Technologies Co. listed in Hong Kong, as well as 29.27% shares of the Great Wall Information Industry Co. Ltd. (originally Hunan Computer Co. Ltd.) that is listed in A-Share. Great Wall Technology is the controlling shareholder of two companies: China Great Wall Computer Shenzhen Co. Ltd. (60.47%) and Shenzhen Kaifa Technology Co. Ltd. (55.96%).

After merging into CEC in 2005, Great Wall Group became the controlling shareholder of four listed companies: Great Wall Technology (HK: 0074), Shenzhen Kaifa Technology (SZ: 000021), Great Wall Computer Shenzhen Co. (SZ: 000066), and Great Wall Information Industry (SZ: 000748). Great Wall's business encompasses three industry divisions: storage service, which includes HSA, disk, and hard disk; computer services, including power, monitor, PC, and server; and finally electronic products, such as HSA, meter, FCR, and memory.

Lu Ming, vice president of CEC, is the chairman and president of Great Wall Technology, who graduated from Wuhan University with BS in computational mathematics in 1976 and from the Chinese Academy of Sciences with a master's degree in computer science in 1981. Lu succeeded Chen Zhaoxiong who became the vice governor of Hunan Province. In addition, Lu also oversees enterprises invested by CEC, serving as the chairman of China Huada Integrated Circuit Design (Group) Co. Shenzhen Aihua Electronics, CEC & Huatsing Microelectronics Engineering Center Co.; vice chairman of China Great Wall Computer Shenzhen Co. and Shanghai Huahong (Group) Co.; and director of China Great Wall Computer (Hong Kong) Holding Ltd. and Shenzhen Kaifa Technology Co. Ltd.

Du Heping, president of Great Wall Technology since 2005, has been working with Great Wall for over 20 years. A graduate in economic management from the Central Party School, he has served as director of Great Wall Electricity, vice president, board chairman, and party secretary of Great Wall Computer and vice president of Great Wall over his tenure.

Challenges and Business Strategies

For the first six months in 2008, Great Wall Technology generated total revenue of RMB 11.69 billion and earnings before tax of RMB 3.7 billion, which represented a sharp fall of 43 percent from the previous

6.4 billion RMB of the same period last year. Because of the downward influence of global economy combined with rising labor cost and drop in selling prices, Great Wall Technology announced on 15 January 2009 the net profit of its subsidiary Great Wall Computer was just 1.2 million RMB in 2008, representing a 90 percent drop when compared with 9.8 million RMB in 2007.

The leadership team at Great Wall Technology believes the current challenge also presents a good opportunity for the group to increase domestic demand and boost its overseas market exploration. To deal with the global financial crisis, Great Wall plans to integrate the scientific outlook on development into corporate operations and further strengthen its technical innovation.

Wei Qian

References

Great Wall Technology Company. 2008 Annual Result Announcement. http://www.greatwall.com.cn/exintranet/ownerarea/groupreport/file/200942222352423332.pdf. Retrieved on 27 April 2009.

Great Wall Computer Shenzhen Co. http://www.greatwall.cn/english/aboutus.asp. Retrieved on 27 April 2009.

Lu, M (2008). Chairman's statement. Great Wall Technology Co. Ltd. http://www.greatwalltech.com.cn/E2.asp. Retrieved on 27 April 2009.

Shenzhen Kaifa Technology Co. http://www.kaifa.com.cn/eng/about/profile.asp. Retrieved on 27 April 2009.

长城科技股份附属公司预计08年业绩大幅下滑 (15 January 2009), 财华社 [Great Wall Technology and its subsidiaries fell sharply in 2008, Caihuanet].

廖春梅 (2005). 中国电子吞并长城集团 (1 August), 人民网 [Liao, C. CEC acquires Great Wall Group].

GREE ELECTRIC APPLIANCES

Corporate Address and Contact Information

Gree Electric Appliances, Inc. of Zhuhai
6 W. Jinji Road
Qianshan, Zhuhai
Guangdong 519070
People's Republic of China
Phone: (86)756-861-4883
Fax: (86)756-861-4998
http://www.gree.com.cn/gree_english/

Gree Electric Appliances Inc. of Zhuhai (珠海格力电器股份有限公司) is the largest air conditioner manufacturer in the world. The state-owned firm has 39,300 employees globally with manufacturing facilities in China, Vietnam, Pakistan, and Brazil. The momentum of the firm's growth was barely affected by the global economic downturn of 2008–2009 with a year-to-year increase in net profit of 65 percent in 2008.

Historical Development

Founded as Zhuhai Haili Cooling Engineering Company Limited in 1989, Gree Electric Appliance was a divisional spin off of the Zhuhai Gree Corporation (Gree Group), one of the largest state-owned enterprises in China. In 1992, it was restructured and renamed Gree Electric Appliances Inc. of Zhuhai. While these two dates (the 1989 "birth" and 1992 "christening") are of interest, Gree Electric was transformed in 1995 by two events. The first was the Gree Group granting Gree Electric the use of the Gree brand. The agreement gave the rights for brand usage for a period of 10 years and required Gree Electric to spend CNY 25 million (US$2.9 million) annually in advertising the brand. The second was the promotion of the then 42-year-old Dong Mingzhu to sales manager. Dong, the youngest of seven siblings, was born in 1954 into a working-class family. A graduate from the Chinese Academy of Social Sciences, Dong began work at Gree as sales assistant and worked her way up to the post of district manager before she took over the position of sales manager. Dong immediately found herself in the middle of a corporate struggle (albeit one of her own design) as she fought to redefine the relationships and roles of the company's sales agents. The conflict pitted established systems based on personal trust and *guanxi* against Dong's vision on the best method for building the Gree Brand. A major agent with sales of CNY 150 million (US$18 million) was terminated. Dong severed ties with her own brother who had sought a lower price for a dealer in return for a commission. Throughout her early years at the helm of the sales department, Dong fought relentlessly to restructure the distribution system and ultimately designed Gree's current system that McKinsey Associates identified as a major competitive advantage in a 2002 industry analysis.

Corporate Structure and Leadership

As a listed company, Gree Electric Appliances was 50.28% held by Zhuhai Gree Group, while Zhuhai Gree Real Estate has 8.38% of shares, and Zhuhai Huasheng Inc. (Group), Shenwan Paris Shengli Jingxuan Security Investment Fund, and Xinghua Security Investment Fund each holds less than 2%.

Dong Mingzhu, who was named president and vice chairman in 2001, remains the most visible of Gree's leaders. One of her books, *Check around the World*, is one of the most popular Chinese business books of all-time and was even made into a television series. She has achieved celebrity status in China and is perennially placed on *Forbes*' and *Fortune*'s lists of the Worlds Most Powerful Women.

The other side of Gree's management coin is Zhu Jianghong, who has served as chairman since the company's founding. It is Zhu's credo of "talk less and practice more" that serves as the cornerstone of Gree's values.

Gree's status as a SOE is not merely a structural classification but a major factor in the company's strategic planning and operations. The firm maintains a very high level of philanthropy and community action. Dong Mingshu will often mention Gree's status as an explanation for actions based upon the belief that the primary responsibilities of an SOE are not profit-based but rather creating sustainable development, generating societal benefits and maintaining the value of state assets. When the price of copper (a key raw material in the overall manufacturing cost of air conditioners) fell in 2007, Dong believed the industry should pass the profits generated by the cost reduction back to consumers. The price reductions were spread to all series of Gree's products in different ranges. In the oligopolistic market, other companies needed to follow suit resulting in an industry-wide price reduction and an example of public policy generated through corporate strategy.

Strategic Overview

In an industry where brand name is a major factor in buyer decision making, Gree has worked exhaustively on building a global brand. In 2005, after what appeared to outsiders to be a long and contentious negotiation, the Gree brand was permanently transferred from Gree Group to Gree Electric.

Gree's strategy has been centered on maintaining a narrow focus on traditional household air conditioners and concentrating on the growth markets of Asia, Southern Europe, and South America. Gree has steadfastly followed a concept of developing strong market presence before moving into production in a target region. Gree has been a major contributor in the growth in Chinese outward FDI, opening production plants in Brazil (2001), Pakistan (2008), and Vietnam (2008).

Traditional air conditioners (also known as reverse-cycle air conditioners) employ a compressor driven heat pump that is either on or off. Temperature is regulated by a thermostat that measures air temperature and switches the compressor on when the ambient air temperature rises too far above the desired temperature and turns the compressor off when the ambient air is below the desired temperature. Since a compressor's speed cannot be varied, the unit is either fully on or off. In contrast to traditional designs, inverter air conditioners use a variable-frequency drive to control the speed of the motor and thus the compressor. Eliminating stop–start cycles increases efficiency, extends the life of components, and helps eliminate sharp fluctuations in the load the air-conditioner places on the power supply. For most households inverters are the long-term preferred option. While initial costs run 40 percent above traditional designs, the higher initial expense is offset by a reduction in energy usage with payback times averaging two years. However, while inverter air conditioners are almost universally recognized as the preferred design, they have not yet found wide acceptance. Except for Japan, inverter air conditioners account for less than 10 percent of the world market.

Although Gree's complete focus on perfecting traditional air conditioners had vaulted Gree to global leadership in the field, the dedication to non-inverter technology had a significant downside. Complying with global energy and environmental standards (including those of the Standardization Administration of China specifically addressing energy-efficiency of air conditioners) employing a non-inverter air-conditioner product line would be extremely difficult. However, it appears that this potential threat was largely neutralized in early 2009, when Gree signed a strategic agreement with Japan's Daikin Industries to jointly develop high-efficiency and energy-saving air conditioners in China. The agreement contains five projects: first, Gree has been contracted to produce 500,000 inverter residential air conditioners under the Daikin brand for the Japanese market; second, forming a joint venture for production of key components such as compressors and electrical components; third, forming a joint venture for production of precision mold designs; fourth, joint production of raw materials and parts; and last, joint development of inverter residential air conditioners that can penetrate the global market.

While Gree is the largest air-conditioner maker in the world, Japan's Daikin holds the biggest share in the global inverter air-conditioning market. The two joint ventures involve a total investment of CNY 910 million (US$133 million). Both of the joint ventures will be managed by Gree (controlling 51% of the projects), which will supply the manufacturing and procurement expertise, while Daikin (controlling 49 percent) will supply the patents and technology.

Neil Slough

References

Colbert, C (2009). Gree Electric Appliances, Inc. of Zhuhai. *Hoover's Company Reviews*.

Developing a Winning Strategy for the Air Conditioner Business in China (20 February 2001). *McKinsey Report*. http://www.cjzlk.com/%E7%BB%BC%E5%90%88%E6%96%87%E6%A1%A3%E5%A4%A7%E5%85%A8/%E7%BB%8F%E8%90%A5%E7%AE%A1%E7%90%86/%E5%8F%91%E5%B1%95%E8%A7%84%E5%88%92/%E9%BA%A6%E8%82%AF%E9%94%A1%E6%88%98%E7%95%A5%E6%8A%A5%E5%91%8A(LG).pdf. Retrieved on 30 June 2009.

Gree Electric Appliances, Inc. of Zhuhai. *Morningstar Investment Research*. http://quicktake.morningstar.com/ StockNet/balance10.aspx?Country=CHN&Symbol=000651. Retrieved on 30 June 2009.

Gree's Dong Mingzhu: A career woman full of great ideas (28 March 2007). *Chief Executive Magazine*. http://www.womenofchina.cn/Profiles/Businesswomen/15359.jsp. Retrieved on 30 June 2009.

Shenzhen Securities Information Co. Ltd. (2008). *China Listed Companies Handbook*. Saratoga, CA: Javvin Press.

GUANGDONG MIDEA ELECTRIC APPLIANCES

Corporate Address and Contact Information

Guangdong Midea Electric Appliances Co. Ltd.
Midea Industrial City
Penglai Road
Beijiao Town, Shunde District
Foshan, Guangdong Province 528311
People's Republic of China
Phone: (86)757-2633-8779
Fax: (86)757-2665-4011
http://global.midea.com.cn/

Commonly known as Midea, Guangdong Midea Electric Appliances Co. Ltd. (广东美的电器股份有限公司) is one of the largest companies in China. The company's product lines include household and commercial air-conditioners, large central air-conditioners, electric fans, electric rice cookers, refrigerators, microwave ovens, water dispensers, washing machines, electric heaters, dishwashers, induction cookers, water heaters, cooking stoves, sterilizers, electric chafing pots, electric ovens, vacuum cleaners, and other small electric appliances. The company also produces intermediate components including compressors, motors, and transformers. Midea has 15 production plants in China, 1 in Vietnam, and more than 20 subsidiaries across Russia, North America, Europe, and Asia. Currently, the company has over 46,000 employees.

Corporate Development

Midea's history is a legendary tale of the opportunities offered by entrepreneurship. In 1968, He Xiangjian and 23 farmers opened a small factory in Guangdong Province producing plastic bottle caps. Collectively, the group had raised a total of CNY 5000 (US$2,000) to start the venture in a small backyard, and slowly increased their production to included plastic cups and plates. By 1977, sales for the operation, known at the time as the Beijiao Commune Plastic Workshop, were approximately CNY 244,000 (US$140,000).

In 1980, the factory started producing electric fans, using the expertise they had gained making component parts for a local state-owned fan maker in Guangzhou. This was the first consumer product produced by the commune, and after a public contest they chose "Midea" as corporate name, which means "beautiful" in Mandarin.

Midea is comprised of five distinct units: the Air-conditioning and Refrigeration Group, the Living Appliances Group, the Appliance Components Group, the Real Estate Unit, and Midea Hong Kong Corp. Midea is a private company, a rarity in China where state-owned enterprises still make up a major part of the economy. Founder He Xiangjian, who is the largest shareholder, serves as chairman of the board and ranks among the 20 richest people in China. Currently, the Midea Group Co. Ltd. under He holds 46.8% of the company, and Morgan Stanley has a minority share of 4.3%, while Foshan Shunde Kalan Industrial Co. holds another 4.2%.

Strategic Overview

Growth came quickly to Midea and sales more than doubled each year in the first four years of the 1980s. However, as the marketplace in mainland China became more competitive, earnings declined, and Midea made two important strategic moves. The first was to shift its focus to export markets in Asia. The second was to enter the home air-conditioner market. In 1985, air conditioners were luxury items used almost exclusively in hotels and modern office buildings, and entry into the market was a daring move by the small company. This decision yielded exceptional results. At the time, there were few mainland firms in the nascent industry and Midea was able to leverage local cost advantages to acquire a respectable market share prior to market entry by other Chinese firms. In 1993, Midea became the first township-based firm to have its shares listed on the Shenzhen Stock Exchange.

Encouraged by its successful entry into air conditioners, Midea began a broad diversification drive across a wide range of household appliances, adding microwave ovens, dishwashers, rice cookers, water dispensers, gas stoves, and soy milk makers to the Midea product mix. While the company produces a broad selection of products for consumer markets, they all share one unwavering trait: the Midea brand. Midea's dedication to a single family branding strategy is unwavering across all product lines. While the brand is well known in China, it has yet to achieve global recognition. The lack of awareness outside of China can be attributed to the fact that two-thirds of the firm's exports are as OEM products manufactured for other companies.

In 2007, Midea opened its first foreign production facility: Midea Industrial Park in Vietnam. Up to that point Midea had focused on optimizing distribution to world markets while avoiding establishing manufacturing operations outside of China. The Vietnam operation aside, Midea still demonstrates a strong belief that the Pearl River Delta region is the single best location for global appliance manufacturing with significant cost advantages arising from the local labor market and preferential government policies. While this centralized production approach has served the company well in gaining market share in China, further foreign manufacturing development may be required to effectively compete globally.

2008 was a busy year for Midea, as it acquired a 25-percent stake in Hefei Royalstar Laundry Equipment Co. from Maytag International Investments for more than 68 million RMB (US$10 million), making Midea the sole shareholder of Royalstar Laundry Equipment. Earlier in 2008, the appliance maker also purchased 24 percent of refrigerator and washing machine manufacturer Wuxi Little Swan. Midea will move quickly to incorporate the acquired technologies and facilities with their current operations. Once these new acquisitions are fully integrated, the Midea — Royalstar — Little Swan amalgamation will challenge Haier Electronics for the market leadership in washing machines in China. Also in 2008, the company announced a 60/40 joint venture deal with air-conditioner manufacturer Carrier to make residential and light-commercial duct-free split AC units exclusively for Carrier. Foshan Midea Carrier Air Conditioning Equipment, the new JV, is the fourth such venture between the two companies.

Midea touts its strong emphasis on Research and Development, which accounts for 3 percent of sales income, as an investment in the future. Alternatively, it can be viewed as the implementation cost of the company's product diversification strategy. Across many of its markets, Midea competes against firms with much more narrowly focused product mixes (for example: Gree in air conditioners and Galanz in microwave ovens). The cross-product benefits of family branding come at the expense of funding R&D across divergent product technologies. Thus far, that strategy has worked well in China with Midea gaining market share in many of its product categories. The question that remains to be answered is whether the strategy can be effectively exported. Most of the growth in the Chinese white goods industry is attributed to penetration of rural markets in the country, a curve that is predicted to begin flattening by 2015.

Neil Slough

References

Developing a Winning Strategy for the Air Conditioner Business in China (20 February 2001). *McKinsey Report.* http://www.cjzlk.com/%E7%BB%BC%E5%90%88%E6%96%87%E6%A1%A3%E5%A4%A7%E5%85%A8/ %E7%BB%8F%E8%90%A5%E7%AE%A1%E7%90%86/%E5%8F%91%E5%B1%95%E8%A7%84%E5%88 %92/%E9%BA%A6%E8%82%AF%E9%94%A1%E6%88%98%E7%95%A5%E6%8A%A5%E5%91%8A(LG). pdf. Retrieved on 30 June 2009.
Oliver, L (2009). Midea Electric Appliances Co. *Hoover's Company Reviews.*
Shenzhen Securities Information Co. Ltd. (2008). *China Listed Companies Handbook.* Saratoga, CA: Javvin Press.

HAIER

Corporate Address and Contact Information

Haier Group Company
1 Haier Road, Hi-Tech Zone
Qingdao, Shandong 266101
People's Republic of China
Phone: (86)532-893-9999
Fax: (86)532-893-8666
www.haier.com

Originally known as Qingdao Refrigerator, Haier Group (青岛海尔股份有限公司) has emerged from the threshold of bankruptcy to establish itself as an internationally renowned company. Currently, the world's fourth largest white-goods manufacturer with nearly $17.8 billion in total sales, Haier manufactures refrigerators, air conditioners, televisions, mobile phones, computers, and other appliances under 15,100 different specifications in 96 product categories. Armed with a brand name strategy implemented by its CEO Zhang Ruimin, the company has been recognized as a global leader in the technology domains of intelligent integrated home furniture, networked home appliances, digitalization, and large-scale integrated circuits. In an ongoing effort to establish itself as a distinguishable brand within a variety of industries, Haier has exported goods to over 100 countries and established joint ventures to branch into other global markets over the past 25 years.

Historical Development

Founded in 1984 with its headquarters in Qingdao, CEO Zhang Ruimin's primary objective was the improvement of product quality. Consequently, his first act was the smashing of 76 products with a sledgehammer to implement his Western-style quality control program. Zhang's philosophy proved to be a blend of international management principles and Chinese wisdom, with the cornerstones of innovation and excellence. Guided by his strategy, Haier has advanced through the brand building, diversification, and internationalization stages, and since 2005, it has embarked on the fourth stage of its rapid development: global branding.

Since its founding in 1984, Haier Group has maintained an average annual growth of 68%, and its sales have increased from RMB 3.5 million to RMB 40.6 billion. This is primarily due to the four stages through which it has advanced. The branding stage ranged from 1984 to 1991, which was characterized by the belief that quality was, and would remain the essence of a sustainable business. In the early stages of China's reform, the market was relatively controlled, and demand was unrelated to product competitiveness but based on the byproduct of a closed system that kept companies from tapping into the enormous potential market for high-quality goods. Consequently, when Haier significantly improved its product quality, it reaped massive benefits in the new market. In the diversification stage (1991–1998), Haier grew from one product to a variety of new products by utilizing the capital operations method of "activating stock fish", a concept in which Haier would merge with an underutilized company and maximize potential through efficient management. During the internationalization stage, ranging from 1998 to 2005, Zhang placed an emphasis on selling products in greater volume to major economic regions through well-established after-sales service and distribution networks. Recently, Haier has initiated its fourth phase of development, the global branding, in which the firm is striving to create a localized Haier brand in each market by promoting the competitiveness of its products and business management, so that it may realize win-win profits with suppliers, customers, and users. So far the firm has already experienced significant success; in 2008 alone, Haier's net profit increased 20.6% and its sales in overseas markets rose 9.8%. Additionally, the company has received a great deal of recognition, as it was ranked first in top 10 global brands, first in Asia's Most Admired Companies List, and 13th in *Forbes*' Reputation Institute Global 200 List.

Main Products and Services

Haier's main products range from general home appliances, audio, video products to communication, IT, and pharmaceutical products. Its four leading product categories include refrigerators, refrigerating cabinets, air conditioners, and washing machines, as each holds over 30% market share. In 2002 alone, Haier held a 35% US market share for large refrigerators and reached $300 million in sales. The company has been successful in European markets as well, gaining a 10% market share in Europe's air-conditioning market.

In addition to its core product lines, Haier offers services including travel, insurance, logistics, and intelligent home integration. Haier's focus on quality and emphasis on meeting customer needs have allowed its emergence as China's leading white goods manufacturer. This is partly attributed to the company's efforts in emphasizing extra sales in its home appliance segment through its joint venture (Haier Suning Selling Company) with Suning Appliance Chains, a China-based home appliance retailer. As the firm further develops innovative capabilities, its product offerings will increase and improve, ultimately propelling it toward achieving its goal of worldwide brand recognition.

Corporate Structure and Leadership

Under Zhang Ruimin, Haier has relied on establishing partnerships with leading chain stores worldwide in an effort to enter its primary markets such as white and brown goods, as well as secondary markets such as mobile phones, plasma televisions, and pharmaceutical goods. In doing so, Haier has been transformed from a vertically integrated company into a decentralized one while maintaining operations in China, the United States, Europe, Africa, and the Middle East, South Asia, the Asia-Pacific, and the ASEAN regions. Moreover, in addition to operating 240 subsidiaries, the firm has established 64 trading companies (19 overseas), 29 manufacturing plants (24 overseas), 8 design centers (5 overseas), and 16 industrial parks (4 overseas). Haier Group's listed subsidiaries include Haier Electronics Group Co. on the Hong Kong Stock Exchange (HKG: 1169) and Qingdao Haier Co. Ltd. on the Shanghai Stock Exchange (SHA: 600690).

Innovation is at the core of Haier's strong and unique corporate culture, as it is guided and developed by advanced concepts, innovative strategies, efficient organization, creative technology, and market orientation. Through prioritizing collectivist participation and superior quality, Zhang Ruimin has developed unique management models that are beginning to be recognized by companies worldwide over a variety of industries. These include OEC management (Overall Every Control and Clear), a market-chain system, individual-goal combination, and the "ball-on-slope theory". OEC management indicates that each of Haier's 50,000 worldwide employees is supervised and spoken to on a daily basis to monitor his or her progress and success. The market-chain is a computerized system concentrated upon order information flow and is operated for logistics and performance to realize the firm's objectives. Thirdly, individual-goal combination emphasizes that every employee is an independent and innovative strategic business unit with the collective goal of achieving primacy in the marketplace. Finally, the "ball-on-slope theory" states that two forces are required to balance success; business management will prevent the firm from falling back, whereas the capacity to innovate with force the firm upwards, thus maintaining a balanced approach to the market. As a consequence of their success, these methods begin to be spread to other companies worldwide, and Haier's corporate structure is becoming more commonly adopted within the industry.

Growth Strategies

With the goal of further enhancing Haier's leadership in the Chinese and global markets and strengthening the reputation of its brand worldwide, the company's leaders have implemented a strategy of not only becoming an international player, but establishing itself as a globalized Haier. Setting its primary objective as meeting customer needs, Haier has aimed to build a brand name internationally and expanding into overseas markets such as Europe in 1990, the Middle East and Africa in 1993, the United States in 1999, and Japan in 2001. Creating partnerships through joint ventures has been Haier's mode of growth. Having already secured a foothold in the home appliances market through partnerships with top local retailers including Wal-Mart, Sam's, Costco, KESA, and Carrefour, Haier is aiming to become a leader in the sale of mobile phones in India through Haier Telecom (India) Ltd., a joint venture with India's Scope Group. Additionally, the company has announced plans to enter the Japanese television market by joining forces with Fujitsu and Hitachi. As Haier operates in a variety of regions, it has also developed a "Three-Thirds Strategy", which outlines that 1/3 of its revenue should in the long run derive from products made and sold in China, 1/3 is from products made in China but exported and the final 1/3 from products made and sold abroad.

Haier's global branding strategy strives to position the company as a local brand in different world markets in conjunction with enhanced product competitiveness and strong corporate operations. In order to do so, the firm has adopted five separate globalization strategies: globalization of design (establish worldwide design centers to consolidate resources from developed countries), globalization of manufacture (develop industrial parks and plants to enable prompt action to satisfy local needs for quality), globalization of marketing (construct 5,000 overseas retail outlets and 10,000 service centers to interact, develop, and further innovate), globalization of purchase (create a public bidding and online purchase site), and globalization of capital operation (lay the foundation for further movement into the international capital market). Haier's overseas expansion has always been based on its domestic success. The company initially establishes its brand name in its current industry, thus creating the opportunity for supplementary and complementary joint ventures worldwide to ultimately gain the leading position in its new markets.

Environment and Industry Challenges

Despite Haier's growing international competitiveness, several challenges and concerns have emerged simultaneously. While the company has been making remarkable strides, it has suffered serious growing pains, as some of Haier's overseas acquisitions have proved to be less than prudent. As a result of diversifying into industries such as finance, personal computers, and real estate, the company appears to be hurting itself due to questionable investments and the lack of experience and reputation within those industries. Another major challenge Haier has confronted is the reputation of Chinese-branded products in the United States and Europe. If the firm is to truly achieve its goal of becoming a global brand, it will need to attract image-conscious consumers who value brand above everything else in addition to progressively improving quality though innovation. As Haier continues to develop joint ventures and expand globally, the company leaders must carefully scrutinize its financial stability.

From the perspective of competition, Haier's main rivals include Whirlpool, Electrolux, and GE Consumer & Industrial. The white-goods industry is extremely competitive worldwide, and Haier's abundance of partnerships could potentially create additional competitors through spin-offs or shared technologies. Finally, international political regulations differ regionally, and as a result, Haier must sufficiently understand the environment of every market within which it operates. This would further help prevent questionable investments in overseas expansions and will allow the firm to target industries that will provide enormous side potential.

Marc Fetscherin

References

Emerging Markets Informative Service: Haier Group Company Financials. Listed Company Financials — China Financial Statement for Listed Manufacturing Companies. http://www.securities.com. Retrieved on 16 April 2009.

Haier Group Company (2007). Corporate Culture. http://www.haier.com/abouthaier/CorporateCulture/index.asp. Retrieved on 16 April 2009.

Haier Group Company (2008). Hoover's Company Records. http://www.hoovers.com. Retrieved on 16 April 2009.

HANDAN IRON & STEEL

Corporate Address and Contact Information

Handan Iron & Steel Company
232 Fu Xing Road

Handan City, Hebei Province 056015
People's Republic of China
Phone: (86)31-0607-2141
Fax: (86)31-0404-1978
www.hgjt.com.cn

Handan Iron & Steel Company (邯郸钢铁股份有限公司) manufactures steel and iron, chiefly hot- and cold-rolled steel, steel bars, rods, and plates. In 2007, the Handan Group produced approximately 8.3 million tons of steel and four million tons of iron.

Reportedly to be 60 percent government-owned, Handan Iron & Steel Co. Ltd. manufactures and sells mostly iron and steel goods. The company's main products are steel billets, steel materials, sintering, and coke products, among others. During the year ending 31 December 2007, the company produced about 4.79 million metric tons of iron ore, 6 million metric tons of steel, and 5.62 million tons of steel materials. In 2007, nearly 86 percent of Handan's total revenues were obtained from the sale of iron, and steel goods. The company distributed its products in both internal and foreign markets. Then, during the year ending 31 December 2008, Handan produced approximately 4.1167 million metric tons of iron, 6.0242 million metric tons of steel, and 5.6086 million metric tons of steel materials.

Historical Development

Handan Iron & Steel Company was founded in 1958. According to the International Iron and Steel Institute, Handan ranks 14th largest of China's and 36th largest company among the world's steel industry. In 2008, the Hebei provincial government combined Handan with Tangshan Iron & Steel, another state-owned company, and other steel factories located in the province to form the steel industry's largest enterprise in the country — now called Hebei Iron & Steel. The new company plans to increase production from its present level of 30 million tons to 50 million tons by 2010.

The company's current leadership team include: Li Lianping, Chairman and General Manager; Li Guiyang and Zhang Jianping, Vice-Chairmen, Ma Chunlin, Deputy General Manager; Zhang Xiaoli, Chief Engineer; and Wang Junjie, Chief Finance Director. Handan Iron & Steel's major subsidiaries are: Wuyang Iron & Steel Co. and Henshai Steel-Pipe Co. Its major competitors are Anshan Iron and Steel, Baosteel, and Jiangsu Shagang among others.

In 2008, Handan Iron & Steel Co. Ltd. reported an attributable net profit of CNY 599.2647 million or CNY 0.213 per share on the main operating turnover of CNY 37.26 billion against an attributable net profit of CNY 961.8657 million or CNY 0.342 per share on the main operating turnover of CNY 26.11 billion for the same period in 2007. The adjusted net profit was CNY 657.0373 million or CNY 0.233 per share for the same period in 2007. The return on net assets was 4.91%; the net cash flow was CNY 0.92 per share against a return on net assets of 7.99%, a net cash flow of CNY 0.45 per share for the same period in 2007.

Main Products and Services

Presently with near 18,000 employees, Handan Iron & Steel Co. Ltd. manufactures and sells iron and steel products throughout China. The primary activities of the company are manufacturing, transforming, and selling eperlan black metal, billets, steel rolling, carbamide, mineral synthesizing, metallurgy, and metal tools. It is also engaged in manufacturing and selling coke and its by-products. Its main products are round bar steel, screw steel, angle steel, channel steel, middle boards, rolling steel, acid picklings, rolling steel galvanizing, and coke.

Handan Iron & Steel is certified according to ISO9002, the GB/T19002, and the ISO9001. The company has the following operations: coke ovens; sinter plant (annual capacity 4 m tons), three blast furnaces (1 m ton), steel-making plants (six basic oxygen converters: three 100-ton and three 20-ton), continuous casting machines (four billet: one 2-strand, two 4-strand, and one 8-strand), two ½-strand bloom/slab, one SMS Demag thin slab (1.3 m ton), rolling mills billet (250,000 tons); SMS Demag compact strip plant (1.2 m tons) with hot and cold rolling facilities; one medium plate (800,000 tons), one SMS Demag cold reversing (1.3 m ton), coil coating lines Danieli Sendzimir hot-dip galvanizing (300,000 tons), Andritz push-pull pickling line (500,000 tons), SMS Demag pickling/tandem line for cold plate, and color coating (120,000 tons).

Business Strategy of Merger and Consolidation

In recent years, the Chinese government has encouraged the consolidation of the steel industry, aiming not only to improve manufacturing but also to eliminate obsolete installations. In 2008, the Hebei provincial government combined Handan with the state-controlled Tangshan Iron & Steel and other steel companies, located in the province, to form a new steel enterprise, called Hebei Iron & Steel. Hence, Tangshan Iron & Steel combined its operations with Chengde Xinxin Vanadium & Titanium and with Handan Iron & Steel. The merger occurred after controllers from Tangshan Iron, Chengde Xinxin, and Handan Iron formulated an agreement in June of that same year, originating the Hebei Iron & Steel Group.

Such decision is in alignment with the central government effort to develop the country's steel companies larger and stronger, aiming both to improve industrial efficiency, and also to reduce pollution and energy consumption. The union of the three companies has allowed an increase in the Hebei Iron & Steel's market participation, as well as a general cost reduction for raw materials and research. The conglomerate's goal is to achieve production of 50 million tons of iron and steel per annum until the end of 2010. As a result of this merger, Baosteel Group announced in early 2009 that the company would withdraw its capital from the joint venture company of Handan Iron and Steel Co. Ltd. so the assets could be sold to Hansteel Group.

Future Growth Plans

In an effort to jump-start the depressed domestic economy, the Chinese central government has recently launched a series of stimulus plans, among them are several large construction and transportation projects. As a result, Handan Iron & Steel Co. Ltd. has successfully won large orders for the Beijing-Shijiazhuang and Beijing-Shanghai High-Speed Railways. In specific, Handan's contract includes 70,373 tons of fine rods and 27,135 tons of fine high-speed wires for the Beijing-Shanghai High-Speed Railway Project, and an order to supply 24,674 tons of fine rods to the Beijing-Shijiazhuang High-Speed Railway Project. The company has already produced nearly 100,000 tons of steel products for the two projects so far, and is delivering the first batch of products.

In 2008, the Handan Steel poured CNY 578.79 million into the energy saving and emission reduction projects, with the former including eight sub-projects and CNY 422.62 million in investments, and the latter of three sub-projects and CNY 156.17 million in investments. As a result of carrying out energy-saving strategies, Handan Iron & Steel Co. Ltd. saved 241,600 tons of standard coal up to the end of October 2008, and fulfilled the original annualized plan of 92,500 tons ahead of schedule. In this way, the Handan Steel speeds up its pace for product mix adjustments. As predicted, the company is likely to phase out obsolete production capacities, including 325 tons of steel-making converters and 4,300 cubic meter blast furnaces etc. by the end of 2010.

Marco Antonio Tourinho Furtado and Tays Torres Ribeiro Chagas

References

BusinessWeek (2008). Handan Iron & Steel Co. Ltd. (600001: Shanghai Stock Exchange). http://investing.business week.com/research/stocks/snapshot/snapshot.asp?ric=600001.SS. Retrieved on 28 December 2008.

Handan Steel saves 0.24 million tonne coal in 10 months (4 December 2008). *Handan Daily*. http://www.handandaily.com/2008/12/handan-steel-saves-024-million-tonne-coal-in-10-months.html. Retrieved on 30 April 2009.

Hille, K (2009). Hebei Steel merger prompts doubt. *Financial Times*, 30 December. http://www.ft.com/cms/s/0/e2fb074c-d690-11dd-9bf7-000077b07658.html. Retrieved on 08 January 2009.

Iron & Steel Works of the World Directory (2009). London: Metal Bulletin Directories.

HARBIN POWER EQUIPMENT

Corporate Address and Contact Information

Harbin Power Equipment Company Limited
Block B, 39 Sandadongli Road
Xiangfang District, Harbin City
Heilongjiang Province 150040
People's Republic of China
Phone: (86)451-8213-5717 or 8213-5727
Fax: (86)451-8213-5700

As a significant player in China's fast-growing energy industry, Harbin Power Equipment Company Limited (哈尔滨动力设备股份有限公司, HPEC) is a major manufacturer of power plant equipment. Based in Harbin, also known as the City of Power, HPEC was formed through the restructuring of Harbin Power Plant Equipment Group Corporation (HPEGC), which is the oldest large-scale power plant equipment manufacturer in the People's Republic of China.

Historical Development

By grouping HPEGC with its subsidiary Harbin Electric Machinery Co. Ltd., Harbin Boilers Co. Ltd., and Harbin Steam Turbine Co. Ltd., HPEC was established on 6 October 1994, and two months later, it was listed on the Hong Kong Stock Exchange (HK: 1133). The company and its subsidiaries are the largest manufacturer of power plant equipment in the PRC, which currently have annual design production capacity of 5,000 MW, of which 4,000 MW is in thermal power equipment and 1,000 MW in hydro power equipment. HPEC possesses a comprehensive range of advanced production and research facilities. Its capabilities in research and development, product manufacturing, and power station construction have been ranked among the top of the power plant equipment-manufacturing industry in China.

Historically, HPEC had to wait a long time for the lights to come on. The company, which builds turbines, boilers, and electric generators for power plants, traces its origins to the early 1950s, shortly after the People's Republic of China was established. Before economic reforms took hold, China's power-supply needs grew modestly, so did HPEC. The situation changed after 2000, when China's rapid industrialization began pushing demand for electricity beyond what the country's creaky infrastructure could supply. After the government ordered a massive push to modernize and expand power production, China's generating capacity climbed 61% from 2000 to 2005, and consequently HPEC's business took off. Since 2004, the company's annual revenue growth has averaged an impressive 79%, mostly due to sales of coal-fired generators, but also because the company has been a supplier to China's most ambitious electrification schemes such as the massive Three Gorges Dam hydroelectric project on the Yangtze River.

Nevertheless, the company is fully aware that its good fortune cannot last forever. Production growth in China's power-equipment industry is expected to slow from an annual average of 55% from 2002 to 2005 to just 3.5% from 2006 to 2010, according to a Citibank report. Therefore, HPEC is developing new products while looking overseas for new customers. Among the promising initiatives is ramping up capacity to build nuclear power generators, which plays into China's efforts to diversify energy sources and reduce dependence on dirty coal-fired plants. According government sources, China will build more than 30 nuclear reactors in the next 15 years.

Nearly 90% of HPEC's revenues are produced within China; however, the company is increasingly striving to move into Asia and Africa, and has eyes on business in the United States and South America, as the international market is becoming more and more important for HPEC. In 2005, a subsidiary of HPEC began to work on a power station in Sudan that is a part of Africa's largest hydropower projects. The company's involvement in Sudan, because of the genocide taken place in Darfur, has made its stock the target for divestment by American-based endowment and public pension funds. Despite the negative publicity, HPEC has recently won contracts for work in Vietnam, Indonesia, Pakistan, the Philippines, and Bangladesh. In 2006, the company generated $3.85 billion in revenue, $429 million in profit, and average revenue growth of 79% in 2004–2006.

Corporate Structure, Main Products, and Services

Harbin Power Equipment has 19 subsidiary companies and 10 affiliated companies. The company's three primary subsidiaries are Harbin Electric Machinery Co. Ltd., Harbin Boiler Co. Ltd., and Harbin Steam Turbine Co. Ltd. The state-owned enterprise, Harbin Power Plant Equipment Group, controls the company through a 60% stake. As the largest power-generating equipment manufacturer, HPEC makes thermal, hydro, and nuclear power equipment, as well as providing engineering, construction, and consulting services related to the power generation sector.

HPEC's principal activities are the manufacturing of thermal and hydropower equipment, and its production ability takes up more than one-third of the domestic production volume in China. Its major products include 300-MW, 600-MW, and 1000-MW boilers, steam turbines, steam turbo-generators, and over 1000-MW nuclear turbines, steam turbo-generators, and heavy-duty gas turbines.

The company also manufactures auxiliary equipment for power stations, AC/DC motors and other products that include control devices, valves, pressure vessels, and axial compressor. Other activities include provision of engineering services and environmental protection services such as industry and sanitary wastewater purification, refuse treatment, and seawater desalination. HPEC also conducts research and development in power equipment engineering technology, develops property, and manages real estate and land investment.

Business Challenges and Growth Strategies

In the domestic market, the major large- and medium-sized enterprises that engage in hydroelectric generating sets manufacturing are HPEC, Dongfang Electric Co. Ltd., Tianjin Alstom Hydro Co. Ltd., Voith Hydro Shanghai Ltd., Toshiba Hydro Power (Hangzhou) Co. Ltd., and GE Hydro Asia Co. Ltd. Among the six companies, HPEC, and Dongfang Electric Co. Ltd. are state-owned enterprises, while Tianjin Alstom Hydro Co. Ltd., Voith Hydro Shanghai Ltd., and Toshiba Hydro Power (Hangzhou) Co. Ltd. are joint-ventures in which the foreign investments control interest. At the end of 2006, GE withdrew from the hydroelectric industry worldwide. GE Hydro Asia Co. Ltd., located in Hangzhou, its only hydroelectric operation in China has already changed the line of production and it no longer produces hydroelectric generating sets.

At present, the market demand of the industry is mainly supplied by the major six manufacturers. The market concentration of the whole industry is quite high and the market is leaning toward monopolistic competition within the six companies. As the two leading Chinese power equipment groups, the products of Dongfang Electric and HPEC cover various kinds of power-generating sets and the two companies steadily occupy the first and second place in the market in recent years. Alstom has continued to increase its investment in the Chinese market, so Tianjin Alstom Hydro Co. Ltd. also enjoys fast growth recently.

Wei Qian

References

Harbin Power Equipment Company Limited http://www.chpec.com/home.asp. Retrieved on 27 April 2009.

Harbin Power Equipment Company Limited (2009). 2008 Annual Report. http://www.chpec.com/syshd/images/upfile/20094278143013626.pdf. Retrieved on 27 April 2009.

Harbin Power Equipment Company Limited (2009). *Wikipedia*. http://en.wikipedia.org/wiki/Harbin_Power_Equipment. Retrieved on 27 April 2009.

Harbin Power Plant Equipment Group Corporation. http://www.hpec.com/index_hd.asp. Retrieved on 27 April 2009.

Harbin Power Equipment Company Limited (2009). Hoover's Company Overview. http://www.hoovers.com/harbin-power-equipment/—ID__149703—/free-co-factsheet.xhtml. Retrieved on 27 April 2009.

Ramzy, A (2007). China's hot new growth companies: Harbin Power Equipment (4 September). *Time*. http://www.time.com/time/specials/2007/article/0,28804,1657601_1657599_1657595,00.html. Retrieved on 27 April 2009.

浙富股份：首次公开发行股票招股意向书摘要 (17 July 2008). *证券时报* [Zhejiang Fuchunjiang Hydropower Equipment Co. Ltd: Extract of initial public offerings prospectus. *Securities Times*].

HENAN SHUANGHUI INVESTMENT & DEVELOPMENT

Corporate Address and Contract Information

Henan Shuanghui Investment & Development Co. Ltd. (000895)
Shuanghui Building
1st Road, Luohe
Henan Province 462000
People's Republic of China
Phone: (86)395-262-2616
Fax: (86)395-262-3398
www.shuanghui.net

Also known as Shineway Group, Henan Shuanghui Investment & Development Co. Ltd. (河南双汇投资发展股份有限公司) is a Chinese state-owned corporation. Headquartered in Luohe, Henan Province, the company is mainly engaged in the processing and sale of meat products. Originally a regional company, Shuanghui has expanded into 12 provinces and municipalities with modern meat processing plants, and established more than 200 sales and logistics centers in 31 provinces and regions across China. In 2007, Shuanghui was ranked 166 among China's top 500 companies, and in 2008, it was ranked 88th among the largest Chinese domestic companies in terms of annual revenues by *Fortune*. Operating under the guiding principles of outstanding quality, high efficiency, innovation, and integrity, the company has been leading the way to help China further define and develop its fast-growing food industry.

Historical Development

The beginning of the Henan Shuanghui Investment & Development Co. could be traced back to 1958, when its first cold warehouse was built in Luohe as a way to process and store perishables. Eleven years later, a meat-processing factory was added, as food shortages during the Cultural Revolution prompted the Chinese government to create the Luohe United Meat Processing Plant that would efficiently process huge amounts of meat. Although, for years, the infrastructure and technology were already in place, it was not until January 1994 that the current Shineway Group was formed. Founded as a joint venture with Chinachem, Shuanghui Group was launched with an initial registered capital of RMB 44.38 million. A year later, the company began to construct what is known as the Shuanghui Food City. When the project was completed in September 1996, 260 million yuan had been invested in the Shuanghui Industrial Park.

Soon after the construction was completed, the important issue of stock ownership reform was tackled. In 1998, Shuanghui Industry became the official corporate name, and the company was successfully listed on the Shenzhen Stock Exchange with 50 million shares. After another round of reorganization, the name of Henan Shuanghui Investment and Development Company was adopted. With an investment of RMB 560 million, the second phase of construction started in 1999 and completed a year later, adding more operational space to the company. Shortly afterwards, Shuanghui started to export meat products to Japan with the approval of the Chinese government.

Based on this experience, Shuanghui began to explore business opportunities with several Japanese companies and in April 2002, Henan Livestock East Ltd. was founded. A joint venture under the control of Shuanghui Investment & Development Co., it enabled the group to produce pork in huge quantities. Around the same time, the company also entered a partnership with American corporate giant DuPont, which led to the formation of DuPont Shuanghui Ltd. In order to maximize production and continue its market growth, Shuanghui Board of Directors decided to invest another RMB 1 billion to further expand the Shuanghui Industrial Park. On 29 June 2007, as the result of state ownership reform, the Chinese government entered a partnership agreement with Goldman Sachs, which became a strategic investor in Henan Shuanghui Group.

Main Products and Services

Henan Shuanghui Investment and Development Co. focuses mainly on the production, processing, and sale of meat products. Ever since the Shineway-branded ham was first launched in 1992, the company has developed many technologies to help with the preservation and packaging of all kinds of meat goods. Such improvements include the usage of PVDC (Poly-Vinylidene Dichloride, specialized plastic wrap) packaging film and the ability to sell both low- and high-temperature meat products. The company is capable of producing in huge quantities ham sausages, fresh or frozen meats, packaging film, and natural seasoning for foods.

Although the company's principal activities are processing and selling meat and foodstuff, Shuanghui also manufactures and sells packaging goods and chemical products, conducts business in bioengineering, breeds livestock, makes investment in food industry, and provides technological advisory, sale agent, logistic, and other related services.

Corporate Structure and Leadership

Like all public companies, Shuanghui Group is governed by a corporate Board of Directors and a set of chief officers who collaboratively make executive decisions. Its leadership team includes Zhang Junjie, chairman; Shi Haitian, vice chairman and general manager; Qi Yongyao, director and secretary; Hu Zhenzhao, CFO; and Wan Long, president and CEO. As with other state-owned enterprises, the company also has a party secretary in charge of political affairs.

Nicknamed the "Godfather of the meat industry" and "China's Chief butcher", Wang Long was first appointed the director of the Luohe United Meat Processing Plant in 1984, after the factory suffered years of losses. Under his leadership, modern management practices were adopted, and advanced meat-processing technologies were gradually introduced, which led to great improvement in operation efficiency, generated new jobs, and helped stabilize the regional economy. For his substantial contributions to the Chinese meat-processing industry, when the group was established in 1994, Wan was named the first chairman of the Henan Shuanghui Investment & Development Co. Ltd.

Shuanghui has 10 major subsidiaries, and a current workforce of 45,000 nationwide. As of December 2008, the company has a total of RMB 70 billion in registered assets. Its market cap is nearly RMB 22 billion, with approximately 606 million shares outstanding while another 312 million shares are closely held.

Business Growth Strategies

To further sustain its impressive market growth, Henan Shuanghui Investment strives to be independently innovative. As a key state enterprise designated by the Chinese State Council since 1999, the company has built state-of-the-art facilities to increase production level while maintaining sufficient quality control. Its laboratories and development teams have been engaging in various researches related to food-processing technologies, which naturally leads to frequent restructuring and industrial upgrades on its current machinery. The company also endeavors to learn and absorb more advanced techniques from developed nations so that it can increase efficiency in the intensive processing of meat products. As a result, more than 200 fresh meat products, 400 seasoning products, and 600 meat-packaging products have been introduced to the Chinese consumers over the years. Through initial introduction of frozen meat products, Shuanghui has successfully developed corporate growth strategies for the Chinese domestic market.

In light of the food safety crisis of recent years, Shuanghui attempts to keeps strict guidelines in management and quality control of its products. The company makes all key decisions based on the current and projected need of various markets and strategic analysis of the Chinese food-processing industry. As a well-respected state corporation with a renowned brand name, the group has passed the ISO9001, ISO14001, and HACCP (Hazard Analysis and Critical Control Point) certifications. By going public, the company has also modernized its industrial management structure and practices. As a result of continual innovation and corporate reconstructing, the company has reached an annual capacity of processing 30 million pigs and 500,000 cattle, generating more than 20 million tons of chicken, 50,000 tons of eggs, and 50,000 tons of plant-based protein. With over RMB 35 billion in annual gross sales, Shuanghui Group has generated various business opportunities for more than 1.5 million farmers surrounding its massive food-processing operations. In addition, the company has established branch offices in Japan,

South Korea, Singapore, and the Philippines, and its recent trade volume in import and export activities has reached over 100 million dollars. Looking forward, Shuanghui's goal is to develop into an even bigger and stronger company, capable of being China's largest and the world's leading meat supplier. Specifically, the company has set an ambitious goal of reaching among the top three corporations of the global meat industry with a gross sale of RMB 50 to 100 billion in the coming years.

Kevin Ding and Wenxian Zhang

References

Henan Shuanghui Investment & Development Co. Ltd. (2005). Company Profile. http://www.shuanghui.net. Retrieved on 15 March 2009.

Henan Shuanghui Investment & Development Co. Ltd. (USA Pink Sheets). Reuters http://www.reuters.com/finance/stocks/companyProfile?symbol=HSUIF.PK. Retrieved on 9 March 2009.

Henan Shuanghui Investment & Development (2008). Company Profile *Wright Reports*. http://wrightreports.ecnext.com/coms2/reportdesc_COMPANY_C156MD200. Retrieved on 19 March 2009.

Henan Shuanghui Investment & Development Company Snapshot (2009). *CI: Corporate Information*. http://www.corporateinformation.com/Company-Snapshot.aspx?cusip=C156MD200. Retrieved on 15 March 2009.

HUADIAN POWER INTERNATIONAL

Corporate Address and Contact Information

Huadian Power International Corporation Limited
14 Jingsan Road
Jinan, Shandong Province 250001
People's Republic of China
Phone: (86)531-8236-6222
Fax: (86)531-8236-6090
www.hdpi.com.cn
hdpi@hdpi.com.cn

Hsuadian Power International Corporation Limited (华电国际电力股份有限公司) is one of the largest independent power producers (IPP) in China. The company's principal activity is the construction and operation of power plants and other business related to power generation. From its IPO in 1999, Huadian's installed capacity has been growing steadily through the acquisition and construction, with an average annual growth rate of approximately 20%. In 2008, the total installed capacity controlled and invested by the company had amounted to 23,293.5 MW, and the total interested installed capacity amounted to 19,578.2 MW. The company produced approximately 100.676 billion kWh of electricity, generating revenues of RMB 29.997 billion during the fiscal year ended December 2008, an increase of 47.47% over 2007.

Historical Development

Formerly named as Shandong International Power Development Company Ltd., Huadian Power International was incorporated on 28 June 1994 in Jinan, Shandong Province. The company was jointly developed by Shandong Electricity Power Corporation (SEPCO), Shandong International Trust and

Investment Corporation (SITIC), China Power Trust and Investment Company Ltd., Shandong Luneng Development Group Co. Ltd., and Zaozhuang City Infrastructure Investment Company. At the time of incorporation, the total share capital of the company was RMB 3.825 billion.

After receiving the approval from the Ministry of Foreign Trade and Economic Cooperation, Huadian became a Sino-foreign investment joint stock company limited by shares incorporated in PRC, and its H-Shares and A-Shares were respectively listed on the Hong Kong Stock Exchange and Shanghai Stock Exchange in June 1999 and February 2005. Currently, there is a share capital of 6.021 billion, of which 1.431 billion shares were circulating H-Shares, representing 23.77% of the company's total issued share capital; while A-Shares are 76.23% of the company's total issued share capital, with a total of 4.59 billion shares.

Among the major shareholders, China Huadian Corporation (CHD) holds 50.60% of the company, while Shandong International Trust Corporation has another 13.30%. China Huadian Corporation is a wholly state-owned enterprise established on the basis of a sum of enterprises and institutions formerly owned by State Power Corporation of China. As a pilot entity approved by the State Council to conduct state-authorized investment, CHD was established on 2002 with a registered capital of RMB 12 billion. Authorized by the state-owned Assets Supervision and Administration Commission, CHD mainly engages in the production and supply of electricity and heat, development of power-related primary energy such as coal, and supply of pertinent technological service. In 2008, China Huadian Corporation had a total installed capacity of 63,020 MW, annual power output was 258.2 billion kWh, and total assets valued at RMB 239 billion. CHD has 3,038 employees, and 23 wholly owned, 40 controlling, and 21 participating affiliated enterprise; and its power plants are distributed in 25 provinces and regions in China, among which 26 power plants are large-scale operations with an installed capacity of over 1,000 MW each. Aiming to become the top power generation enterprise in China, and among the top 500 enterprises of the world, China Huadian Corporation seeks to increase its installed capacity to 80,000 MW by the end of 2010, with annual power output of over 400 billion kWh, and annual profits reaching 6 billion RMB.

Corporate Structure and Leadership

As of 2008, Huadian Power International wholly owned or controlled a total of 27 power plants and companies, among them: Zouxian Plant, Shiliquan Plant, Laicheng Plant, Huadian Zouxian Power, Huadian Qingdao Power, Huadian Weifang Power, Huadian Zibo Power, Huadian Zhangqiu Power, Huadian Tengzhou Xinyuan Power, Huadian Laizhou Wind Power, Huadian Ningxia Lingwu Power, Ningxia Zhongning Power, Huadian Ningxia Ningdong Wind Power, Anhui Huadian Suzhou Power, Anhui Huadian Wuhu Power, Anhui Chizhou Jiuhua Power, Huadian Suzhou Biomass Energy Power, Huadian Xinxiang Power, Sichuan Guangan Power, Sichuan Huadian Luding Hydropower, Sichuan Luzhou Chuannan Power, Huadian Inner Mongolia Kailu Wind Power, Hangzhou Huadian Banshan Power, Hebei Huadian Shijiazhuang Thermal Power, Hebei Huarui Energy Group Corporation, Huadian Luohe Power, and China Huadian Group New Energy Development Company Limited.

Huadian Power International is governed by a Board of Directors, with Yun Gongmin serves as the current chairman. Born in 1950 and graduated from the elite Tsinghua University, Yun has over 30 years of experience in public administration and industry management, who is also the general manager of China Huadian Corporation. Other board members include: Chen Feihu (vice chairman), Meng Fanli, Chen Jianhua, Wang Yingli, Chen Bin, Zhang Tonglin, and Chu Yu (executive directors); and the independent non-executive directors are Wang Yuesheng, Hao Shuchen, Ning Jiming, and Yang Jinguan. In addition, there is a Board of Supervisors that includes Li Xiaopeng, Peng Xingyu, and Zheng Feixue. Among the senior management, Chen Jianhua is the current general manager, with Xie Yun as chief engineer.

Development Strategies

Huadian Power International defines its mission to provide the safe, clean, reliable, and low-cost electricity for the society, and to pursue the harmonious unification of the shareholders' value, the society responsibility, and the staff interest. Its operating model is to develop, construct, acquire, manage, and operate the large-scale power plants in way of controlling or occupying completely in China, and the generated electricity will be supplied to customers through the power grids in various cities and regions.

Among the chief development strategies of the company is the regional development strategy, through which Huadian seeks to strengthen its businesses in Shandong Province with a view of expanding to other regions in China and international markets, appropriately centralized its operations geographically, and integrate its short-term development with its long-term development. Furthermore, Huadian has begun to pursue an industry-development strategy by focusing on the development of thermal power-generating units with large capacity, efficiency, and environment conservation in nature, expanding the business of heat and electricity co-generation and hydro power projects appropriately, and acquiring new source of energy and investing in high-tech new energy power projects. In addition, Huadian has formulated its development implementation strategy to carry out acquisition as well as construction of new plants with emphasis on economic benefits and scale.

Specifically, the company seeks to devote itself to its main electricity generation and other relevant industries. With electricity generation as its core, Huadian's priority is to develop large capacity, high-efficient, environmental-friendly power operations, while properly developing upper reaches and downstream sectors that are closely related with electricity industry. The company believes the best way to beat the mounting competitions is by increasing and developing its core business while reducing of cost of its operation and taking a lead in technologies. Although the company suffered an operational loss in 2008 due to high fuel cost, government price control, and the global economic recession, the company still plans to pursue its new development and acquisition strategies swiftly. By doing so, Huadian hopes to reach a large operational scale and build up a first-class modern company in the coming years.

Wenxian Zhang

References

China Huadian Corporation (2008). Brief introduction of China Huadian. http://eng.chd.com.cn/channel.do?cmd= show&id=475. Retrieved on 5 August 2009.

Huadian Power International Corporation Limited (2009). Company Profile. http://www.hdpi.com.cn/est/TZ/GSGK/ about.aspx. Retrieved on 5 August 2009.

Huadian Power International Corporation Limited (2009). 2008 Annual report. http://www.hdpi.com.cn/est/WebPad_ client/Upload/20094993742.pdf. Retrieved on 5 August 2009.

Reuters (2009). Huadian Power International Corporation Limited http://www.reuters.com/finance/stocks/overview? symbol=600027.SS. Retrieved on 5 August 2009.

HUANENG POWER INTERNATIONAL

Corporate Address and Contact Information

Huaneng Power International, Inc.
West Wing, Building C

Tianyin Mansion
2C South Fuxingmen Avenue
Xicheng District, Beijing 100031
People's Republic of China
Phone: (86)10-6649-1999/1114
Fax: (86)10-6649-1888
http://www.hpi.com.cn/

Huaneng Power International, Inc. (华能国际电力控股有限公司), commonly known as Huaneng (HPI), and its subsidiaries develop, construct, operate, and manage large thermal power plants throughout China. An established player in the fast-growing Chinese energy segment, Huaneng is administered by the State Council of the People's Republic of China, and is one of the five largest power producers in China. Headquartered in Beijing, China, Huaneng employs about 22,900 people. During 2008, the company together with its subsidiaries generated approximately 184.6 billion kWh.

Historical Development

Established in June 1994, Huaneng completed a global initial public offering in October of the same year with the issuance of 1.25 billion foreign shares. Such shares, represented by 31.25 million American Depository Receipts (ADR), became listed on the New York Stock Exchange (Ticker symbol: HNP). In January 1998, the company became listed on the Hong Kong Stock Exchange (Stock code: 0902), raising US$140 million. The offering was named the "Best Straight Equity Offering" of the year by *Finance Asia*. In November 2001, Huaneng successfully issued 350 million A-shares on the Shanghai Stock Exchange (600011). Currently, the company has approximately 12.06 billion total shares outstanding. HPI's parent company, Huaneng International Power Development Corporation (HIPDC), was established in 1985. HIPDC has a 42% economic interest in Huaneng Power but controls 70% of voting rights. Any joint ventures between HIPDC and investment companies are controlled by local governments with HIPDC power plants. Since HIPDC is a state-owned enterprise, all executive officers are appointed by the Chinese central government.

HPI provides electricity supply to customers through grid operators where the power plants are located. It currently owns 17 operating power plants and has controlling interests in 13 operating power plants and minority interests in five operating power companies. Such power plants are located in 12 of China's provinces, including Liaoning, Hebei, Shanxi, Shandong, Henan, Fujian, Jiangsu, Zhejiang, Guangdong, Jiangxi, Gansu, Hunan, and two municipalities, including Shanghai and Chongqing. The group also has a wholly owned power generation company in Singapore. Its electricity generation business covers the Northeast China Grid, the North China Grid, the Northwest China Grid, the East China Grid, the Central China, and the South China Grid.

Measured by capacity, Huaneng is the largest of China's five independent power producers, or IPPs. The others are Datang International Power Generation (HK: 0991), Huadian Power International (HK: 1071), China Resources Power Holdings (HK: 0836), and China Power International Development (HK: 2380).

Corporate Structure, Products, and Services

Huaneng's vision and mission are based on the principles of market, production safety, operating efficiency, competitiveness, and shareholders' interest. With development as the main theme, the company aims to become a world-class independent power producer with stable and long-term growth prospects, solid foundations, and first-rate management.

Huaneng is governed by the Board of Directors, which consists of ten executive directors and five independent directors, with Cao Peixi as chair, who also serves as chairman of HIPDC and CEO of Huaneng Group. Born in 1955 and a member of the Chinese Communist Party, Cao is a senior engineer with a degree in electronic engineering from Shandong University, and had worked as deputy director of Qingdao Power Plant and vice president of Shandong Power Group. In addition, there is a six-member Board of Supervisors with Guo Junming as chair, and four committees focusing on strategy, audit, nomination, remuneration, and evaluation. HPI's current CEO is Liu Guoyue, with Zhou Hui as CFO and Zhao Ping as chief engineer.

Huaneng Power International engages in the investment, planting, operation, and management of power plants, with a special focus on the development, construction, and operation of coal-fired power plants. Its principal activity includes generating and selling electric power, with a total generation capacity of more than 33,000 MW on an equity basis. The group provides electricity supply to customers through grid operators where the operating plants are located.

Utilizing modern technology and equipment, and using international as well as domestic capital, Huaneng mainly engages in the development, construction, and operation of large power plants. Among its achievements, the company introduced China's first 600-MW supercritical generating unit. Huaneng Dalian Power Plant is the first power plant in China to receive the title of "First-Rate Thermal Power Plant". Huaneng Yuhuan Power Plant has the first operational ultra-supercritical coal-fired unit in China with 1000 MW of capacity. In addition, the full labor productivity of the company ranks among the best in domestic power industry. In 2000, the company was awarded the title of "First-Rate Power Company in China" by State Power Corporation. Riding the economic wave of the country and through persistent enterprising and steady operation, Huaneng's operating scale continued to rise and profit continued to grow, and its competitiveness became ever more strong over the years. As of 31 December 2008, HPI has a total asset of US$24.276 billion. The company has a growth margin of 19.6, and its five-year growth rate in sales is 23.6%, as compared with 3.63% of industry average.

Challenges and Growth Strategies

Known for its significant presence in China with strong power generation assets, HPI has seen a steady increase in its revenues until recently. Although the year 2007 showed an increase in revenues by 12.3%, the revenues declined in 2008 due to slow economy, sluggish growth in its electricity volume, and higher coal and fuel costs. Analysts predict modest growth for HPI in the coming years. Among the several strategies proposed, HPI's economies of scale for centralized coal procurement for the company are instrumental in reducing coal procurement costs, transportation costs, and storage loss. It also aims to promote coal blending and firing optimization to off-set the price increase, further reduce the oil consumption of certain power plants through enhancing the operating efficiency, and reduce unit coal consumption through optimizing the operational mode of the generating units.

Huaneng's planned capital expenditures for 2008–2010 exceeded CNY 10 billion. Historically, robust economic expansion and an aggressive acquisition strategy have fueled rapid growth at HPI, which also resulted in new development and expansion of existing plants, as the company had made a substantial number of acquisitions since its inception. Recently, Huaneng has announced the completion of the receipt of 100% equity interest in SinoSing Power from the China Huaneng Group. In addition, the company received the approval for equity interests in Huaneng Nanjing Jinling Power. The National Development and Reform Commission has also approved the project of one 1,000-MW domestic ultra-supercritical coal-fired generating unit at Huaneng Jinling Power Plant. HPI's aggressive acquisition strategy combined with its relationship with Chinese government no doubt provides protection from stiff competition. However, this protection also comes with a heavy cost. The State Regulatory Commission of China retains control over setting the electricity tariffs and has never reduced its prices after increasing them. Hence cost increases may be difficult to pass on to consumers. While the growing Chinese electricity market and its strategic market, expansion initiatives have showcased its presence more stronger than before, HPI continues to face challenges in the areas of strict government regulations, slower power industry reforms, and lack of government tax incentives.

Huaneng's success can be attributed to use of advanced equipment, efficient generating units, and steadily operating power plants coupled with high-quality employee base and experienced management team, standardized corporate governance structure, and scientific decision-making mechanism, with strategically located power generating assets and bright market prospect. In addition, HPI's sound creditworthiness both domestically and internationally with rich capital market operating experience has no doubt made HPI China's largest producer of thermal power. Among its recognitions, *Fortune Magazine* in 2006 ranked HPI 24 among Top 100 Listed Enterprises in China; *South China Morning Post* named HPI as one of the Top 50 State-Owned Enterprises; and *Finance Asia* named HPI the ninth Best Managed Company and fifth in Commitment to Strong Dividend Payments.

Looking into the future, Huaneng will continue to seek further development based on the principle of placing equal emphasis on acquisition and development, expansion and green-field, coal-fired and alternative energy sources, domestic and internal capital, and resources. In the mean time, the company is committed to enhance management control and cost control, raise efficiency, so as to continuously increase shareholder's equity, and maintain long-term and steady development. Specifically, Huaneng seeks to establish a sound management structure with reference to the requirements of a modern enterprise; to enhance the company's operating efficiency by actively expanding markets, strengthening production safety, as well as focusing on environmental protection and cost controls; to speed up development by seizing opportunities and to improve capital management; to maintain the company's leading positions in technological facilities, workforce productivity, and management quality by developing technology innovation; and to develop the company into a major enterprise with "solid-foundations, first-rate management" comparable with the world's best independent power producers.

Kevin B. Lowe and Wenxian Zhang

References

Huaneng Power International, Inc. (2009). Annual Report. http://www.hpi.com.cn/investor/announcement/announcement_detal.jsp?id=1276. Retrieved on 29 June 2009.

Huaneng Power International, Inc. (2009). Company Profile. http://www.hpi.com.cn. Retrieved on 29 June 2009.

Huaneng Power International, Inc. (2009). Financial Reports. http://www.hpi.com.cn/management/financial/index.jsp. Retrieved on 29 June 2009.

Huaneng Power International, Inc. (2009). Press Release. http://www.hpi.com.cn/investor/pressrelease/index.jsp. Retrieved on 29 June 2009.

Morningstar (2009). Huaneng Power International, Inc. http://quote.morningstar.com/Quote/Quote.aspx?ticker=HNP. Retrieved on 29 June 2009.

HUAWEI TECHNOLOGIES

Corporate Address and Contact Information

Huawei Technologies Co. Ltd.
Bantian, Longgang District
Shenzhen 518129
People's Republic of China
Phone: (86)755-2878-0808
http://www.huawei.com/

Huawei Technologies Co. Ltd. (华为技术有限公司) is one of the best examples of a successful Chinese high-technology firm with private ownership and no significant background as a state-owned firm. Founded in 1988, almost a decade after the beginnings of economic reform, Huawei continues to be located in Shenzhen. However, it is one of China's most important transnational firms with operations in more than 100 countries and derives nearly three-fourths of its revenues from abroad. Huawei operates in one of the most important and most global high-technology industries: networking telecommunications equipment. The transformation of communications — think of the Internet and mobile phones — in the past 30 years has created a dramatically new and dynamic competitive environment, from which Huawei has become one of the most important firms.

Historical Development and Corporate Leadership

The founder and current CEO of Huawei is Ren Zhengfei, and the company has been decidedly shaped by his experience and philosophy. Born in 1944, Ren Zhengfei once served as an officer in the People's Liberation Army. This and the philosophy of guerrilla war developed by Mao Zedong were important in the development of Huawei. Using a military-style form of organization, Huawei is known for its hierarchical organization, driven style and the intense dedication of its employees. Moreover, the tactic of guerrilla-warfare strategy in which the rural areas are used as a base for surrounding and taking the cities was adapted for Huawei. Like Mao, Huawei focused its initial efforts in China's rural areas, where the very strong competition from global telecommunications firms was weakest. Only later, after building this rural base, did Huawei begin operating in Chinese cities.

Though Huawei is a privately owned firm, with no background of state ownership, it has benefited greatly from the telecommunications strategy of the Chinese government. Originally, Huawei operated as a distributor of telecommunications switches. However, the Chinese government was committed to obtaining the knowledge and technology needed to permit Chinese firms to produce these devices and develop a domestic telecommunications industry. This was achieved in the mid-1980s through a series of joint ventures arranged by the government with foreign telecommunications firms, who were given access to the Chinese market in return for transferring the knowledge and technology for production, development, service, and marketing. A research institute established by the Chinese military, the government communications ministry and the state-owned equipment manufacturer was the focus of efforts to apply and develop the newly acquired knowledge to develop digital technologies. Huawei was able to attract engineers from the state-owned firm set up to manufacture digital switches and thereby benefit from the knowledge and technology transfer and R&D process. Huawei also benefited from the Chinese government efforts to shift purchase of telecommunication equipment away from imports and toward indigenous firms.

Using these advantages and leveraging the knowledge and technology, Huawei was able to make swift advances. In 1993, the company developed its own product, a digital telephone switch. Though well behind the global technology frontier, this product was very advanced for the Chinese market, especially for rural China, where transnational corporation penetration was weak and Chinese firms had considerable advantages. With government encouragement, Huawei began exporting in 1996 and quickly established its position in Africa and in Russia. Huawei has been especially successful in markets with no previous landline telecommunications systems.

Main Products, Services, and Growth Strategies

Today, Huawei offers hardware, software and services for broadband core networks, transport networks, radio access networks, data communications, and has begun selling handset devices. Huawei has been innovative in adopting a new corporate strategy: becoming a "solutions provider" instead of just a network sales company in the mid-1990s. This is an example of a local organizational innovation, based on adopting ideas from Western firms, ideas that were new to Chinese firms. Management consultants at IBM were hired and this led to changes in Huawei's product development strategy, management structure, and a new emphasis on R&D and supply chain management. IBM supplied the computer and networking systems for supply chain management and this allowed Huawei to adapt to the new global competitive environment with improved on-time delivery of products and lean inventory management. These change cascaded across Huawei's Chinese supply chain, forcing new practices by the company's suppliers. Huawei also worked to develop a system of products that could be sold together as a package, thereby raising profit margins. As a result, Huawei has mostly made the transition from a low-cost, low-quality seller of products, to a higher-quality innovator in less well-served parts of the world, to a position of aggressive pricing of quality communications systems based on an established brand and quality service. Huawei is especially competitive in Africa, where it is recognized for its products and service and for several high-profile training centers. Efforts are in process to leverage the success in Africa into the European and US markets. In fall 2008, Huawei won a Canadian contract for installation of a high-speed packet access overlay.

Huawei's success in domestic and global competition, especially in a fast-changing and dynamic industry, is impressive. This is a consequence of strong management and the extremely rapid growth in telecommunications, especially in China. Between 1998 and 2005, the Chinese telecommunication industry grew at a rate of 33% per year. From 1998 to 2008, Huawei employees grew from 800 to 83,000, and in 2008, Huawei reported sales of $23 billion, up five-fold from 2003. Profits in 2008 were $1.15 billion, up only two-fold from 2003. The company predicts sales growth of 29% for 2009. Though the greatest part of Huawei sales have recently come through exports, the large and rapid build out for a 3G wireless network in China will lead to a greater role for domestic revenues.

Huawei is very atypical for a developing nation firm, with a heavy commitment of resources to research and development; about 10% of sales are devoted to R&D and nearly 45% of its employees are working in R&D. The labor costs of R&D are much lower in China and Huawei has been able to leverage this advantage to provide customized solutions for customers. The results of R&D investment are impressive and can be seen in the large number of patents and patent applications by Huawei. In

2008, the World Intellectual Property Organization ranked Huawei as the fourth largest patent applicant in the world. These knowledge capabilities also result in an array of strategic alliances and joint ventures and in the establishment of several R&D centers abroad.

Business Challenges

Huawei has significant competition, both inside China and in global markets. ZTE, founded in 1985, is the second largest Chinese telecommunications equipment manufacturer. Huawei accounts for 23% and ZTE 15% of the Chinese telecommunications market. In second and fourth place are foreign firms, Ericsson with 22% and Nokia-Siemens with just less than 15%. Huawei and other Chinese firms such as ZTE have benefited from ready access to capital from state-owned Chinese banks to finance purchases by customers. These arrangements are not available to foreign telecommunications sellers operating in China.

Huawei Technologies is well positioned for continued exceptional growth. It is the most important firm in China's rapidly growing telecommunications market, has a very significant position and experience in many emerging markets, devotes considerable resources to successful R&D, and has made inroads into advanced markets in Europe and Canada. The combination of lower costs and good technology, along with operating as a Chinese firm in the Chinese market, gives Huawei a strong competitive position. The ability to win business in the United States faces considerable competition along with concerns over the role of the Chinese government in Huawei's operations. In 2008, Huawei was forced to abandon its effort to purchase a 16.5% ownership of the American firm 3Com, after political opposition on national security grounds. Nonetheless, Huawei is likely to become an important player in the US market because of its competitive strengths.

Thomas D. Lairson

References

Aguiar, M *et al.* (2009). The 2009 BCG 100 new global challengers. *Boston Consulting Group Report* (January), 25.

Chang, C *et al.* (2009). Huawei Technologies: A trailblazer in Africa. *Knowledge@Wharton*, 20 April. http://knowledge.wharton.upenn.edu/article.cfm?articleid=2211. Retrieved on 22 May 2009.

Chao, L (2009). China's telecom-gear makers, once laggards at home, pass foreign rivals. *Wall Street Journal*, 10 April, B. 1.

Chao, L (2009). Huawei bucks recession. *Wall Street Journal*, 22 April.

Gadiesh, O and T Vestring (2008). The consequences of China's rising global heavyweights. *MIT Sloan Management Review*, 49.3 (Spring): 10–11.

Hille, K (2009). Huawei looks to state-backed vendor financing. *Financial Times*, 22 April.

Hille, K and A Parker (2009). Upwardly mobile — Huawei. *Financial Times*, 20 March.

Mu, Q and K Lee (2005). Knowledge diffusion, market segmentation and technological catch-up: The case of the telecommunication industry in China. *Research Policy*, 34: 759–783.

Sharma, A and S Silver (2009). Huawei tries to crack U.S. market: Chinese telecom supplier wins Cox contract, is finalist for Clearwire deal. *Wall Street Journal*, 26 March, B.2.

Teagarden, M and HK Dong (2009). Learning from dragons who are learning from us: Developmental lessons from China's global companies. *Organizational Dynamics*, 38(1): 73–81.

Tucker, S (2008). Case study: Huawei of China takes stock after a frustrating year. *Financial Times*, 25 November.

HUNAN NONFERROUS METALS HOLDING GROUP

Corporate Address and Contact Information

Hunan Nonferrous Metals Holding Group Co. Ltd.
342 Laodong Road West
Changsha, Hunan Province 410015
People's Republic of China
Phone: (86)731-538-5559
Fax: (86)731-518-0558
http://www.hng.com.cn
hng@hng.com.cn

Hunan Nonferrous Metals Holding Group Co. Ltd. (湖南有色金属股份有限公司), also known as Hunan Nonferrous Group (HNG), was founded on 24 August 2004. As a large state-owned corporation under the administration of Hunan Province, People's Republic of China, HNG is one of the top 500 Chinese enterprises and one of the top 500 Chinese manufacturing enterprises with a specialty in the mining, processing, and sale of nonferrous metals. Hunan Nonferrous Metals Corporation Limited is a subsidiary of Hunan Nonferrous Metals Holding Group Co. Ltd.

China's Nonferrous Metal Industry and HNG's Main Products

The term nonferrous is used to indicate metals other than iron (steel and pig iron) and alloys (such as stainless steel) that do not contain an appreciable amount of iron. The primary Standard Industrial Code (SIC) for this industry is metal ores, not elsewhere classified. The nonferrous metal industry has experienced years of rapid growth in China. Several large corporations, in particular, have taken initiative in this rapid growth, including the Aluminum Corporation of China (in the electrolyte aluminum industry), Zijin Mining Group (within the gold market), as well as Tongling Nonferrous Metals Group Holdings Co., Jiangxi Copper Industry Co., and Yunnan Copper Industry Co. China's investment in overseas markets by its nonferrous metal producers is increasingly active, but still at an initial stage. Industry observers consider it inevitable that they will participate in global competition in the future. At the same time, growth has slowed down recently due to, among other factors, rising costs and economic slowdown.

HNG is an investment holding company that engages in the mining, processing, and sale of nonferrous metals. It produces cemented carbides, zinc, and antimony in the People's Republic of China, as well as lead, silver, indium, tantalum, and niobium. HNG also manufactures hard alloys and refractory metal compounds; imports and exports nonferrous metals, trades hard alloys, tungsten, and molybdenum products; and manufactures chemical products. The company is based in Changsha, capitol city of Hunan Province.

HNG enjoys the resource advantages of nonferrous metals. The company owns the largest tungsten reserve globally, which accounts for 20% of the world deposit, mainly scattered in Shizhuyuan Mine (reputed as "Nonferrous Metals Museum of the World") and the century-old Yaogangxian Mine (known as "the fourth largest scheelite mine in the world"). In addition, HNG has over 300,000 tons in bismuth reserve, also the largest in the world, and its annual production of bismuth concentrates is 1,000 tons. Moreover, HNG owns rich antimony reserve, which is distributed at the 100-year-long Hsikwangshan Mine (known as "Antimony Capital of the World"). HNG's annual production in antimony concentrates is nearly 20,000 tons.

HNG is the largest integrated producer of nonferrous metals (excluding aluminum) in China in terms of gross production. The company has the mining rights of major minerals such as lead, zinc, tungsten, antimony, bismuth, and fluorite in Hunan Province. It integrates surveying, mining, dressing, smelting, research and development, processing, and value-added processing; combines technology, process, and trade; and is a well-known product and service provider in China for many types of nonferrous metals and their value-added processing products.

Corporate Structure and Leadership

Currently, HNG has 10 subsidiaries. Through the successful IPO of its holding subsidiary — Hunan Nonferrous Metals Co. Ltd. (HNC) — on the Hong Kong Stock Exchange, in March 2006, HNG entered the international capital market. HNC was founded through a reorganization of Zhuzhou Smelter Group Co. Ltd. (Zhuye Group), Zhuzhou Cemented Carbides Group Co. Ltd. (Zhuying Group), Hsikwangshan Twinkling Star Antimony Co. Ltd., Hunan Shizhuyuan Nonferrous Metals Co. Ltd., and Huangshaping Branch of HNC. In a strategic attempt to consolidate the Chinese nonferrous industry, HNC successfully acquired China Tungsten and High Tech Materials Company and controlled Zigong Cemented Carbides Co. in 2006.

As an investment holding company, HNG is governed by a Board of Directors. The top leaders of the corporation include: He Renchun, chairman of HNG, who also serves as the head secretary of Leading Party Group; Cao Xiuyun, director and general manager, who is also vice chairman of HNC; and Zeng Shaoxiong, director and executive deputy general manager of HNG.

Business Strategies

HNG defines its corporate mission as to generate and boost the value of nonferrous metals through sustainable development. HNG's core values include trustworthiness, openness to the development of a global industry, and cooperation as a base of win-win outcomes. By focusing on innovation and harmonious balance between human and nature, HNG is always searching for business opportunities in forward-looking development and industrial diversifications, a strategy that if fully implemented, will likely to sharpen its international competitive edge and forge its ambitious drive for global brand development in coming years.

The short-term goal of HNG is restructuring, integrating, and optimally distributing the various nonferrous industrial resources, operating according to the standards of modem enterprise system, and developing the company into a multinational corporation with outstanding core operation, comprehensive strength in Hunan and China and relatively strong competitive edge within the nonferrous industry. By providing high-quality products and services for the society, the company seeks to make contributions to the national economic development and Hunan's industrialization process.

From a long-term perspective, HNG strives to develop into a top 500 enterprises in the world, and one of the nonferrous metal multinationals with the strongest international competitive advantage in China by the year 2020. It targets to own abundant nonferrous metal reserves, the largest lead zinc smelting and deep processing production enterprise, and the largest cemented carbides-manufacturing enterprise in China. In addition, the company aims to become the strongest and internationally recognized cemented carbides-cutting tools products and service provider in China, the most influential and comprehensive antimony corporation in the world, and one of the internationally advanced mining research and production bases among the nonferrous industry.

Competing on the global landscape, HNG has some unique advantages. Its reserves in antimony, lead, zinc, and fluorite are abundant; its bismuth reserve ranks the first in the world, while tungsten also tops the international reserve. With over 5,000 technical personnel who have generated over 260 national patents, and another 100 plus technology-related patents under examination, the company holds a leading position in technology, equipment, and R&D capability in China. Since HNG already owns a series of top and well-known brands in China that include *Torch*, *Diamond*, *Great Wall*, *Hsikwangshan*, *XiangLv*, and *Shizhuyuan*, its key growth strategy is to vertically integrate industrial chain running from upstream exploration, mining, dressing, to the midstream smelting and to the downstream refining and value-added processing.

Maria Nathan and Hao Jiao

References

China's Non-ferrous Metal Industry Report (2008). *ReportLinker.* http://www.reportlinker.com/p095618/China-Non-Ferrous-Metal-Industry-Report-2008.html. Retrieved on 21 March 2009.

Hunan Nonferrous Metals Holding Group Co. (2008). Brief introduction to the enterprise. http://www.hng.com.cn/English/index.asp. Retrieved on 21 March 2009.

HUNAN VALIN STEEL

Corporate Address and Contact Information

Hunan Valin Steel Co. Ltd.
20th Floor, Hualing Building
269 Furong Zhong Road
Changsha, Hunan Province 410011
People's Republic of China
Phone: (86)731-8256-5961
Fax: (86)731-8224-5196
http://www.valin.cn, http://www.chinavalin.com

Hunan Valin Steel Co. Ltd. (湖南华菱钢铁股份有限公司) is located in Changsha, capital city of Hunan Province in south-central China with recorded history of 3,000 years. The company primarily engages in smelting, manufacture, and sale of iron, steel, as well as nonferrous metal products, and distributes its products in domestic and overseas markets. As of 31 December 2008, the company had 12 subsidiaries, which involved in smelting of steel and nonferrous metal products, trading of relevant equipment, as well as financing services.

Historical Development

Hunan Valin Steel Co. Ltd., formerly known as Hunan Valin Steel Tube & Wire Co. Ltd., was formed in 1999 as a way to save from bankruptcy three of Hunan's key steel enterprises: Xiangtan Iron & Steel Group Co. Ltd., Lianyuan Iron & Steel Group, and Hengyang Steel Group.

In 2005, Hunan Valin Steel Co. Ltd. sold about one-third ownership to ArcelorMittal. This was a very important deal, as ArcelorMittal is the largest producer of steel in Europe, North and South Americas, and Africa, and the second largest steel producer in the Commonwealth of Independent States (CIS) region that includes countries of former Soviet Republics, and has a growing presence in Asia, particularly in China. Through its partner ArcelorMittal, Hunan Valin Steel Co. Ltd. now has access to worldwide markets and a great deal of steel-making expertise.

In early 2008, Hunan Valin Steel Co. Ltd. acquired the assets of Chinese state-owned Hunan Hualing Iron & Steel Group Co. Ltd., an iron and steel products manufacturer and wholesaler. The assets consisted of 12.27% stake in Hunan Hualing Xiangtan Iron & Steel Co. Ltd., 6.23% stake in Hunan Hualing Lianyuan Iron & Steel Co. Ltd., and 10.55% stake in Hunan Hualing Liangang Thin Board Co. Ltd. To raise capital in 2009, Hunan Valin Steel Co. Ltd. plans to sell up to RMB 3 billion in new shares to its partner firm, ArcelorMittal and its parent (holding) company, Hunan Valin Iron & Steel Group. Hunan Valin Steel Co. Ltd. announced in January 2009 that it would take full ownership of and upgrade the technology at subsidiaries Xiangtan Steel and Lianyuan Steel through a share deal.

Main Products, Corporate Structure, and Leadership

Hunan Valin Steel Co. Ltd. is a China-based company primarily engaged in the smelting, manufacture, and sale of iron and steel products, as well as nonferrous metal products. The company produces wide- and heavy-steel plates, hot- and cold-rolled steel plates, galvanized plates, steel wires, rods, pipes, strips, and slabs; copper plate pipes and inner-twisted pipes, and aluminum products. Its markets are primarily in the construction sector, with product distributions mostly to southern China and limited exports to the United States, South Korea, and Europe. Other steel demand at Hunan Valin Steel Co. Ltd. comes from durable goods manufacturers such as automobiles, machinery providers, container fabricators, and construction firms. The company has annual capacity of 10.8 million tons of steel products, and yearly output is approximately 9 million tons.

As a public company, Hunan Valin Steel Co. Ltd. is listed on the Shenzhen Stock Exchange (000932). Majority shareholders are the People's Republic of China, Hunan Valin Group, and ArcelorMittal. Officers of the firm are: Li Xiaowei (chairman), Cao Huiquan (president, CEO and director), Tan Jiujun (CFO, deputy general manager, and director), Jean-Paul Georges Schuler (chief operating officer and director), and Wang Jun (deputy general manager, secretary, and director).

Business Strategies and Development Plans

The profitability of firms in the steelmaking industry depends on efficient operations. Hunan Valin Steel Co. Ltd. seems to be strongly focused upon improving the efficiency and cost effectiveness of its operations, judging by the recent investments and strategic joint ventures it has made. By investing in iron ore-mining companies, Hunan Valin Steel Co. Ltd. reduces its weakness of limited iron ore supplies. The joint ventures with controlling shareholders, Hunan Valin Group and ArcelorMittal also allow the firm to draw upon the technology, efficiency, and supply chains of these industry leaders, further solidifying, Hunan Valin Group's success as one of the top 10 steel producers in China.

Hunan Valin Steel Co. Ltd. enjoys brand name recognition. Thus, the company gives high priority to promotion of its brand. It also enjoys first-rate production equipment and facilities. To make the most of these tangible and intangible assets, the firm has linked its managers' annual salaries to the group's economic returns. This should provide great incentive for management to increase work efficiency and keep costs down.

Looking forward, Hunan Valin Steel Co. Ltd. hopes to build on its 2008 sales of $5.36 billion and utilize its 32,084 employees productively and efficiently. To continue to grow, the firm needs cash and secure sources of iron ore. The recent issue of shares to the Hunan Valin Group and ArcelorMittal will help with cash resources. The company will also obtain partial ownership Xiangtan Steel and 5.01% stake in Lianyuan Steel to Valin Steel to increase their market share.

To solidify long-term ore availability, Hunan Valin Steel Co. Ltd. has been pursuing a series of investments in overseas resource companies that, along with joint ventures and partnerships with firms in Australia and China, may lead to competitive advantages. The firm is also getting help from its parent, Hunan Valin Iron & Steel Group, with deals for iron ore with Australian suppliers Fortescue Metals Group Ltd. and Golden West. These raw material deals will help develop iron ore mines to assure a steady supply at competitive prices.

Future Challenges

Hunan Valin Steel faces a difficult future, as the worldwide recession is causing great difficulties within the Chinese steel industry: demand has fallen and prices have been cut to hold market share. Of 26 steel mills in the PRC, 12 predict 2009 profit declines and 14 expect losses. Hunan Valin Steel Co. Ltd. predicts over RMB 100 million losses in 2009. Steel prices fell 40 percent and then recovered 15 percent and are starting to stabilize. As with all of the large steel companies in the PRC, Hunan Valin Steel Co. Ltd. is expected to grow through mergers and acquisitions at least through 2010. This will be difficult with foreign exchange rate fluctuations, increased costs for raw materials, and falling product prices. The firm also faces the realities of the international marketplace where the United States and Europe are taking measures to stabilize their own steel producers by setting increased import duties and requirements for use of in-country steel suppliers.

James P. Gilbert

References

Alon, I and JR McIntyre (eds.) (2008). *Globalization of Chinese Enterprises*. New York: Palgrave Macmillan.

Chen, J (2009). China plans to create three steel giants. *New York Times*, 21 February. LexisNexis Academic, 26 January 2009.

Chiu, N and C Chan (2009). China Life warns of 50 percent profit fall amid share market slide. *South China Morning Post*, 22 January, Business, p. 1. Lexus-Nexus Academic, 3 March 2009.

De Kretser, A (2009). China tries to rein in steel overcapacity. *The Australian Financial Review*, 2 March. LexisNexis Academic, 3 March 2009.

Holland, T (2009). Steelmakers' outlook not as strong as investors believe. *South China Morning Post*, 30 January, Business, p. 8. Lexus-Nexus Academic, 1 February 2009.

Hunan Valin Steel Tube & Wire acquires Hunan Hualing Iron-assests privatized by People's Republic of China (30 April 2008). *Thomson Financial Mergers & Acquisitions*. www.alacrastore.com/storecontent/Thomson_M&A/Hunan_Valin_Steel_Tube_Wire_acquires_Hunan_Hualing_Iron_Asts_privatized_by_Peoples_Republic_of_China-1943130040. Retrieved on 14 August 2009.

Li, Sun (2003). Li Xiaowei's "Third Mode" SOE management. *China Today* (August). www.chinatoday.com.cn/English/e2003/e20038/8p47.htm. Retrieved on 21 August 2009.

Lu, H (2009). Valin Steel to wholly own, upgrade subsidiaries via share issue. *Metal Bulletin*, 6 January. LexisNexis Academic, 12 January 2009.

Steel mills may suffer huge loss in H1 — Report (23 July 2009). *China Securities Journal*. http://steelmillsoftheworld.com/news/newsdisplay_moreover.asp?slno=15695. Retrieved on 12 August 2009.

INDUSTRIAL AND COMMERCIAL BANK OF CHINA

Corporate Address and Contact Information

Industrial and Commercial Bank of China Ltd.
55 Fuxingmennei Street
Xicheng District
Beijing 100140
People's Republic of China
Phone: (86)10-6610-6114
www.icbc.com.cn

Industrial and Commercial Bank of China (ICBC中国工商银行股份有限公司), founded on 1 January 1984, is the largest and most internationally influential commercial bank among its Chinese counterparts. Either in terms of net profits or aggregate market value, ICBC is ranked top of the other global financial enterprises, and seventh among 1,000 major international banks from the tier-1 capital size. ICBC, like the other Chinese state-owned banks, was once well known for its huge non-performing loans and poor operating results. With China's deepening economic reform, the bank has done remarkably in the improvement of assets quality and business efficiency, particularly after the restructuring and listing in the stock exchange market. ICBC holds leading positions in many of its business sectors and in spite of the global financial crisis, the bank still delivered a brilliant performance. In 2008, ICBC's profit after tax was RMB 111.2 billion (USD 16.35 billion), 35.2% up from the previous year, the sixth consecutive year of high growth since 2003, which makes ICBC one of the world's fastest growing international banks.

Historical Development

ICBC has experienced three stages in its corporate development. The bank traced its history back to 25 years ago when China was opening its door to the outside world. At that time, Deng Xiaoping expressed in plain language his expectation to the Chinese banking industry, run the banks as real ones. The goal of the reform was to transfer a bank from the "nation's financial cashier" to a profit-oriented corporation with modern corporate structure governed by the market rules.

Before the banking reform, the People's Bank of China used to be the most exclusive and comprehensive financial institute in the country. Therefore, during the first stage of the financial institutional reform a two-level banking system was to be built. In September 1983, the Chinese State Council made a decision that People's Bank of China should be responsible for the duties of a Central Bank, and on 1 January 1984, ICBC was set up to carry out the business of credits for industrial and commercial businesses, as well as savings originally done by People's Bank of China. Since then the old and highly integrated financial system was broken. With the establishment of three other state-owned banks, Agricultural Bank of China, Construction Bank of China, and Bank of China, marked the official establishment of the new, two-level financial system in China. Through strong government supports and because of the swift development of the Chinese economy, ICBC has built a huge service network covering major cities around China while serving mainly for urban corporate and individual customers, and its product ranges has been greatly extended. As a result, ICBC held dominant positions in the basic banking sectors such as deposits, loans, and remittance among its counterparts. However, the various reformative measures from the initial stage only contributed to the awareness of antonymous management.

ICBC still acted like a policy bank, as it was a primary channel for the state's macro-economic regulations, mainly due to the underdeveloped financial market at that time. As a result, a huge amount of non-performing loans were piled up.

The second stage of development began in 1993. In December of that year, the third session of the 14th Congress of the Chinese Communist Party proposed the establishment of the socialist market economy system. In July 1995, the law of the Chinese Commercial Banks was issued, which signified the beginning of transformation of ICBC and other state-owned banks into commercial ones. A series of reformative measures on corporate governance, asset management, business efficiency, internal control, and cost reduction were carried out. However, the reform of state-owed enterprises and the Asian financial crisis in 1997 greatly increased the non-performing assets of those banks. Although the government made efforts to supplement capitals and strip off bad assets, ICBC was still struggle to survive. At the end of 2003, the bank showed negative in its capital adequacy rate.

The year 2005 marked the beginning of the third stage of the bank's reform. In April, the central government approved the proposed shareholding reform of ICBC. In order to have a clear ownership, a new Central Huijin Investment Corporation was established to act as a contributive representative of the state's capital; and then Huijin injected RMB 15 billion (USD 2.2 billion) to ICBC, which helped improve the financial status of the bank. On 28 October 2005, ICBC was restructured from a solely state-owned bank to a joint-stock company and officially changed its name to the Industrial and Commercial Bank of China Ltd. On 27 October 2006, it was listed simultaneously on the Shanghai and Hong Kong Stock Exchanges. Since then ICBC has been on a fast track of development. By the end of September 2008, the equity structure of ICBC is 70.6% by the state-owned shares, 22.2% by the National Social Security fund as well as public, and 7.2% by overseas strategic investors.

ICBC also aims to grow globally. On 31 December 2003, ICBC took over Fortis Bank Asia HK (100%), and a year later the Chinese Mercantile Bank (100%) was acquired. Other recent major purchases include: Bank Halim of Indonesia (90%) on 8 December 2006; Seng Heng Bank of Macau (79.93%) on 29 August 2007; Standard Bank of South Africa (20%) on 25 October 2007; and JEC Investment Co. of Hong Kong (40%) on 13 November 2007. ICBC has been cooperating closely with Goldman Sachs Group, American Express, and Allianz Group, in corporate governance, risk management, non-performing loans management, staff training and financial transactions, bankcards, and other business areas.

By the end of the first quarter in 2009, ICBC continues to show a decline of the non-performing loans to 1.97%, a further drop of 0.32% than before. During the same period, its provision coverage rate keeps on rising 1.87% up to 132.02%, which demonstrates a stronger capability to hedge risks.

Corporate Structure and Services

ICBC follows the modern corporate governance structure with the shareholders meeting at the top, under which are the Board of Directors and Board of Supervisors. Committees such as auditing, risk management, strategy, and nomination remuneration work with Board of Directors to provide professional consulting to the bank. In order to closely monitor and control over the bank's operations, Internal Audit Bureau was established along with more committees such as financial checkup, branch organization management, information technology approval, asset and liability management, risk management, business creation, and credit approval. Under senior management, marketing product departments, risk management departments, integration management departments, and support and assurance departments take responsibility for their own business, each of which has smaller departments under it such as corporate business, international business, e-banking, credit management, credit approval, finance and accounting, management information, operation management, retiree management, etc. Up to the end of 2008, the bank include 5 direct branches, 30 Tier-1 branches, 27 business centers of branches, 385 Tier-2 branches, 3,055 Tier-1 sub branches, and 12,952 local business networks. Furthermore, the bank has two domestic holding subsidiaries, namely ICBC Credit Suisse Asset Management Co. Ltd., and ICBC Financial Leasing Co. Ltd. ICBC has expanded its overseas network to 15 countries and regions around the world, totaling 134 branches and subsidiaries. In addition, ICBC has corresponding relationship with 1,358 banks in 122 countries and regions.

As the biggest commercial bank in China, ICBC has now more than 380,000 staff, providing approximately 3,000 financial products and services for about 190 million individual customers and 3.10 million corporate customers. Apart from the basic business sectors, it is now placing itself in advantageous positions in many other newly developed areas of services.

ICBC offers a great variety of financial products for its corporate customers, 13 categories in all, including corporate deposit, financing lease, global services, financial products, investment banking, institutional banking, small and medium enterprises services, loan financing, bill business, clearing and settlement service, corporate e-banking, assets custody business, and corporate annuity service.

For personal finances, ICBC develops itself to be "the First Retail Bank" in China. ICBC divides its personal banking services into five categories, investment and financing, personal loan, personal e-banking business, convenient banking, and deposit. By the end of the first quarter of 2009, ICBC's balance of deposits has hit RMB 9.1 trillion (USD 1.34 trillion), an increase of nearly RMB 900 billion (USD 132.35billion) from the end of last year to become the bank with the largest customer deposits in the world.

ICBC is the largest credit card issuing bank with the most complete card categories in China. ICBC's bank cards in issue exceeded 238 million with amount of consumption close to RMB 800 billion (USD 117.64 billion) by the end of 2008, among which are over 39 million credit cards with amount of consumption surpassing RMB 250 billion (USD 36.76 billion), reinforcing the bank's market leading position.

After a decade of development, ICBC has grown to be the top asset custody bank in China with its custody amount to RMB 1,000 billion (USD 147 billion). In addition, ICBC is the largest e-banking in China with its trading volume reaching RMB 129,000 billion (USD 18,971 billion), accounting for 43% of its total trading volume. Furthermore, ICBC holds a leading position in financing, annuity, investment banking, and cash management, as its business covers comprehensive areas such as currency, capitals, and insurance.

Since October 2005, Mr. Jiang Jianqing has served as ICBC's chairman and executive director, who received a master's degree in engineering and a doctorate degree in management from Shanghai Jiaotong University. The senior management team includes: Yang Kaisheng (president) and Zhang Furong, Niu Ximing, Wang Lili, Li Xiaopeng, and Yi Huiman (vice presidents).

Growth Strategies

ICBC aims to consolidate its market leadership in China, and in the meantime seeks to forge it into a world-class financial institution, that is, to build ICBC into a most profitable, most preeminent, and most respected commercial bank. In order to achieve this goal, ICBC strives to: develop high-growth and non-credit business to diversify the revenue structure and asset mix; extend moderately the credit business and improve the credit portfolio; promote the customer mix and profitability by further customer segmentation, targeted marketing, and quality customer service; strategically expand the traditional branch network and e-banking service to further marketing capabilities; continue to upgrade the risk management and internal control capabilities; leverage its partnerships with strategic investors; and finally improve employees' performance through incentive schemes and human resources development.

To achieve what the bank envisions, ICBC believes that its scale economy would bring about extraordinary benefits. Up to the end of 2008, ICBC was the first in total assets (USD 1,435 billion), first in total loans (USD 672.4 billion), and first in total deposits (USD 1,209.3 billion). The scale economy is also shown in its extensive distribution network with 16,386 physical outlets, 7,085 self-service banks, 28,600 ATMs and huge e-banking transaction volume, and strong and quality customer base with 3.10 million corporate customers, 190 million personal customers, 4.55 million elite club accounts, 1.44 million corporate Internet banking customers, and 56.72 million personal Internet banking customers. The bank will surely gain early starter's advantages from its strategic transition.

Xiaorong Zhu

References

Industrial and Commercial Bank of China Limited (2009). Company Profile. http://www.icbc.com.cn/ICBC/About%20Us/Brief%20Introduction/. Retrieved on 30 April 2009.

姜，建清 (2009). 风雨砥砺 铸就辉煌. *中国金融家* 1, 22–28 [Jiang, J. Successes from Struggles and Hardships. *Chinese Financier*].

王，松奇 (2008). *中国商业银行竞争力报告*. 北京: 社会科学文献出版社 [Wang, S. *Annual Report on Competitiveness of China's Commercial Banks (2007)*. Beijing: Social Sciences Academic Press].

谢，平 (2009). 国有商业银行改革三部曲: 从经营到产权. *金融与保险* 3, 16–18 [Xie, P. A reform trilogy for the state-owned commercial banks: From operation to ownership. *Finance and Insurance*].

中国建设银行研究部课题组 (2008). *中国商业银行发展报告*. 北京: 中国金融出版社 [Project Group of Research Department from Construction Bank of China, *China Commercial Bank Development Report*. Beijing: China Financial Press House].

INDUSTRIAL BANK

Corporate Address and Contact Information

Industrial Bank Joint-Stock Corporation Limited
No. 154 Hudong Road
Fuzhou 350003
People's Republic of China
Phone: (86)591-8783-9338
Fax: (86)591-8784-1932
http://www.cib.com.cn/netbank/en/index.html

Headquartered in Fuzhou City, Fujian Province, the former Fujian Industrial Bank (福建兴业银行) was established on 26 August 1988 as one of the first batch of joint-stock commercial banks approved by the State Council and the People's Bank of China. In March 2003, after undergoing a series of restructurings, it was renamed to Industrial Bank Joint-Stock Corporation Limited (兴业银行股份有限公司), or more commonly the Industrial Bank Co. (IBC). On 5 February 2007, Industrial Bank was listed on Shanghai Stock Exchange (601166) with total registered capital amount RMB 5 billion.

Main Products and Services

As a commercial bank in China, IBC provides a wide range of personal, corporate, and institutional products and services. Its main business activities include deposit accounts, provision of loans, local and international payments and settlements, bills acceptance and discounting, underwriting, purchase and sales of government bonds and financial bonds, inter-bank placements and borrowings, settlement and sales of foreign currencies, and other banking activities approved by the China Banking Regulatory Commission (CBRC).

Currently, IBC has almost 20,000 employees working in approximately 40 branches and 400 sub-branches in 40 cities throughout China. A total of 140,834 shareholders hold five billion shares on issue with a market capitalization of RMB 124.8 billion (USD 18.3 billion) as of May 2009. Major shareholders are Fujian Provincial Department of Finance (20.4%) and Hang Seng Bank Limited (12.78%). IBC total assets at the end of 2008 were RMB 1.02 trillion (USD 149.5 billion), up 19.9% from the previous year. In 2007, IBC was placed 260th globally in terms of tier-1 capital by *The Banker* magazine.

Corporate Governance

Mr. Gao Jianping, Chairman since June 2004, presides over a board comprising 13 directors, five of whom are independent. In line with the Chinese government's policy measures, great improvement has been made in the bank's corporate governance in recent years. The bank has built up a framework of five committees with direct accountability to the Board of Directors: Executive Committee, Risk Management Committee, Audit Committee, Related Party Transaction Control Committee, and the Nomination, Remuneration, and Evaluation Committee. Five independent directors have been appointed to the board with international experience, which contributed significantly in changes to the board's composition. In addition, four regional credit review and approval centers have been set up in Shanghai, Beijing, Guangzhou, and Fuzhou and five audit sub-departments in Beijing, Shanghai, Shenzhen, Fuzhou, and Xiamen.

The bank maintains a relatively flat structure that is both specialized and centralized and where front, middle, and back offices are separated. The divisional structure comprises Retail Banking Headquarters, Financial Markets Department, Credit Card Center, Asset Custody Department, VIC (Very Important Clients) Department, and Investment Banking Department, all of which are headquartered in either Beijing or Shanghai. Management centers support the three major business segments: institutional banking, corporate banking, and channel development.

Financial Performance and Corporate Social Responsibility

While the economic downturn had a negative impact on the Chinese banking industry in general, IBC results in 2008 were outstanding. Operating income was RMB 29.8 billion (USD 4.4 billion), up 35.3%, with a commensurate surge in operating profit to RMB 14 billion (USD 2.1 billion). Earnings per share rose 29.7% to RMB 2.3, with net assets per share up 26.0% to RMB 9.8.

During the same year, IBC continued its outstanding performance in relation to return on average equity (25.90%), and was named the "Best Bank in Mainland China for ROE" for the second year running in the "2008 Competitiveness Rankings of Asian Banks". IBC's asset quality remained sound, with its non-performing loan ratio reduced to 1.06% as of September 2008, against China's industry average of 2.45%. The bank's capital adequacy ratio stands at 11.24% as of December 2008, well above the minimum regulatory requirement of 8%.

IBC has been at the forefront of Corporate Social Responsibility (CSR) initiatives in China, winning many awards for wide-ranging projects related to poverty alleviation, education, disaster relief, energy saving, emission reduction, environment protection, and other social public utilities. In June 2007, the bank joined the UN Environment Program Finance Initiative and was the first Chinese financial institution to adopt the "Equator Principles" to promote green credit programs. Both of these initiatives require signatory institutions to consider environmental and social issues when financing development projects.

Key Business Drivers

In the context of the global financial crisis, the challenges facing IBC differ from those faced by financial institutions in more developed economies. The complex financial instruments that set-off worldwide financial calamity had, until then, played little part in the bank's growth or investment strategies. The crisis will, nevertheless, have its impact in the months and years ahead as Chinese regulators continue to micromanage operations at domestic banks, a policy known as "Hongguan Tiaokong", or "Macroeconomic Control and Adjustment".

The balance between social responsibility, supporting rapidly evolving government policies, and maintaining asset quality will be a major challenge for IBC, which will likely elicit considerable incongruence in its strategic decisions. As credit expansion is critical to sustaining China's growth, most of the funds will come from banks, often via directives from the national government. Local governments, too, are placing pressure on banks to support infrastructure works, most of which offer only long-term profit opportunities. The enticement to misallocate resources will be strong for all participants in the financial sector.

In recent years, IBC has had a proven record of strong credit management by bringing non-performing loans well below the national average. While it may be reasonable to expect a similar superior performance from IBC during the current international crisis, the Chinese banking industry is yet to be fully tested on its risk-management competencies. New technologies, new procedures, and a shortage of experienced managers and personnel signal potential problems. Theory and practice are quite often very different, especially in these exceptional times.

While the global economy is a major focus as we face a new decade, the entrance of foreign multinationals is also a major driver of industry growth and change. It is expected that future growth and profitability will substantially come from retail, small business lending, and fee-based businesses where foreign banks have superior skills and experience. The foreign banks are keen to exploit strategic gaps created by China's rapidly expanding consumer needs, limited product and service offerings, and the poor customer service offered by domestic participants.

IBC and its local competitors need also to contend with converging markets — especially in insurance — and the introduction of increasingly sophisticated and innovative financial products. A significant deficit in management skills and an inexperienced workforce underscores the difficulties faced by the bank during this period of rapid industry change.

Business Strategies

IBC has identified the following key strategic issues in the years ahead.

Restructuring

The bank is seeking to develop its dynamic capabilities to optimize strategic opportunities in the rapidly evolving market. While mergers, acquisitions, and related diversification, appear to be strategic options within the industry, IBC has not yet signaled their intentions.

Enhanced marketing capabilities

In order to protect existing business, the bank is focusing on developing new products and services such as wealth management and integrated financial solutions. Key channels such as corporate and third-party deposits have been given increased priority. Service scope and quality is to be extended through expansion of online banking, telephone banking, VIP services, and mobile banking.

Strengthened financial management

The bank is striving to consolidate its capital base by strengthening its risk management, internal controls, and resource allocation. Less reliance is to be placed on loan income through promotion of a more diversified income structure via multi-channel marketing. An increased contribution is being sought from intermediaries such as agencies, and trade and consulting businesses. In addition, newly established fund management and futures departments and increased interbank funds will support a stronger and more diversified capital base.

Technological progress

IBC is committed to upgrade technologies and develop the much-needed expertise required to optimize the value of that technology.

Operational advancement

All departments are committed to developing and implementing global standards in their operations. The bank's Six Sigma implementation underpins all of its quality initiatives.

Human resource development

IBC has recognized the importance of human capital to its continuing success, and is committed to develop a corporate culture that supports innovation and sustainable growth.

In brief, Industrial Bank Co. appears well placed to exit the current global financial crisis in a comparatively stronger position than today. The bank's future success may depend on two main factors: first, its ability to balance social responsibilities — as defined by central and local governments — with maintenance of its hard-won asset quality; second, the success in internationalizing all areas of its operations in the coming years.

Lin Song and Terence R. Egan

References

Bekier, MM and K Lam (2005). What Chinese consumers want from banks? *The McKinsey Quarterly* (27 June).

Brennand, G, T Tang, and D Beal (2005). *Banking on China: Where to Place the Chips?* Boston Consulting Group.

China Industrial Bank (2009). *Annual Report.* http://download.cib.com.cn/netbank/download/en/2008en.zip. Retrieved on 25 March 2009.

Foreign banks have landed in China, but the local competition may prove tougher than expected (I August 2007). Knowledge at Wharton http://www.knowledgeatwharton.com.cn/index.cfm?fa=viewArticle&articleID=1680&languageid=1. Retrieved on 25 March 2009.

Industrial Bank Co. Ltd. Profile and history. http://www.cib.com.cn/netbank/en/About_IB/Porfile_x_History.html. Retrieved on 25 March 2009.

Klamann E (2009). *China's Industrial Bank 2008 Profit Rises 32 pct* (18 January). Reuters http://www.reuters.com/article/rbssBanks/idUSSHA26342920090118. Retrieved on 2 May 2009.

Kynge, J (2006). *China Shakes the World*. New York: Houghton Mifflin Harcourt.

INNER MONGOLIA BAOTOU STEEL UNION

Corporate Address and Contact Information

Inner Mongolia Baotou Steel Union Co.
East Baogang Info Building
Hexi Industrial Zone, Kun District
Baotou, Inner Mongolia 014010
People's Republic of China
Phone: (86)472-218-9528
Fax: (86)472-218-9530
http://www.btsteel.com/

Inner Mongolia Baotou Steel Union Company (内蒙古包钢钢联股份有限公司) is a subsidiary of Baotou Iron and Steel Group in the People's Republic of China. Baotou Iron and Steel Group, shortly known as Baotou Steel, is the largest steel company in Inner Mongolia and a leading producer of iron and steel in northern China. Further, it possesses a huge scientific research facility for analysis and production of rare earth in China. Baotou Steel has two public-listed companies — Inner Mongolia Baotou Steel Union Company and Inner Mongolia Baotou Steel Rare-Earth Hi-Tech.

Historical Development

Although Inner Mongolia Baotou Steel Union Company was established in the People's Republic of China only on 29 June 1999, the Baogang Group has a much longer history. Headquartered in Baotou City, Inner Mongolia, the Baotou Iron and Steel Company was formed in 1954. It was restructured in 1998 from which two listed companies mentioned about were established and were listed on the Shanghai Stock Exchange as A-Shares. Baogang Group owns 61.2% of stakes in Inner Mongolia Baotou Steel Union Company (Annual Report 2008). The Baotou region in northwest China is a unique resource for iron and rare earth materials. The Baiyunebo Mine in this area possesses an exceptional intergrowth of iron and rare earth elements, with the iron reserve being the largest in northwest China, and its rare earth reserve is the biggest in the world. Availability of thorium and niobium reserves is considered as the second largest in the world. Due to the presence of this mine, Baotou gained the name as the Capital of Rare Earth in the world, and Baotou Steel Union has since grown to be the top enterprise in the Autonomous Region of Inner Mongolia.

Baogang Group had established two national rare earth research institutes, the Baogang Rare Earth Research Institute and the Ruike National Engineering Center of Rare Earth Metallurgy and Function Materials. In recent years, it had furnished the magnetic spectrograph for the Discovery Space Shuttle of the United States. Moreover, it had provided highly important magnetic materials for the Shenzhou Spacecraft and Chang'e I Carrier Rocket of China.

Corporate Leadership, Main Products, and Services

Mr. Cui Chen is the chairman of Inner Mongolia Baotou Steel Union, Cao Zhongkui and Liu Yuying are directors, while Jing Han is an independent director. Guo Jinglong, Liu Yufeng, and Liu Rui are deputy general managers. Guo Jinglong is also a director and board secretary and Xie Meiling is the CFO. At the end of 2007, the total assets of the group amounted to 57.2 billion RMB.

Inner Mongolia Baotou Steel Union has the capacity to produce 10 million tons of iron and steel each year. Its production lines are capable of producing cold- and hot-rolled strips, heavy steel plates, heavy rail, seamless pipes, large-scale beams, bars, and wire rods. The company has one of the only three rail production units in the country, and its seamless pipe production base is also one of the biggest in China, manufactured to several specifications and varieties. The product portfolio includes the manufacture of 1,112 specifications and 55 varieties of steel products such as slab, seamless pipe, and heavy rail. The company possesses the largest Continuous Strip Production (CSP) base in northwest China.

The total sales revenue of Inner Mongolia Baotou Steel Union had exceeded 40 billion RMB with a net profit of 0.92 billion RMB in 2008 (Annual Report, 2008). In the rare earth field, it produces more than 7,000 tons of hydrometallurgy rare earth products converted from oxide. The company manufactures 200 specifications and 80 varieties of rare earth products, apart from 28 specifications and 26 varieties of metallurgical coke and byproducts of coke. Baotou Steel Union also engages in coal-fired power generation projects, and manufactures steel billets, steel wires, steel plates for shipbuilding, boilers, containers, and engineering machinery, apart from structural and tool steel plates. The Baiyuebo Brand rare earth products had become quite famous throughout the world.

Challenges and Business Strategies

Inner Mongolia Baotou Steel Union is operating in a specialized industrial environment. Hence, it enjoys certain advantages compared to other industries. Both in China and in overseas markets, it plays a significant role in the rare earth industry. The rare earth oxide output caters to 40% of the Chinese market requirements; praseodymium and neodymium production accounts for 30% of the local market, while Nd-Fe-B, polishing powder, and negative powder productions amount to 20% of the Chinese market supply. Since Baotou Steel is located in an important transportation hub that connects the northwest and northeast China, it is assured of ample resources of coal and electricity. This gives the company a competitive advantage. In spite of production dominance and advantageous location, Baotou Steel had been having difficult times due to the high cost of coal and rising cost of electric power. During 2008, the net profit declined a whopping 47.3% from 2007 to 920 million RMB. On the other hand, the operating revenue grew 64.81% in 2008 to 44.12 billion RMB.

Even though the Chinese economy has been slowing down due to the impact of the global recession, the company plans to improve its production and profitability through self-innovation and scientific approach. The CSP plant is the first authoritative training base in Asia and second in the world. It had been providing technical support and supervision in CSP projects and seamless pipe production to several foreign companies. Its technical advances in high-speed rail manufacturing and CSP have enabled it to win twice the National Award for Science and Technology in China.

To strengthen its position in the industry, Baotou Steel has entered into a strategic alliance and structural agreement with Baoshan Iron & Steel (Group) Co. Ltd. This had helped Baogang to fortify the partnership with the Chinese and overseas raw material suppliers. Furthermore, the company had established sales subsidiaries and after-sales service branches in 13 provinces in China. In addition, it had also opened sales offices in Japan, United States, and other countries.

Currently, Inner Mongolia Baotou Steel Union is concentrating on environment protection and energy savings as part of its sustainable operations. It has established an eco-industrial park, and has been named as one of the first groups for establishing recycling experimental units in China. The company is the first corporation in the country to use the blast furnace dry dusting process in the entire iron and steel industry, and is ranked among the top 50 Energy Green Enterprises in China.

For further growth in future, Baotou Steel is planning to optimize the product mix for improving the seamless pipe market share and tap the potential for steel plate market. It also strives to focus on pollutant reduction and energy saving through total system improvement. The company expects to achieve sales income and total assets value of $10 billion at the end of the 11th five-year period (2006–2010) of planning. To support and realize this ambitious target, Baotou Steel seeks to utilize innovations in science and technology in the coming years.

Amir Shoham and Hui He

References

Baotou Iron and Steel Group (15 November 2006). *China Daily*. http://www.chinadaily.com.cn/bizchina/2006-11/15/content_734141.htm. Retrieved on 19 May 2009.

Baotou Steel Group. Brief introduction of Baogang. http://www.btsteel.com/. Retrieved on 19 May 2009.

Inner Mongolia Baotou Steel's net profit plunged 47.3% in 2008 (17 April 2009). China Knowledge http://www.chinaknowledge.com/Newswires/News_Detail.aspx?type=1&NewsID=22832. Retrieved on 19 May 2009.

Inner Mongolian Baotou Steel Union Co. Ltd. (NBB: IMBA F). Mergent Online. Retrieved on May 3, 2009.

Inner Mongolian Baotou Steel Union Co. Ltd. Annual Report 2008 (English). Mergent Online. Retrieved on May 3, 2009.

Inner Mongolia Baotou Steel Union (2008). *Annual Report*. http://www.cninfo.com.cn/finalpage/2009-04-16/51323533.PDF. Retrieved on 20 November 2009.

JIANGXI COPPER

Corporate Address and Contact Information

Jiangxi Copper Corporation
15 Yejin Avenue
Guixi City, Jiangxi Province 335424
People's Republic of China
Phone: (86)701-3777-070
Fax: (86)701-3777-656
www.jxcc.com

Jiangxi Copper Corporation (江西铜业股份有限公司), founded in July 1979, is a large integrated enterprise in the non-ferrous metals industry of China. Its operation covers copper mining, milling, smelting, and processing. The company, based in East China's Jiangxi province, has a main subsidiary Jiangxi Copper Company Limited (JCC) and 93 other affiliates. Jiangxi Copper Company Limited is dually listed on the Hong Kong and Shanghai Stock Exchanges. In 2007, the total asset of the company was over RMB 26 billion, with more than 34,000 employees. The company possesses most copper, coexisting and associated mineral resources in the whole industry — with the top five copper mines in China all belong to Jiangxi Copper, and its products have been exported to over 30 countries.

Historical Development

More than 2,000 years ago China started copper smelting, and today the copper industry has become one of the most important pillars to the country's economy, as 91 percent of the industries need copper.

Thirty years ago, Jiangxi Copper Corporation was founded as a state-owned factory. In its history, the company experienced four rounds of reforms with regards to the belonging relationship with four different government organizations in the following sequence: the National Management Bureau of Ferrous Metals Industry, China Ferrous Corporation, China Copper Lead Zinc Corporation, and the Jiangxi provincial government. After three decades of development, Jiangxi Copper Corporation establishes itself as the flagship of China's copper industry. Today, the company's copper cathode production capacity is among the top three in the copper industry worldwide. It leads the copper industry in China in terms of total asset, gross sales and net profit and ranks 87th among China's top 500 enterprises.

With the global economic development, the consumption of refined copper has been rising rapidly worldwide, and China is the key factor to determine such a climb. Studies of copper consumption show that copper consumption in developing countries such as China and India rose considerably from 1980 to 2008. The United States was the leading copper consumer until 2002, then its top position in refined copper usage was overtaken by China due to the country's booming economy that contributed to a tripling of its annual refined copper consumption. Thus, as the giant leader of Chinese copper industry, Jiangxi Copper Corporation had to take on more responsibilities to meet the country's demands.

According to its development plan, Jiangxi Copper Corporation needed to form an annual production capacity of 200,000 tons by the end of 1990s, which required an investment of several billion RMB. Instead of asking for money from the government, the company decided to fund the expansion with overseas financing. In 1997, Jiangxi Copper was listed on the London and Hong Kong Stock Exchanges, which made it the first Chinese mining company listed abroad. In same year, the company's capital debt ratio decreased from 78 percent to 40 percent. Since then, Jiangxi Copper Corporation has conducted six capital operations, accumulatively raising RMB 12 billion, which helped the company expand rapidly both in China and overseas. The company's total asset had climbed from RMB 335 million in 1979 to RMB 42.3 billion at present.

Jiangxi Copper Corporation's current products include: high pure copper cathodes under copper products, selenium powder, rhenium powder, 1# Te spindle No. 1 and high pure Te under rare dispersion metal products, gold ingot and silver ingot under PM products, arsenic trioxide, sulfuric acid and sulfur concentrate under chemical products, copper wire, and copper rod and electrolytic copper foil under processed copper products.

In addition to its business efforts, Jiangxi Copper Corporation realizes that protecting the environment in which it operates is pivotal to its sustainable development. The company has been paying great attention to energy saving and emission reduction. Its main subsidiary, Jiangxi Copper Company Limited (JCC), received the 2005 Green Oriented Enterprise Environmental Prize of the Chinese Environmental Award issued by China Environmental Protection Foundation.

Corporate Structure and Leadership

Headquartered in Guixi, Jiangxi Province, the company's main subsidiary, Jiangxi Copper Company Limited, consists of Dexing Copper Mine, Yongping Copper Mine, Wushan Copper Mine, and Guixi Smelter, and 93 affiliates such as JCC Copper Products Company Ltd., JCC-Yates Copper Foil

Company Ltd., JCC Finance Company, JCC Shenzhen South Company, JCC (Dexing) Mining New Technology Company, JCC (Guixi) New Materials Company, JCC (Guixi) Logistics Company, Dongtong Mining Company, Chengmenshan Copper Mine, and Jinrui Futures & Brokerage Company.

As such a giant, Jiangxi Copper Corporation's operation platform and management system faced severe challenges. The facts that there were many layers of management and that the company has its subsidiaries and many affiliates that are located at different parts of China made it very difficult for the company to leverage its plan and control systems and to balance between centralization and decentralization, which, as the company keeps growing rapidly, became particularly critical to its future development. One of the main solutions was to build up an ERP (enterprise resource planning) system to manage and coordinate all the resources, information, and functions of the company. In addition, other reforms conducted in 2008 included: improving the company's operation system and management regulations, putting more efforts in organization integration, streamlining the management tier between general office and second-level units so as to shorten management chain, fully utilizing internal human resources, and improving management efficiency and staff assessment management mechanism.

Li Yihuang is the current president of Jiangxi Copper Corporation and chairman of JCC, who also serves as deputy party secretary of the company. Other senior leaders include Li Baomin (party secretary), Wang Chiwei, Li Ping, Long Ziping, and Liu Yuewei (vice presidents), Hu Faliang (union chief), Gan Chengjiu (chief account), Liu Jianghao (chief engineer), and Wu Jinxing (CFO).

Challenges and Business Strategies

Copper is the second strategic resource being undersupplied for China; thus, the country has to depend heavily on copper imports because of its growing demand for the consumption. Many economists have warned that excessively relying on the overseas resource can restrict China's copper development, which presented a major challenge to Jiangxi Copper Corporation, the leader of the industry.

Accordingly, Jiangxi Copper Corporation adopted several strategies. On the one hand, the company continues to improve its technology to reach the advanced level of copper mining and manufacturing in the world. For instance, through technology innovations, the company's subsidiary, Jiangxi Copper Company Ltd. greatly upgraded the capacity of its major product — copper cathode — which exceeded 800,000 tons per year by the end of 2008. Its by-products such as gold, silver, and sulfuric acid have also experienced remarkable increases with respect to the production capacity.

On the other hand, in order to secure a steady supply of copper and meet the rapid development of Chinese economy, the company has been adopting the resource development strategies through investing in joint ventures in both China and overseas. In 2007, together with China Minmetals Non-Ferrous Metals Co. Ltd., the company acquired Northern Peru Copper Corp., which was a Vancouver-and-Lima-based copper exploration company that controls the Galeno copper, gold, and molybdenum project, the adjacent Hilorico gold deposit and the Pashpap copper and molybdenum deposit. In 2008, Jiangxi Copper, together with China Metallurgical Group Corporation, jointly obtained the right to develop the largest Afghan copper mine, Aynak Copper Mine. The mergers and acquisitions in both China and overseas increased the company's copper resources from 7.95 million tons to 15 million tons. In addition, the indirect control of the copper resources reached 10 million tons. It is estimated that by the end of 2012, Jiangxi Copper Corporation will greatly decrease the volume it needs to import from foreign countries.

Another strategy that Jiangxi Copper Corporation gradually carried forward was to enhance its position as a mineral enterprise by developing its copper-related multi-metal business, which also helped improve the company's performance.

In 2009, the total asset of Jiangxi Copper Corporation reaches RMB 42.3 billion, 126 times more than it was in 1979, when it was founded. With the company's rapid development, Jiangxi Copper Corporation will continue to make significant contributions to China's economic growth in the coming years.

Michael A. Moodian, Margaret Minnis, and Yifang Zhang

References

Datamonitor (2008). Metals & mining in China: Industry profile.

Jiangxi Copper Company Ltd. (2008). Summary of annual report 2007. http://www.hkexnews.hk/listedco/listconews/sehk/20080326/LTN20080326162.pdf. Retrieved on 2 July 2009.

Jiangxi Copper Corp. Ltd. (2009). Company profile. http://www.jxcc.com/english/product.html. Retrieved on 2 July 2009.

Jiangxi Copper Corp. Ltd. (2009). News Center. http://www.jxcc.com/Html/30y/2009/05/197220090507182700.html. Retrieved on July 2, 2009.

Jiangxi Copper Company Limited Announces 2008 Annual Results (1 April 2009). ACN Newswire. http://www.finanznachrichten.de/nachrichten-2009-04/13518500-jiangxi-copper-company-limited-announces-2008-annual-results-011.htm. Retrieved on 2 July 2009.

USGS Mineral Resources Program (2009). http://pubs.usgs.gov/fs/2009/3031/FS2009-3031.pdf. Retrieved on 2 July 2009.

高价时代中国铜业的内忧外患 (2006). 中国科学院预测研究中心研究报告 [*Chinese Copper Industry's Challenges in a High-Price Era.* Report Series *of the Center for Forecasting Research,* Chinese Academy of Sciences] http://www.cefs.ac.cn/reports.files/express/reports-final/%E9%A2%84%E6%B5%8B%E7%A0%94%E7%A9%B6%E6%8A%A5%E5%91%8A19.pdf. Retrieved on 1 July 2009.

江铜三十年做大做强跻身世界铜产业前列的启示：挺起中国铜工业的脊梁 (26 June 2009). [The implication of Jiangxi Copper's rapid growth over the past three decades: Building the backbone of the Chinese copper industry. Jiangxi Nonferrous Metals Information Network] http://www.jxys.gov.cn/view.asp?NewsNo=00032220. Retrieved on 2 July 2009.

新中大国际 ERP 助力江西铜业管理案例 (2 July 2009). [The case study of ERP boosting Jiangxi Copper Corporation's management system] http://solution.it365.com/139/7833639.shtml. Retrieved on 2 July 2009.

JINAN STEEL

Corporate Address and Contact Information

Jinan Steel Group Co. Ltd.
21 Gongyebeilu Road
Jinan, Shandong Province
People's Republic of China
Fax: (86)531-8886-6029
http://www.jigang.com.cn
jigang@jigang.com.cn

Jinan Steel Group Co. Ltd. (济南钢铁股份有限公司) has a history of more than 50 years. Currently, the group has a workforce of 38,000 and its total assets have reached 50 billion RMB. Focusing primarily on medium plate, hot-rolled sheet, cold-rolled sheet, and so on, Jinan Steel in 2008 produced 11 million tons of steel, 10 million tons of iron, and 10 million tons of rolled steel, which included one million tons of steel for exportation. Jinan Steel is one the top 100 China Blue-Chip Companies, Top 10 Blue-chip Companies in Steel Industry, and Top 100 Taurus Award Powers of Chinese Listed companies. In addition, the group has obtained series of awards related to environmental protection, such as the national forestation model unit, and clean production and environmentally friendly enterprise of China steel industry.

Historical Development

The history of Jinan Steel could be divided into four periods. The first period (1958–1983) saw the founding and slow development of the initial combined enterprises of iron, steel, rolled steels under the planned economy background. The construction on its Medium Plate Plant was started in 1959, and a year later, it was put to operation with designed output of 150,000 tons. In April 1968, the first 8-M^3 pellet vertical furnace in China was put to production in Jinan Steel, which enhanced production to nearly three times comparing with the standard steel output before. By the time when China declared the economic reform and opened to the outside world in the late 1970s, Jinan Steel possessed annual output of steel 320,000 tons, which until 1983 was still ranked medium to lower level among the Chinese regional steel works.

The second period took place from 1984 to 1997, when Jinan Steel implemented a new system in which the factory directors or managers assuming direct responsibilities. Through technical advancement, merging, and by tapping into internal potential, the company went on a track of fast growth, and with its advantage in medium plate market Jinan Steel became one of the three regional steel powers. By 1991, Jinan Steel yielded one million tons of steel per year; and in year 1993, it was ranked 51st among Top 500 Largest Chinese Industry Companies. During the same year, clean production was also adopted with the aim of reducing industrial pollution. A year later, Jinan Iron and Steel Group Corporation were formed with 110 domestic and overseas subsidiaries. The group's main business focuses on mines, smelting, mechanical processing, and refractory materials, while its joint stock companies engage in retailing, finance, medical service, real estate, etc. by 1996, Jinan Steel had grown to become a huge trans-regional steel conglomerate with two million tons of annual steel production.

Since the early 1990s, Jinan Steel had been facing the challenges of higher cost and environmental issues as with other Chinese steel companies. By the end of 1997, Jinan Steel was severely affected by the deflation policy and the Southeast Asian financial crisis, which marked a new stage of readjustment (1997–2000) in Jinan's Development. After a new leadership team was put in place, the company focused on improving technical processing and low-level operation standards, and gradually became the largest production base of medium plate in China. By 2000, its annual production reached over three million tons, and the company entered the current stage of development. Three years later, Jinan Steel won the National Quality Management Prize and broke five million tons of annual steel output. In 2004, its annual production ranked ninth in China.

On 29 June 2004, Jinan Steel Co. Ltd. was listed on the Shanghai Stock Exchange. During the same year, the company built its gas-steam combined cycle generating unit, and became one of the first-generation enterprises utilizing cycle power generation. A year later, its annual steel output ranked 7th in China, and 24th among the global crude steed makers. On 17 March 2008, Jinan Steel merged with Laiwu Steel Group and registered as Shandong Steel Group. On 20 March, the company renamed itself to Jinan Steel Group Co. Ltd.

Corporate Structure and Leadership

From 1997 to 2007 Jinan Steel experienced one of the fastest development periods in the company history, as the group was listed on the Chinese stock market while its annual production exceeded 10 million tons. The success to a large part was due to the leadership of Li Changshun, an MBA from the Graduate School of China University of Science and Technology. Li, who was born in 1946, started his career in Jinan Steel from in 1967, and undertook the senior leadership role since 1984. In 1997, Li was appointed the general manager when Jinan Steel was severely affected by the domestic deflation policy and the Southeast Asian financial crisis. By implementing a strategy of product quality and lower cost, Li led Jinan Steel to surpass three million tons annual output in 2000. By the time when Wang Jun succeeded him in late 2007, Jinan Steel was ranked eighth in annual production in China.

Jinan Steel has two forms of subsidiaries. One has direct connection with steel, such as Jinan Iron & Steel Co. Ltd. and Jinan Steel International Trade Co. Ltd. Founded in 1999, Jinan Steel International Trade focuses on import and export business, overseas investment, international bidding, labor output, etc., while Jinan Steel Sales Co. Ltd. is responsible for the domestic sales. The other form is 28 non-steel subsidiaries dealing with mechanical processing and manufacture, metallurgical construction, logistics, new-style building materials, real estate, etc. Some of those hold leading positions in China or in Shandong Province, such as Jinan Baode Truck Transportation Co. Ltd., Jinan Luxin New-Style Building Material Co. Ltd., and Shandong Ductile Iron Pipe Co. Ltd.

Main Products and Services

Jinan Steel's core product of has been the medium plate, which makes up nearly 50% of the company turnover. In 2008, it has about 3.5 million tons of production and 13% market share in China in term of medium plate. To ensure its leading position, in 2009, Jinan Steel has invested a new production line with an estimated annual production of six million tons in medium plate after the investment. Serving primarily the domestic market via the direct sales method, the medium plate is mainly supplied to shipbuilding, boiler, automobile, and engineering machinery industry. Among them, the shipbuilding industry accounts for about 50% the demand. Other steel products include: hot-rolled ribbed bar and plain round bar, plate blank, continuous casting billet, and steel for automobile beams.

Under its long-term market leading strategy, Jinan Steel also provides production-on-demand service to its industry clients in shipbuilding, pressure vessels, engineering machinery, and infrastructure construction. Striving to meet the customized need of categories, specifications, and performance, Jinan Steel has gradually enhanced its market share in various segments of low-alloy and high-strength steel plate, boiler plates, hull plates, and so on.

As a huge steel company with various subsidiaries, Jinan Steel operates not only in steel production but also in related industries such as trading, exportation and importation, investment, R&D, gas supplying, product development, mechanical processing and manufacture, metallurgical construction, logistics, new-style building materials, real estate, and services. Jinan Steel adopts ISO2000 quality management system, and was awarded the National Quality Management Prize in 2003. The company has a top-ranked R&D team in the country, and its hull plate won accreditations from 10 classification societies of China, England, France, Japan, Germany, the United States, Norway, Korea, Italy, and Holland, and has been exported to more than 50 countries and regions.

Challenges and Business Strategies

Benefited from the booming Chinese economy, Jinan Steel experienced tremendous growth since 1984. However, the company has recently been affected by the global economic slowdown. Great changes have taken place in both the domestic and international markets in 2008, and the company's profit experienced a decrease of 60.13%. The key challenges are derived from increasing steel players both at home and aboard, continuous pressure for cost and environmental protection, and transformation from production orientation to customer orientation.

As a key medium plate steel producer in China, Jinan Steel faces many existing or potential competitors in the domestic market, which include Nanjing Iron Steel Union Co. Ltd., Magang (Group) Holding Co. Ltd., Baosteel, Anshan Iron Steel Group Corporation, Liuzhou Iron Steel (Group) Company (Liuzhou Steel), Anyang Iron Steel (Group) Co. Ltd. (Anyang Steel), Chongqing Iron Steel (Group) Co. Ltd. (Chongqing Steel), and so on. In recent years, some private steel works have also added low price pressure to Jinan Steel alike. Furthermore, Jinan Steel faces great challenges from international players such as Nippon Steel in both export and domestic markets.

Cost and environmental issues have become major concerns for Jinan Steel in recent years. Today, nearly 80% of its iron ore are imported. However, Jinan Steel achieved first-class cost control, primarily through more than 80 technical innovation programs. From 1995, Jinan Steel launched its project in building a resource-conserving and environmentally friendly steel conglomerate. The program was divided into three periods: during the first period (1995–1999), the company concentrated on energy conservation and consumption; in the second period (2000–2002), clean production became the central point; in the third period (2003–2005), Jinan Steel focused on recycling economy. By the end of the program, the group's comprehensive energy consumption per ton decreased 44%, while industrial dust discharge decreased 84%.

China has an enormous market potential for medium plate steel products with an imbalanced supply structure. While the general item supply is sufficient, the high value-added items are depended on importation. Since 1999, Jinan Steel determined to update its low value-added plate into high value-added line. In addition to its technical and product innovations, the company also modified its marketing strategy from production orientation to market orientation.

Based on market needs, Jinan Steel develops the following growth strategies: low-cost strategy, sustainable development strategy, premium strategy, talent strategy, and IT-driven strategy. These strategies clearly reflect the changing needs and challenges from the market. Through energy saving and technical innovation tactics, the company strives to accomplish low-cost and sustainable development plan. Through customer orientation and customer satisfaction program, the group seeks to fulfill the premium strategy. As regard to the talent strategy, Jinan Steel establishes education fund for employees to further their education, and pursues three talent growing routes with management, technical professional, and technical operations. In term of its IT-driven strategy, the company has adopted such an approach since 2002 by implementing Oracle database and ERP (enterprise resources planning) system into its operation.

Shiqiang (Kenny) Wang

References

Jinan Steel Group Co. Ltd. (2007). *Group Introduction* http://www.jigang.com.cn/invinfo/WEB_SIDE/jtjs.jsp. Retrieved on 1 May 2009.

The great charming of scientific and technical development (24 November 2004). *Science & Technology Daily*.

心系发展写风流：记济南钢铁集团总公司党委书记总经理李长顺 (3 June 2005) [Li Changshun, party secretary and general manager of Jinan Steel Group]. http://www.mos.gov.cn/Template/article/csr_display.jsp?mid=200506 30014352. Retrieved on 1 May 2009.

JISCO

Corporate Address and Contact Information

Jiuquan Iron & Steel (Group) Co. Ltd.
Chengxin Plaza, E. Xiongguan Road
Jiayuguan, Gansu Province 735100
People's Republic of China
Phone: (86)937-671-5577
Fax: (86)937-622-6872
http://www.jiugang.com

Located in Gansu Province, Jiuquan Iron & Steel (Group) Co. Ltd. (JISCO 甘肃酒钢集团有限公司) is a large-scale enterprise group with a total asset of RMB 40 billion and 38,000 employees. JISCO consists of about 50 companies among which there are 22 subsidiaries. The group has sales offices in Jiayuguan, Lanzhou, Xi'an, Yinchuan, Urumchi, Taiyuan, Zhengzhou, Tianjin, Chengdu, Wuxi, Foshan, and Shanghai, as well as branch offices in South Africa, Mongolia, and the Philippines. JISCO's sale revenue reached $2.622 billion in 2008, and is the largest steel manufacturer and complex in Northwestern China. During the same year the company was ranked 16th among the Chinese steel enterprises and 88th among the top 500 Chinese manufacturers.

Corporate Development and Structure

Founded in 1958, Jiuquan Iron & Steel was one the key projects during China's First Five-Year Plan (1953–1957). Over the years, the company has established three manufacturing sites in Jiayuguan, Lanzhou, and Yicheng (Shanxi Province), with a combined capacity of eight million tons each year. Since 1985, JISCO has been ranked among the top 500 Chinese enterprises. After going through corporate restructuring and ownership reform, Jiuquan Iron & Steel was listed on the Shanghai Stock Exchange on 20 December 2000. In a four year period, JISCO Hongxing's business income increased from RMB 2.073 billion to 5.892 billion, and the total assets from RMB 1.891 billion to 3.818 billion, which represented increases of 184% and 102%, respectively.

To meet the requirement of modern enterprise system, JISCO is governed by a Board of Directors, with Ma Honglie serves as current chairman and Zang Qiuhua as president. The main subsidiaries include: Gansu JISCO Hongxing Iron & Steel Stock Co. Ltd., JISCO Metallurgical Company, JISCO Mechanical Manufacturing Corporation, Guiyou Property Service Company, Dashun Logistic Company, JISCO Hongda Construction Material Company, Hongfeng Industry Corporation, Deliyuan Company, JISCO Hospital, and Saiyahongyun Automobile Sale and Service Company. The following graph illustrates JISCO's governance structure.

Main Products and Services

JISCO's main iron and steel products include various wires and rods, rolled steel plates, and bars. Included among its high-speed wire and rod coils are plain carbon steel, high carbon steel, cotton steel,

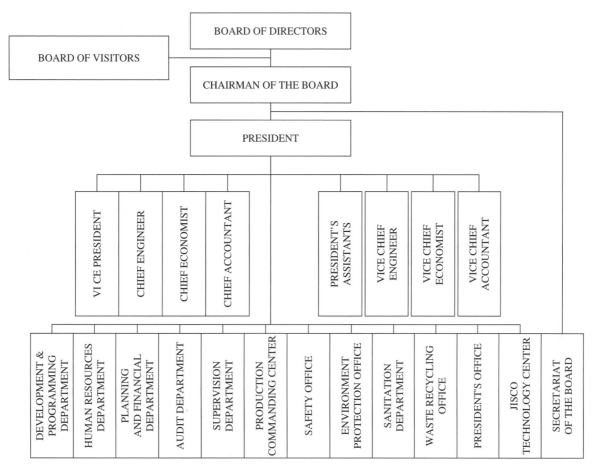

Figure 5. Corporate structure of JISCO.

Source: http://www.jiugang.com.

cold forged steel, cotton binding wire, welding rod, and wire. The company also produces large quantities of medium and heavy plates, which include carbon steel plate, ship plate, coiler steel, vessel steel, low alloy steel, bridge steel, auto beam steel and pipeline steel. Its hot-rolled strip coil products include high quality carbon steel structure and stainless steel. Those products have passed the third-party attestation for ISO9001:2000 quality management system, and the metallurgical production process has been assured with ISO14000 environment system. JISCO's products have been widely used in construction, welding, shipbuilding, automobile manufacturing, and transportation.

Although its operation mainly focuses on steel industry, as a conglomerate JISCO also engages in various other businesses at different areas, including power generation, mechanical manufacture, electrical manufacture and repair, refractory and chemistry, cement and construction materials, steel structure, welding material, industrial and civil architecture, metallurgical engineering, vehicle transportation, logistics, real estate, industry automation, environment protection, high-tech farming, medical service, vocational education, catering, and industrial tourism.

Challenges and Business Strategies

Chinese Iron & Steel industry, severely affected by the worldwide industrial recession in 2008–2009, will face new challenges in the coming years because of the need for technique upgrade, market complicacy, resource shortage, and rising competitions. Specifically in 2008, JISCO suffered a huge dip in net profit, largely due to the economic crisis with shrinking market demands and reduced prices in steel products. Within China, Jiuquan Iron & Steel competes mainly with other regional steel enterprises, among them: Anshan Iron and Steel, Chongqing Iron and Steel, Wuhan Iron & Steel, Jiangsu Shagang Group, Tangshan Iron and Steel, Hunan Valin Iron & Steel Group, Shougang Corporation, Qingdao Iron and Steel Group, and Taiyuan Iron and Steel. Demand for iron and steel products comes largely from the manufacturers of durable goods such as motor vehicles, machinery, containers, and construction steel. The profitability of individual companies depends largely on efficient operations, because most products are commodities sold based on price.

JISCO's development plans consist of the resource strategy, diversification strategy, differentiation strategy, extroversion strategy, and capital strategy. In order to improve productivity and reduce inefficiency, JISCO's old three-level structure (group company, plants, and shops) has been changed into new two-level structure (group company and production processes), and production commanding center was established in 2003. In addition, in an attempt to boost its core competence, JISCO separated its auxiliary activities from the iron and steel operations, and let all subsidiaries assume sole responsibility for losses and profits. As a large state-owned enterprise with 50 years of history, JISCO had redundant employees, which presented a major challenge to its further development. However, through a systematic review in recent years, a total of 23,000 positions were eliminated from the company.

During the 11th-Five-Year Planning period (2007–2012), JISCO has focused on building a human-based and technology-oriented framework of "scientific development". In order to achieve its goal of "excellent product, superior quality, and high benefit", the company sought to deepen its enterprise reform and adjust the industrial structure, while upgrading its technology, optimizing the product mix, and putting more emphasis on the value-added projects. Specifically, JISCO attempted to take the advantage of local resources and accelerate production adjustment, hoping to increase its steel making capability to 10 million tons by 2010.

In addition, JISCO made efforts to attract new strategic investors, develop the non-steel industries, and improve its administration and management efficiency. In particular, JISCO sought to enhance development diversity, implement advanced management concepts into its operations and foster the growth of key auxiliary industries. Guided by the principles of diversification and sustainable development, the company also expanded into the fields of trade, logistics, high-tech modern agriculture, etc. Aiming to become an international group enterprise in the coming years, JISCO will make the strategic investment in business operations that are characterized with resource predominance, fast growth opportunities, or complementary advantages.

Qun Du

References

Hoovers (2009). Jiuquan Iron & Steel (Group) Co. Ltd. http://www.hoovers.com/jiuquan-iron-and-steel/—ID__154120—/free-co-factsheet.xhtml. Retrieved on 8 August 2009.

Jiuquan Iron & Steel (Group) Co. (2009). Group Profile. http://www.jiugang.com/structure/ywlm/ezjjg/gp. Retrieved on 8 August 2009.

Jiuquan Steel 2008 net profit dips by 96%YoY (29 April 2009). *Steel Guru* [9 August 2009].

LAIWU STEEL

Corporation Address and Contact Information

Laiwu Steel Group Co. Ltd.
38 Youyi Street
Gangcheng District
Laiwu, Shandong Province
People's Republic of China
Phone: (86)643-682-0114
www.laigang.com

Ranked among the top 10 steel works in the country, Laiwu Steel Group Co. Ltd. (莱芜钢铁集团有限公司) has annual steel output over 10 million tons. In 2007, Laiwu Steel's total assets have reached RMB 62 billion with 25 subsidiary companies. It is also the holding company of two listed companies and one securities firm. Laiwu Steel is one of the biggest production bases of H-beam, pinion steel, and power metallurgy in China. Its business spectrum has also covered mining and extraction, steel structure building, real estate, cement, fire-retardant material, transportation and logistics, chemistry, and so on. Laiwu Steel's involvements in capital market are noteworthy. After becoming the holding company of Luyin Investment Group, Laiwu Steel acquired Qilu Securities, and then restructured Tiantong Securities.

Historical Development

From its founding in 1970, Laiwu Steel grew slowly and by 1979, it only yielded 45 tons in output. Since then the company experienced three periods of rapid development. During the first period (1979–1986), at the beginning of 1983, the management team was shocked and inspired by the household contract responsibility system and decided to eliminate the deficit within one year. Through effective reform measures, Laiwu Steel made 1.1 million RMB annual profits and marched into a new era.

The second period (1986–2000) was marked by utilizing foreign investment and share holding reform. In 1986, China decided to invite foreign investment for a steel expansion project of 10 million tons. Laiwu Steel grasped this opportunity to speed up its development and won support from both the provincial and central governments. After its plan was approved on 19 October 1986, Laiwu Steel engaged in tough negotiations with the Asia Bank and reached an agreement three years later. On 21 April 1992, a loan agreement of USD 253 million was officially signed, which was one the first loan agreements of the 10 million steel expansion project. Laiwu Steel deployed this investment into mines, steel making, steel rolling, and facility enhancement. The appraisal of medium section steel equipment was completed in May 1999, which marked the conclusion of the expansion project with foreign investment. As a result, Laiwu Steel possessed the annual production capacity of two million tons steel and became a large-scale steel corporation. During the negotiation with the Asia Bank, the shareholding restructure became a key cooperation factor. Therefore, on 30 December 1992, two production branches were listed for shareholding restructure experiment and on 28 August 1997, the whole group went through an IPO on the Shanghai Stock Exchange, and began its operation in the Chinese capital market.

From 2000, Laiwu Steel began a new era of fast development with great market opportunities and challenges. By reallocating internal resources and exploring the potential of the existing system, Laiwu Steel increased 1.3 million tons of steel output and enhanced the output of its four rolling production lines to over four million tons afterwards. H sections, deformed steel bars, and strip steel have emerged to become competitive products. In March 2003, the National Development and Reform Commission (NDRC) approved Laiwu Steel's Large Scale H Sections Project. From 2003 to 2005, Laiwu Steel ranked first nationally in terms of speed of increase in steel production and grew to be the first steel enterprise of 10 million tons in Shandong Province. In 2007, it occupied the ninth position among national metallurgy enterprises. In 2008, it merged with Jinan Steel to form the Shandong Iron & Steel Group.

Corporate Structure and Leadership

Laiwu Steel Group and its subsidiaries mainly operate in three areas: iron and steel products, iron- and steel-related service, and capital market. Laiwu Steel Iron and Steel Co. Ltd. is a listed company, which specially deals with iron and steel products, such as H-beams pinion steel and etc. Laiwu Steel's iron and steel service business typically deals with metallurgy engineering, construction project, and automation engineering. Shandong Metallurgical Design Institute was established in March 1959 and joined Laiwu Steel Group Ltd. in July 1997. Shandong Laigang Construction Co. Ltd., a wholly owned subsidiary of Laiwu Steel Group, was established in November 2002. Laigang Electronics Ltd. is a subsidiary dealing with electronic design, IT consulting and implementation, and automation control system. In addition, Laiwu Steel actives in capital market through its listed holding company Luyin Investment.

A senior engineer and a representative of the 14th, 15th, and 16th Congress of the Chinese Communist Party, Jiang Kaiwen was the former president of Laiwu Steel. After graduated from the Beijing University of Aeronautics & Astronautics in 1970, Jiang started working for Laiwu Steel since 1976, and became the secretary of party committee in 1991 and its president in 2000. Under his leadership, the company formulated the strategy of "winning by developing and speed". By 2004, Laiwu Steel had 25 subsidiaries and the total assets reached RMB 30 billion. After undergoing process optimization, its steel production was raised from 2 million tons in 1999 to 3.85 million tons in 2004; the sales revenue compared with that of 1999 increased 6 times from RMB 4.5 billion to 30.1 billion.

In addition, Jiang adhered to the concept of "co-winning between enterprise and employees and society". With the challenge of unfavorable reemployment conditions, he promised not to dismiss surplus personnel and not to make a worker suffer from laid-off. Hence, he advocated the development of the non-steel industry, which in turn helped boost growth opportunities for both individuals and the firm. As a result, the per-capita income of employees rose as a rate of more than RMB 2,000 per year and reached RMB 25,754 in 2004. Furthermore, Laiwu Steel sought to build a study-oriented, ecology-oriented, and sustainable enterprise. As a responsible corporate citizen, the company also contributed to charity programs such as the Hope Project and Wenchuan Earthquake relief efforts and so on.

Due to the efforts of Jiang and all the employees, Laiwu Steel ranked 78 among the domestic top 500 enterprises with the operating revenue RMB 30.1 billion in 2005. And Jiang was named an "Outstanding Entrepreneur" in 2004 and "The Most Attentive Entrepreneur" in 2007. After Jiang stepped down in February 2008, Song Lanxiang was appointed as his successor. This change of leadership took place simultaneously as Jinan Steel and Laiwu Steel joined the force to form Shandong Iron & Steel Group.

Products and Services

Laiwu Steel's key business focuses on steel products in four categories. First, steel bars, e.g., hot-rolled ribbed steel bar, round steel, rock bolt steel, etc. Laiwu Steel was one of the early enterprises that acquired the licenses for the production of HRB-400, HRB-500 grade steel in China. Its products were chosen by many major projects such as the Beijing Olympic Games and Beijing-Shanghai Express

Railway. Second, steel slates and strips with CE, FPC (Factory Production Control) accreditations, e.g., wide steel strip, narrow steel strip, cold-rolled sheet, etc. These products are widely used in wield pipes, pressure vessel, and shipbuilding industries and exported to European Union, South America, and South-East Asia. Third, formed steel, e.g., H-beam applicable with various international standards. Laiwu steel is one of largest scale H-beam production bases in China with most complete specifications. Its EU standard H-beam for nuclear power stations fills a gap in Chinese production line. Finally, the company deals with special steel with a history of more than 40 years and mainly serves mechanical and automobile industry, including carbon structural steel, structural alloy steel, pinion steel, and bearing steel. Among those, pinion steel has become the top-selling product for five years in China. China First Auto Works and Ford are among its account clients.

Besides iron and steel products, Laiwu Steel also provides extensive services through its subsidiaries. The company offers advanced design in metallurgy and engineering design in construction field, and its design projects include mines, sintering machines, coke-oven plants, blast furnaces, and so on. Recently, Laiwu Steel also expands into steel construction, real estate, and new building materials. Its green energy-saving buildings have constructed in many cities in China. Laiwu Steel's achievement in IT and automation engineering is also notable. It is listed among the top PLC (programmable logic controller) and DCS (distributed control system) experiment bases in China, and its blast production lines and related control systems have been exported to India, Malaysia, and so on.

In China steel industry, Laiwu Steel took the lead to pass ISO9001 quality management system certification, ISO14001 environment management system certification, and OHSAS 18001 occupational safety and health management systems certification in the nationwide metallurgy and machinery industries.

Challenges and Business Strategies

Affected by the trend of globalization, Laiwu Steel faces challenges from home and aboard. Within China, it primarily competes with Magang (Group) Holding Co. Ltd., Baosteel, Wuhan Iron & Steel Group Corp., and Changzhi Iron & Steel Group Co. Ltd., which mainly focus on medium- and low-level steel markets; in the world, Laiwu Steel mainly competes with Arcelor Mittal (MT), Inchon Iron & Steel, Nippon Steel Corporation, and so on, which mainly focus on high-end steel market where China relies on importation. Some of the global steel giants also plan to invest in China to enhance their market share. Among them, the Korean competitors are especially notable for their huge H-beam output.

Laiwu Steel puts special emphasis on building a learning organization and a corporate culture of innovation. It has adopted the theory of learning organization to reform the corporate management and improve the thinking and behaviors of the company and employees. This strategy was implemented as early as 2000, which led to more than 750 programs in technical and management innovations being initiated and implemented. As the most important strategy for building its competitive advantage, those various innovative measures contributed to its rapid development. Consequently, within six years, Laiwu Steel's output jumped from 2 million tons to 10 million tons.

Recently, Laiwu Steel has been negatively affected by the global economy downturn. Facing such a challenge, Laiwu Steel has modified its strategy toward the high technical level and high value-added products through management improvement and technical innovations. From January to August 2008, nearly 40% of its sales were generated from high end products. Among them, the EU standard H formed steel for nuclear power stations has been delivered to its customer. Next, Laiwu Steel has enforced the cost control to every strategic unit even individual employees. Consequently, energy and emission saving became more prominent as a way to reduce cost and increase revenue. Finally, Laiwu Steel has switched to a customer-orientated strategy. It offers customized product and professional service through deep research to meet the customer needs. Beijing-Shanghai Express Railway has proved the success of this strategy, as 15 of 21 stations will be built with the steel supplied by Laiwu Steel.

Lujin (Regina) Huang and Shiqiang (Kenny) Wang

References

Laiwu Steel Group Co. Ltd. http://www.google.com/finance?q=SHA:600102. Retrieved on 1 June 2009.

刘传佳，王利峰 (2008). 沂蒙西麓，走出一支钢铁劲旅: 莱钢三十年发展纪实. *中国冶金报*, 23 December. [Liu, C and L Wang. A steel force on the west side of Mt. Yimeng: Thirty years of development of Laiwu Steel part I]. http://www.laigang.com/lgnews/view2.asp?id=2961. Retrieved on 22 June 2009.

刘传佳，王利峰 (2008). 解读科学发展密码: 莱钢三十年发展纪实. *中国冶金报*, 25 December. [Liu, C and L Wang. Interpreting the secret of scientific development: Thirty years of development of Laiwu Steel part II]. http://www.laigang.com/lgnews/view2.asp?id=2962. Retrieved on 22 June 2009.

LENOVO GROUP

Corporate Address and Contact Information

Lenovo Group Ltd.
6 Shangdi Chuangye Road
Haidian District, Beijing 100085
People's Republic of China
Phone: (86)10-5886-8888
www.lenovo.com

Lenovo (联想集团有限公司) is the fourth largest firm in the global PC market with global market share 7.6% in 2007. As the best-selling brand in the world's second-largest PC market — China, and a global leader in the PC market, Lenovo develops, manufactures, and markets cutting-edge, high-quality PC products and offers value-added professional services. In the 2007/2008 fiscal year, Lenovo's sales increased by 17% compared with last year to approximately US$16.352 billion, and the gross profit margin for the year was 15%. The group had a steady improvement with profit before taxation (excluding the cost of strategic restructuring actions) increased significantly by 237% to US$5.6 billion, and the profit attributable to shareholders totaled US$0.484 billion, up 201% from the previous year.

Historical Development

Lenovo experienced three stages of development in its corporate history. During the initial domestic dominance stage (1984–1997), it took Lenovo 14 years to become the No. 1 in PC business in China via local distribution of foreign brands and marketing its own products. In 1984, with RMB 200,000 (US$25,000) in seed money from the Chinese Academy of Sciences, Liu Chuanzhi and 10 other engineers and researchers set up shop in a small, one-story bungalow in Beijing. The founding of the company, Legend, which offered service such as installation of computers, examination of imported computer as well as training beginners, marked the new era of consumer PCs in China. Since 1987, Lenovo expanded its commercial activities to include both trade and distribution, becoming the first distributor of

AST. Through the distribution of foreign made PCs, Lenovo not only accumulated the necessary funds but also learned how to organize sales channels and sell personal computers.

In 1991, Lenovo acquired the license for production of personal computers, and began to manufacture PC with its own brand. In 1993, Lenovo became China's largest domestic manufacturer of personal computers, next to AST and Compaq. Meanwhile, Lenovo expanded and strengthened its R&D activities by establishing three large-scale manufacturing bases to develop its own capacity. By 1994, Lenovo was trading on the Hong Kong Stock Exchange; four years later, it produced its one-millionth personal computer. In 1997, Lenovo become the top manufacturer in Chinese PC market.

During the second, restructuring stage (1998–2003), it took Lenovo four years to restructure its business offering and internal organization, including corporate spin-off, diversification, and ownership reform. After became the biggest dealer of personal computer in the Asia-Pacific region (excluding Japan) in 1999, Lenovo strived to engage innovations and meet the consumer needs in more segment markets. In particular, two R&D centers were established: with the first one focusing the development of the current technologies including server, notebook, consumer IT, business desktops, and so on; and the second concentrating on future technologies.

During the third, globalization stage (2004–present), Lenovo began to aggressively pursue its globalization goal of joining the rank of the top 500 companies in the world with a well-known global brand. In 2005, Lenovo merged with the IBM's PC business, and within three years turned the unit that previously generated an annual loss of US$0.2 billion into a profit. Lenovo's turnover jumped from US$3 billion to US$17 billion, and its goal of doubling the profit established three years ago was easily reached with the increase in global computer sales.

Main Products and Services

Globally, Lenovo offers customers ThinkPad notebooks and ThinkCentre desktops, featuring the ThinkVantage Technologies software tools, as well as ThinkVision monitors and a full line of PC accessories and options. Within China, Lenovo delivers a set of servers, peripherals, and digital products. With its cutting-edge technology, customer friendly features, and personalized design solutions, Lenovo's PC products are well received and capture 30% of market share in China. In the 2007/08 fiscal year, its notebook accounted for more than 58% of total sales around the world. Lenovo has also expanded its product lines to digital cameras, printers, cell phones, set-top boxes, and network equipment, demonstrating diversified characteristics.

In October 2007, ThinkPad's logo was switched from IBM to Lenovo all over the world, and its global sales of notebook in the fiscal year raised by about 36%, market share increased to 7.8%; desktop computers accounted for about 41% of its total sales, increased by 13%, while the global market increased by only 4%. Through the successful integration of product platform, Lenovo has made a significant upgrade of its competitiveness and profitability in the global market, since its product complexity has been reduced and the cost-effectiveness improved. Nevertheless, as a result of intense market competition, its mobile phone business recorded total sales of about US$436 million, down 28.7% compared with 2007. In March 2008, Lenovo sold this division to a private equity.

Corporate Structure and Leadership

As an MNC, Lenovo is headquartered in Raleigh (the United States), and has branches in 66 countries and sales operations in more than 50 countries around the world. Lenovo is a global company with major research centers in Beijing, Shanghai, and Shenzhen, China; Yamato, Japan; and Research Triangle

Park, North Carolina (the United States); and primary operational hubs in Beijing, Research Triangle Park, Singapore and Paris. Lenovo operates manufacturing and/or assembly facilities in China, India, the United States and Mexico (and soon in Europe) with a total of approximately 25,000 employees in 2007. To tide over the recent economic crisis, Lenovo announced a global restructuring in January 2009, streamlining the organizational structure in EMEA (Europe, the Middle East, and Africa) and the Americas, which expected to result in a saving of US$300 million.

In two decades, founder Liu Chuanzhi has successfully transformed Lenovo from a small state-owned enterprise into a flagship joint-stock conglomerate that is largely owned by overseas investors. Under Liu, Lenovo established an option plan and incentive mechanism, which enabled a large number of young people embark on the first line of leadership positions. Meanwhile, Liu combined the modern Western management theories with the practice of Chinese enterprises, and put forward management ideas such as "a roof model of corporate governance theory". Liu's core philosophy is to "build a team, set a strategy, and organize a team". People believe such a practical and effective approach has contributed to Lenovo's success as a large modern company with international competitive edge.

Business Strategies and International Expansion

To further expand its business, Lenovo has developed a comprehensive five-part strategy. First, the company plans to accelerate its international process. As early as 2000, Lenovo had put forward a strategic objective of being a "ministrant, high-tech, and internationalized" company. In order to achieve such a goal, Lenovo introduced a three-step strategy of globalization: the first step is to change its brand name to Lenovo in 2003, taking the "Le" from Legend, a nod to its heritage, and adding "novo", the Latin word for "new", to reflect the spirit of innovation at the core of the company. A year later, the corporate name was changed from Legend to Lenovo as well. The second step is to acquire IBM's PC business, which Liu remarked: "The group's brand will be well propagated by the worldwide shock of Lenovo's acquisition of IBM's business". The third step is to break into the global market through the Olympic Games. Lenovo selected strategic alliances or joint ventures with global corporations, such as Visa, Coca-Cola, Disney, Pacific Century Cyber Works, and so on, as its entry model, which effectively reduced the risk of international expansion and shortened the time to enter the target market.

Second, Lenovo seeks to optimize the process of supply chain. In order to increase the efficiency of its global supply chain, Lenovo makes strong commitment to continuously improve its management process and has so far achieved remarkable progress. By simplifying its global supply chain infrastructure including its logistics network, Lenovo further enhanced its service capacity by 10%, with each computer's cost of end-to-end supply chain reduced by 17% as compared with 2008.

Third, Lenovo strives to refocus its corporate attention on the key and emerging markets in the world. In 2008, consumer PC accounted for above 42% of the global PC market. The key for Lenovo is to expand its business scale by replicating the successful experience in China to the other areas. In this regard, Lenovo has won an impressive array of contracts in India and ASEAN countries through effective marketing strategies. Lenovo also outperformed the industry in key emerging markets such as Russia, Mexico, Brazil, and Turkey. Meanwhile, Lenovo has made important progress in adjusting to the changing market conditions and has accelerated its expansion in the fast-growing industry segments, with a belief that such rapid growth is expected to continue in the coming years.

Fourth, Lenovo attempts to expand both relational and transactional business models. In 2008, Lenovo's relational business increased in all areas. After making efforts on the adjustment of customer segmentation and customer relational management, Lenovo's profitability has been raised by a large margin. In the future, Lenovo's business focus will remain on providing services to key customers and improving the share in the medium-sized enterprises market. In contrast, in 2008, Lenovo's transactional business accounted for 35% of the sales of global PC market (excluded the Greater China region). Looking forward, to maintain sustainable growth, Lenovo will continue to develop its business partners through marketing activities, accelerate the development of emerging markets, and enhance the performance ability in some countries, as well as to expand the productivity and the channel coverage of its sale teams.

Finally, Lenovo aims to establish a global brand. In 2008, Lenovo has done a superb job in marketing and brand building by sponsoring the Olympic Games, AT&T Williams Formula One team and the NBA games. To raise the awareness and image of the brand, the group launched a publicity campaign for two of its major products, which has in turn helped enhance Lenovo's brand visualization: ThinkPad ultra-slim X300 made the cover of *BusinessWeek* as soon as it appeared on the market, and IdeaPad U110 won three major awards on International Consumer Electronics Show in Las Vegas, the United States. Through those efforts, Lenovo has made a deeper impression in the international arenas and gained rapid recognition, consequently the image of Lenovo brand has been improved by 13% according to one survey.

Future Challenges

Global economic slowdown has affected all industries and in all countries in 2008. As a result the worldwide PC market recorded a drop in unit shipment, and Lenovo's PC shipments dropped 4.7%, and its overall performance lagged behind the industry shipment growth. Looking forward, Lenovo begins to implement a major restructuring that includes a reduction of 11% of its workforce and a renewed focus on the emerging markets such as China, which currently accounts for more than 40% of its revenue. With its continual and aggressive efforts in internationalization, Lenovo will likely play an increasingly significant role in the global computer and high-tech market in the coming years.

Sixian Zhou, Bing Ren, and Sunny Li Sun

References

Golden Sachs Report (2009). What Lenovo needs: Strengthening ThinkPad, cost down in IdeaPad.

Lenovo Group Ltd. (2008). *Annual Report*. http://www.pc.ibm.com/ww/lenovo/pdf/07_08/Lenovo_2007-08_Annual_Report_Final_E.pdf. Retrieved on 24 April 2009.

Li, P (2007). Toward an integrated theory of multinational evolution: The evidence of Chinese multinational enterprises as latecomers. *Journal of International Management*, 13(3): 296–318.

Liu, CZ (2007). Lenovo: An example of globalization of Chinese enterprises. *Journal of International Business*, 38(4): 573–577.

Spencer, J and L Chao (2008). Lenovo goes global, but not without strife, *Wall Street Journal*, 4 November.

白思迪，谢伟 (2008). *联想集团有限公司对动态战略匹配的追求*. 北京: 北京大学出版社 [Bai, S and W Xie. *Lenovo's Pursuit of Dynamic Strategies*. Beijing: Peking University Press].

LIUZHOU IRON AND STEEL

Corporate Address and Contact Information

Liuzhou Iron & Steel Co. Ltd.
117 Beique Road
Liubei District
Liuzhou, Guangxi 545002

People's Republic of China
Phone: (86)772-259-3658
Fax: (86)772-259-5998
www.liusteel.com

Liuzhou Iron & Steel Co. Ltd. (柳州钢铁股份有限公司), hereinafter referred to by its English moniker "Liuzhou Steel", is best known in China by its abbreviated nickname "Liu Steel" (柳钢). Located in the industrial city of Liuzhou, Guangxi Zhuang Autonomous Region in Southwestern China, Liuzhou Steel is one of the country's growing national champions — state-owned corporations slated for development into industrial global multinationals with significant domestic ties, large blocks of state ownership while offering market opportunities such as public listing of stocks through operational subsidiaries. Stocks of a listed subsidiary of Liuzhou Steel are available on the Shanghai Stock Exchange.

Historical Development

Since its inception in 1958, Liuzhou Steel has developed total assets of more than RMB 22 billion of primarily state-owned large iron and steel enterprises, including industry-derivative businesses based on iron and steel, engineering design, construction installation, machinery manufacturing, automobile transport, tourism, commerce, housing real estate, environmental protection, cement, and other industries. The company employs more than 14,000 people, including a large number of all kinds of professional and technical personnel.

In 2006, Liuzhou Steel produced more than 5 million tons of iron, steel, and timber products, with its primary holdings grossing more than RMB 20 billion. During the year ending 31 December 2008, the most recent year for which numbers are available, Liuzhou Steel produced approximately 6.09 million metric tons of steel, 3.57 million metric tons of steel products, and 5.54 million tons of iron. In terms of global annual output of iron and steel enterprises, Liuzhou Steel was ranked No. 53 by the China National Bureau of Statistics and in terms of the country's 500 largest business groups, Liuzhou Steel was ranked No. 146. While Liuzhou Steel's 2007 ranking in the top 500 Chinese enterprises dropped to No. 187, it grew to be the largest industrial enterprise in Guangxi. Liuzhou Iron and Steel has won numerous Chinese domestic awards, including the award for National Civilized Unit, the award for National Quality and Efficiency of Advanced Enterprises, the award for National Quality Management of Advanced Enterprises, the award for National Contract and Re-credit Enterprises, and the Honorary Title of Advanced Units, to name a few.

Main Products, Services, and Corporate Leadership

Liuzhou Steel's principal activities are the producing, refining, processing and selling of steel and its by-products along with significant interests in the industries derivative of the aforementioned activities that include refining and selling iron, coking products and by-products, exporting self-produced products and technologies, importing of materials, machinery, equipment, apparatus, and parts for production, and research and processing of imported materials. In its activities in the manufacture and sale of steel products, Liuzhou Steel offers steel billets and small steel sections, as well as median steel plates including common carbon plates, low steel alloy boards, ship boards, boiler plates, and pressure vessel plates. The company distributes its products internationally from its stronghold of Guangxi and neighboring Guangdong Province in China.

Guangxi Liuzhou Iron & Steel (Group) Company CEO and party secretary Chen Yongnan (1951–) is a Guangxi native from the county of Bobai. A party member with extensive local contacts and strong dedication to his home province, he joined Liuzhou Steel in 1970. Chen is a 1990 graduate of the Guangxi Institute of Economic Management; he has since obtained a master's degree and has been honored with a "Senior Economist" title. Under his leadership, Liuzhou Steel has seen double-digit growth through 2007. More recently, with the economic downturn, his leadership has also carried out mill reconfigurations and the concurrent closing of old factories and opening of new factories.

Challenges and Business Strategies

Liuzhou Steel is facing numerous challenges as it moves forward and develops into a national and international steel products competitor. Return on net assets for 2008 was just 0.33% against 19.89% for the same period in 2007. The net income of RMB 998 million from 2007 dipped to just 15.5 million in 2008. The global steel marketplace is highly competitive and the industry as a whole is generally dominated by massive multinational conglomerates with strong nationalistic ties based on the support and often outright state ownership of many of their component companies. China's steel industry is no different and the country is committed to developing its own national champions in the steel industry. This commitment, however, has led to over development of capacity within China relative to the global demand for steel products. In particular, 2008 was a difficult year for the global steel industry, as the worldwide economic downturn led to steep declines in the demand for steel on an international scale. In an industry such as steel production, which requires significant long-term capital investment in infrastructure, it is difficult to react to unexpected market fluctuations.

Liuzhou Steel's 2008 performance can be seen as a reflection of the Chinese national policy toward the domestic steel industry. China has taken the approach of continuing to press for the modernization and expansion of new steel plants while limiting excess capacity by concurrently closing down older, most often outdated and environmentally less desirable mills. On a macro level, this is no doubt a solid strategy for development of China's industry as a whole — limiting capacity while modernizing processes and improving environmental impacts. At the micro level, individual companies such as Liuzhou Steel are faced with sudden, unexpected profit drops and even losses. China is undergoing a wave of mergers and acquisitions in its steel industry as larger producers are encouraged to buy out and smaller rivals. Liuzhou Steel has not been unaffected — the Wuhan Steel Group (one of China's largest state-owned steel groups) has purchased into the parent company of Liuzhou Steel and 2008 has also seen many of the new mills in China being built and operated as joint ventures between large producers. Additionally, state-owned enterprises, with their high labor inefficiencies are susceptible to social upheaval and political unrest when business decisions such as closing plants or limiting production have dramatic impacts on local populations. Liuzhou Steel, as both a national and regional champion, must balance its development against its role as a major state-owned employer in a relatively impoverished and less economically developed region of China.

Michael J. Miske

References

Hornby, L (2009). SW China's Guangxi makes room for new steel mill. *Reuters*, 16 January. http://www.reuters.com/article/rbssSteel/idUSPEK30320720090116. Retrieved on 26 August 2009.

Reuters (2009). Liuzhou Iron & Steel Co. Ltd. Financial Statements. http://www.reuters.com/finance/stocks/income Statement?stmtType=INC&perType=INT&symbol=LIUZF.PK. Retrieved on 26 August 2009.

柳州钢铁股份有限公司 (2009). 公司概况 [Liuzhou Iron & Steel Co. Ltd. Company Profile] http://www.liusteel.com/about/about.htm. Retrieved on 26 August 2009.

MAANSHAN IRON & STEEL

Corporate Address and Contact Information

Maanshan Iron and Steel Co. Ltd.
8 Hongqi Zhong Road
Maanshan, Anhui Province 243003
People's Republic of China
Phone: (86)555-288-8158
Fax: (86)555-288-7284
http://www.magang.com.hk/index.asp

Maanshan Iron & Steel Co. Ltd. (马鞍山钢铁股份有限公司) is located in Maanshan, Anhui Province in east-central China, which was settled in 205 BC and is one of China's smallest provinces. The area surrounding the city is fertile, being watered by the Huai and Yangtze rivers, and has abundant in natural resources of iron, coal, and copper. Out of this agricultural center has risen one of the largest iron and steel complexes in China — Maanshan Iron & Steel Co. Ltd. (also known as Masteel).

Historical Development

More than 55 years of hard work has gone into the development of the Maanshan Iron & Steel Co. Ltd. The firm was established and started production in early 1953 as the Maanshan Iron Mining Plant. Five years later, the Maanshan Iron & Steel Company was founded and inspected by Chairman Mao in the fall of 1959. From its earliest days Masteel has promoted environmentally clean production with no leakage operations, and the firm was honored with the name "a flower of Jiangnan" (south part of the Yangtze).

The 1980s brought new technologies to the firm, as nine national super-grade blast furnaces were put in operation and the first high-speed wire and rod mills brought world attention to Masteel. In 1992, the firm became a Chinese national super-large enterprise following visits by Premier Li Peng and General Secretary Jiang Zemin. A year later Masteel regrouped and was able to raise RMB 6.4 billion through shareholder equity, allowing them to divide into the Magang Holding Company and Maanshan Iron & Steel Company Ltd.

By installing a 2,500-cubic-meter blast furnace in 1994, Masteel emerged on the world market as a Sino-foreign limited liability company certified by the National Foreign Trade and Economic Commission. ISO9002 quality certification followed in 1997, and new processes were developed for train wheel production and the first H-beam in China was rolled in 1998. In the same year, Magang Holding Company was renamed Magang (Group) Holding Company Ltd., indicating an increased presence in the industry.

Developments in both hot rolling and cold rolling of thin strip steel in 2001 and 2002 was a key to the restructuring of the firm's core business and sent the firm into the super-large enterprise group. In the next two years (2003–2004), key process developments brought online additional high-speed wire lines, pig iron blast furnaces; cold- and hot-rolled thin coiled-steel lines; and the first hot-dip galvanized coil production was started.

Main Products and Services

Iron, steel, and rolled products produced by Maanshan Iron & Steel Co. Ltd. fall into four categories: steel plates, section steel, wire rods, and train wheels. All of the four main product lines are ISO9001 quality certified.

Masteel produces hot-rolled thin plates, which are used in the automobile, construction, and machinery industries, while cold-rolled thin plates support light industries such as home appliances and automotive small parts production. High-grade galvanized plates manufactured at Masteel plates are used by firms in the home appliance, eating utensil, and construction industries. Coiled plates are used by construction and steel window frame industries among others, while medium plates are used in the manufacturing of shipbuilding, pressurized vessels, containers, and heavy plates form the sides of ships.

Maanshan Iron & Steel Co. Ltd. holds the patent on shock and fire-resistant H-shaped steel used on construction. Its H-shaped section steel is used for drilling platforms, railways, ships, and a wide variety of steel structures that require strength and ridged forms. The company is proud of its quality and certifications in this business area, having been awarded the "Golden Cup Prize in Quality Metal Products" by the Chinese Construction Materials Enterprise Management Association.

A core technology for Masteel is high-efficiency, low-cost cold-forged steel with wire-softening treatment. This patented line produces high-speed wire rods and the hot-rolled reinforcing steel that is used in armored concrete construction, strand steel wires, and spring steel wires. The quality of these product lines is so high that the General Administration of Quality Supervision, Inspection, and Quarantine of the PRC has honored the firm by acclaiming "The First Lot of Quality Products Exempted from Inspection" certification.

Train wheel production includes wheel and rims used for railway transportation, port machinery, petrochemical industries, and the aerospace industry. Maanshan Iron & Steel Co. Ltd. leads the industry and holds the patent and core technology for train wheels used for high-speed railroads.

Corporate Leadership and Structure

Masteel is led by a trio of executives: Gu Jianguo is president of Magang (Group) Holding Co. Ltd. and chairman of the Board of Maanshan Iron & Steel Co. Ltd., while Gu Zhanggen is secretary of party committee of Magang (Group) Holding Co. Ltd., and Zhu Changqiu is president of Maanshan Iron & Steel Co. Ltd.

The firm has approximately 70,000 active employees who produce about 8 million tons of steel each year, generating assets around 80 billion RMB. Approximately 90 percent of Masteel output stays in the PRC while the rest is shipped to nearly 50 countries. Maanshan Iron & Steel Co. Ltd. is a state-owned enterprise and operates on its behalf as well as the behalf of Magang (Group) Holding Co. Ltd. As a major shareholder for Maanshan Iron & Steel Co. Ltd., the Chinese government selected Masteel as one of the nine pilot enterprises in the country to be listed overseas. As a result, the company issued H-shares on the Hong Kong Stock Exchange in 1993, and RMB common shares were also listed on the Shanghai Stock Exchange (SSE) during 1993 and 1994. The company further issued bonds with warrants on the SSE in 2006. Magang (Group) Holding Co. Ltd. is a controlling shareholder of the company.

Business Strategies

Quality products are the primary differentiation strategy for Masteel. The firm is actively engaged in a strategy to create an internationally competitive business model. During its history, Maanshan Iron & Steel Co. Ltd. has utilized a series of Five-Year Plans; it is currently in its eleventh. According to company reports, this plan completed its initial stage of technological renovation and structural adjustment in 2007. Masteel now looks to strengthen and expand its core iron and steel business. This strategy is illustrated by the expansion of its train wheel-rolling system, silicon steel production line, large-scale roll production line, and the forged steel production line.

Other key strategic initiatives include increasing competitiveness in its thin-plate lines, which now has a 5-million ton annual capacity. As a key feature in its Eleventh Five-Year Plan during 2007–2012, the firm seeks to increase its core iron and steel business. The dynamic nature of Masteel strategy in the raw material and fuel market initiates is also observed, as the company is developing Strategic partnerships with suppliers to promote the logistics flow of Chinese production of spare parts and components with the goal of reducing costs.

Along with other Chinese firms, Masteel is looking to strengthen its management of intellectual property with the goal of incentivizing in this area. Maanshan Iron & Steel Co. Ltd. hopes to integrate its internal research in technical innovation areas of construction. To respond to Chinese infrastructure plans, the firm looks to expand its capacity of train wheel rolling system, steel production line, and forged steel production line. These expansions should also help in developing external markets and expand the firm's market shares.

Maanshan Iron & Steel Co. Ltd. has been included in one of the state's second group of recycling economy pilot enterprise programs. Masteel's strategy here is to strengthen its quantitative management of resources leading to the development of energy consumption statistics and utilization enhanced plans. The company hopes to implement an all-staff incentive system to focus attention on energy consumption and emission reduction. Another goal of those conservation initiatives is to develop the firm into a state-graded environmentally friendly enterprise.

Future Development Plans

Operations at Masteel continue to focus on product quality and the optimization of product mix. These are critical initiatives that are made more difficult in the midst of a worldwide recession. Specifically, the company is focusing on the following developmental areas: accelerating product research and development in the thin plate production area; reducing costs and expenses; raising the abilities in technological innovation; cultivating and expanding new profit growth sources; pushing ahead energy conservation and emissions reduction; and strengthening environmental protection.

Masteel has established joint ventures with the 17th China Metallurgical Construction Co. Ltd., Chery Automobile Co. Ltd., and Foshan Shunde Shungeng Material Supply Co. Ltd., all which should add leverage to the current product lines. Growth is certainly a strong possibility with the Chery Automobile Company joint venture, as Chery is the largest independent Chinese auto manufacturer and one of the fastest growing automobile fabricators in the world.

Given the large capacity of the company's iron and steel lines, the firm imports about 80 percent of its iron ore, and struggles with its rising costs. The increasing expenses of these ore imports and the additional shipping fees have led to cost-reduction strategies such as standardization efforts and brand marketing efforts. Company leaders are examining both technical and management standards to improve operations and reduce costs.

Masteel's Role in the Chinese and Global Economies

Maanshan Iron & Steel Co. Ltd. is the second largest producer and marketer of iron and steel in the People's Republic of China. Masteel is challenged by the 2009 worldwide economic recession. Global demand is down for steel products and this is expected to reduce international orders. Further, the United States of America and the European Union are imposing import restrictions and tariffs on all foreign-produced steel. International automobile-manufacturing and ship-building industries are also experiencing demand reductions. Thus, the Chinese steel industry as a whole is over capacity. Chinese steel mills have the capacity to produce approximately 600 million tons of steel a year, while domestic demand is about only 450 million tons. Masteel is responding to these challenges by pursuing a low-cost strategy. The firm hopes that the infrastructure stimulus spearheaded in Beijing will stimulate demand for steel products domestically.

Approximately, 90 percent of its current production is used in the PRC. Masteel needs to develop its offshore sales if it is to grow in the short run. Beijing has stimulus initiatives in place that should help develop additional internal demand for steel. Nonetheless, Chinese private construction, new car sales, and shipyard construction are having difficult times. Overall internal demand is likely to drop, as will international demand since these same industries are under stress worldwide. In early 2009, the European Union placed a 25-percent duty on imports of steel reinforcing bars from China, and other such tariffs may be implemented before the world economies rebound. Overall, it appears that Masteel will continue to deal with high cost pressures, difficulties in reducing iron ore prices, and low internal and international demand for its products.

James P. Gilbert

References

Alon, I and JR McIntyre (eds.) (2008). *Globalization of Chinese Enterprises*. New York: Palgrave Macmillan.

Holland, T (2009). Steelmakers' outlook not as strong as investors believe. *South China Morning Post*, 30 January, Business, p. 8. Lexus-Nexus Academic [7 February 2009].

Maanshan Iron & Steel Company Limited (2009). 2008 Annual Report. www.magang.com.hk/eng/report.asp. Retrieved on 7 February 2009.

Maanshan Iron & Steel Company Limited (2007). Company Profile. www.magang.com.hk/eng/companypofile.asp. Retrieved on 7 February 2009.

Zhang, W and I Alon (eds.) (2009). *Biographical Dictionary of New Chinese Entrepreneurs and Business Leaders*. Northampton, MA: Edward Elgar Publishing.

NANJING IRON & STEEL

Corporate Address and Contact Information

Nanjing Iron & Steel Company
Xiejiadian, Liuhe District
Nanjing, Jiangsu 210035
People's Republic of China
Phone: (86)25-5707-3114
www.njsteel.com.cn

Nanjing Iron & Steel United Company Ltd. (NISCO United 南京钢铁股份有限公司) is a joint venture established by the Nanjing Iron and Steel Group and the Fosun Group in 2003. It includes ferrous metals pressing and melting, as well as steel goods trade. Located in the center of eastern China, NISCO is among the largest in the steel market. The company produces over one million tons of medium steel plates, and one million tons of heavy steel plates and strips per year.

Historical Development

The Nanjing Iron & Steel United Co. Ltd. is a company with short history. Its predecessor, founded in 1958, was incorporated in 2003 into a new group in partnership with the Fosun Group. According to the agreement, NISCO's capital was formed by: 40% of the Nanjing Iron & Steel Group Co. Ltd.; 30% of the Shanghai Fosun High-Tech Co. Ltd.; 20% of the Shanghai Fosun Industrial & Investment Co. Ltd; and 10% of the Shanghai Guangxing Sci-Tech Development Co. Ltd. On 28 April 2009, the company discontinued its trading of shares for a shareholding restructuring. According to an *International Iron and Steel Institute* ranking, Nanjing Iron & Steel was the 20th largest company in the Chinese steel industry and the 53rd largest in the world in 2007 (the 57th largest in the world in 2006).

The current leadership team of NISCO United include: Yang Siming, chief executive officer; Yang Zhenhe, vice president; and Diao Yuechuan, chief engineer. The company is sited and has its headquarters in Nanjing, Jiangsu Province. With a current staff of 5,338 employees, Nanjing Iron & Steel owns 11 subsidiaries and an associated company working in the steel products market, including the Nanjing Iron & Steel International Trade Co. Ltd. and the Wuxi Jinxin Steel-Rolling Co. Ltd. NISCO shares have been traded on the Shanghai Stock Exchange since 2000.

Main Products and Services

NISCO is a medium-sized steel manufacturer, with an average production capacity of 6.5 million tons in 2008 (5.9 million tons in 2007). Its production has reached as high as 4.97 million tons of steel, 5.14 million tons of pig iron, and 4.25 million tons of steel goods, which were sold in both domestic and international markets. According to the *Iron & Steel Works of the World Directory* (2009), the company has a capacity of four million tons in iron ore production.

NISCO's main activities are ferrous metals pressing and smelting, and sales of steel goods, billets, pig iron, and other steel materials. The company also produces and sells coke. Its main products include: carbon steel — wire rod, reinforcing bars, round bars, hot-rolled uncoated hoop and strip, medium plates, heavy plates, hot-rolled uncoated sheet/coil, wire; alloy steel (other than stainless) — round bars, hot-rolled hoop and strip, wire; bearing steel; spring steel; and tool steel.

The company structure includes the following operations: coke ovens; sinter plant; iron ore, palletizing plant; blast furnaces (one 2,000 cu. meter); steel-making plant (one top- and bottom-blowing 150-ton basic oxygen converter); 100-ton electric, arc furnace; VAR (Vacuum Arc Remelting) refining plant; and wire rod, medium plate, and strip/sheet rolling mills.

At present, the company operates the widest slab caster in the world (3,250-mm wide by 150-mm thick), as well as a more conventional caster (2,300-mm wide by up to 260-mm thick), and a multi-strand bloom caster. The Nanjing Iron & Steel United Co. owns certifications in quality management systems (ISO9001:2000) and environmental management systems (ISO14001).

Challenges and Business Strategies

The Nanjing Iron & Steel United Co. has several major competitors within the Chinese domestic steel market, among them: Anshan Iron and Steel, located in Anshan; Baosteel, in Shanghai; and Jiangsu Shagang, in *Zhangjiagang*. NISCO sells its products primarily in Nanjing, Shanghai, Hangzhou, Beijing, as well as Guangdong Province, all in China.

NISCO is China's second largest producer of medium and heavy plate, fifth largest producer of high-value-added steel for oil pipelines, and fourth largest producer of ship-plate steel. In 2007, NISCO ranked fifth, fourth and first in its profit per ton, profit per capital, and ROI (returns on investment), respectively. NISCO's major products include medium and heavy plate, welding and wiring equipment and materials, and iron strips. NISCO's medium plate and its medium and heavy plate production system have won a CE (Conformité Européenne) authentication.

NISCO has been constantly optimizing and diversifying its product mix to embrace more high-value-added products. Its largely experienced and ambitious team is an integral part of its competitive advantage in the corporate market. Nevertheless, like all the steel mills in China, Nanjing Iron & Steel Co. Ltd. was affected by the 2008 market crisis — including cost increases for raw materials and the international financial crisis at the end of the year. Hence, although its operational revenues increased 28% in the year — to a total of RMB 28.35 billion, its profits dropped as much as 88.08% — to 17.98 million dollars, or RMB 0.07 per share.

For 2009, the company previews a small increase in production — up to 5.12 million tons of steel, 5.33 million tons of pig iron, and 4.31 million tons of rolled steel. Nonetheless, revenue is estimated to be lower than in 2008 — a total of RMB 23.99 billion, or a 15.37% reduction — due to price reductions of its products.

Future Growth Plans

The company has just announced some investment plans focused on a new line of products of low-carbon bainite, wide and medium plate, which have been approved by the Jiangxi Science & Technology Bureau, and the Finance Commission of Jiangsu Province. Such investments total up to RMB 370 million, yielding a production capacity of 0.5 million tons of low-carbon bainite wide and medium plate per year. The project includes the development of 28 technology patents and 19 invention patents. All these technological efforts have allowed the company's mastery of 8 key technologies, and 18 new products in 5 varieties.

Low-carbon bainite steel has properties of high strength, high tenacity, good welding, and low cost. NISCO expects that this new line of products may contribute to overcome the current difficulties originating from the world's financial crisis. It believes that these new products will bring in a net profit of RMB 419 million to the company, which still achieving sales revenue of RMB 4.058 billion.

In February 2009, the company announced the delivery of an initial batch of steel plates for the first offshore wind energy installations of the Shanghai Donghai Bridge Offshore Wind Farm Project. This wind farm stands in two lines, a thousand meters from the Shanghai Donghai Bridge. It is expected that the farm will be installed with a gross capacity of 100,000 kW and will produce 260m kWh of electricity per year. In the near future, NISCO's bottom line will likely be positively affected by its substantial contribution toward the construction of this project.

Marco Antonio Tourinho Furtado and Tays Torres Ribeiro Chagas

References

BusinessWeek (2008). Nanjing Iron & Steel United Co. Ltd. (600282: Shanghai Stock Exchange). http://investing. businessweek.com/research/stocks/snapshot/snapshot.asp?ric=600282.SS. Retrieved on 19 December 2008.

Iron & Steel Works of the World Directory (2009). London: Metal Bulletin Directories. Nanjing Steel sells plate to China 1st offshore wind project (11 March 2009). http://en.chinasteelnet.com/html/Steelmills-dynamic/200903/12.html. Retrieved on 4 May 2009.

Wright Investors' Service (2008). Nanjing Iron & Steel United Co. Ltd. http://wrightreports.ecnext.com/coms2/reportdesc_COMPANY_C156VV200. Retrieved on 16 December 2008.

Yu, H (2009). Nanjing Iron & Steel profits down 88%. *China Daily*, 11 March. http://www.chinadaily.com.cn/bizchina/2009-03/11/content_7568028.htm. Retrieved on 4 May 2009.

PANZHIHUA NEW STEEL & VANADIUM

Corporate Address and Contact Information

Panzhihua New Steel and Vanadium
Xiangyang Village Eastern District
Panzhihua City
Sichuan Province 617067
People's Republic of China
Phone: (86)81-2339-2044
Fax: (86)81-2339-3992
www.pzhsteel.com.cn

Panzhihua New Steel & Vanadium Company Limited (攀枝花新钢钒股份有限公司) is a subsidiary of Panzhihua Iron and Steel Group. Panzhihua's principal activities are manufacturing and trading of steel and steel products that consist of hot-rolling steel plates and steel belt. Other activities include the manufacturing and trading of vanadium products and ferroalloy, conducting of overtime activity, and project inspection. In addition, the company has import and export operations.

Corporate Development

Located in Panzhihua, Sichuan Province, which is rich in vanadium and titanium ore resources, the company was founded in 1965. Since then Panzhihua Iron & Steel Group Co. Ltd. has developed into a large modern steel enterprise. It was listed on the Shenzhen Stock Exchange in 1996. Formerly known as Pangang Group Steel Plate Co. the corporate name was changed to Panzhihua New Steel & Vanadium Co. Ltd. in 1998. According to the *International Iron and Steel Institute*, Panzhihua Iron & Steel Group Co. Ltd. is the 17th largest in China and the 45th largest company among the world steel industry in 2007.

Hong Jibi is the current chairman and general manager of Panzhihua Iron and Steel. With more than 20,000 employees, Panzhihua New Steel & Vanadium Company Limited is a public company, and has Pangang Chengdu Seamless Steel Tube Co. and Pangang Group International Economic & Trading Co. Ltd. as its major subsidiaries.

In April and May 2009, the company reported two asset changes. The first was the sale of 22.1 million shares to Shanghai Automotive Industry Corporation (SAIC), the largest automaker in China in terms of sales, making SAIC a 5.52-percent shareholder. The second was the merge of all its listed Panzhihua Steel into a group-listing-deal worth RMB 7.19 billion, which involved Chongqing Titanium and Sichuan Changcheng Special Steel, with 37.7 billion yuan in annual sales and 1.69 billion yuan annual profit. Despite the earthquake and others problems, the company produced 5.46 million tons of iron, 4.94 million tons of steel, and 213,100 tons of vanadium slag in 2008.

Main Products and Services

With an annual production capacity of 7.8 million tons, the primary business activities of Panzhihua New Steel & Vanadium Co. Ltd. include: iron, steel, and vanadium smelting and processing; steel press forging; and provision of metallurgical technology development, consultancy, and services. The company's products include cold-rolled products, hot-rolling steel plates, steel belts, vanadium iron, vanadium slag, railway tracks, vanadium pentoxide, electrode flat steel, VN alloy, vanadium trioxide, steel plates, auto girder frame steel, low alloy steel, ship steel plates, petroleum pipeline steel, boiler steel, carbon steel, plain carbon steel, and ferroalloy. It also manufactures oxygen, hydrogen, nitrogen, argon, and steam among others.

Panzhihua Iron and Steel has the following operations: sinter plant; four blaste furnaces; steel-making plant (three 120-ton basic oxygen converters); refining plant (one SMS Demag ladle furnace); one RH vacuum degassing unit; continuous casting machines; rolling mills (one 7-stand universal heavy section); basr; wire rods; one wide hot strip/sheet; one cold reversing; coil coating lines; zinc-aluminum galvanizing; color coating; and pickling line (300,000 tons). In addition, Panzhihua has mine operations, one of which has a 1.08 billion ton ore reserve.

Challenges and Business Strategies

Nowadays, Panzhihua has become the largest production base in railway steel and seamless pipe in southwestern China, as well as the second largest vanadium products producer in the world. During the year ending on 31 December 2007, the company generated approximately 83 percent of its total' revenue from steel and related products. With the effects of the Sichuan earthquake and the world financial crisis, Panzhihua New Steel and Vanadium Co. lost RMB 430 million in 2008, a fall of 145% from a profit of 950 million in 2007.

Despite the worldwide financial crisis and the major Sichuan earthquake, the company did not dismiss workers. However, the impact of the earthquakes made it necessary for the company to acquire a loan of RMB 20 billion from the Bank of China for its reconstruction efforts. More recently, the company reported that it has formed a new venture with German industrial gas company, Messer Griesheim Investment Co. Ltd., to establish a gas-producing company, in which Messer will hold a 60% stake in the joint venture along with a capital injection of RMB 300 million. The new unit will produce and sell various kinds of industrial gases.

As the biggest steel company in resource-rich southwestern China, the company is seen as one of the steel companies to be part of the sector-wide reform initiative; and with the right vision and strategic moves, Panzhihua could be among the largest Chinese steel companies in the near future.

Marco Antonio Tourinho Furtado and Tays Torres Ribeiro Chagas

References

BusinessWeek (2008). Panzhihua New Steel & Vanadium Co. Ltd. (Shenzhen: 000629). http://investing.businessweek.com/research/stocks/snapshot/snapshot_article.asp?ric=000629.SZ. Retrieved on 15 December 2008.

China to cap steel output at 460m tons in 2009 (23 March 2009). *China Daily*. http://www.chinadaily.com.cn/bizchina/2009-03/23/content_7606526.htm. Retrieved on 27 March 2009.

The Chinese steel industry will raise the annexation reorganization tide (21 September 2008). http://www.scanji.com/english/news_show.asp?id=642. Retrieved on 12 may 2009.

Iron & Steel Works of the World Directory (2009). London: Metal Bulletin Directories.

Mao, L (2008). Bank of China offers 25 billion yuan lifeline for firms. *China Daily*, 4 June. http://www.chinadaily.com.cn/bizchina/2008-06/04/content_6735039.htm. Retrieved on 27 March 2009.

Panzhihua New Steel says two earthquakes damage factory, mines (1 September 2008). http://www.chinamining.org/companies/2008-09-01/12202233852d16776.html. Retrieved on 20 March 2009.

Zhou, Y (2009). Steelmakers' earnings drop on weak demand. *China Daily,* 24 February. http://www.chinadaily.com.cn/bizchina/2009-02/24/content_7505529.htm. Retrieved on 12 May 2009.

PETROCHINA

Corporate Address and Contact Information

PetroChina Company Limited
World Tower
16 Ande Road
Dongcheng District, Beijing
People's Republic of China
Phone: 86(10)-8488-6270
Fax: 86(10)-8488-6260
http://www.petrochina.com.cn/petrochina/

PetroChina Company Limited (中国石油天然气股份有限公司) is the listed arm of state-owned China National Petroleum Corporation (CNPC), the biggest oil producer in China. With one of the largest sales revenue in the country, PetroChina is not only the dominant producer and distributor in the Chinese domestic oil and gas industry, but also one of the largest oil companies in the world.

Historical Development

As part of the restructuring of CNPC, PetroChina was established as a joint stock company with limited liabilities on 5 November 1999, with CNPC as the sole sponsor and controlling shareholder of PetroChina. CNPC itself is a large state-owned enterprise managed by the investment organs of the State-owned Assets Supervision and Administration Commission (SASAC) under the Chinese State Council. Through the restructuring, CNPC injected into PetroChina most of the assets and liabilities relating to CNPC's exploration and production, refining and marketing, chemicals, and natural gas businesses.

On 7 April 2000, the American Depositary Shares (ADS) and H-Shares of PetroChina were listed on the New York Stock Exchange (stock code: PTR) and the Hong Kong Stock Exchange (stock code: 857), respectively; and on 5 November 2007, it was also listed on Shanghai Stock Exchange (stock code: 601857). By the end of 2007, CNPC possessed 86.29% of PetroChina shares.

As one of the most profitable companies in Asia, PetroChina could credit its success to its corporate management, but to a large extent this could also be attributed to its near duopoly on the wholesale and retail business of oil products it shared with Sinopec in China. In recent years, PetroChina has come under scrutiny from international organizations for its part in trading with the Sudanese government, which is allegedly responsible for the ongoing genocide in Darfur. Because of its link to Sudan through parent company CNPC, several institutional investors such as Harvard, Yale, and Fidelity Investments decided to divest from both PetroChina and Sinopec. Despite the setback, in May 2007, the company announced that it had made China's largest oil find in a decade off the country's northeast coast, in an oilfield named Jidong Nanpu in Bohai Bay; and on 10 December 2007, PetroChina became a Hang Seng Index Constituent Stock.

For its excellent corporate governance and high profitability, PetroChina has won wide recognitions in the international capital market. It ranked seventh among the "2005 Global Top 50 Petroleum Companies" by the *American Petroleum Intelligence Weekly*, first in "2006 Top 50 Asian Enterprises" by *BusinessWeek*, sixth in "2006 Global Top 250 Energy Companies", first in Asia-Pacific region for the past five years by Platts, an authority in global energy sector, and "the First Most Profitable Company in Asia in 2006" by *FinanceAsia*.

Corporate Structure

PetroChina has four key divisions including exploration and production (14 enterprises), refining and marketing (38 enterprises), chemicals and marketing (13 enterprises), and natural gas and pipeline (five enterprises). The group also owns three institutes: PetroChina Planning and Engineering Institute, PetroChina Exploration and Development Research Institute, and Petrochemical Research Institute. PetroChina international Co. Ltd. is also controlled by the group. Since its founding, PetroChina has established and improved standard corporate governance structure. The shareholders' meeting, the Board of Directors and the Supervisory Committee of the company operate independently in accordance with the Articles of Association under the Company Law of the PRC.

Main Products and Services

PetroChina engages in a wide range of activities related to oil and natural gas, including: exploration, development, production, and marketing of crude oil and natural gas; refining, transportation, storage, and marketing of crude oil and oil products; the production and marketing of primary petrochemical products, derivative chemicals, and other chemicals; and transportation of natural gas, crude oil, and refined oil; and marketing of natural gas.

PetroChina along with its subsidiaries is the largest oil and gas producer and seller in China, occupying a leading position in the oil and gas industry with one of the largest oil revenues in the PRC and the world. Its operation covers all key sectors in the petroleum and petrochemical industry. PetroChina's integrated business chain ranges from exploration and production of crude oil and natural gas in the upper stream to the refining, chemicals, pipelining, and marketing in the middle and down streams, which greatly improves its operation efficiency, reduces costs, and enhances the core competitiveness and overall counter-risk capability.

PetroChina has made great progress in terms of global expansion. In 2006, its overseas proved oil and gas reserves accounted for 5.5% and 1.5% of its own total production capacity, respectively, and the overseas oil and gas production in 2006 accounted for 6% and 3% of its own total production capacity total, respectively; and by 2007, its exploration and development business extended to 11 foreign countries and regions.

Chinese Oil Industry, Challenges, and Strategies

As one of the essential energy sources in modern world, petroleum is closely related to both the national interest and people's livelihood, and the oil industry is an important foundation of the national economy in China. Since the reform began in the late 1970s, China's rapid economic development has led to the growing demand for energy. As the oil industry is a highly centralized fund industry and a high-risk investment field, how to reasonably determine the scale of investment, and funding for higher return on investment, is a common concern for oil companies. Although China's main oil fields are in depression, potential still exists in future development.

In 2005, China produced 181.5 million tons in crude oil output, an increase of 3.7% compared to that in 2004. The net imports of crude oil were 118.75 million tons, a mere 1.2 % increase, while that of refined oil product was 17.42 million tons, which represented a decrease of 34% compared with the previous year. In 2007, the growth of China's domestic oil production declined, but the natural gas output growth accelerated. In 2008, crude oil output turned to be 189 million tons, keeping a sustainable growth.

Under the guiding principle of scientific development, PetroChina strives to implement three strategies of resources, markets, and internationalization. In order to develop itself into an international energy company with strong competitiveness, the company has designed a two-phase strategy: in Phase 1, during China's 11th Five-Year Plan (2007–2012), the company plans to focus on its core businesses, keep developing emerging energy businesses, enhance comprehensive strength in China and strive to achieve sustainable, effective and rapid development; in Phase 2, the company will seek to further consolidate its leading role in China and reap major gains in international operations. By significantly improving its competitive power in international market, raising its rank in global oil companies and achieving a profit growth and return on investment equal to that of the international level in the industry, PetroChina sees itself to become one of the most important global producers and distributors of petroleum and petrochemical products by 2020.

To achieve such ambitious goals, PetroChina has established a research and development system with supporting specialties and strong technological focus, which include three major research institutes at the corporate level, and 47 regional research institutes and the related key laboratories and experimental bases. By 2006, the number of personnel engaged in research and development has reached 17,737. In order to foster a system for scientific and technological innovations, PetroChina has developed corporate rules and procedures related to scientific planning, project management, research funds, and intellectual property and award management, as well as significantly increased its scientific and technological investment in recent years.

William X. Wei

References

PetroChina (2009). Annual Report. http://www.petrochina.com.cn/resource/EngPdf/xwygg/ew_20090415_annual_report.pdf. Retrieved on 26 April 2009.

PetroChina (2008). Company Profile. http://www.petrochina.com.cn/Ptr/About_PetroChina/Company_Profile/. Retrieved on 26 April 2009.

Wikipedia (2009). China National Petroleum Corporation. http://en.wikipedia.org/wiki/China_National_Petroleum_Corporation. Retrieved on 26 April 2009.

Wikipedia (2009). PetroChina. http://en.wikipedia.org/wiki/PetroChina. Retrieved on 26 April 2009.

PICC PROPERTY & CASUALTY

Corporate Address and Contact Information

PICC Property & Casualty Company Ltd.
69 Dongheyan Street
Xuanwu District

Beijing 100052
People's Republic of China.
Phone: (86)10-6315-6688
Fax: (86)10-6303-3589
http://www.piccnet.com.cn/english/gszleng/

PICC Property & Casualty Company Ltd. (中国人民财产保险股份有限公司), or PICC P&C for short, is a major component of the People's Insurance Company of China Holdings Company (中国人民保险集团公司). PICC is a state-owned enterprise under the control of the central government of the People's Republic of China. Besides PICC P&C, the holding company has eight subsidiaries with business ranging from property and casualty insurance, life insurance, health insurance, asset management, and insurance brokerage. As the largest casualty insurance entity in mainland China, PICC Property & Casualty offers all major types of insurance products and services except life insurance. It was listed on the Hong Kong Stock Exchange on 6 November 2003, which became the first state-owned Chinese financial enterprise listed in overseas market. In 2008, the *Forbes* ranked PICC P&C at number 911 of its Global 2000 List.

Historical Development

In 1949, the Chinese government established a state-owned insurance company under the name of People's Insurance Company of China; in 1996, the name was changed to PICC Holding Company and four subsidiaries were set up. In 2003, PICC was reorganized, when PICC Property & Casualty and PICC Asset Management Company were established as separate subsidiaries. Today, PICC has developed into a comprehensive insurance and financial company with over 4,500 branches all over the country; and most of the international insurance organizations have designated PICC Property & Casualty as their agent in China, including the reputed Lloyd's of London. On 6 November 2003, PICC P&C was listed on the Hong Kong Stock Exchange under the symbol SEHK: 2328, with 3.456 billion H-Shares issued. Currently, American International Group (AIG) is holding 9.9% of the stock of PICC.

In 2005, PICC entered into a joint venture arrangement with Sumitomo Life Insurance Co. of Japan to form PICC Life Insurance Co., which was designed to sell insurance products that include savings-oriented endowment insurance. In March 2009, PICC P&C announced an intention to increase the share capital of its associated firm, PICC Life Insurance Company Ltd. At present, it holds 28% of the PICC Life registered capital, but the holdings would be reduced to around 14% after the capital increase in PICC Life. PICC P&C would not participate in the capital increase in any manner.

Corporate Leadership, Main Products, and Services

The Board of Directors of PICC Property & Casualty consists of 11 members, with Dr. Wu Yan as the chairman and executive director, and Wang Yicheng as the vice chairman. Other members include Tse Sze-Wing Edmund, Zhou Shurui, Li Tao, and Wu Gaolian, while Cheng Wai Chee Christopher, Lu Zhengfei, Luk Kin Yu Peter, and Ding Ningning serve as independent non-executive directors, and Liu Zhenghuan as board secretary. As of 30 June 2008, the company had 7,686 million RMB registered, issued, and fully paid domestic shares and 3,456 million H-Shares.

Despite its short history, PICC Property & Casualty has been offering various types of insurance products and services in China, except life insurance services. It provides casualty insurance, short-term health insurance and accidental injury insurance, motor vehicle insurance, homeowners insurance, commercial property insurance, and cargo insurance. The cargo insurance division provides insurance for vessels, crafts, and other conveyances. The accidental injury and health insurance products cover accidental injuries and medical expenses. In addition, the company also undertakes agricultural insurance, liability insurance, hull insurance, and surety insurance, as well as investment application and fund application services. PICC P&C's insurance products are denominated both in RMB, the Chinese currency, and in foreign currencies. It further undertakes reinsurance of all the above insurance products. The fund application and investment businesses are carried out in accordance with the Chinese laws and regulations. Additionally, the company has been the chief or sole insurance underwriter for several major projects in China, such as the northeast Sichuan gas field, the Shanghai-Sichuan DC power transmission line for the State Grid Corporation, the Chinasat-9 satellite, the Dalian-Harbin Railway, and the Fuqing Nuclear Power Plant.

The "PICC" brand is highly reputed and recognized in the Chinese insurance market. The company enjoyed around 45% of the insurance market share in China in 2006. It values customer satisfaction and gives top priority for product development as well as claims management. Compared to its competitors, PICC P&C's e-commerce platform with a high-level of technical expertise in information dissemination helps it to achieve superior client retention standard. In 2008, Sina Finance awarded the Golden Kylin Award of "Insurance Corporation of the Year" to the company; SOHU selected it as the "Property & Casualty Insurance Company with the Best Services"; and the *21st Century Business Herald* named it the "Most Competitive Non-Life Insurance Company in Asia" in its 2008 Asian Insurance Competency Raking.

Challenges and Business Strategies

PICC P&C is operating in a business environment where insurance and financial companies owned by the state are dominant. Hence, it takes adequate care that its activities and dealings with other enterprises follow the rules and regulations of the government, especially the supervising entity — China Insurance Supervision Commission — and the company has established pricing structures of its insurance policies accordingly. The rapid growth of the insurance business had been sustained by the prudent policies undertaken and executed by the management. In the six months ending June 2008, the turnover increased to 58,970 million RMB, climbing 19.2% from the same period of the previous year. As of 30 June 2008, the market share of the Chinese non-life insurance market held by the company was 43.3%. However, during 2008, PICC P&C and its subsidiaries suffered a net loss. The catastrophic snowstorms that occurred in Southern China and the devastating earthquake that shook Wenchuan on 12 May were the chief reasons for the erosion in profits.

To improve its operating financial strength, the company had arranged a 10-year revolving credit facility of 10 billion RMB in August 2003 with China Development Bank. However, it had not drawn down any amount under this facility as of 30 June 2008, as it had been meeting the working capital needs from the cash that had been generated from the operating activities, and the working capital level had been maintained at an adequate and satisfactory level. In the near future, the company still plans to meet the working capital requirements from internal generation of cash.

According to the Chinese insurance regulations and laws, insurance companies are required to maintain minimum solvency margins and provide for certain reserves and funds. To comply with these provisions, PICC P&C should have maintained a minimum solvency margin of 12,404 million RMB. However, the actual margin maintained was 14,920 million RMB, an adequacy ratio of 120.3%. The gearing ration, representing the total liabilities, excluding subordinated debts, divided by total assets, was 84.1% as on 30 June 2008, which represented an increase of 5.8% from 31 December 2007. Moreover, the annual premium income exceeded 100 billion RMB, a historical milestone for the company.

Looking forward, PICC P&C believes that the Chinese domestic insurance market will grow further, riding on the high-growth rate registered by the Chinese economy. To sustain the growth and augment it further, the company plans to strengthen its product line development, employ professional teams, and improve client services capabilities; at the same time, it will implement strict cost-cutting measures and supervise claims management effectively to improve the profitability. It will also take measures to improve risk-management strategies in underwriting management, application of funds, and reinsurance arrangements.

Amir Shoham and Hui He

References

PICC P&C (2009). 2008 Annual Report. http://www.piccnet.com.cn/english/yjggeng/P020090415609361638576.pdf. Retrieved on 19 May 2009.

PICC P&C. Corporate governance. http://www.piccnet.com.cn/english/gszleng/. Retrieved on 19 May 2009.

PICC P&C Co. Ltd. (NBB: PICC F). Mergent Online. Retrieved on May 17, 2009.

PICC Property & Casualty. EconomyWatch. http://www.economywatch.com/companies/forbes-list/china/picc-property-casualty.html. Retrieved on 19 May 2009.

PING AN INSURANCE (GROUP) COMPANY OF CHINA

Corporate Address and Contact Information

Ping An Insurance (Group) Company of China Ltd. (SIC: 6311/6719; NAICS: 524113/551112)
Ping An Building
3 Bagua Road
Shenzhen, Guangdong Province
People's Republic of China
Phone: (86)755-8226-2888
Fax: (86)755-8243-1029
www.pingan.com
IR@pingan.com.cn

Ping An Insurance (Group) Company of China Ltd. (中国平安保险(集团)股份有限公司) is the second largest insurer (by premium income) in PRC. Commonly known as Ping An, it is ranked 141 in 2009 "*Forbes Global 2000*", in which it out beats all the other non-state-owned enterprises (non-SOEs) from mainland China. Headquartered in Shenzhen, the first special economic zone in China, Ping An is the first insurer that integrates various financial services (securities brokerage, trust and investment, commercial banking, asset management, and corporate pension business) into its core insurance operations. Ping An has been an important player in the Chinese financial industry, where global competitors begin to flow in over the passing years after China joining the WTO and loosening its restrictions on the domestic financial market.

Historical Development

Headquartered in Shenzhen, Guangdong Province, Ping An was established in 1988 by the China Merchants Company and the Industrial and Commercial Bank of China as a shareholding company.

"Ping An" means "safety and peace" in Chinese, which represents the theme of the company. Ever since its incorporation, it has become a household brand in China. In June 2004, Ping An issued H-Shares on the Hong Kong Stock Exchange under the name "Ping An" and stock code "2318". Three years later, in 2007, Ping An debuted trading of its A-Shares on the Shanghai Stock Exchange under the name "Ping An of China" and stock code "601318". However, it has not been providing American Depositary Receipt (ADR) for US investors.

With more than 20 years in the business, Ping An has successfully turned its P&C insurance business into a billion dollar multi-product, multi-service financial conglomerate. Currently, Ping An has developed an extensive customer base of over 39 million individuals and approximately 2 million corporate customers through its distribution network, one of the largest in China. Ping An's integrated financial structure enables the company to match a wide range of financial products and services to the needs of an expanding customer base. The growth of Ping An comes from its straightforward strategies: diversifying and innovating; absorbing investments from the global market; and getting involved in the global financial market.

In the mid-1990s, when China has just begun opening up, Ping An was one of the few companies that provided financial products and services to individuals and corporate customers. By introducing various products and new services, Ping An gradually builds up its reputation as the innovative non-SOE in the country. Ping An also took the advantage of attracting oversea investments, which boost the rapid development of the company. In 1994, Ping An received investments from Morgan Stanley and Goldman Sachs, as the two firms were seeking to enter the Chinese financial market. It is the first time that an insurance company in mainland China received strategic investment from overseas companies. Beside those investments, Ping An received another substantial equity interest from HSBC in 2002. In addition to attracting investments worldwide, Ping An also plays a relatively active role in the global financial market. In the early 2008, Ping An invested in Fortis Investments, a Dutch-Belgium financial group and acquired an aggregate 4.81% equity interests in Fortis. Unfortunately, due to the unforeseen global financial crisis in 2008, Ping An lost RMB 22.79 billion in its Fortis investment for the significant drop in Fortis shares. This resulted in Ping An's substantial loss in 2008. Its net profit fell 97.5% to RMB 0.48 billion, while its revenue fell 31.1% to RMB 95.19 billion.

Despite the setback by the global financial crisis, Ping An's insurance business income rose 20% to RMB 98.01 billion in 2008. During the same year, it has been continually ranked among the "*Forbes* Global 2000" (No. 293), and for the first time listed in "*Fortune* 500" (No. 462), in which it was also ranked first among all Chinese private companies; in the following year, Ping An's rank was jumped to No. 141 in "*Forbes* Global 2000" list. Even with the recent loss, Ping An remains fundamentally sound and continues to seek growth in its other investments and business. According to the company report, in 2008, Ping An's cross-selling accounted for 50.5% of newly issued bank credit cards and 14.3% of the premium income for the property and casualty insurance business. In the same year, it also launched the Ping An One Account Management Services and Ping An Wanlitong Loyalty Points Program to accelerate its integrated financial strategy.

Corporate Structure

Ping An is the holding company of the following subsidiary companies (as shown in Figure 6): Ping An Life Insurance Company of China Ltd. (Ping An Life); Ping An Property & Casualty Insurance Company of China Ltd. (Ping An Property & Casualty); Ping An Annuity Insurance Company of China Ltd.; Ping An Asset Management Company Ltd.; Ping An Health Insurance Company of China Ltd.; China Ping An Insurance Overseas (Holdings) Limited; China Ping An Trust & Investment Company Ltd., and Ping An

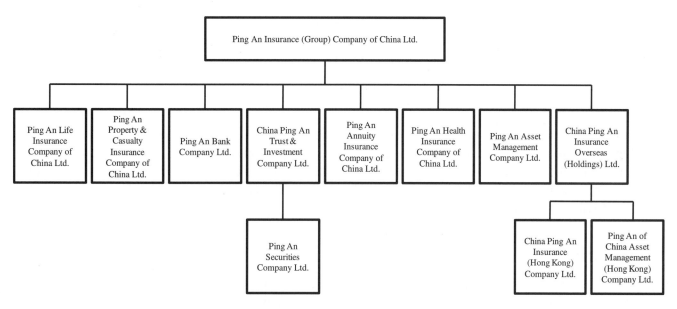

Figure 6. Corporate structure.

Source: Adapted from Ping An company website http://www.pingan.com.

Bank. China Ping An Trust & Investment Company Ltd. holds Ping An Securities Company; and Ping An Overseas holds China Ping An Insurance (Hong Kong) Company Ltd., and Ping An of China Asset Management (Hong Kong) Company Ltd.

As the leading non-SOE in China, Ping An is the first Chinese insurer to have introduced foreign investors into its shareholding structure. Its service team includes over 40 million individual clients and about two million corporate clients. It has about 356,000 life insurance sales agents, over 83,000 full-time employees, and more than 3,000 branch and sub-branch units and sales offices. Operating along the principle of "Group Holdings, Segment Operation, Segment Supervision, Group Listing", Ping An has been able to ensure the group as a whole is moving toward its goal, upon the foundation that unites strategy, branding, and corporate culture.

Main Products and Services

Ping An provides financial services including insurance coverage, investment and wealth management. It has been concentrated on three core business over the decades — insurance, banking, and asset management. Following its strategy on offering various financial products and services while focusing on life, property, and casualty insurance products, Ping An explores for overseas opportunities and invests in innovative products such as Wanlitong and One Account to enhance its competitive advantages.

Insurance business

Ping An has successfully implemented a strategy that focuses on "Reaching New Heights" and resulted in a record premium income of RMB 102.37 billion in the life insurance business in 2008, making Ping An Life the second largest life insurance company in China in terms of premium income, accounting for 10.9% of the national aggregate. For the recent swine flu crisis, Ping An also develops a (H1N1) flu-tailored product to satisfy the needs of the individuals and companies. This product includes main insurance liability and affixation insurance liability, with a 15-day waiting period, which is half the period compared to other ordinary health insurance products.

Banking business

Ping An Bank, formally known as Shenzhen Ping An Bank, has a network across major cities in China, such as Shenzhen, Shanghai, Fuzhou, Quanzhou, Xiamen, and Hangzhou. Ping An's credit card business broke the record for first-year card issuance in China with the accumulated number of credit cards in circulation exceeding 1.5 million by end of 2008. Net profit from the banking business amounted to RMB 1.44 billion in 2008.

Investment business

Ping An is the first mainland China insurance company to obtain regulatory approval to invest up to 15% of its total assets in overseas market. In 2008, the group achieved substantial increase in income from the trust business. Total investment income from trust business surged 58.5% to reach RMB 1.32 billion in 2008. Net profit from its trust business increased significantly to RMB 1.21 billion from RMB 0.74 billion in 2007.

Ping An is also actively involved in social activities to help the Chinese community. By the end of 2008, Ping An had participated in the building and planning of 78 Hope Primary Schools in China. It has held its education programs giving away study grants to 1,430 students in the past five years. Ping An has donated over RMB 1 million to support "China Children Protection and Education Program" for six years in a row. Ping An has also mobilized blood donation among its staff for the past seven years. It provides accident and critical illness insurance coverage for those who donated hemopoietic stem cells (HSC) starting in 2003 and until 2010. Following the Sichuan earthquake on 12 May 2008, Ping An and its employees donated more than RMB 75 million to the relief funds for the devastated areas.

Challenges and Business Strategies

The 2008 global financial crisis prompted Ping An to rethink the relationship between risk and reward. Although Ping An experienced the turbulent markets recently, equity analysts expect that the business environment will be "stable" and "back to normal" in the following years. Having learned a costly lesson, corporate leaders do not have an immediate plan to go global and seek overseas investment opportunities in the short term; instead, Ping An will take measures to enhance and reinforce risk management in the pursuit of long-term stable returns. In addition, Ping An will adjust its investment portfolios to tackle current financial difficulties.

Looking forward, the executives of Ping An will concentrate more on asset-liability management while making investment decisions in the future. Ping An will focus on diversifying its risks, enhancing its profitability and expanding its asset scale. By setting such a goal, the company's asset management subsidiary, Ping An Asset Management, will take the lead in investing insurance funds in the Beijing-Shanghai High-Speed Railway, as an example of direct investment that helps broaden Ping An's investment channel.

Hao Chen

References

A.M. Best Company, Inc. (2009). Stung by Fortis stake, Ping An looks to control portfolio risks. *BestWire Services.*

Chen, HY (2008). The Ping An–Fortis deal: Who really wins? *Caijing Magazine*, 3 April. http://english.caijing.com.cn/2008-04-03/100055137.html. Retrieved on 22 May 2009.

Deutsche Bank and CIRC (2009). Leading life insurers in China, 2008. *Market Share Reporter*, 2 September.

Forbes (2008). *Forbes* 2000 Company List. http://www.forbes.com/lists/2008/18/biz_2000global08_The-Global-2000_MktVal.html. Retrieved on 25 May 2009.

Forbes (2009). *Forbes* 2000 Company List. http://www.forbes.com/2009/04/08/worlds-largest-companies-business-global-09-global_land.html. Retrieved on 25 May 2009.

Ping An Insurance (Group) Company of China Ltd. (2009). Fact Sheet. http://www.pingan.com/investor/en/summary.jsp. Retrieved on 22 May 2009.

SinoCast (2009). Ping An launches a (HINI) flu-tailored product. *SinoCast Daily Business Beat.* http://www.sinocast.com/readbeatarticle.do?id=24302. Retrieved on 25 May 2009.

SHANGHAI AUTOMOTIVE

Corporate Address and Contact Information

Shanghai Automotive Industry Corporation (Group) (SIC — 3711; NAIC — 336111)
489 Weihai Road
Jing'an District, Shanghai 200041
People's Republic of China
Phone: (86)21-2201-1688
Fax: (86)21-2201-1188
http://www.saicgroup.com/

Shanghai Automotive Industry Corporation (SAIC, 上海汽车工业(集团)总公司), is one of the "Big Three" Chinese automakers. As a state-owned enterprise, SAIC ranks first in sales volume in China and owns about 50 plants in the Shanghai region alone. Through holding 88.83% of the equity of SAIC Motor Co., the company is mainly engaged in manufacturing, sales, research and development, and investment in passenger cars, commercial vehicles, and components, as well as related trade services and financial business. Historically, SAIC's operations were entirely based on its relationships with General Motors and Volkswagen, but in recent years, the company has introduced its first independently developed model in an effort to achieve record growth and international expansion.

Historical Development

From the birth of its first branded car in 1958, Shanghai Automotive Industry Corporation (Group) has played a significant role in the development and growth of the Chinese auto industry. Following severe economic setbacks stemming from the Great Leap Forward and the Cultural Revolution, China's new leader, Deng Xiaoping, initiated an era of reform in 1978 stressing the development of heavy industry as a crucial component of reviving the nation. In 1985, the Chinese government declared the automobile industry a "pillar" industry to be targeted for financial and developmental assistance. As a result of such great attention, SAIC introduced its first Shanghai Volkswagen (SVW) product in the same year. This proved to be a crucial step in establishing the company as a top automobile producer in China, as it rolled out its first Shanghai General Motors (SGM) product in 1997 and ultimately its first independently developed model in 2006.

SAIC has always grasped opportunities emerging from the implementation of an opening-up policy and rapid national economic growth. The firm has focused on business scale expansion, technical capability promotion, and industrial upgrade in developing itself from a local enterprise into the ranks of the "Big Three". In 2004, Shanghai Automotive became a member of the *Fortune* Global 500, where it was ranked 461st. Currently, SAIC is ranked 373rd and it has become the largest Chinese automotive corporation in the domestic market. The company has recently displayed aspirations of becoming an international automaker, as it hired the former head of GM China, Phil Murtaugh, while additionally launching its first independently developed brand. Success rapidly followed, as its export business grew 174% over the following year and a long-term export intent agreement was signed with Chile. SAIC experienced even greater growth in 2007, as its total export volume reached 22,000 units (a 225% increase), its domestic market share reached 18.5%, and it became the first Chinese auto group to run cross-country assets operations with its five overseas branches in North America, Europe, Japan, Hong Kong, and Korea. SAIC has established these branches in an effort to cooperate with other world-renowned brands and to seek opportunities in the OEM and AM market. SAIC USA, for example, is engaged in the production of auto parts and components and SAIC Europe designs and develops high-tech products including customized hardware and software. The company further utilizes the advantages of worldwide purchasing process to import materials from companies of SAIC Group at a preferential price. Shanghai Automotive has benefited from the rapid growth of both the economy and the industry, as an increasing amount of the population, particularly the emerging Chinese middle class, is beginning to purchase automobiles.

Main Products and Services

In the last few years, Shanghai Automotive Industry Corporation has been heavily investing in developing its independent models to sell in both the domestic and global markets. Following its "low cost, high quality" strategy, SAIC's main products and services include passenger vehicles, commercial vehicles, parts and components, and service and trade. Other products that the company manufactures include vehicles such as motorcycles and tractors. Shanghai Automotive sold 1.69 million units in 2007, occupying 18.5% of the domestic market share. Passenger vehicles totaled 1.137 million units and commercial vehicles reached 553,000 units, increasing by 24.3% and 29%, respectively.

Besides its core business of passenger and commercial vehicles, SAIC has developed a components business to supply global OEMs. It has already joined with over 30 well-known suppliers in industries ranging from power train, trim and lighting, air-conditioning, electronic appliances, and stamped parts. Additionally, Shanghai Automotive has established a service and trade business covering 23 fields such as logistics, international trade, sales, service, real estate, asset operation, and IT procurement. These supplemental businesses have allowed the company to establish differentiated advantages that have ultimately helped to promote the competitive capability of SAIC. Consequently, Shanghai Automotive has constructed a positive brand image, which has ultimately driven the company toward establishing itself as a leader within the domestic automotive market.

Corporate Structure and Leadership

Under the leadership of its President/Director Shen Jianhua and Chairman of the Board Hu Maoyuan, Shanghai Automotive is engaged in the production of passenger cars, trucks, buses, motorcycles, and tractors in addition to other operations such as car leasing, auto parts wholesale and retail, and financing.

The company's core businesses are organized into six segments: vehicle, selective auto components, auto finance, manufacturing business, service and trade business, and other investments. SAIC maintains its headquarters in Shanghai with other production bases in Liuzhou, Chongqing, Yantai, Shenyang, Qingdao, Yizheng, and Nanjing. Additionally, the company has established branches in the United States (Detroit), Germany (Hamburg), the United Kingdom (Longbridge), Hong Kong, Japan (Tokyo), and Korea (Seoul). SAIC has a production base and a technical center in the United Kingdom, and its other international branches are devoted to the promotion of understanding, communication, and cooperation between the company and other global automotive giants in an effort to seek future business opportunities.

Shanghai Automotive has approached the automotive market with a strategy of contributing equal concentration to independent R&D and global cooperation. It does this through strengthening partnerships with global OEMs (11 companies), core components companies (3 companies), and automotive finance companies (1 company), while also pushing its R&D through the establishment of state-level, municipal-level, and engineering centers jointly run with domestic research institutions. SAIC has two key joint ventures, one with Volkswagen and another with GM, while additionally owning 51% of Korean carmaker Ssangyong Motor and 10% of GM Daewoo. In 2007, as part of a government attempt to consolidate the auto business and prepare for international sales, SAIC combined its production operations with those of Nanjing Automobile Corporation, and in 2008, transferred ownership of its auto parts operation over to fellow state-owned firm Shanghai Bashi Industrial.

SAIC has established its vision based on the satisfaction of its customers, the interest of its shareholders, and the harmony of the nation's society through its dedication to outstanding brands, brilliant employees, core competitive competencies, and international operation capabilities. The firm's corporate culture consists of two key components: a management mode of everyone being a business manager that ultimately strengthens leadership and generates synergy, and the 4-S concept (Study, Sino-foreign JVs' interest goes first, Standardization, and Spring). Additionally, Shanghai Automotive has constructed a four-tiered theme of practice: cost is the first competitive power, technology is the first productive force, talented people are the first resource, and systems and mechanisms are the first motive power. Through these core values, SAIC's objective is to create a brand of excellence with a globalization insight, to establish technical and operational systems that are conducive to sustainable development, to enhance its core competencies for international business operations, to build itself into an automotive enterprise that takes the leading position in China and has an international influence, and to create the maximum value for consumers, investors, and society as a whole.

Growth Strategies

With the goal of ranking itself among the world's major auto conglomerates and doubling its vehicle sales volume by 2020, Shanghai Automotive plans to build up to 30 models including SUVs, hybrids, compacts, and mid-sized vehicles to export abroad. The company's plans to make cars independently of GM and Volkswagen will not interfere with its cooperation with those companies. Through a product differentiation strategy, and the establishment of business cooperation with renowned brands, SAIC is striving to support the synchronous growth of vehicles in a market in which only 4% of the population owns an automobile. As the Chinese economy continues to grow, there will be an emerging middle-class accounting for about 300 to 400 million people. In light of high-saving rates in China, the ensuing increase in demand has been identified by Shanghai Automotive, and the firm is preparing for it. SAIC also endeavors to increase its business through a "scientific development concept", which consists of rapid industrial restructuring, intensified technical development, enhancing innovative capability, the conservation of resources, and a focus on the transformation of economic growth. Through an efficient combination of independent R&D and global cooperation, Shanghai Automotive has already built an extensive consumer base and established relationships with many large business groups and companies that are strategically important to China's economy.

By actively implementing the "going out" policy, SAIC became the first Chinese auto group to run cross-country assets. SAIC has set up five overseas branches in North America, Europe, Japan, and Korea for the import and export of components and finished cars. Additionally, SAIC established SAIC Motor UK Technical Centre in 2007 to develop a self-owned brand by taking the advantage of global resources. These are a few of the major steps being taken in the process of ultimately establishing itself as a global auto conglomerate in the long term.

Environment and Industry Challenges

With the continual reforms in financial institutions and SOEs, SAIC has encountered many new rivals, both foreign and domestic. Within China, Shanghai Automotive competes with Chery Automobile, Geely Auto, Dongfeng Motor Group, and China First Automotive Group among others. Globally, the company's competitors include Toyota, Nissan, Ford Motor, or Honda, for example. When China was admitted into the World Trade Organization (WTO) in 2001, the nation's automotive industry opened further up for foreign competitors, threatening SAIC's dominant position in the market. Political, economic, and social instability also provide significant challenges. Unsolved political tensions under China's fourth generation leaders and diverging incentives between central and local governments have created a sense of anxiety within the political environment as the government has become reliant upon the industry for revenue and employment. From an economic perspective, a debt-ridden financial segment, combined with an inefficient SOE sector, have resulted in escalating unemployment and growing regional income inequality. The financial crisis, the world economy and undervalued *Yuan*, it is imperative that these economic obstacles in China be resolved so that the company may continue its success story not only domestically but also internationally. Geo-strategic challenges have also materialized, as China's historical disputes with neighboring countries and accusations of increasing protectionist policies have threatened the performance of the industry.

Within the automotive industry, the government's new policy toward improving energy efficiency and reducing emissions has had a serious impact on domestic companies. Price liberalization and tax controls have been common, and the emergence of new fuel economy standards has proved to be a challenge. Those new policies have threatened high-end manufacturers within the domestic market, which generally lack key-process knowledge and technical know-how. However, through government initiatives to promote domestic technology, companies such as Shanghai Automotive are receiving funds for R&D spending, thus spurring the industry's competitiveness. This government assistance, combined with the corporate strategies of SAIC, are critical in the company's ultimate goal of becoming a leading international auto conglomerate.

Marc Fetscherin

References

Ni, J (2005). Automotive Management Briefing: *Development of China's Automotive Industry*, S.M. Wu Manufacturing Research Center, University of Michigan. http://www.cargroup.org/mbs2005/documents/JunNiChinaAutomotive TraverseCity.pdf. Retrieved on 16 April 2009.

Shanghai Automotive Industry Corporation (Group) (2007). Annual Report. http://www.saicgroup.com/English/sqjt/gsnb/2007njtnb/gzhg/index.shtml. Retrieved on 16 April 2009.

Shanghai Automotive Industry Corporation (Group) (2007). Corporate Profile. http://www.saicgroup.com/English/sqjt/gsjs/index.shtml. Retrieved on 16 April 2009.

Shanghai Automotive Industry Corporation (Group), Hoover's Company Records. http://www.hoovers.com. Retrieved on 16 April 2009.

SHANGHAI CONSTRUCTION

Corporate Address and Contact Information

Shanghai Construction Co. Ltd.
33 Fushan Road, Pudong New District
Shanghai 200120
People's Republic of China
Phone: (86)21-6887-2178
Fax: (86)21-5879-5500
http://www.shconstruction.cn

As one of the leading developers within Shanghai, Shanghai Construction Co. Ltd. (上海建工股份有限公司), is principally involved with the construction and engineering services of residential buildings in the People's Republic of China. The company's other major business activities include the design and development of industrial buildings, civil buildings, subways, and public utilities.

Corporate Development

Formed in 1998, Shanghai Construction Co. Ltd. is part of the Shanghai Construction Group, a state-owned construction corporation whose majority shareholder is the Shanghai Municipal Government. On 23 June 1998, the company was listed on the Shanghai Stock Exchange (600170), after Shanghai Construction Group reconstructed its nine subsidiaries. Of the total registered capital of RMB 719 million, 406 million are held by the state, while the rest shares are flowing on the market. As of 31 December 2008, the company had a net asset of RMB 3.78 billion. Besides Shanghai Construction Group, other major shareholders of the company are various investment funds of large Chinese state-owned banks that include China Construction Bank, Industrial and Commerce Bank of China, Chinese Social Security Fund, Bank of China, Agricultural Bank of China, and China Life Insurance.

Currently, Shanghai Construction Co. Ltd. has seven wholly owned subsidiaries: Shanghai First Construction Company Limited, Shanghai Second Construction Company Limited, Shanghai Fourth, Fifth, and Seventh Construction Co. Ltd., Shanghai Building Decoration Engineering Co. Ltd., and Shanghai Construction Design and Research Institute Limited. In recent years, Shanghai Construction has become the controlling shareholder of the following three companies: Shanghai Tongsan Highway Co. Ltd., Shanghai Central Belt Way Construction Co. Ltd., and Huzhou Xinkaiyuan Co. Ltd. Moreover, the company has made significant investments in Shanghai MBT High-Tech Construction Co. Ltd., Shanghai Huqingping Highway Construction Co. Ltd., and Dongfang Securities.

Shanghai Construction Co. is governed by a nine-member Board of Directors, with Xu Zheng serves as the chair, who also is the CEO and deputy party secretary of Shanghai Construction Group. Other directors include Liu Guolin (vice chairman), Lin Jinsheng (president), Fan Zhongwei, Xia Jun and Xiao Changsong, while independent, non-executive directors are Tan Qikun, Wu Hongbing and Hou Qin. In addition, the company has an eight-member Board of Supervisors, with Jiang Zhiquan serves as chair.

Main Products and Services

Shanghai Construction Co. Ltd. designs and constructs regular and high-rise residential buildings, industrial buildings, civil buildings, expressways, subways, and public utilities. The company's residential building products include three categories: common residential buildings, residential buildings with 30–50 floors and residential buildings over 50 floors. The company is also involved in building decoration, general contracting, advisory services, manufacturing and marketing equipment and materials, machinery equipment leasing, extracting stone materials, and maintaining and administering expressways. Shanghai Construction and its subsidiaries have been involved in many landmark projects in the metropolitan area in recent years, among them: the Pudong International Airport, Shanghai Maglev Train, Jinmao Tower, Shanghai Grand Theatre, Shanghai Museum, Pearl of the Orient TV Tower, Shanghai International Conference Center, Shanghai Science and Technology Hall, Shanghai Oriental Arts Center, Shanghai Stadium, Shanghai Sports Center, International Race Track, Shanghai High-Rise Expressway, South Train Station, Donghai Bridge, Lupu Bridge, and World Financial Center, which is the tallest building in China. The company also participated in the construction of the National Grand Theatre in Beijing, and operates its businesses in other domestic markets and in Macau and Russia. For the quality of its construction, the company has received several top awards in China during recent years.

The company currently employs approximately 9,200 employees. For the year ending 2008, the company had contracts valued at CNY 44.85 billion, accounting for approximately 47% of its operating revenue for the year. With a goal to obtain CNY 46 billion worth of contracts in 2009, the company expects to take advantage of an increased amount of opportunities from the 2010 Shanghai World Expo. For the same year, the company had total revenue of RMB 30.573 billion and net income of 302 million.

Challenges and Business Strategies

Asia's rapid economic expansion is creating a construction boom of a magnitude seldom seen before, offering tremendous growth potential for Shanghai Construction Co. Ltd. in the coming years. With construction being the single largest industry in the world, Asia represents the second-largest market, accounting for approximately 31% of the world's total, compared with 35% for North America and 29% for Western Europe. China's construction industry accounts for 6.6% of the country's gross domestic product (GDP) and the fourth largest industry in the country.

One of the most significant challenges facing construction companies in Asia stems from China's construction industry being controlled by the government. As all land is property of the state, land-use projects must gain government approval, which can often present a challenge. In addition, corrupt business practices can often be found within the industry due to the unusually heavy influence of the Chinese government in the awarding of many contracts. With bribery and fraud commonly taking place within the industry, bribes can often amount to as much as 30% of an entire project's value, substantially raising the cost of the project. While the country does have strong penalties in place for official corruption (up to the death penalty), China's corruption problem within the construction industry remains widespread. In addition, another significant challenge facing Shanghai Construction Co. is the construction industry's strong tendency to follow economic cycles. With the industry being closely tied to the economic growth of the nation, this leaves construction companies highly vulnerable to an economy that is often strongly affected by monetary and fiscal policies.

Finally, a highly competitive environment presents a strong challenge to Shanghai Construction. Low-entry barriers, fragmentation, and high-exit costs all contribute to a country with a large number of competitors within the industry. As of 2002, there were nearly 100,000 construction enterprises in China. The five largest construction companies in China (all owned by the state) are China Railway Engineering Corp., China State Construction Engineering, China Communications Group, China Metallurgical Group Corp., and Shanghai Construction General Co.

Overall, the company expects strong and stable growth within the coming years, benefiting from an increased number of contracts and decreased raw material prices, with an increased amount of contracts originating from domestic cities, including Wuxi, Guangzhou, and Shenyang. In addition, the company will seek further growth opportunities through continued exploration of overseas business, with many Asian construction companies already beginning to gain contracts in the Middle East and Africa. It is possible that the company's projects may soon extend to North America, as the company recently began exploring the option to participate in the multibillion-dollar recovering effort taking place in New Orleans.

Matt Amick and Wenxian Zhang

References

Hoovers (2009). Shanghai Construction Co. http://www.hoovers.com/shanghai-construction/—ID__154125—/free-co-factsheet.xhtml. Retrieved on 24 June 2009.

New Orleans in talks with Chinese firms (12 April 2008). *The Globe and Mail.*

Scully, V (2007). Global industry surveys: Construction and engineering — Asia. *Standard & Poor's*, May.

Shanghai Construction Co. (2009). Company Profile. http://www.shconstruction.cn/About.aspx. Retrieved on 15 July 2009.

Shanghai Construction expects stable growth in coming years (6 April 2009). *SinoCast.* http://www.shihua.com.cn. Retrieved on 7 July 2009.

SHANGHAI ELECTRIC

Corporate Address and Contact Information

Shanghai Electric Group Co. Ltd.
30F, Shanghai Maxdo Center
8 Xingyi Road
Shanghai 200336
People's Republic of China
Phone: (86)21-5208-2266
Fax: (86)21-5208-2103
http://www.shanghai-electric.com/en/index.asp

Shanghai Electric Group Co. Ltd. (上海电气集团股份有限公司) is one of the oldest and largest mechanical and electrical equipment manufacturers in China. Although Shanghai Electric Group was officially established in March 2004, the history of one of its subsidiaries could be traced back to 1880. Major investors of Shanghai Electric include Shanghai Electric General Co., Guangdong Pearl River Investment Co., Fuxi Investment Holding Co., Shenergy Group Co., Shanghai Baosteel and Shantou Mingguang Investment Co. Since most of those investors are state-owned and Shanghai Electric (Group) General Co. took 62.3% of the stake, Shanghai Electric was in fact controlled by the Chinese government. On 28 April 2005, Shanghai Electric was successfully listed on the Hong Kong Stock Exchange. The company currently has more than 40,000 employees in its 60 subsidiaries.

Historical Development

Shanghai Electric is one of the largest comprehensive equipment manufacturers in China. In 1949, all the main mechanical equipment manufacturing businesses were under the governance of Shanghai Heavy Industry Bureau (later renamed to Shanghai Mechanical and Electric Equipment Administration Bureau). In 1985, Shanghai Electric United Co., the former body of Shanghai Electric (Group), was established. Ten years later, Shanghai Mechanical and Electric Equipment Administration Bureau was restructured and merged with Shanghai Electric (Group) General Co.

Entering the new millennium, Shanghai Electric experienced enormous growth by focusing on innovation, brand building, high-end market development, utilization of automation systems to upgrade its traditional industries, extreme-environment equipment manufacturing and services, and new business development. In 2004, Shanghai Electric (Group) General Co. reshuffled its assets and invited various investors to form the Shanghai Electric Group. Because of its successful human resource management, corporate image building as well as product development, the company won the trust from both the Chinese government and business customers. Shanghai Electric therefore involved in many important projects in China, which in turn generated many new growth opportunities for the group. Through state banks and self financing, Shanghai Electric was able to facilitate the key technology development, and along the way company leaders and managers gained valuable experiences in R&D, marketing, sales, and corporate operations. In 2007, the company's net assets amounted to 28.5 billion RMB. In 2008, sales revenue was 58.9 billion RMB with net profits of 3.64 billion.

Main Products and Services

Shanghai Electric has a wide product portfolio. Its main businesses include power generation, environment protection, power transmission, machine tools, heavy machinery, elevator, transportation, printing and package machine, trade and investment, finance, and mechanical and electrical engineering. Shanghai Electric also participates in manufacturing refrigerating air-conditioning equipment, wood-base panel machinery, wood-base panel, welding equipment, and engineering machinery. In addition, the company conducts various EPC (Engineering, Procurement, and Construction) projects. Those projects require Shanghai Electric to not only produce relevant equipment but also offer engineering, procurement, and construction services, which in fact have transformed the company from a manufacturer to a consultant or a solution provider.

Shanghai Electric owns powerful research resources and, due to its state-owned nature, is able to receive financial support from various financial institutes. These pave ways to its well-performed technology development and capital operations. The production of thermal power equipment by Shanghai Electric has been ranked first in the world for years, so is its capacity of elevator manufacturing per factory. The company's market shares of printing and packaging equipment, refrigerating and air-conditioning machinery, and programmed engineering machinery also top the relevant industries in the Chinese domestic markets.

Strategies and Future Challenges

The growth of Shanghai Electric can be attributed to its strategies in R&D and brand development, while governmental support serves as the third pillar for its success.

Shanghai Electric has been investing in technology innovation since its founding in 2004. The company adopted a "focus" strategy in its main businesses to quickly manage the current portfolio and obtain updated techniques in the world. Concentrating all the relevant technical and human resources on a few fields made these businesses reach economic scales in a short run. New products therefore could be developed in a faster pace compared with those of its competitors. Unlike diversification strategies adopted by some Chinese companies, Shanghai Electric picked up related businesses into its business portfolio. These businesses cross-enrich with each other and build up a network of interrelated products. Integrating global resource, focusing on strategic industry development, and encouraging innovation activities among subsidiaries, divisions, and individuals led to a series of breakthroughs. The first 6,000-kW fossil-fueled power generating unit, the first cooling gas turbine generator of the world, the first 300-mW nuclear power generating unit of China, the first large ship-use crankshaft of China, and the first 1,000-mW ultra super-critical fossil-fueled power generating units of China were all produced by Shanghai Electric.

Shanghai Electric has not only endeavored to build up a physically (corporate structure and products) competent company but also put more attentions to brand and communication development. In 2003, Shanghai Electric terminated its multi-brand strategy where each subsidiary could use self-designed trademarks in its products, and asked all its member companies to set the Shanghai Electric brand as the only acceptable corporate logo. In joint ventures, a duel-brand or major-minor-brand strategy was adopted. Partners' trademarks could be shown on the jointly developed products. However, the Shanghai Electric trademark must accompany theirs or dominate the joint image. Consequently, the coverage of Shanghai Electric brand in its major businesses and products increased greatly, and its "reliable, trustful, and amiable" image was thus solidly established.

As one of the largest state-owned companies, Shanghai Electric was strongly supported by the Chinese government, especially the Shanghai municipal government. Due to its economic scale, governmental investment, technology development capacity, and the ability and experiences to complete large projects, most of such infrastructure contracts in the fields of power generation, transportation, and power transmission were obtained by Shanghai Electric. Competing with GE, Siemens, Mitsubishi, and other world-class enterprises, Shanghai Electric successfully built an international image of a Chinese heavy industry manufacturer. While Shanghai Electric enjoys the strong support from the government, the company also closely follows the national policy in its development plans. Environmental protection businesses, wind power projects in China, large-scaled marine tooling and transportation equipment manufacturing are all demonstrating this trend. In light of the continual and rapid development of the country's economy, Shanghai Electric as one of the key companies in China will likely enjoy a bright future in the coming decade.

Dong Bian

References

Bian, D (2008). Shanghai Electric Group: A state-owned legend. Working case study.

Shanghai Electric Group Co. Ltd (2006, 2007, 2008). Annual Reports. http://www.shanghai-electric.com/en/notice.asp?re=2. Retrieved on 18 June 2009.

SHANGHAI FRIENDSHIP

Corporate Address and Contact Information

Shanghai Friendship Group Co. Ltd.
8/F No. 518, Shangcheng Road
Pudong District
Shanghai 200120
People's Republic of China
Phone: (86)021-5879-2123
http://www.shfriendship.com.cn

Shanghai Friendship Group Incorporated Company (上海友谊集团股份有限公司), formerly known as Shanghai Friendship & Overseas Chinese Company Limited (上海友谊华侨公司), is a Shanghai-based large chain enterprise with commercial retail as its main business, and is currently a listed company with the largest retail volume in China.

Historical Development

The firm was established in Shanghai in 1952 and restructured as a company limited by shares in 1993. The group's main subsidiary, Lianhua Supermarket, has been consistently ranked as the nation's number one in sales volume. Lianhua also achieved a few other "first" in China's domestic retail industry, among them: the first large-scale chain supermarket in China; the first enterprise in domestic supermarket industry that passed the inspection of ISO9002 International Quality System; the enterprise with largest number of chain stores in China; and the first chain supermarket that employed e-commerce system.

Friendship Department Store, another subsidiary of Friendship Group, is a parent company of several wholly owned entities or joint ventures, including Shanghai Friendship Shop and Hongqiao Friendship Shopping Center. Friendship Department Store's branches are mainly located in Shanghai's prosperous business districts and main residential areas. Friendship Department Store currently occupies a total business area of over 100 thousand square meters, and sells more than 80,000 different commodities covering both medium and high ends of market needs, hence builds up a high degree of recognition both home and abroad. Friendship-South Shopping Mall, which possesses a gigantic business area of 80,000 square meters, is the first shopping mall in Shanghai.

The group's A-Shares and B-Shares were listed and traded on Shanghai Stock Exchange on 4 February 1994 and 5 January 1994, respectively. In December 2000, the group was renamed to take its current corporate name. The abbreviated name and listing code for Friendship Group's A-Shares are "*Youyi Gufen*" and 600827. The abbreviated name and listing code for its B-Shares are "*Youyi B Gu*" and 900923.

Corporate Structure, Leadership, and Main Services

The group's administrative structure ensures that the company runs effectively.

The corporate leadership team of the group as of May 2009 is composed of Wang Zhongnan, board chairman; Zhang Yongfang, CFO; Zhong Huajun, supervisory committee chair; and Huang Zhencheng, director and general manager.

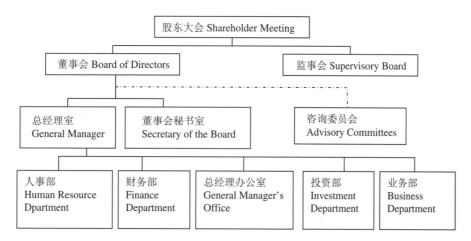

Figure 7. Corporate structure of Shanghai Friendship Group.

Shanghai Friendship Group's principal activities are operating and retailing of supermarkets and department stores. Other activities include leasing of properties, selling of construction materials, retailing of arts, crafts, antique, general goods, and clothing, retailing and wholesaling of knitted and textile products, and operating of restaurants and provision of advertising services. The group's operations are mainly carried out in metropolitan Shanghai with plans to expand across China.

Business Strategies and Corporate Culture

The company has established an incentive mechanism based on position performance. In 2000, the company shifted from a traditional department store to a retail and chain operation mode. In specific, the group decided to focus on four core businesses as pivots supporting the corporate development: first, food and commodities supermarkets with Lianhua Supermarket as its flagship store, which is currently the largest chain supermarket in China; second, specific-commodity-oriented shopping malls with Homemart Decoration Materials Supermarket Co. Ltd. (Homemart) as its flagship mall; third, department stores of modern and brand name commodities with Shanghai Friendship Department Store as its flagship store; and last, community shopping centers supported with modernized logistics, resource allocation, and e-commerce system with Friendship Shopping Center as its flagship center.

Beginning from 2001, the company has launched its nationwide market development strategies, which included development of core businesses as first priority, strengthening the company's presence in Shanghai's local market and having more operation on the national market, promoting core competitiveness, expanding capital operation, and aggressively recruiting talents.

Comparing with other firms in the sector, Shanghai Friendship Group has certain brand advantage. It owns domestically renowned business brands as well as commodity brands such as *Lianhua*, *Friendship*, and *Homemart*. The company has a logistic delivery and management system, which is more advanced than its peers. Over the years, the company's core technology in the fields of purchase, logistic delivery, settlement, information, network, etc. has been continuously improved, which has further strengthened its overall competitiveness. Looking forward, the group will focus its exploring and expanding efforts toward national market, and increase its occupation rate in domestic market. The final goal is to reshape its corporate structure, managing procedure, operation flow, information system, and enterprise culture more adaptable to the national market.

The company attaches great importance to encouraging teamwork spirit and has formed its corporate culture with main features including innovation, honesty, and career devotion. The company's management concepts include maintaining special features, pursuing quality, expanding development potentials, and value creation. Recognizing that its success is largely dependent on its employees, Shanghai Friendship has emphasized education and training for its employees.

Recent Development and Challenges

For 2008, the company reported net profit attributable to group of RMB 139.81 million or RMB 0.326 per share on main operating turnover of RMB 25,563.73 million, against net profit attributable to group of RMB 306.32 million or RMB 0.714 per share on main operating turnover of RMB 22,935.68 million for the same period in the previous year. The company reported adjusted net profit attributable to group of RMB 139.17 million or RMB 0.324 per share, against RMB 0.260 per share for the same period in the previous year, and net cash flow per share of RMB 5.869 against net cash flow per share of RMB 6.493 for the same period a year ago. Return on net assets was 6.204%, comparing with 10.035% for the same period a year ago. For the full year, the company plans to pay dividend of RMB 0.05 per share.

After China's entry into the WTO, competition between domestic large-scale chain supermarkets and foreign-funded retailing conglomerates has been heightened, and competition within industry has also become more intense. As restriction on foreign capital's entry into the domestic market has been lifted, liquidation, merger, and reorganization will likely become important forms of expansion in the coming years. In light of these recent developments, the company plans to consolidate its competitiveness and take up new challenges to survive and succeed in the large and still growing retail market in China.

Zhiqun Zhu

References

BusinessWeek (2009). Shanghai Friendship Group Incorporated Company. http://investing.businessweek.com/research/stocks/snapshot/snapshot.asp?ric=600827.SS. Retrieved on 16 May 2009.

Introduction of Shanghai Friendship Group Incorporated Company. www.friendship.lhok.com/gongsijieshao/gongsijieshao.doc. Retrieved on 16 May 2009.

Shanghai Friendship Group Incorporated Company (2008). Annual Report. http://www.friendship.lhok.com/files/600827_2008_1.pdf. Retrieved on 16 May 2009.

SHANGHAI MATERIAL TRADING

Corporate Address and Contact Information

Shanghai Material Trading Co. Ltd.
325 South Suzhou Road
Shanghai 200120
People's Republic of China
Telephone: (00)86-21-6323-1818
Fax: (00)86-21-6323-0703
http://www.600822sh.com/Newsabout.asp

Shanghai Material Trading Centre Company Limited (SMTC 上海物资贸易股份有限公司) primarily engages in the trading of fuel, general trading, and the management of hotels and properties. Other activities include rental of automobiles, metal, steel, petrochemicals and other goods, operation of hotels, service exhibition, commission agent, provision of property management services, and property development.

Corporate Development

The marketization of China since 1978, with the reforms introduced under the leadership of Deng Xiaoping, has had a profound impact both on the country's economy and on the behavior of enterprises within an environment which was once almost wholly dominated by state actors. After Deng Xiaoping's Southern Tour in 1992, when he reenergized the liberalization of the Chinese economy and the privatization process, Shanghai Material Trading Co. Ltd. came into existence as a state-owned entity. In December 1993, SMTC became a limited shareholding company with a capital of USD 325 million. It was floated on the Shanghai Stock Exchange only a few months later in February 1994. Such speed indicates that the intention was always to create a listed company with a highly flexible trading philosophy that was able to deploy capital in areas with commercially high returns. That has proved to be the case.

The company divides its operations into three areas: general trading (which includes metal, petrol, cars, metals, etc), property and hotels, and fuel trading. In fact, according to a report in 2001, the revenues generated by trading in each of these areas divide almost half between general trading and fuel trading (with fuel making up the bulk), and only 1% coming from property. The company also engages in the manufacture and sale of wood, special glasses, and other household products. It has a market capitalization in 2008 of USD 250 million, and 1,930 employees, and although it had business interests in Beijing, and other PRC cities, its main focus was in Shanghai. It was overwhelmingly a domestic trading company, with hardly any foreign interests — something testified to by the fact that its website is wholly in Chinese, and mentions no subsidiaries even in Hong Kong. The chairman of the board for the company was Lu Yongming, with Wu Jianhua as his deputy and general manager. In 2008, it had sales of USD 400 million, and 252 million issued shares.

For the full year of 2008, Shanghai Material Trading Co. Ltd. reported net profit of CNY 70.78 million or CNY 0.28 per share on main operating turnover of CNY 32.92 billion against the net profit attributable to group of CNY 73.65 million or CNY 0.29 per share on main operating turnover of CNY 30.04 billion for the previous year. Adjusted net profit attributable to group was CNY 44.08 million for 2008. Adjusted earnings per share for 2008 was CNY 0.174 against CNY 0.185 for the previous year. The net cash flow for 2008 was CNY 0.9 against negative net cash flow of CNY 1.16 in 2007. The return on net assets for 2008 was 9.67% against 9.33% in 2007.

Growth Strategies

By 2009, SMTC was already the largest commercial trading center in China. But it had a number of new plans for expansion, with reports in May 2009 that it had issued from 30 to 100 million new shares to institutional investors, including an offer for 30% of these to controlling shareholder Shanghai Bailian Group. This was to finance the Bailian Oil Fuel Depot project, although it was subject to the approval by the China Securities Regulatory Commission. The Bailian Oil Depot in Shanghai Chemical Industrial Park, which owns Shanghai Fuel Company Ltd., was launched on 11 May 2009. This expansion of interest in fuel trading was accompanied by a refocus in its property interests, with reports of a shift from residential to commercial property. SMTC already has USD 1.5 million committed to the Beijing Sanlitun project in 2007. But its main interests were in 200,000 square meters of residential projects, with only 100,000 square meters in commercial up to 2009. In May 2009, in a deal with one of China's largest real estate developers, it committed to a shift away from residential into commercial. At the same time, the company also increased its activity in the trading of non-ferrous metal material trading, with speculation that it was planning to become China's largest spot market for non-ferrous metals and fuel oil.

Kerry Brown

References

BusinessWeek (2009). Shanghai Material Trading Centre Co. Ltd. http://investing.businessweek.com/research/stocks/snapshot/snapshot.asp?ric=600822.SS. Retrieved on 10 June 2009.

Shanghai Material Trading launches oil park in SCIP (10 May 2009). *China Knowledge*. http://news.alibaba.com/article/detail/business-in-china/100099846-1-shanghai-material-trading-launches-oil.html. Retrieved on 10 June 2009.

Shanghai Material Trading Centre turns to realty giant (8 May 2009). *SinoCast Daily*. http://www.zibb.com/article/5279617/Shanghai+Material+Trading+Centre+Turns+to+Realty+Giant. Retrieved on 10 June 2009.

SHANGHAI PUDONG DEVELOPMENT BANK

Corporate Address and Contact Information

Shanghai Pudong Development Bank Co. Ltd.
12 Zhongshan East One Road
Shanghai 200002
People's Republic of China
Phone: (86)21-6361-1226
Fax: (86)21-6323-0807
www.spdb.com.cn

Shanghai Pudong Development Bank Co. Ltd. (SPDB, 上海浦东发展银行) is a commercial bank headquartered in Shanghai, which was established shortly after the Chinese government decided to develop Shanghai's new Pudong district in the early 1990s. It aims to transform Pudong into an international financial hub that will contribute to China's economic development and social progress.

Though a relatively new bank, SPDB has made stellar achievements since it was founded in 1993. It was ranked among the top three Chinese banks by *The Asian Banker* magazine in 2007, joining the rank of the China Merchant Bank and the Bank of China; at the same time, the British magazine *Bankers* nominated SPDB as one of the top 10 Chinese banks, and ranked it number 191 among the top 1,000 world banks based on core capital, number eight among all Chinese banks based on tier one capital and number three among joint-stock commercial banks in China. In addition, through a creditability poll co-conducted by *Public Security News* and *Sina Finance*, the bank also gained the honor as one of the top 10 listed companies of being worth investing and top 10 listed companies with best share reform. In March 2007, the company was awarded as one of the top 50 worth-investing listed companies at the annual conference of Chinese stock investors.

Historical Development

Incorporated on 9 January 1993, SPDB issued a 400 million A-Share offer on 23 September 1993 on the Shanghai Stock Exchange. With both the Chinese Central Bank and China Securities Regulatory Commission's approval, it became the first public shareholding commercial bank in China since the enactment of the country's Commercial Bank Law and the Securities Law. On 10 November 1999, an additional issue of 320 million shares was listed on the Shanghai Stock Exchange, and the bank's registered capital reached RMB 2.41 billion.

In 2003, Citigroup bought 5% stake in SPDB, which was diluted into 3.779% later. In 2005, Citigroup planned to increase its holdings to 19.9%, a goal that has not yet completed as of 2009. Citigroup's shares in SPDB became tradable by the end of 2008, and the holdings were believed to be liquidated.

By the end of 2007, the bank's total assets reached RMB 9149.80 billion, the outstanding balance of all deposits stood at RMB 7634.73 billion, with outstanding loans of RMB 5509.88 billion, and after-tax profits totaled RMB 54.99 billion. The bank has set up 30 directly subordinate branches in Shanghai, Beijing, Tianjin, Chongqing, Hangzhou, Nanjing, Guangzhou, Shenzhen, Kunming, Zhengzhou, Dalian, Jinan, Xian, Chengdu, Shenyang, Wuhan, Taiyuan, Changsha, Harbin, Ningbo, Suzhou, Wenzhou, Wuhu, etc., with a total of over 400 business network sites.

According to the bank's annual financial report for 2008, its net profit increased by 127.61% year-over-year to RMB 12.516 billion, while its earnings per share increased by 127.7% to RMB 2.21. By 31 December 2008, the total assets of SPDB had reached about RMB 1.309 trillion, an increase of 43.11% compared with the same period of 2007; its average return on assets was 1.13%, increasing by 0.44 percentage points over the previous year; and its revenue during the entire year of 2008 reached RMB 34.561 billion, increasing by RMB 8.684 billion over 2007 with a rate of increase was 33.56%.

With regard to the several key indexes that are used to value the performance of business banks, the bank's capital adequacy ratio was 9.06%, decreasing by 0.09%; its non-performing loan ratio was 1.21%, decreasing by 0.25%; and its provision coverage ratio for non-performing loans was 192.49%, an increase of 1.41%.

Corporate Leadership, Main Products, and Services

Fu Jianhua is the current president of SPDB, who has been vice chairman since May 2007 and the head of the bank since August 2006. Before joining SPDB, Fu had served as the chairman of the Bank of Shanghai. Along with Fu's appointment in May 2007, Ji Xiaohui was named the chairman of SPDB. Ji used to be chairman of the Shanghai International Group before joining SPDB, and served as the head of the Shanghai Branch of the Industrial and Commercial Bank of China (ICBC). Other key figures in the leadership team include Zhu Shiyin, vice chairman of SPDB, who is also serving as president of Shanghai State-owned Asset Management Co. Ltd.

The SPDB's products and services are offered through three business divisions: personal banking, featuring the Orient Cards, private deposits, and private loans; corporate banking, including corporate deposit accounts, financing, asset custody, annuity, and offshore businesses; and intermediate business, including credit card and point of sale (POS) businesses. SPDB also offers Internet-banking and telephone-banking services. From its headquarters on Shanghai's historic Bund — the previous HSBC Building — SPDB commands over 400 branches and network offices across the country and a representative office in Hong Kong as of mid-2009.

SPDB provides various financial products and services to corporations and individuals in China. The bank primarily engages in generating deposits and originating loans. Its deposit products include time deposits, demand deposits, corporate fixed deposits, and current savings deposits. The bank's lending activities comprise short-, mid-, and long-term loans. It also engages in handling domestic and international settlements; discounting bills and notes in domestic and foreign exchange; issuing financial bonds; acting as agent for the issuing, encashment, underwriting, and trading of state bonds; conducting inter-bank lending, etc.

SPDB offers its clients personal banking, corporate banking, and inter-bank business products (treasury and markets). Personal-banking products include saving products, leisure banking card, individual FX trading, mortgage loan, online payment, electronic ticket, bank securities express, open-ended fund, instant message, car mortgage, and easy remittance. Treasury and market services include RMB-structured deposit, USD-CNY exchanges, vanilla option, and premium deposits. Corporate-banking services include offshore banking, non-bank financial institutions, trade finance, occupational pension, correspondent banking, investment banking, and assets custody. Banking businesses have become more competitive in China. To better cater to the needs of its customers, SPDB plans to expand its online services.

Business Challenges

Though it suffered a sharp drop in its share price due to financial uncertainty among investors and financial traders, SPDB has been affected marginally by the 2008–2009 global financial crisis and it posted net profit of RMB 2.96 billion for the first quarter of 2009, up 5.29% from a year earlier.

China is determined to develop Shanghai into a global financial center rivaling New York and London by 2020. Shanghai has long-lobbied Beijing for more support to achieve this objective. The inevitable adjustment to the international financial order as a result of the global financial crisis presented a great opportunity for China and for Shanghai. Among all the supportive policies approved by China's State Council in the aftermath of the global financial crisis, the most crucial one is the pilot for RMB settlement.

In 2005, the Chinese State Council chose Shanghai and Shenzhen as pilots for offshore RMB financial business. In Shanghai, the business is conducted by the Bank of Communications and SPDB. A strong impetus for Shanghai's rise is the growing strength of the RMB, which is gradually becoming a hard currency. Shanghai has become the center for RMB settlement, RMB asset pricing, and RMB wealth management. In light of this development, in the coming years, SPDB will face both a challenge and an opportunity to play a leadership role in China's financial reforms and in turning Shanghai into a global financial center.

Zhiqun Zhu

References

Citigroup not to sell Shanghai Pudong Development Bank stake (9 January 2009). SinoCast Daily. http://www.tradingmarkets.com/.site/news/Stock%20News/2116773/. Retrieved on 16 May 2009.

Financial Times (2009). Shanghai Pudong Development Bank Co. Ltd. http://markets.ft.com/tearsheets/businessProfile.asp?s=CN:600000. Retrieved on 16 May 2009.

Pudong Development Bank net profit up 127.61% in 2008 (24 April 2009). China Retail News. http://www.chinaretailnews.com/2009/04/24/2583-pudong-development-bank-net-profit-up-12761-in-2008/. Retrieved on 16 May 2009.

Shanghai Pudong Development Bank (2008). Annual Report. http://www.spdb.com.cn/res/200807/0711_16001_3255.pdf. Retrieved on 16 May 2009.

SHANGHAI ZHENHUA PORT MACHINERY

Corporate Address and Contact Information

Shanghai Zhenhua Port Machinery Company Ltd.
3470 South Pudong Road
Shanghai 2000125
People's Republic of China
Phone: (86)21-5039-0727
Fax: (86)21-5839-7000
http://www.zpmc.com

Shanghai Zhenhua Port Machinery (Group) Company Ltd. (ZPMC 上海振华港口机械) is the world's largest manufacturer of cranes and large steel structures. The group's principal activities are manufacturing, selling, and installation of port machineries, project vessels, steel structure and related spare parts, and accessories. Quayside container cranes and Rubber Tired Gantries (RTG) are Zhenhua's core products, and the company has six production and assembly bases located in southern China. As a large state-owned listing corporation, ZPMC's operations are carried out not only in China but also in Asia, America, Europe, Africa, and Oceania.

Historical Development

In the last three decades, China's logistics sector has risen from being one of the least developed, to becoming one of the most dynamic and fastest expanding in the world. The development of the Port of Shanghai typifies this, rising from being a moribund backwater during the late Maoist period up to 1976, to its river and deepwater port being ranked in 2006 for the first time as the world's largest and busiest, shipping more containers than Singapore and Hong Kong, its closest competitors. This is a direct result of the immense attention given to the export-orientated economic growth model used by the Chinese over the last three decades, with massive amounts of goods now shipped from Chinese ports to markets in the United States, Asia, and Europe, and increasing amounts to Africa.

Shanghai Zhenhua Port Machinery Company is highly representative of the industries that China has had to build up to support its burgeoning shipbuilding and port sectors. Typically for its sector the company is state-owned. ZPMC was founded in February 1992, just before China's exports started to expand massively as a result of government policy supporting foreign investment in export-orientated manufacturing industries. But Zhenhua has a complex ownership structure. As of 2009, ZPMC is a subsidiary of the China Communications Construction Company (CCCC — 中國交通建設), itself a state-owned infrastructure and construction company established in mainland China in 2005 from the merger of China Harbor Engineering Company Group and China Road and Bridge Group. CCCC is a serious player, and has real clout. In 2008, it ranked as the largest port construction and design company in China, the largest dredging company in China and the third largest in the world, and the largest state-owned mainland Chinese infrastructure enterprise listed on the Hong Kong Stock Exchange. As a sign of how strategically important CCCC is, some of its stock was bought by prominent Hong Kong business people such as Li Ka Shing, Lee Shau Kee, Joseph Lau, Robert Kuok, and Alwaleed bin Talal, during its initial public offering (IPO) in December 2006. China Life Insurance Group, Chow Tai Fook Group, and Government of Singapore Investment Corporation were its strategic stockholders.

ZPMC itself was partially listed on the Shanghai Stock Exchange B-Index, which allowed foreign investment, issuing one billion shares for USD one billion in August 1997. In December 2000, Zhenhua was listed on the Shanghai A-Index with 88 million shares at one RMB each share, allowing local holdings. In December 2004, it issued a second tranche of 114 million A-Shares, and another 125 million shares in October 2007. According to the Shanghai Municipal Government's report, ZPMC's output value increased at an annual rate of 30%–50% since 1996. In 2007, ZPMC had sales of just over USD 2 billion, and a market capitalization of USD 2.4 billion, with net income of USD 274 million.

Main Products and Services

ZPMC specialises in designing, manufacturing, and erecting large steel structures, such as container cranes, rubber tyre gantry cranes, bulk material ship loaders, bucket wheel stackers and reclaimers, and steel bridges. Other activities include leasing of self-manufactured container cranes, provision of marine forwarding services with specific vessels for container cranes, and the contracting of steel structure projects. According to the survey made by *World Cargo News* in England, ZPMC has had the biggest order book for large container cranes every year from 2000 to 2007. The company employs 800 engineers engaged in mechanical, electrical, and hydraulic design and in its own designated research and development department. It also has 2000 certified welders, 400 of whom hold international welding certificates. ZPMC's products are in use in 54 countries and regions around the world, and operations of the group are carried out at over 160 terminals worldwide. According to the company, it has supplied 1,000 quayside container cranes, 1,650 RTGs, and numerous non-standard large port machineries. ZPMC has achieved annual capacity supplying 160 quayside container cranes, and 200,000 tons of large steel bridge structures. ZPMC designed and fabricated the first set of quayside container cranes in the world that can handle twin 40′ containers. The company has also been successful in producing double trolley quayside container cranes and has supplied large bridge structures to the United States and Canada, and over 100,000 tons of steel for the Donghai Bridge, Shanghai. In 1999, ZPMC was granted the certificate from the American Institute of Steel Constructions (AISC) for steel structure fabrication, one of only two certificates issued in China.

Corporate Structure and Business Strategies

The company currently has six manufacturing bases: Jiangyin, Changzhou, Changxing, Zhangjiang, Nanhui, and Nantong Base. The company also has four professional corollary companies: Zhenhua Fengcheng Brake Co., Zhenhua Shenyang Outdoor Elevator Co., Zhenhua Changzhou Panel Co., and Zhenhua Ningbo Transmission Mechanism Co. In 2001, ZPMC completed the first phase of the construction of a large port machinery production base on Changxing Island, at the mouth of Yangtze River, with a total area of one million square meters and a coastline of 3,500 meters. It plans to expand the production scope and start a development on the manufacture of offshore heavy-duty equipment.

From 1990, ZPMC has had a European agency, ZPMC Europe, located in Holland, and directed by Van den Broek, employing 40 people, most of them are service engineers. It provides technical services for its customers here. There is also a similar agency in the United States.

The current vice president, chief engineer, and executive director since 18 March 2004 is Yan Yunfun, who was the former deputy chief engineer, manager of machinery design, as well as deputy head of the technical department. He holds a master's degree in engineering management. Other company personnel since April 2007 include Chairman Zhou Jichang, Vice Chairman Guan Tongxian, Chief Financial Officer Yu Wang, and Vice Chairs Zhou Jianbo, Zhou Qi, Dai Wenkai, Zhai Liang, and Fei Guo.

In October 2003, Xinhua Far East China Credit Ratings (Xinhua Far East), a Chinese government service ranking credit risk among Chinese corporations using international standards, downgraded the long-term credit rating of ZPMC from AAA to BBB, but said that the rating outlook remains stable. Xinhua Far East stated that while it had:

> Noticed that although the Company's operating scale has expanded, its profit margin has declined due to price competition arising from intensified competition among global port machinery manufacturers and price rises in raw materials, such as steel and oil. Moreover, Zhenhua's accounts receivable have been high, resulting in a mediocre cash flow. Debt has been increasing as sluggish operations have not effectively generated cash flow, and construction of the production base still requires large investment. As a result, the Company has been in an operation mode with high debt, thus largely increasing Zhenhua's financial risk.

By February 2009, however, ZPMC's position had improved considerably. Judged in 2005 by *Forbes* as one of the best "small companies in Asia", it gained, according to the official government paper in China, the *People's Daily*, "the world's largest order for bulk handling machinery", from a Brazilian company. "The signing of the contract is a milestone for ZPMC", read the report, indicating it has successfully entered the international market for large-sized bulk goods handling machinery. With contracts in South Africa, Dubai Ports, and similar plaudits in Europe for being a well-run business supplying good quality products, ZPMC looked in rude health, with global assets of USD 450 million, even while the worldwide shipping sector was in recession. To sustain its growth over a long run, ZPMC's main focus is now on increasing its research and development capacity to come up with not only new goods, but ones that are environmentally friendly and energy efficient, both in production and in their use. It shares these aims with many other Chinese corporations in the coming years.

Kerry Brown

References

Forbes Online (2005). Shanghai Zhenhua Port Machinery. http://www.forbes.com/lists/2005/24/QFP8.html. Retrieved on 28 February 2009.

Shanghai Foreign Economic Relation & Trade Commission (2005). Looking back and forward in the past 12 years. *Investment Shanghai*. http://www.investment.gov.cn/2005-10-27/1130425544452.html. Retrieved on 28 February 2009.

Shanghai Zhenhua Port Machinery (Group) Co. Ltd. Downgrades to BBB from A- (30 October 2003). http://www.prnewswire.com/cgi-bin/stories.pl?ACCT=104&STORY=/www/story/10-30-2003/0002047932&EDATE=. Retrieved on 31 May 2009.

ZPMC (2006). About Us. http://www.zpmc.com/article_detail.asp?Article_ID=82&Column_ID=41. Retrieved on 31 May 2009.

ZPMC books US$2.03B in first half (12 July 2008). *World Cargo News*. http://www.worldcargonews.com/htm/w20080712.989863.htm. Retrieved on 31 May 2009.

ZPMC wins World's largest bulk goods handling order (18 February 2009). *Peoples Daily*. http://english.people.com.cn/90001/90776/90884/6595637.html. Retrieved on 10 June 2009.

SHANXI TAIGANG STAINLESS STEEL

Corporation Address and Contact Information

Shanxi Taigang Stainless Steel Co. Ltd.
2 Jiancaoping Street
Taiyuan, Shanxi Province
People's Republic of China
Phone: (86)351-301-7728
Fax: (86)351-301-7729
http://tgbx.368info.com
tgbx@tisco.com.cn

Shanxi Taigang Stainless Steel Co. Ltd. (山西太钢不锈钢股份有限公司) is located in Taiyuan, Shanxi Province, adjacent to Beijing. Nicknamed the "coal sea" of China, Shanxi Province has enriched coal, electricity, and mineral reserves that provide the steel industry with rich energy resources. Taigang Stainless Steel was established and listed after reconstructing the productive assets of Taiyuan Iron & Steel (Group) Co. Ltd. (TISCO) in 1998. Eight years later, Taigang Stainless Steel took over the main assets of TISCO and increased its output capacity to 10 million tons of steel and 3 million tons of stainless steel. It has become one of the global stainless steel enterprises with the largest production capacity, advanced technology and equipment, and the most complete varieties of different specifications. Taigang Stainless Steel possesses over 700 items of core technology in stainless steel area, and its stainless products have been widely adopted in many important projects in China, such as the Olympic Games, the Three Gorges Project, etc. As one of the most famous Chinese brands, Taigang's stainless steel products are also well received in the international market.

Historical Development

Although Taigang Stainless Steel was only incorporated in 1998, its history could be traced back to 1952, when its parent company TISCO produced the first furnace of stainless steel. The first stage of its development (1952–1985) is marked by the first stainless steel plank production line, the first argon oxygen decarburizing furnace, the first slab caster of stainless steel in China, although during this period TISCO only has the production capacity of one million tons of steel.

During the second stage (1985–2001), TISCO endeavored to develop itself into the top stainless steel company in China. Series of technical reconstruction projects were implemented including one modern stainless steel production line. Facing a hard time in the 1990s, TISCO sought the state support of national debt of RMB 5 billion to update its stainless steel production system. In 1996, it introduced 20 Rolls Sendzimir mill and built up the cold-rolling sheet production line with advanced international standard. In 1998, Taigang Stainless Steel was officially established and listed on the Shenzhen Stock Exchange, and the raised funds helped the company to update its production lines of cold-rolling mill.

During the third stage (2001–present), after China joined the WTO, along with great market demand, Taigang Stainless Steel faced severe challenges from home and abroad. After systematic research of the stainless steel market in China, Taigang Stainless Steel launched a drive to build the most competitive stainless steel company in the global market. In 2002, Taigang Stainless Steel adopted the most advanced steel-making technology of three-step route (EAF/LD(MRP)/VOD). After reaching a production output of one million tons, the company became one of the top 10 stainless steel powers in the world.

From 2004 to 2006, with support from the government, Taigang Stainless Steel invested more than RMB 30 billion in the new stainless steel and auxiliary projects. As a result, its production capability of stainless steel reached 3 million tons and the company grew to be the largest stainless steel enterprise in the world. In June 2006, the main assets of TISCO were purchased by Taigang Stainless Steel. After the acquisition, besides its main focus on the stainless steel industry, the company grew to become a dynamic enterprise in resource development, further processing, and so on.

Corporate Leadership

The leadership of Taigang Stainless Steel has passed three generations. Under the first generation (1998–2002), which includes Liu Yutang as president and Miao Hanjin the general manager, Taigang Stainless strove to become the top stainless steel company in China. The second generation (2002–2008) includes Chen Chuanping as president and Miao Hanjin and Chai Zhiyong as general managers. Under their leadership, Taigang Stainless Steel grew from a famous Chinese brand to a global giant in stainless steel.

A graduate of Shenyang Industrial College with a major in metal casting, Chen Chuanping earned his master of science from Xi'an Jiaotong University. He is known for his high level of quality awareness and attention to details. In August 2008, Taigang Stainless Steel held a meeting in which all management personnel from the medium level up must present, where 276 tons of sub-quality stainless steel sheet and cold-rolled silicon steel were displayed. As noted by Chen: "Haier was early to destroy the defect refrigerators, we have been late to destroy the defect steel." The event marked the beginning of the drive for high-quality products, and the detail-oriented work spirit and the preciseness have gradually become the corporate cultures of Taigang Stainless Steel.

After Chen was elected the vice governor of Shanxi Province, the third generation of leadership team was put in place in April 2008, which includes Li Xiaobo as president and Liu Fuxing as general manager. A graduate of Beijing University of Science and Technology and Beijing University, Li rose from low-level positions and has years of working experience with Taigang Stainless Steel.

Main Products and Services

Focusing mainly on stainless steel, Taigang Stainless Steel possesses an annual production capacity of 3 million tons. Its stainless steel, stainless clad plate, cold-rolled silicon steel, and other five products hold the largest market shares in China, serving oil, railway, automobile, shipbuilding, container, and coinage industries.

Taigang's stainless steel products include three categories: cold rolling, hot rolling, and profile. The cold-rolling category contains eight sub-categories of stainless steel that are widely used in refrigerator container, water box, shipbuilding, auto exhaust system, etc. The hot-rolling category includes five sub-categories: duplex stainless steel, heat-resistance stainless steel for industry furnace, nuclear power stations and reaction furnace, hydroelectricity stainless steel for flow passage components, and hot coil for railway trucks. The profile category includes five sub-categories: weld steel tube, seamless pipe, tube blank, weld wire rod, and filament and microfilament wire rod. Both its cold- and hot-rolling duplex stainless planks are accredited by the CCS (China Classification Society), GL (Germanischer Lloyd), LR (Lloyd's Registers), ABS (American Bureau of Shipping), and BV (Bureau Veritas).

Taigang Stainless Steel's another main product is carbon steel, which is used for steel wheel and axle carbon steel in the auto industry, oil ribs, furnace and pressure vessels, power stations, ships, molds, air bottle, and so on. Taigang Stainless Steel's services mainly include: design for material, performance and specification according to customer needs, accurate delivery time, and technical support to customer in material and technology problems around the clock. The company has more than six processing and distribution centers in China and three overseas subsidiaries in Europe, Southeast Asia, and North America. After taking over the main productive assets of TISCO, Taigang further extended its business to resource development, further processing, investment, and medical and hotel services.

Challenges and Business Strategies

Since 1985, Taigang Stainless Steel enjoyed a fast development, stimulated by the great demand of stainless steel associated with the rapid economic development in China. However, the competition has grown increasingly fierce, as Taigang Stainless Steel moves to become a global giant in stainless steel industry. Domestically, the supply is obviously more than the current demand, and China has changed from an imported country to a supplying country. Within China, Taigang Stainless Steel mainly competes with Baosteel Stainless Steel and Zhangpu Stainless Steel; in the international market, it competes with Arcelor-Mittal, POSCO, JFE, ThyssenKrupp, Sumikin & Nippon, etc.

Taigang Stainless Steel has adopted a leading and focus strategy in its niche stainless steel market. The company has decided to first build the top stainless steel company in China, and then grow to become the No. 1 stainless steel company in the world. Following this strategy, Taigang developed four major tactics: high quality orientation, customer satisfaction and service, technical and management innovation, and people-oriented corporate culture. In the past, the uneven quality had badly damaged the corporate image of Taigang Stainless Steel while fake brands co-existed in the market. In 2002, Taigang Stainless Steel decided to pay premium attention to the product quality by destroying 276 tons of defect stainless steel products. Supported by Quality Control, ISO, Six Sigma, and series of quality movement, the company has substantially improved the quality of its products.

Furthermore, Taigang has adopted "customer first" as its ongoing marketing strategy. Listening to customers needs has been a practice among management personnel, and the company also implemented the Three Dimension Market Segmentation Method according to different regions, sales channels, and consumption levels of customers. In aspect of technical and management innovation, Taigang Stainless Steel has made more than 70 breakthroughs and set up awards for technical and managerial innovation program in strategic business units (SBU). In order to build a people-oriented corporate culture, Taigang Stainless Steel bundled quality training and attention to detail to its workers that later became a part of its core values. In the ensuing years the company has carried out 515 Talent Project and 262 evaluation system: "515" stands for training 50 management executives, 100 senior technical experts, and 500 senior technical workers; while "262" stands for monthly evaluation by proportion of and 20% excellent employees, 60% eligible employees, and 20% poor performance employees. In addition, Taigang Stainless Steel has sought to fulfill its corporate social responsibility (CSR) by building an energy-saving program and becoming an environmental friendly corporate citizen in recent years.

In late 2008, Taigang Stainless Steel faced the most severe challenge in its corporate history. Accordingly, the company has modified its strategies toward acquisitions, high-end products, and dynamic operations. Given its key position and with strong government support, despite the global slowdown, it is expected that the company will continue to play an important role in the country's economic development and in the international steel market in the coming years.

Lujin (Regina) Huang and Shiqiang (Kenny) Wang

References

Shanxi Taigang Stainless Steel Co. Ltd. (2009). *Annual Report 2008.* http://tgbx.368info.com/show.jsp?id=2206. Retrieved on 25 June 2009.

TISCO (2009), Company Profile. http://www.tisco.com.cn/show.jsp?id=23. Retrieved on 25 June 2009.

技术创新成就太钢集团世界之最 (20 September 2007). *网络报* [Technical Innovations led TISCO to become a top enterprise in the world]. http://society.people.com.cn/GB/6294141.html. Retrieved on 25 June 2009.

SICHUAN CHANGHONG ELECTRIC

Corporate Address and Contact Information

Sichuan Changhong Electric Co. Ltd.
35 East Mianxing Road
High-Tech Park, Mianyang
Sichuan Province 621000
People's Republic of China
Phone: (86)816-241-0306
Fax: (86)816-241-6135
http://www.changhong.com/changhong_en/changhong_global.htm

Sichuan Changhong Electric Co. Ltd. (四川长虹电器股份有限公司) is principally engaged in the manufacture and distribution of household appliances. However, unlike the other leading Chinese producers of white goods, Changhong is located in the interior rather than the coastal area. Naturally, its initial growth strategy focused on establishing a strong foothold in the countryside. To more effectively fan out into the urban markets and meet rising export demand, Changhong eventually built a manufacturing base in Guangdong Province in 2003.

Historical Development

When Changhong's predecessor was established in 1958, the beginning of China's second Five-Year-Plan, its role was to produce military supplies. Production gradually shifted to consumer goods in the 1980s. Capitalizing on its experience in making screens for military systems, the company obtained permission to produce color televisions in 1985; by 1992, it became the first Chinese company to produce one million sets of TVs. While TVs remain Changhong's primary business today, its product line has broadened to include air-conditioners, audio/video equipment, information technology goods, electronic components, and others.

Economic reforms also brought ownership reforms, and in 1988, Sichuan Changhong Electric Co. Ltd. was established. Six years later Changhong became a publicly traded company on the Shanghai Stock Exchange, but the Sichuan Changhong Electron Group — an entity 100% owned by the government of Mianyang City — remained the main stockholder with 53.63% of the shares. In 2000, Changhong sought to diversify shareholding structure by reducing its state-owned shares, but the drive was soon suspended due to the local government's interference.

The business strategies pursued by Changhong were primarily shaped by two of its leaders: President Ni Runfeng, who served from 1985 to 2004, and his successor Zhao Yong. Consistent with its state-owned enterprise status, Zhao was not only a former Changhong executive but also the former deputy mayor of Mianyang. Although both of them took the helm when they were in their early 40s, the strategies they pursued could not be more different.

Ni made Changhong the King of Color TVs in China by staging vicious price wars. In the end, this "weapon of choice" crippled a once promising business as years of aggressive price cutting eliminated profits and funds for R&D investments. Although Changhong had a commanding lead in market share, it remained stuck in the low-end segment while foreign brands dominated the small but fast-growing high end of the market. Slowed growth, coupled with the city government's pressure to quickly revive its star business, prompted Changhong to venture abroad and Ni to waive routine checks on the creditworthiness of its agent. Chonghong agreed, in spite of Apex's dubious reputations, to fund the supply of goods and get paid after the agent had collected from retailers; that arrangement left Chonghong unable to collect receivables totaling hundreds of millions. Worse, although these exports did boost sales, their profit margins were close to zero. The Apex debacle resulted in a boardroom coup, and Ni was sacked. Gone was also Ni's strategy of growing market share at all costs. The Tsinghua University trained successor Zhao Yong began to push for quality-driven growth and innovations in 2005. Dr. Zhao was ready to make bold technology bets; his ultimate goal was to transform Changhong from an appliance maker to a technology juggernaut.

Business Strategies

Fierce competition among Chinese TV manufacturers caused the price of flat-panel TVs to plunge by 30% in 2006, even market leader Changhong came to admit that large sales volumes did not necessarily guarantee profits. In a shareholder meeting that year, Zhao proposed production of plasma display panels (PDP). His idea was greeted with scepticism both inside and outside the company because the sales ratio of LCD TV sets to PDP TV sets was about 9:1 in China. The global trends were similar, and the market potentials of PDP seemed limited.

Betting on PDP was a contrarian approach, but Zhao saw it as a catalyst to usher in quality-driven growth. Technical merits of PDP aside, lower patent threshold and lower capital requirements would enable Changhong to enter the business more easily. Most importantly, the cost structure of producing PDP TVs favored Changhong. For example, the LCD screen alone accounted for 60–70% of the panel module price while driver circuits made up the rest of the total cost of a LCD TV, but display panels accounted for less costs in PDP TVs than the driver circuits, which Changhong happened to specialize in, and this would afford the company a substantial cost advantage. On the contrary, direct competition in the LCD TV market with rivals that also controlled the bulk of LCD panel supply would be a dead end because they could easily squeeze their competitors by pushing up panel prices while slashing prices of TVs. The only way for Changhong to break this stranglehold was to get vertically integrated as well. In fact, Changhong's ambitions went beyond extending to the upstream industrial chain and securing core components, it intended to build a PDP industrial cluster in China.

Zhao set off this high stake gamble because he believed leadership in PDP production would be crucial to bringing down the price of plasma TV, to which home computers and the Internet could be linked. Zhao's long-term vision was to restructure Changhong into a 3C (consumer electronics, computers, and communications) business, and more specifically a pioneer in integrated digital media platform for home infotainment. PDP production would be a means to realizing this grand plan.

In April 2007, Changhong formally obtained approval from the National Development and Reform Commission for establishing the first PDP production line in China. To get such a capital-intensive project off the ground, the Mianyang government would fund as much as RMB 2.8 billion and the provincial government of Sichuan another RMB 700 million. Changhong's owners eagerly support the project because its success could help transform the industrial landscape of the city of Mianyang, Sichuan, and even the country. The provincial authorities are counting on this project to develop Sichuan's electronic information industry into an important player on the national level and power their "Strong Province in Industry" strategy (工业强省战略). Changhong's ambitious project, by establishing a local supply base of core components and developing capabilities for the entire value chain, could expedite the process of industrial upgrade and strategic transformation of China's household appliance industry.

Risks and Challenges

Changhong and its supporters remain optimistic about the project, but it will be an uphill battle. By 2008, even Hitachi and Pioneer, the world's fourth and the fifth largest plasma TV makers, decided to quit panel production and buy from larger vendor such as Panasonic. Sales of LCD TVs continue to lead PDP TV by a ratio of 9:1. The continuous fall in LCD panel price will make LCD TVs more attractive to buyers than PDP TVs. Also, although the PDP patent threshold is lower in terms of number, these patents are controlled by a tightly knitted group headed by Panasonic. Barriers to independent innovations remain high. The Vice President of China's Electronics Association recently expressed worries that the provincial and city authorities might not get any returns for their investments because of the poor marketing prospects of PDP.

However, with so much hope pinned on this trophy project, will it be shut down even if it turned out to be a wrong bet? The ability to enlist government help is crucial to the realization of Changhong's ambitions, but the patronage could also be a double-edged sword. For example, government ownership can bring pressure and interference, such as that witnessed in the late 1990s when the TV producers tried to call off their price wars. Instead of forcing industry consolidation, governments heavily dependent on tax revenues calculated on sales volume rather than profits kept production lines running. Some analysts suggest that many executives in Changhong realized there were problems with this, but they did not stop it and could not stop it.

Changhong's size may contribute to its woes but also save it from downfall. Because of its status as a dominant employer and a provider of tax revenues, failure could trigger social unrests. This explains why Changhong, despite is recklessness, was rescued from the costly Apex fiasco. However, will the government's readiness to bail out Changhong lead to moral hazard?

Some critics argue that Zhao's PDP investment is just as irrational as Ni's cooperation with Apex before. Ni pushed for an ambitious overseas strategy because the city and provincial government were proud to hold up Changhong, and to some extent that put pressure on Changhong to deliver results. Changhong's being beholden to the state makes it highly dependent on specific appointed leaders rather than sound corporate governance, but the tangle of financial, managerial, and political interests in fact demands more oversight.

Carmencita Cheung

References

Buckley, C (2005). Political tones to problems of TV maker In China. *New York Times*, 1 January.

COCPDP (2007a). Changhong's risk move: Investment on PDP is not a war of itself. Sichuan COC Display Devices Co. Ltd., 23 June. http://www.cocpdp.com/ecoc/3343_3494.htm. Retrieved on 7 June 2009.

COCPDP (2007b). Changhong shows to the world that the first plasma panel production line in China has been started to construct. Sichuan COC Display Devices Co. Ltd., 19 July. http://www.cocpdp.com/ecoc/3343_3477.htm. Retrieved on 7 June 2009.

Jia, H (2002). Changhong to expand overseas presence. *China Daily Business Weekly*, 31 December.

郎朗 (2009). 四川彩电业转型路径之辩. *21世纪经济报*, 20 March [Láng, L. Sichuan Changhong's transformation in color TV production. *21st Century Economic Herald*].

李壮 (2008). 四川长虹再挺等离子恐将陷入困境. *华夏时报*, 11 October [Lǐ, Z. Sichuan Changhong may be in jeopardy by sticking to its PDP strategies. *Huaxia Times*].

Zhang, ZJ and D Zhou (2006). The Art of price war: A perspective from China. http://knowledge.wharton.upenn.edu/papers/1330.pdf. Retrieved on 7 June 2009.

SINA

Corporate Address and Contact Information

Sina Corporation
Room 1802 United Plaza
1468 Nanjing Road West
Shanghai 200040
People's Republic of China
Phone: (86)21-6289-5678
Fax: (86)21-6279-3803
http://www.sina.com

The development of the Internet and of Internet-based firms in China is closely tied to the political evolution of the Chinese government and thinking about a broad array of issues, ranging from private Chinese firms to censorship to interaction among Chinese citizens. Initially, the Chinese government attempted permanently to block sites such as Google and heavily censored discussion forums but retreated when this proved both technically impossible and counterproductive to economic activities. Likewise, the use of the Internet for propaganda has become more sophisticated shifting from undisguised government distributed media to less obvious use of media outlets who agree to manage the availability of information according to government standards. Chinese and Western Internet companies alike have little choice but to cooperate with the Chinese government to control access to banned information. In addition, the Chinese government has a series of sophisticated technical arrangements — usually referred to as the "Great Chinese Firewall" — that make accessing banned information difficult. Nonetheless, the Chinese government also understands the immense importance of the Internet for economic development.

Sina and the Chinese Internet

This is the environment in which Internet companies operate in China and it has a particular effect on firms that are predominantly providers of information and entertainment. Such is the case for Sina (新浪), one of the largest and most important of the Chinese portals or prime access points for the Internet. Notwithstanding the restrictions, Chinese are able to access and use the vast majority of information and entertainment on the Internet and Sina is a main source of organizing and providing this material to a rapidly growing audience of users.

Though the content of this interaction on the Internet and via mobile phones is monitored and controlled by both Sina and the Chinese government, some believe the new features of the Internet will have dramatic effects on authoritarian states. The Internet is creating a public space in China where new forms of culture are being defined. For the first time, very large numbers of Chinese are able to create and express ideas and share these with each other. The size of these communities is approaching a level beyond governmental control, as witnessed by constant efforts to test the envelope of control and diminish its scope. There is a remarkable level of openness in the Chinese Internet and the point of no return may have already been passed.

Sina's Origins

Sina is not a typical Chinese firm. It was formed in 1999 through a merger of Chinese-oriented websites run in the West, and in 2001 the corporate headquarters was move to Beijing. Sina is a privately owned company listed on NASDAQ and lacks any past as a state-owned or sponsored firm. The initial public offering was in 2000. Insider ownership is about 10% of 56 million outstanding shares, with the vast majority of shares held by Western institutions and mutual funds. Thus, the preponderant source of capital and ownership for Sina is Western. Sina's upper management retains this Western affiliation, with most having some Western education. Major competitors in China include Netease and Sohu. Sina's market capitalization was $1.6 billion in mid-2009, reflecting substantial growth in revenues and earnings and expectations of continued growth in the Chinese Internet business space.

Business Operations

Sina has several businesses built around the Chinese Internet. Founded in 1999, Sina operates a Chinese language information and entertainment website, often referred to as a web portal, focused on users inside and outside China. Sina has been a main provider of information and entertainment for Chinese users of the web. Its business strategy has been to attract a large audience to its site with varied content and sell advertising based on the number of users. Because this business model — selling ads on web pages — is thought to be a declining Internet strategy, Sina has moved aggressively in other directions. The company also has expanded its offerings into many of the features of Web 2.0, a set of new Internet capabilities involving user created content and use of the Internet to foster much richer forms of user interaction. For example, Sina has moved into social networking via Sina brands that facilitate users' exchange of information, photos and messages, form communities, use instant messaging, and post blogs and podcasts.

Because mobile phones are so important in China, including as a primary means for accessing the Internet, Sina, since 2002, has also been involved in providing services and content for this market segment. Sina offers a customized subscription for various forms of content and services for mobile phones. These include short message service (SMS), multimedia message service (MMS) and Internet capabilities, such as news, weather, ringtones, dating services, interactive games, and Internet access. In addition, Sina.net helps business and government organize and deliver marketing and information campaigns over the Internet and via mobile phones. This system creates a variety of means for interacting with an audience, including customer relationship management.

Certainly the most dramatic and risky venture for Sina is the move beyond the Internet with the purchase of Focus Media for about US$1 billion in Sina common stock. Focus Media operates an advertising business in China cities through small LCD screens and large LED billboards. This purchase is only for the digital outdoor advertising part of Focus Media. The combination of an Internet firm with an old media advertising firm seems odd and has been criticized by many. However, Sina management expects this will lead to cross synergies by having an alternate outlet for Sina's content and add to its audience for raising advertising rates.

Prospects for Sina

The Chinese Internet market, buoyed by the 2008 Olympics, is growing very rapidly. The number of Internet users in China passed that in the United States in 2008 and totaled more than 300 million in early 2009. Because this represents only 20% of potential users and Chinese incomes are also growing rapidly, there is much growth left. In monetary terms, this market is relatively small; however, growing very quickly. When advertising, gaming, and other forms of e-commerce are added, the Chinese Internet generated about $2.2 billion in revenue in the third quarter of 2008. This is an increase of 50% above the level in 2007.

Sina's revenue and earnings generally track growth in the Chinese Internet market. For 2008, Sina's revenue grew by 50% to $370 billion, though in the fourth quarter growth rates slowed following the Olympics. Advertising accounts for just over two-thirds of revenues. Net income for 2008 rose by 54% to $89 million.

Sina will be challenged to retain and grow its position as the largest web portal in China, largely because this market is changing rapidly. Most business models for Chinese Internet firms, also true for Sina, were developed in the United States. This may well change with continuing growth of the size and diversity of Chinese Internet users. New business models may well emerge from China and suited to this market, perhaps based on mobile devices.

Thomas D. Lairson

References

Batjargal, B (2007). Internet entrepreneurship: Social capital, human capital and human performance of Internet ventures in China. *Research Policy*, 36: 605-618.

China's Internet market size totaled CNY 14.63 billion (7 November 2008). *SinoCast China Business Daily News*.

Fallows, J (2008). The connection has been reset. *The Atlantic Online* (March). http://www.theatlantic.com/doc/200803/chinese-firewall. Retrieved on 28 May 2009.

Kuo, K (2009). Blogs, bulletin boards and business. *China Business Review* (January–February), 28–31.

Reporters without Borders (2009). China. http://www.rsf.org/article.php3?id_article=10749. Retrieved on 1 June 2009.

Shambaugh, D (2007). China's propaganda system: Institutions, processes and efficacy. *The China Journal*, 57 (January): 25–58.

Sina reports preliminary fourth quarter and fiscal year 2008 financial results (16 March 2009). http://corp.sina.com.cn/eng/news/2009-03-17/95.html. Retrieved on 1 June 2009.

Wang, T (2008). Sina faces uphill battle in digital media. *Forbes Online* (23 December). http://www.forbes.com/2008/12/23/sina-focus-media-markets-equity-cx_twdd_1223markets2.html?partner=whiteglove_google. Retrieved on 28 May 2009.

Update on the number of China Internet users (19 April 2009). *China Internet Watch*. http://www.chinainternet-watch.com/138/china-internet-users/. Retrieved on 24 May 2009.

Yang, G (2003). The co-evolution of the Internet and civil society in China. *Asian Survey*, 43(3) (May/June): 405–422.

Yahoo Finance (2009). Sina Corp. http://finance.yahoo.com/q/mh?s=SINA. Retrieved on 28 May 2009.

SINOCHEM INTERNATIONAL

Corporate Address and Contact Information

Sinochem International Co. Ltd.
18/F, Jinmao Tower
No. 88 Century Boulevard
Pudong District
Shanghai 200121
People's Republic of China
Phone: (86)21-6104-8666
Fax: (86)21-5049-0909
http://www.sinochemintl.com

In December 1998, Sinochem International Corporation (中化国际股份有限公司), which was derived from the business of rubber, plastics, chemical products, logistics, and transportation operations of Sinochem Corporation, was founded in Beijing; and in 2000, it was listed on the Shanghai Stock Exchange with 120 million A-Shares issued, raising 946 million RNB. As one of the key enterprises under the supervision of the State-owned Assets Supervision and Administration Commission (SASAC) of the State Council, Sinochem Corporation has been named to the *Fortune* Global 500 list for 18 times, ranking the 257th in 2008.

Historical Development

China Import Co., which later became the Sinochem Corporation, was established on 1 March 1950 as the first state-owned import and export enterprise specializing in foreign trade. A year later, China Import & Export Co. was established based on China Import Co. and North China Trading Co., engaging mainly in foreign trade with Western countries and importing necessities for domestic production and consumption. In the 1950s, the company had built up trading relationship with hundreds of clients in more than 40 countries and regions. Under the planned economy, the growth in export and the establishment of import channels for international oil and chemical products enabled Sinochem to become a specialized import and export company dealing with oil and chemicals trading in China.

On 1 January 1961, China Import & Export Co. formally changed its name to China National Chemicals Import & Export Corporation. By 1965, the number of countries and regions that established trading relationship with Sinochem had topped 90; the export portfolio had increased to 300 from mere 30 with total export volume of US$80 million. In 1973, Sinochem exported its first shipment of crude oil to Japan, and later on to Brazil, Singapore, and US markets. By 1975, Sinochem's export portfolio was enriched to 400 products, with total export volume of US$214 million.

In the 1980s, Sinochem further expanded its export business of domestic chemical products while guaranteeing the country's assignment, and set up a batch of associated economic entities, which significantly boosted its export growth of chemical products. By 1986, the export volume had reached US$708 million with annual trading volume ranking top in the industry. At the end of 1987, Sinochem received green light from the State Council for its international expansion. After seven years' development, Sinochem evolved into a multinational company with cross-industry, multi-functional, comprehensive, and international operation, and was ranked among the *Fortune* Global 500 companies for the first time in 1989, one of the earliest Chinese enterprises named on the prestigious list.

In 1994, Sinochem also received governmental approval for its plan to build up a comprehensive trading company, combining the functions of trading, industry, technology, finance, and information with trade at the core. After successfully offsetting the blow of the Asian financial crisis in 1998, and with the economic globalization and deepening reform of China's market economy, Sinochem began to conduct market-oriented strategy and carry out strategic transformation. In 1999, Sinochem launched management improvement project and stepped on a brand new development track. A year later, Sinochem became a key enterprise under the direct control of the State Council, and Sinochem International (600500), with Sinochem as the holding company, successfully went public on the Shanghai Stock Exchange.

On 22 January 2002, Sinochem signed an agreement with Petroleum Geo-Services (PGS), acquiring a PGS subsidiary, Atlantis. It is the first oil field acquired by Sinochem, which marked a breakthrough in its upstream extension strategy of oil business. On the basis of the year 2003, Sinochem proposed in 2004 to double its net assets and net income in five years. By 2005, Sinochem's performance far exceeded the benchmark set by SASAC, accomplishing its financial target of doubling net profit, three years ahead of the schedule. In 2008, Sinochem still maintained a steady and sound growth stance, with the revenue exceeding RMB 300 billion and the profit before tax over RMB 8.7 billion.

Corporate Structure

Sinochem International Corporation was jointly founded by Sinochem Corporation and five other initiators in Beijing on 21 December 1998, with a total share capital of RMB 558.975 million. On 1 March 2000, Sinochem International issued 120 million common shares on the Shanghai Stock Exchange, with Sinochem Corporation as the controlling shareholder. In 2001, Sinochem International strategically relocated its headquarters to the Jinmao Tower in Shanghai.

The Sinochem Group consists of Sinochem Petroleum Exploration and Production Co. Ltd., the oil group, the fertilizer group, China National Seed Group Corporation, Sinochem International, Shenyang Research Institute of Chemical Industry, Zhejiang Petrochemical Building Material Co. Ltd., Sinochem Hong Kong (Group) Co. Ltd., and Sinochem Plastics Company. It also has domestic operation group, financial companies, Franshion Properties, overseas subsidiaries, and some other associated companies.

Main Products, Services, and Business Strategies

In recent years, Sinochem International has been pursuing the development strategies of extending to industrial upstream and downstream; also, the company endeavors on its transformation from a foreign trade agent company to an integrated solution supplier with sound marketing capability and stable profitability. With the continuous advancement of the four-core operating sectors: rubber, chemical engineering, metallurgy energy, and chemical logistics, the company has customers in over 100 countries and regions around the world, and the sales revenue of USD 1.9 billion.

In the business sector of chemical logistics, the company has consolidated and expanded its competitive advantages to a great extent. During the recent years, the scale of operation and the service capacity of its subordinated maritime shipping companies have been improved rapidly, with the actual tonnage of marine shipping achieved 1.54 million tons, of which 410,000 tons come from the internal customers. Long-term shipping orders has been conducted with the majority of high-end customers, such as Shanghai Saike, Shell China, and Nanjing Yangba, with its market share increased gradually, which reached over 21% in the high-end market of internal trade shipping. Sinochem possessed 19 specialized chemical vessels, with shipping capacity of 102,600 tons in 2005, which ranked the first place in the domestic liquefied chemical products industry.

In the field of rubber business, the company's market share in natural rubber sales has been ranked the first place for several years. Besides the consolidation and enhancement of its leading position in current trade marketing, the company facilitates the integration strength in the expansion to upstream resources. As for natural rubber, the company has, through investment, mergers and acquisitions, become the dominate shareholder of Hainan Sinochem Enlian, Yunnan Xishuangbanna Sinochem Enlian, and other projects, and formed initial strategic layout in domestic non-governmental rubber resource integration. Based on the cooperation with the aforementioned two agricultural reclamation groups, the company realized the differentiated development of product and technology, which has facilitated its competitive advantage in the acquisition of domestic natural rubber and product technological services; for synthetic rubber, the company has consolidated and expanded the strategic alliances with such core suppliers as Exxon Mobil, Thai Rubber, etc., and greatly enhanced the marketing and technological service capacities via firming upstream resources and high-efficient marketing channels; meanwhile, through the integration of marketing, industry, technology, and branding in rubber business, the company's customer-oriented services have been greatly promoted, with the embedding of supplier system with transnational tyre corporations, such as Michelin, Bridgestone, and Goodyear, as well as domestic tyre enterprises such as Shanghai Tyre, Guizhou Tyre, etc. Moreover, in order to manage the risk of price fluctuation and achieve sustainable growth in rubber business, the company vigorously promotes new brands and the development of new products.

As to the traditional chemical business, Sinochem maintains its competitive edge in the trade distribution field, with its export volume of paraffin amounting to 8% of the total volume nationwide, and the import volume of pesticide taking 10% of the total domestic import volume. In addition, with fundamental chemical and plastic business as the major integral parts of Eastern China regions, pigment, paraffin, specialty chemicals, and rare metals take up considerable market shares. Since 2005, under its guiding principle of "pursuit of the leading segmentation field", the company has undertaken reconstruction on the traditional chemical business sector, and has defined and enriched its operations in the export of agro-chemical and specialty chemical products, with PVC and chemical segmentation products as the key and integrating with elements such as technology, industry, and marketing. As a result of restructuring, fine chemical laboratories have been built in line with international standards.

In light of China's rising demand for energy in the coming years, Sinochem's outlook seems fairly bright. Under the current leadership, Sinochem's R&D initiatives have achieved a number of patented inventions, the construction of new plants is going smoothly as a number of fine chemicals plants is coming on-stream, significant investments in chemicals logistics have been made with shore tanks and tankers fleet, the Taicang Chemical Park development project also gained substantial pre-development progress. All these initiatives would provide the company with a solid foundation for speedy progress in future.

Compared with PetroChina, Sinochem has an obvious advantage in integration as a chemical enterprise, especially in product manufacturing and sales, although its oil gas reserves and explorations are not as large as those of PetroChina. As one of China's largest oil producers and marketers, Sinochem possesses 26 refineries, 22 regional sales companies of petroleum products, and 1 lubricant manufacturer. The company's retail network is holding a competitive position in Northern China, while rapidly expanding to the East and the South.

William X. Wei

References

Sinochem International Co. (2008). Annual Report. http://www.sinochemintl.com.cn/cn/3invest/report/ 二OO八年年度报告.pdf. Retrieved on 26 April 2009.

Sinochem International Co. Company Profile. http://www.sinochemintl.com/en/index_en.asp. Retrieved on 26 April 2009.

Sinochem Corporation (2007). Annual Report. http://www.sinochem.com/Portals/5/nianbao/2007英文年报.pdf. Retrieved on 26 April 2009.

Sinochem Corporation. Corporate Profile. http://www.sinochem.com/tabid/615/Default.aspx. Retrieved on 26 April 2009.

SINOFERT

Corporate Address and Contact Information

Sinofert Holdings Limited
F10, Central Tower
Chemsunny World Trade Center
28 Fuxinmen Nei Road
Beijing 100031
People's Republic of China
Phone: (86)10-5956-9601
www.sinofert.com

Sinofert Holdings Limited (中化化肥控股有限公司) is one of the largest fertilizer manufacturers, the largest fertilizer distributor, and the largest supplier of imported fertilizers in China. Sinochem Corporation, one of the biggest state-owned corporations in China, controls about three quarters of the company. In 2008, Sinofert owned holdings in 13 fertilizer makers across China and operated 1,860 sales outlets.

Scope and Products

The history of Sinofert Holdings can be traced back to 1993 when Sinochem Fertilizer was established by Sinochem Corporation. At that time, Sinochem was the only enterprise in China approved to import and export fertilizer products. In 2005, Sinofert acquired the Sinochem fertilizer business, and Sinochem Hong Kong Holdings Limited became a listed company on the Hong Kong Stock Exchange. In December 2006, the company became Sinofert Holdings Limited.

Sinofert's operations encompass R&D, production, import and export, procurement, distribution, wholesale and retail of fertilizer raw materials and products, and other agriculture-related products and services. Currently, the company manufactures diammonium phosphate, monoammonium phosphate, compound fertilizer, potassium chloride, potassium sulfate, carbamide, ammonium hydrogen carbonate, and others. In 2004, the State Administration for Industry & Commerce authorized the Sinochem brand as the fertilizer industry's "Nationwide Name Brand", a premier status within the industry.

Corporate Structure and Management

Sinochem Corporation remains the ultimate controlling shareholder with approximately 52% of issued stock. The other substantial shareholder is Potash Corporation of Saskatchewan Inc., a Canadian company and the largest potash producer in the world. As regard to corporate leadership, Liu Deshu is the current chairman, who joined the company in April 2004 and presides over a board of ten members including two executive directors, five non-executive directors, and three independent non-executive directors.

Sinofert's governance structure includes an audit committee, a cremuneration committee and, a nomination committee, which reviews the structure, size, and composition of the Board. Sinofert employs 11,100 people including those employed by controlled entities such as Qinghai Salt Lake Potash Co. Ltd. (18.5% ownership) and Guizhou Xinxin Industrial and Agricultural Trading Co. Ltd. (30% ownership).

The company operates a vertically integrated business model and continues to expand and develop both its downstream and upstream activities through the entire fertilizer industry chain. Sinofert maintains a decentralized management system in which each store is managed individually and ultimate responsibility for each product devolves to a single manager.

Sinofert has stated that its strong focus on improvements to risk management, internal control systems, and business processes has laid a solid foundation against the global financial crisis and that this has enabled it to make timely adjustments to its financing strategy in line with rapidly changing government policy and market conditions.

The group's social programs in 2008 included 4,200 agrichemical service activities such as fertilization skill lectures and field instruction. In addition, more than 1,000 "Sinofert Scientific Fertilization Pilot Villages" have been established, and in cooperation with the Ministry of Agriculture, 114 "Model Villages" have also been set up across the country. In the wider social context, Sinofert has been a major contributor to programs and initiatives related to natural disasters and poverty alleviation in China.

Competitive Strengths and Financial Performance

Sinofert's competitiveness is largely reflected in the strength and management of its networks. For example, the group has established a diversified, multi-channel procurement network. Its distribution network includes more than 600 transit warehouses and 2,010 distribution centers, covering 90% of the country's arable land area. Sinofert's sales network has the largest coverage in China, which includes 17 branch companies and 1,672 sales outlets. The company pays great attention to the synergistic integration of production, supply, and sales networks. Other competitive advantages include its extensive range of products and agrichemical services, the strength of its *SINOCHEM* brand, its strategic alliances, and several exclusive distribution and sales contracts.

In 2008, Sinofert's turnover was RMB 4.5 billion (USD 659.6 million), up 59.9%, on sales volume of 16.2 million tons, up 8%. This was supported by an increase of 48% in the average selling price of fertilizers. As a result, Sinofert further strengthened its position as China's largest fertilizer distributor. During the same year, sales volume of imported fertilizers amounted to 4.17 million tons (26% of the group total). The contribution of domestically produced fertilizers continued to increase, now comprising 70% of the group's sales volume.

Net profit attributable to shareholders in 2008 was RMB 1.9 billion (USD 278.5 million), up 198.3% with earnings per share at RMB 0.27, up 156.3%. Revenue from investments amounted to RMB 336 million (USD 49.2 million), up 19.1%, while return on equity rose to 13.7% as compared to 8.54% in 2007.

Market Overview and Business Challenges

In 2008, unprecedented fluctuations were seen in global fertilizer markets. Fertilizer prices climbed sharply as a consequence of market demand and the soaring cost of petroleum, natural gas, and sulfur. During the recent years, Sinofert also faced an adverse situation in the potash market with a significant increase in the price of imported potash fertilizers and, concurrently, slumping market demand. The group managed to overcome these difficulties by readjusting operational strategies and by developing a tailor-made product mix to better serve the needs of customers. In spite of the adverse conditions, the company's potash market share rose to more than 55% in China.

Furthermore, the expansion of ammonium chloride operations contributed to a new growth segment for the company's nitrogen operations with sales volumes increasing by 29% in 2008. Meanwhile, in response to the global financial crisis, the government has increased subsidies to rural areas, improved farmers' access to bank lending, and placed a minimum purchase price on rice amounting to an increase of 16% for 2009, as compared to 13% in 2008, all of which bodes well for the fertilizer industry's future.

Potash is a heavily capital intensive business, which requires major long-term capital investments, making it one of the most exclusive and attractive mass mining products. Internationally, the market appears to be consolidating through a series of both friendly and hostile M&As. While demand appears to continue its growth trend, supply disruptions could easily cause disruptive price growth. For example, the droughts that are affecting many of the most fertile parts of the world could be the catalyst for such a supply disruption. Central and northeastern China are in the midst of a severe drought that could quickly push prices up in the short term. In their internal operations, Sinofert faces opposing pressures in improving management skills, while at the same time, continuing its transformation into a globally competitive international organization.

Growth Opportunities and Strategies

In China, the population is still increasing, the food consumption pattern is diversifying, and the demand for grains is growing at a steady pace, all of which augur well for national fertilizer usage. In light of the current global economic recession, the Chinese government has strived to create a favorable environment for the industry by earmarking RMB 123 billion (USD 18 billion) in 2009 for various rural subsidies. Fertilizer pricing controls have also been relaxed and overall export taxes on fertilizers have been reduced.

Sinofert Holdings is in the process of transforming from a foreign trade-oriented company to a marketing service and industrial service-oriented enterprise. It will continue its industry focus on fertilizers, pesticide and seed production, supply, and sale. During the 1990s, the group learned some hard lessons through the sale, merger, or cessation of more than 400 diversified businesses. This would seem to assure Sinofert's unremitting focus on its core businesses and is further reinforced by its recent M&A activities and alliances. These are expected to be a continuing feature of the forward and backward integration strategies that will underpin its expansion plans.

Optimization of internal controls and systems, including new technologies, is considered critical to achievement of business goals. Sinofert has invested heavily to establish ERP (enterprise resources planning) and DMS (dealer management system) platforms to ensure smooth communication between all sales points and obstacle-free strategy implementation. Sinofert continues to focus on a distribution-centered marketing strategy to protect and enhance its *SINOCHEM* brand. The customer base of the distribution network has also been consolidated and the customer structure optimized. Among the group's 32,000 customers, the ratio of township-level customers — a critical growth segment — increased to 82% in 2008, as compared to 77% in 2007.

Sinofert's goal is to develop a superior sales-service team that covers all major agricultural regions nationwide. The company will also continue to develop international alliances to address local fertilizer product shortages. Through careful investment in R&D and development of its existing team of senior experts — including alliances with China Agricultural University and the Chinese Academy of Agricultural Sciences — Sinofert seeks to maintain its lead in scientific fertilization.

In recent times, Sinofert Holdings Limited has achieved strong growth in revenues, profits, and market share while also demonstrating leadership in the internationalization of its operations. As we enter a new decade, Sinofert appears to be well placed to weather both the macro and industry challenges that lie ahead.

Lin Song and Terence R Egan

References

Campbell, K (2009). Potash essential to feed the world's growing billions (23 January). *Mining Weekly*. http://www.miningweekly.com/article/potash-essential-to-feed-the-worlds-growing-billions-2009-01-23. Retrieved on 25 March 2009.

Sinofert Holdings Limited announces 2008 annual results (24 March 2009). *PR Newswire*. http://news.prnewswire.com/DisplayReleaseContent.aspx?ACCT=104&STORY=/www/story/03-24-2009/0004994174&EDATE=. Retrieved on 20 May 2009.

Sergeant, B (2009). Hell, of a kind, breaks loose in potash (27 February). Mineweb. http://www.mineweb.com/mineweb/view/mineweb/en/page72102?oid=79327&sn=Detail. Retrieved on 5 May 2009.

Sinofert Holdings Limited (2008). *Annual Report*. http://www.sinofert.com/english/tzzx/cfbg_nei.php?id=8. Retrieved on 20 May 2009.

Sinofert Holdings Limited. Corporate Overview. http://www.sinofert.com/english/gywm/gsjj.php. Retrieved on 10 February 2009.

SINOPEC SHANGHAI PETROCHEMICAL

Corporate Address and Contact Information

Sinopec Shanghai Petrochemical Company Limited
48 Jinyi Road
Jinshan District, Shanghai 200540
People's Republic of China
Phone: (86)21-5237-7880, 5794-3143
Fax: (86)21-5237-5091, 5794-0050
http://www.spc.com.cn
spc@spc.com.cn

Sinopec Shanghai Petrochemical Company Limited (SPC, 中国石化上海石油化工股份有限公司) was incorporated in 1993. As a China-based company located in Shanghai's Jinshan District, SPC employs over 22,922 people as of 2008, and its common stocks have been listed on the Shanghai (600688) and Hong Kong Stock Exchange (0338). The company is a major manufacturer in high synthetic petrochemicals in China, and processes crude oil into a range of products that include synthetic fibers, resins and plastics, intermediate petrochemicals, and petroleum products. As one of the subsidiaries of China Petroleum & Chemical Corporation (Sinopec Corp.), SPC is considered one of the largest and most important refining-chemical integrated petrochemical companies in China.

Historical Development

SPC evolved from the original Shanghai Petrochemical Complex established in 1972. The company was among the first Chinese companies listed on the stock exchanges in Hong Kong and New York. Over its history, the company went through four phases of large-scale development, which started in Jinshanwei, Hangzhou Bay in 1974, and ended with the start-up of Phase Four project in April 2002.

In the first phase, starting 1 January 1974, the company established a large petrochemical and synthetic fiber production base within three years; by 1977, 18 major plants for the production of ethylene, polyester fiber, PVA fiber, acrylic fiber, and plastics were put into production and supplied the nation with 1 meter synthetic fabric raw material per capital, achieving an annual profit of RMB 500 million. During Phase Two (1980–1985), the crude oil utilization rate increased from less than 30% to 43%; the company produced 3 meters synthetic fabric raw material per capital, and generated over RMB 1 billion of profit and tax annually. In Phase Three (May 1987 to April 1992), a RMB 6 billion project was launched, which further raised the crude oil utilization rate from 43% to more than 62%. As a result, the ethylene production reached 450,000 tons per year, and 1.7 billion RMB of profit and tax were realized. SPC also went through a major transformation from only a synthetic fiber producer to a manufacturer of petroleum products, petrochemicals, synthetic fibers, and plastics, and therewith became one of the largest petrochemical production bases in China. The last phase started in June 2000 and completed two years later. With an investment of 5.2 billion RMB, the project allowed SPC to quadruple its production capacities, enhance technological know-how, and raise corporate revenue among other things.

Main Products and Services

By the end of 2007, the company has built up a large crude oil processing capacity of 14 million tons, an ethylene production capacity of 950,000 tons, a refined oil products and petrochemicals production capacity of 5.48 million tons, a synthetic fiber feedstock and synthetic fibers production capacity of 1.38 million tons and a synthetic resins and plastic products capacity of 950,000 tons. Moreover, SPC has its own utilities system, environmental protection system, loadings, and un-loadings handling facilities for marine and inland waterway, railway, and highway transportation.

SPC's main products are in the following four categories. The first one is refined oil products such as gasoline, diesel, jet fuel, and LPG (liquefied petroleum gas) among others. The second product group is the petrochemicals, such as ethylene, propylene, butadiene, benzene, toluene, paraxylene, PTA (purified terephthalic acid), acrylonitrile, ethylene glycol, ethylene oxide, C5 fraction, acetic acid, and vinyl acetate, among others. The third category is synthetic resins and plastics such as polyethylene, polypropylene, polyester chips, and polyvinyl alcohol, among others. The last is synthetic fibers such as acrylic staple, acrylic top, polyester staple, polyester filament, and polyester industry yarn. By the end of 2008, synthetic fibers accounted for 6.17%, resins 25.03%, plastics and intermediate petrochemicals 17.31%, petroleum products 46.44% and all other product categories 5.05% of total net sales, respectively.

Corporate Culture

Under the leadership of Chairman and President Rong Guangdao, Sinopec Shanghai Petrochemical Company Limited is dedicated to its corporate responsibility, sustainable development, international exchange, and cooperation. SPC operates under the guiding principle of "returning to the society with the best of all", and defines its corporate culture as "hard-working, truth-seeking, improvement, and dedication", which was first introduced in the 1980s. The company has a four-word motto: "Justice, Integrity, Harmony, and Industriousness", and its leadership team targets high quality as a criterion for the best performance in management. Aiming to become the leading petrochemical enterprise in the world, SPC expects all employees to work hard in all their pursuits, acquire necessary knowledge, and demonstrate professionalism through passion, honesty, and self-discipline. With a strong belief that there is always some room for further improvement, especially when it comes to the customer needs for services and products, SPC is dedicated to work hard for this self-improvement process and to share universal values, which in turn will benefit both the company and the whole society in the long run.

Growth Strategies

SPC's strategic goal is to be a competent modern oil provider, not only in domestic terms, but also in overseas. In addition, the company plans to continually improve its production to ensure both quantitative and qualitative development. More specifically, SPC seeks to be regarded as a competitive leader on international levels and the leader of the refining industry in China by the year 2010. By then, it plans to process more than 12 million ton crude oil every year, while still maintaining an annual production capacity of 1 million ton ethylene, 0.95 million ton synthetic resin and plastics, and 1.40 million ton chemical fiber raw material and synthetic fiber. A key asset to this mission is the international exchange and cooperation relationships SPC has built up over the years. For instance, in an agreement on technical training with OAO (Otkrytoe Aktsionernoe Obschestvo) Polyef in Russia, 21 Russian technicians received a 42-day technical training at SPC's Polyester Division and in 2004, 23 technicians from the National Petrochemical Co. of Islamic Republic of Iran received a 35-day technical training at the Refining & Petrochemical Division.

SPC has made enormous efforts to continually rejuvenate the petrochemical industry. The company has received many prizes for enhancing its shareholder value and providing customers with quality products and good services. In 2001 and 2002, SPC received a certificate as a "company which values the credit and abides by the contract" issued by the State Industry and Commerce Administration Bureau. In 2004, SPC was awarded the China's Foreign Economic and Trade Enterprise with AAA Grade in credit issued by the Ministry of Commerce, and the National Consumer Satisfied Enterprise issued by the China Quality Management Association. In 2005, SPC was awarded the honorary title of National Model Enterprise, and in the following SPC was named the State Occupational Sanitation Model Enterprise and ranked the 26th among the Top 100 Chinese Listed Companies by *Fortune*.

By strategically positioning itself to be a top-tier enterprise in the country and striving to be among the most advanced in the world, SPC is accelerating the construction of its structural adjustment projects. The company seeks to continuously optimize its business structure and gradually build up its international competitiveness through implementing overall cost leadership strategy in all aspects and instigating advanced managerial concept in all its operations.

Industrial and Environmental Challenges

In recent years, the company has been facing a major challenge in the fluctuation of the oil price. At many times when the price of the oil reached higher, the price of its petrochemical products had to increase as well. A second area of concern, especially in regard to the production of chemical materials, is the environmental impact. The petrochemical industry, which generates massive useless materials, is a key stakeholder in environment protection. Facing such challenges, and recognizing the balance between the endless potentials of human resources and the limit of natural resources, SPC is dedicated to using its resources with much care. In 2008, the company launched the "National Environment-Friendly Enterprise" program as a way to contribute to the establishment of an energy-saving and environment-friendly society in China. The goal is to promote a clean production, prevent industrial pollution, and protect ecological environment. According to the Ministry of Environmental Protections, there are 22 basic requirements for an environment-friendly enterprise designation, which SPC plans to meet in five phases, including: the mobilization of a leadership team, the analysis of the gap, the plan development and the implementation, self-evaluation and report, and the acceptance check. Furthermore, SPC, the Jinshan District and the Shanghai Chemical Industry Park also reached an agreement to establish a national environmental protection model district with "safety, greenness, and harmony" as the goal.

Mareike Hoffschmidt-Fetscherin

References

Reuters (2009). Key developments for Sinopec Shanghai Petrochemical Company Limited. http://www.reuters.com/finance/stocks/keyDevelopments?symbol=SHI.N. Retrieved on 1 June 2009.

Sinopec Shanghai Petrochemical Company Limited. Company Profile. http://www.spc.com.cn/enspc/spc/alllook.php?Cid=83&Dlev=1. Retrieved on 1 June 2009.

SINOTRANS

Corporate Address and Contact Information

China National Foreign Trade Transportation (Group) Corporation
Sinotrans Plaza A
No. A43 Xizhimen Bei Avenue
Haidian District, Beijing 100044
People's Republic of China
Phone: (86)10-6229-5900
Fax: (86)10-6229-5901
www.sinotrans.com

Sinotrans is the English name for China's largest transport and logistics corporate group, the China National Foreign Trade Transportation (Group) Corporation (中国对外贸易运输集团总公司). Sinotrans activities include logistical services, freight forwarding, express courier services, shipping agency, storage and terminal services, trucking, and marine transportation. Supported by advanced information technology and well-trained staff, Sinotrans offers comprehensive services to its clients in all major global markets.

Historical Development

Established in 1950, Sinotrans has evolved as China's leading provider of comprehensive transportation services. In China, Sinotrans has been responsible for a number of "firsts" such as the introduction of the first container shipping service in 1973, launching the first sea-rail multimodal transport service in 1977, offering the first international multimodal transport service achieving a direct "door-to-door" service using "one-ticket-only" system in 1980, starting the first air express business in 1980, and initiating the first chained container transport in 1980.

Since 1980, Sinotrans has established subsidiaries in the United States, Canada, Hong Kong, South Korea, Japan, and Germany. Joint-venturing with DHL, UPS, and other corporations, Sinotrans established an international air transport network throughout China. In its international joint ventures, Sinotrans follows a "win-win" policy to enhance mutual gains of the venture partners while offering superior services to clients.

Sinotrans witnessed strong revenue growth during 2003–2007. Revenues grew at a *Compound Annual Growth Rate* (CAGR) of 22%, from RMB 17.3 billion (USD 2.3 billion) in 2003 to RMB 38.9 billion (USD 5.2 billion) in 2007. By 2007, Sinotrans had 97 subsidiaries, 1,161 domestic companies, 114 oversea companies, and the total revenue has reached RMB 57.7 billion. By 2009, Sinotrans was the largest international freight forwarding company, the largest air cargo and international express agency, the second largest shipping agency, and the third largest shipping company in China.

Corporate Structure

In 1997, Sinotrans initiated market-based capitalization and restructuring of its operations. By 2007, there were three listed companies focused on two core businesses — integrated logistics and shipping.

Sinotrans Air Transportation Development Co. Ltd. (中外运空运发展股份有限公司) was the first listed company in Sinotrans Group, officially founded on 11 October 1999 and listed on the Shanghai Stock Exchange (600270) on 28 December 2000.

Focusing on integrated logistics, Sinotrans Limited (中国外运股份有限公司) was established on 20 November 2002 by incorporating core businesses, assets, and staff from the major coastal, riverside, and strategic regions of Sinotrans, and listed on the Hong Kong Exchange (0598) on 13 February 2003.

As a specialized subsidiary of Sinotrans, Sinotrans Shipping Ltd. (中外运航运有限公司) was founded in Hong Kong on 13 January 2003 to strengthen shipping services and listed on the Hong Kong Exchange (0368) on 23 November 2007.

Sinotrans also established important joint ventures with key international partners. In 1986, Sinotrans formed DHL–Sinotrans, a 50/50 joint venture with DHL, the German express delivery and logistics giant. By 2008, DHL–Sinotrans had developed the largest air express services network in China covering 320 cities, with 56 joint ventures, 150 locations, and 6,000 employees.

Business Strategies

China's transportation and logistics industries have traditionally been fragmented and unsophisticated, with little strategic focus. This has given a competitive edge to global players who have continued to encroach on new and existing Chinese business by using non-Chinese Third-Party Logistics (3PLs) and local, independent carriers. In a move to combat this trend, Beijing has given Sinotrans virtually unlimited resources to spearhead modernization of China's logistics and transportation industries. To meet this challenge, Sinotrans has formulated specific strategies.

Asset realignment

Sinotrans traditionally competed by managing the movement of industrial products such as petroleum and heavy industrial equipment. Recently, Sinotrans has realigned its assets to compete in the commercial and retail logistics, and expanded its markets through mergers and acquisitions. In 2008,

Sinotrans merged with Wuhan-based Chinese Changjiang National Shipping Group (CSG), China's largest river (or "short-sea") shipping company, to form Sinotrans CSC Group. This consolidation creates more efficient intermodal air-, land- and water-borne transport linkages. Sinotrans also entered into partnership with another government-owned company, COSCO, a large ocean shipping company that operates as well as builds vessels. In 2009, Sinotrans started merging its operations with yet another transportation giant, China Yangtze Transportation (Group) Corporation.

Sinotrans is moving away from its traditional large industrial market and betting on the dry bulk vessel business to achieve growth. Sinotrans has committed over $388 billion to purchase 10 new vessels from COSCO. With these vessels, Sinotrans will boost capacity of its shipping subsidiary to 3.3 million deadweight tons (dwt) by 2011 from 1.7 million dwt in 2008. With globally tight credit, it is unlikely that competitors can match this move. Despite the economic downturn, Sinotrans strategy appears to be working. Dry bulk vessel charter business is experiencing strong growth and is responsible for doubling Sinotrans net profit from $141 million in 2007 to $347 million in 2008. Sinotrans should maintain its historical double-digit financial growth through 2009, even with the economic downturn. As the company grows its dry bulk business, it is simultaneously reducing its capacity in petroleum shipping. In 2009, Sinotrans sold three of its single-hull petroleum carriers for $40 million.

Management and marketing systems

From a managerial perspective, Sinotrans positions itself as a Just-In-Time (JIT) logistics company. Its challenge is to develop the infrastructure and expertise to fully support JIT. Several obstacles need to be overcome. First, the Chinese culture in general is not customer-focused, a fundamental aspect of JIT. For smooth JIT logistics, Sinotrans has to develop a formal demand management system that ensures explicit and implicit customer requirements are translated and communicated throughout the organization. Second, while the Chinese education system delivers graduates with excellent analytical skills, there is a paucity of education in logistics and supply chain management strategies. Specific supply chain strategies are required to support JIT. Sinotrans needs to promote logistics education to support a full JIT program. Third, the transportation infrastructure must be well developed and robust to support JIT. The Chinese infrastructure — while advancing — is still relatively deficient when viewed on a national scale. Therefore, even with proper strategy and cultural support, true JIT service is possible only in a few urban areas of China. Fourth, the company has inconsistent service, often generating customer complaints. One reason is that Sinotrans has not incorporated key performance indicators (KPIs) in its JIT system. KPIs are negotiated as part of the customer relationship management (CRM) process and are used to translate customer expectations throughout the supply chain. The CRM specifies remediation and emergency procedures in case of KPI degradation or performance failure.

Sinotrans is in the process of developing global-training and professional-certification programs. The American Society of Transportation and Logistics (AST&L) has opened an office in Hong Kong to train Chinese professionals in contemporary logistics. AST&L trained individuals can apply for the certification in transportation and logistics (CTL). Such certification not only diffuses knowledge throughout the company but also works as marketing tool to attract new US and European business.

Future Challenges

While foreign companies strengthen their supply chains in China to leverage the country's low labor costs, they face many challenges. Foreign firms are limited in where they can source because of China's overburdened and underdeveloped physical infrastructure beyond the key East Coast hubs, its under-funded state-owned distribution companies, its fragmented distribution and logistics industry, and the powerful regional protectionist practices. Additionally, foreign firms encounter bureaucratic barriers to legally importing goods, selling products and services, and efficient servicing of products. To overcome these, foreign companies often find "workarounds" (Jiang, 2002). The role of Sinotrans is to minimize or limit these restrictions for foreign and domestic companies and to eliminate the need for them to bypass the Chinese system. Common workarounds entail clustering with other foreign firms, using non-Chinese 3PLs, exploiting local carriers, and the "one-day trip to Hong Kong" effect. Such trips are used to avoid import duties on goods sold in China by foreign companies by transshipping them out of China to regional ports such as Busan (South Korea) and Hong Kong, and then returning them to China as non-tariff goods.

Despite recent restructuring, Sinotrans is still a Chinese state-owned 3PL service intermediary, and thus faces political uncertainty of government interference. For example, Sinotrans has attempted to respond to increased market pressure by insulating its technical core business through short-run strategies, but politics often reverse such decisions.

To properly support its JIT strategy, Sinotrans must develop Carrier Rationalization Programs in its procurement process. Also known as Carrier Selection or Vendor Qualification, the programs are part of contemporary Supplier Relationship Management programs. Sinotrans uses over 250 different carriers. The typical Western JIT system negotiates with a relative few (usually 10–20) carriers. Using fewer carriers would give Sinotrans the purchasing power necessary to enforce customer requirements and enhance service levels in exchange for qualified carriers receiving a much larger share of its business.

The Sinotrans Warehouse Management System (WMS) is more sophisticated than given credit for. While it is not at the level of a Manhattan-style WMS system, it does perform deconsolidation and consolidation services for National Retail Transportation (NRT). These services are primarily performed for the retail apparel industry in Southern China, and the electronics and chemical industries in the North. Factors such as lack of documentation, reliable data, standardized record-keeping and reporting practices, and some cultural aversions to information sharing, however, make analysis and decision making more subjective than is necessary. For example, Sinotrans does not use warehouse pricing techniques commonly used in contemporary logistics, which are based on SKU complexity, level of activity, access and security requirements. Pricing strategies thus do not fully support financial objectives. Nor does Sinotrans subscribe to the Western practice of early discounting to attract new business, because the associated short-term loses are not culturally acceptable in China.

The lack of reliable and sufficient data also inhibits the development of Decision Support Systems to improve supply chains. For example, Logistics Network Modeling and Optimization activities that minimize logistics costs are not employed by Sinotrans. This severely hampers a manager's ability to make informed decisions.

Conceptual Perspective on Sinotrans Development

Sinotrans' business strategies, including apparent suboptimal aspects, are explainable in terms of classical organizational theory (Parsons, 1970; Thompson, 1967). Uncertainties occur at three organizational levels — technical, managerial, and institutional — and are often dealt with using rational, natural, or open business perspectives. The rational perspective values effectiveness and efficiency, which is operable only in closed formal systems — as, for example, in a planned and command economy. Global systems are open, however. Therefore, rational systems may work only at a technical level where formality is essential. This partially explains why Sinotrans strives to insulate its technical core from external uncertainties. At a managerial level, as China opens its logistics markets to foreign firms,

Sinotrans managers are forced to take on a naturalist perspective, where only the strong and adaptable survive. Flexible, informal structures — even with some loss of control — help organizations adapt. This explains why Sinotrans seeks to grow through risky acquisitions and mergers, hoping to internalize expertise, assets, and resources much faster than slow internal transformation. Sinotrans is realigning its assets to expand into the commercial and retail industries, diversifying its service and revenue portfolio. For Sinotrans, natural-adaptive managerial level could mediate between the open institutional level and the closed technical level to maintain informal structures that are flexible and difficult to replicate by competitors — and thus ensure organizational survival.

Nikhilesh Dholakia, Douglas N. Hales, and Miao Zhao

References

Buckley, PJ, J Clegg, and H Tan (2008). Organization and action in a Chinese state-owned service intermediary: The case of Sinotrans. *Journal of Chinese Economic and Business Studies*, 6(1): 23–48.

Jiang, G (2002). How international firms are coping with supply chain issues in China. *Supply Chain Management: An International Journal*, 7(4): 184–188.

Parsons, T (1970). *The Structure of Social Actions — Volume 2*, 2nd edition. Glencoe IL: Free Press.

Thompson, JD (1967). *Organizations in Action: Social Science Bases of Administrative Theory*. New York: McGraw-Hill.

SINOTRUK

Corporate Address and Contact Information

Sinotruk, Limited
China National Heavy Duty Truck Group Co. Ltd.
Dangjiazhuang, Shizhong District
Jinan, Shandong Province 250116
People's Republic of China
Phone: (86)531-8558-7586
http://www.Sinotruk.com.cn/en/index.asp, http://www.Sinotruk.com/

Sinotruk Group is located in Jinan, Shandong Province, which is the cradle and leading production base of the heavy-duty truck industry in China. Owned by China National Heavy Duty Truck Group Co. Ltd. (中国重汽有限公司), Sinotruk is famous for developing and manufacturing the first heavy-duty truck in China, for successful introducing the "STEYR" heavy-duty truck production project, and for setting up a joint venture with VOLVO to manufacture the heavy-duty trucks with advanced technologies.

Historical Development

Third largest heavy-duty truck manufacturer in China, Sinotruk was founded in 2004 based on Jinan Automobile Works (JAW). Established in 1935, JAW mainly manufactured spare parts of trucks. In 1956, it began to develop plans for manufacturing heavy-duty trucks and in April 1963, HUANGHE branded model JN150 vehicle with payload 8 tons was launched, which marked the history that heavy-duty truck was produced for the first time in China. Since then, Sinotruk has manufactured several hundred thousand units of heavy-duty trucks, making an important contribution to the Chinese economic development.

Sinotruk also possesses a listed company under the same name. On 18 January 2001, through a number of reforms and restructures, Sinotruk built a new corporate structure to improve its operations. Since the reorganization, Sinotruk has raised its sales profit from 6.2 billion to 23 billion RMB. The production and selling of truck CBU (completely built-up) raised from 7,000 to 45,000, the market share was increased from less than 4% to 18% and reached three "first" records in China: first in the segment of heavy tractors sold in China, first in the segment of large power engine (over 300 hp) sold in China, and first in the segment of heavy duty truck equipped with engine (more than 10 liter) in China. On 15 July 2005, Sinotruk ranked 17th of the top 500 mechanical companies in China.

From 2004 to 2005, several national leaders, including Wu Bangguo, Wang Zhaoguo and Wu Yi, visited Sinotruk in succession, and all praised the development of Sinotruk while putting forward ardent expectations. Since then Sinotruk has invested RMB 4 billion to more than 100 programs to ensure its quality and scale of production are on par with advanced enterprises in the world. Jinan Industrial Area, Chongqing Industrial Area, and Zhangqiu Industrial Area have been built up in succession; the digital frame line, new assembly line, Howo welding line, and painting line have been put into use, all are the result of implementation of advanced technologies into corporate operations. The production capacity of Jinan Power Co. Ltd., after an investment of nearly RMB 1 billion, reaches 60,000 units. Meanwhile a time-featured engine has been developed for heavy-duty truck, which represents the top level of 10-liter emission engine in China, and thus establishes the technical criterion for upgrade in truck CBU technology. Through this process, Sinotruk was able to absorb the advanced technologies of the heavy-duty trucks around the world, and has successfully developed a series of heavy-duty trucks such as Howo, Steyr King, Golden Prince, Haojun, Haoyun, Huanghe Commander, Huanghe General, and so on, which altogether represent more than 1,380 models. In addition, Sinotruk also pays a great attention to the intellectual property protection, and has filed and received more than 600 patents in technology advancement.

Corporate Structure, Products, and Services

Currently, in Jinan region, Sinotruk has Jinan Truck Co. Ltd., Jinan Commercial Vehicle Co. Ltd., Jinan Power Co. Ltd., Jinan Axle Co. Ltd., Jinan Special Vehicle Co. Ltd., Jinan Bus Co. Ltd., and Huawo Truck Co. Ltd., which are responsible for manufacturing and assembling of truck CBU, making and processing of engine, axle, gearbox, wheel, propeller shaft, cab trimming, seat, components and parts, and producing bus and special vehicle. In Shandong Province, there are Qingdao Special Vehicle Company, Taian Wuyue Special Vehicle Company, Jining Refitting Vehicle Company, and Jinan Park Machine Company, responsible for manufacturing of special trucks and refitting trucks. Out of Shandong, there are Hangzhou Truck Engine Works of Jinan Power Co. Ltd., Chongqing Fuel Pump & Nozzle Factory, and so on. The Technical Development Center at the Jinan headquarters, which is a state-level enterprise technical center, provides technical support for the R&D of Sinotruk's products and services. Besides the core truck business, Sinotruk has been managing subsidiaries such as real estate, import and export, finance, property management, etc.

The company's principal subsidiaries specialize in the research, development, and manufacturing of heavy-duty trucks and related key parts and components, including engines, cabins, axles, steel frames, and gearboxes. The company operates in three segments: trucks, which includes the manufacture and sale; engines, also including both the manufacture and sale; and finance, which includes taking deposits from member companies, facilitating borrowings for member companies, discounting notes of member companies and providing entrusted loan and entrusted investment between member companies. Its other group operations mainly comprise the sale of design and research service. On 31 May 2008, Sinotruk (Hong Kong) Limited acquired 60% of equity interest in Liuzhou Yunli Special Vehicle Co. Ltd.

Sinotruk produces six main lines of heavy-duty trucks, which are Howo, Steyr King, Steyr, Gold Prince, Haojun, and Huanghe Commander. Currently, the company has built up key parts into an intact product platform of heavy truck assemblies and components such as cab, engine, axle, clutch, propeller shaft, balance shaft, which contributes greatly to its core competitive advantage of complete vehicle of all series.

Business Strategies

Sinotruk, one of the country's largest heavy-truck makers, manufactured and sold 15,000 heavy trucks in March 2008, creating a new trend in monthly production and sales in China's heavy truck segment. The company has set its goal to make and sell 125,000–135,000 vehicles in 2008 and to gross RMB 45 billion in sales. To achieve this target, Sinotruk started to enhance its whole portfolio of products and to implement the energy efficiency strategy in late 2007.

At the beginning of 2008, the truck maker's new models were well received soon after their launch in the domestic market. In January and February, despite the natural disasters in some parts of China, 17,500 units of these models were sold and 31,249 units were ordered. The demand for Sinotruk's vehicles has now begun to exceed the supply. The company took effective measures to cope with the disruption in the supply links of auto parts caused by the snowstorms in Southern China in the first two months of 2008.

Sinotruk began marketing its Hong Kong IPO (SEHK-3808) in November 2007, aiming to use the funds raised for boosting its manufacturing capacity by more than half by 2010. The truck maker seeks to turn its funding advantage into a driver of faster growth, broader expansion, and stronger competitiveness. In the first quarter of 2008, Sinotruk invested RMB 500,000 in technical innovation to boost its capacity for greater achievements in the future. Furthermore, Sinotruk has established a truck-making joint venture with Volvo, the world's second-largest truck manufacturer. The Chinese truck maker's two engine production lines in Hangzhou and Jinan in Eastern China have an annual capacity of 200,000 units. With the addition of the third assembly line of its subsidiary Jinan Truck Company, the group has so far increased its assembly capacity by 50%.

In recent years, Sinotruk has pursued an internationalization strategy, actively developing the overseas market and strengthening its international competition strength. In specific, Sinotruk seeks to gradually internationalize its product, market, capital, mechanism, and brand. In 2005, Sinotruk exported 3,546 units of its truck CBU model, which alone generated foreign exchange income over USD 100 million. In all aspects of its operation from the development of new product and technical craft to energy saving, financial control, purchase, and material flow reconstructing, Sinotruk endeavors to implement its high quality and low cost strategies. Consequently, in a five-year period, the cost of each vehicle was reduced RMB 10,000. With its technology, brand, cost, human sources, and networks, Sinotruk has built a competitive advantage and growth potential in the heavy truck market in the coming years.

Tom Tao

References

China automotive technology center. *China Automotive Yearbook* (2005, 2006, and 2007). Tianjin: China.

Introduction of China National Heavy Duty Truck Group Co. Ltd. http://www.Sinotruk.com.cn/en/index2.htm. Retrieved on 21 June 2009.

Sinotruk (2008). *Interim Annual Report 2008*. http://www.Sinotruk.com/pdf/UploadPdfs/1220434221236.pdf. Retrieved on 21 June 2009.

Sinotruk (Hong Kong) Limited Company Profile. http://www.google.com/finance?q=HKG:3808. Retrieved on 21 June 2009.

SUNING APPLIANCE CHAIN STORE

Corporate Address and Contact Information

Suning Appliance Chain Store Group
68 Huaihai Road
Nanjing, Jiangsu Province 210005
People's Republic of China
Phone: (86)025-8441-8888
Fax: (86)025-8446-7008
http://www.cnsuning.com/include/english/

Suning Appliance Chain Store Group (苏宁电器连锁集团股份有限公司) is one of the largest retailers in China and the country's second biggest home and appliance and consumer electronics retailer. Listed on the Shenzhen Stock Exchange since July 2004, the company also provides repair and installation services for appliance and electronic products. As of 2009, Suning operates approximately 800 stores in 29 provinces across China.

Historical Development

Founded in 1990 by Zhang Jindong at the age of 27 along with his brother Zhang Guiping, Suning originally began as a single, small air-conditioning shop on Ninghai Road in Nanjing. Zhang Jindong was a former Chinese literature major and a graduate of Nanjing Normal University. Soon after his brother left the company to begin a very successful venture in property development, Zhang has stayed the course and led the company over the past 18 years through a strong focus on providing superior service both in the company's retail stores and post-purchase warranty offerings.

Suning has also benefited greatly from an increasingly strengthening infrastructure across Asia. As power grids continue to be developed and transformed in China's rural areas, a stronger infrastructure and reduced electricity charges have encouraged rural consumers to buy an increased amount of household appliances. In addition, social and technological advances, an overall enhanced quality of life, and an increased focus on health and safety (largely due to SARS outbreaks in recent years) by many Chinese have benefitted the white goods industry in Asia and helped fuel Suning's growth over the past two decades. Finally, government subsidies have helped drive the appliance industry in China. The country's "home appliances to the countryside plan", initiated in December 2008, provides a 13-percent subsidy to farmers who buy designated brands of color TV sets, refrigerators, and mobile phones in 12 provinces across China.

Corporate Structure, Main Products, and Services

During the past few years, Suning's management team has demonstrated an extremely strong focus on increasing company efficiencies and effectiveness as the chain has undergone rapid growth. In October 2006,

Suning put into place a new corporate structure, composed of the company's headquarters (located in Nanjing), management head offices (which oversee the various business regions where the company has stores), subsidiaries, and chain stores. With a structure modeled after a three-tier matrix management system, the company's realignment not only allowed for more stable growth for the future but also enabled greater alignment and sharing of physical and intellectual resources, as the company has continued to expand its base of stores. As of 2009, the company has ballooned to operate approximately 800 retail shops in 178 cities and 29 provinces throughout China, with stores in major regions including Shanghai, Beijing, Guangdong, Zhejiang, Anhui, Shaanxi, Fujian, Jiangsu, Hunan, and Shanxi, and employs more than 100,000 employees.

The company's principal activities are chain selling and servicing household appliances, electric products, office equipment, and telecom equipment. Other activities include developing, selling, and system integrating computer software; Internet information service; chain selling general merchandise, bicycle, electric moped, motorcycle, and automobile; industrial investment; place rental; counter rental; domestic products exhibit service; enterprise image strategy; economic information consultation service; and personal training and business agent service. Total revenue for Suning for the year ending 2008 was RMB 49.896 billion with a total net income of 2.17 billion.

Challenges and Business Strategies

After China's entry into the World Trade Organization and the end of its five-year protection period, the company is likely to face increased competition from abroad and continues to operate in a highly competitive landscape. As of 2009, Suning's major competitor is Gome Electrical Appliances, which currently stands as the country's largest retailer with over 1,300 stores across China. Together, Gome and Suning control less than 20% of the $75 billion consumer-appliance market that is expected to reach $100 billion by 2010. Best Buy Co., the largest US consumer appliance retailer, purchased Jiangsu Five Star in early 2006 to become China's fourth largest appliance and electronics retail chain. As there are low to moderate entry barriers into the appliance retail industry in Asia with several direct and very strong competitors already in place, a challenging business environment exists within China's home appliance retail market.

An important element of Suning's future success and a potential strong differentiator for the company in the future is its warranty extension offerings, which are provided to customers for an additional charge on many of the products sold in stores. Announced in September 2008, Suning called it the "Sunshine Package Service Program", under which the company consumers will be able to receive repair and replacement for hard-to-repair products. Through managing the logistics of both a call center and its own maintenance and replacement services, Suning has positioned itself as a unique retailer in that it will be offering both the retail product as well as an extended warranty service. This will allow Suning to achieve a competitive advantage through being one of the few retailers in China that both sells and services its products without the use of outside companies. This strategy not only provides a unique product mix offering but also allows the company to provide strong post-purchase service. Such a service used to be limited and only has been offered by foreign companies that often did not customize service standards according to the habits of Chinese consumers. This warranty service offering likely will not only provide a strong competitive advantage over other national appliance retailers in the coming years but also help further position Suning as a long-lasting brand in the mind of consumers through its ability to offer maintenance plans for products that the company retails.

Suning has consistently sought out new channels and initiatives to drive increased sales of its products. In 2006, Suning launched its e-business, breaking into the online sales arena. While sales in the first couple of years have paled in comparison to that from its traditional channels (having generated approximately US 13.6 million in online sales in 2007), this will serve as a strong avenue for continued sales growth as infrastructure across China strengthens and a growing number of consumers look to the Internet to purchase goods. In 2009, the company partnered with eight domestic banks to roll out an "easy buy" purchase plan that allows Suning's customers to purchase home appliances with no down payments or handling fees and zero interest. In the same year, in partnership with China's Ministry of Commerce to boost credit card spending and drive economic growth, the company also began to encourage the use of credit cards at its retail stores, a measure estimated to bring in additional sales of CNY 1 billion. The company plans to gradually extend credit card services across China throughout 2009.

Looking ahead, the company has plans to continue its aggressive growth, with a goal of adding over 180 to 200 stores annually across China and Hong Kong. In addition, Suning has initiated plans to potentially enter into the appliance-manufacturing business, allowing the company to become increasingly vertically integrated. In late 2008, the chain began building a technology park in Nanjing, the capital city of Jiangsu Province. Combining information technologies, research and development, and production of home appliances, this technology park in Nanjing will serve as a logistical base for its chain stores in cities around the Yangtze River Delta in East China.

Matt Amick

References

Ding, Q (2008). Suning Appliance on expansion spree. *China Daily*, 5 December.

Home appliances makers catch their breath as rural sales boom (31 May 2009). *People's Daily*. http://english.peopledaily.com.cn/90001/90776/90884/6668512.html. Retrieved on 24 June 2009.

Ramzy, A (2007). Suning Appliance: China's hot new growth companies. *Time*, 30 August.

Retailers focus on high end products (25 May 2009). *Shanghai Daily*. http://www.china.org.cn/business/2009-05/25/content_17829777.htm. Retrieved on 24 June 2009.

Suning upgrades warranty services in China (23 September 2008). *China Tech News*. http://www.chinatech-news.com/2008/09/23/7593-suning-upgrades-electronics-warranty-services-in-china/. Retrieved on 1 May 2009.

Suning (2009). Annual Report 2008. http://www.cnsuning.com/investors/report/nd/images/20090302/761.pdf. Retrieved on 24 June 2009.

Suning (2009). Company Profile. http://www.cnsuning.com/include/english/C-jianjie.html. Retrieved on 24 June 2009.

Top home appliance chains expand (3 February 2005). *China Daily*. http://mdjnkj.china.com.cn/english/BAT/119662.htm. Retrieved on 6 July 2009.

TANGSHAN IRON & STEEL

Corporate Address and Contact Information

Tangshan Iron and Steel Co. Ltd.
9 Binhe Road
Tangshan, Hebei Province 063016

People's Republic of China
Phone: (86)315-270-2409
Fax: (86)315-270-2449
http://www.tangsteel.com.cn/

Tangshan Iron & Steel Co. Ltd. (唐山钢铁集团有限公司) was founded in 1994 and is headquartered in Tangshan, Hebei Province, the People's Republic of China. The firm is owned by Tangshan Iron and Steel Group Company Limited (holding company), also known as Tangsteel. Tangshan Iron & Steel Co. Ltd. is a smelter, processor, and seller of iron and steel products.

Historical Development

Tangshan Iron & Steel Co. Ltd. is a relatively new firm, having been organized in 1994 when Tangshan in northeast Hebei Provence was rebuilt. The city was completely destroyed by a massive earthquake on 28 July 1976, with an estimated 250,000 people killed.

The Tangshan Iron & Steel Co. Ltd. was listed on the Shenzhen Stock Exchange (SZSE: 000709) in 1997. In early 2004, the company partnered with Wuhan Iron & Steel Group, Maanshan Iron & Steel Co. Ltd., and Sha-steel Group to set up a joint venture with BHP Billiton's (a global energy firm) iron ore mine — thus, assuring a 40-percent stake, or 12 million ton of ore deliveries to these Chinese producers. In April 2005, Tangshan Iron & Steel Co. Ltd. announced an agreement to acquire a 75-percent stake in Tangshan Gangxin Iron Plate Co. and Tangshan Hengchang Iron Plate Co.

In 2006, Tangshan Iron & Steel Co. Ltd. merged with Xuanhua Iron & Steel Group and Chengde Iron and Steel Group to form New Tangsteel Iron and Steel Group. Also in 2006, Tangshan Iron & Steel International Co. Ltd. was established by the Tangshan Iron & Steel Group Co. Ltd., Xuanhua Iron & Steel Group Liability Co. Ltd., and Chengde Iron & Steel Group Co. Ltd. This move was seen by financial observers as signifying another step toward industry consolidation taking place throughout China.

To continue to expand plant and capacity, Tangshan Iron & Steel Co. Ltd. issued RMB 3 billion worth of five-year convertible bonds in 2008. During the same year, after more than five months of debate among Hebei Province leadership, New Tangsteel Iron and Steel Group merged with Handan Iron & Steel Corp. (Hansteel) to form Hebei Iron and Steel Group, which is the largest steel maker in China and the fifth largest in the world. The new group has an annual iron and steel production capacity of 30 million tons. The Chinese government which controls 60 percent of the firm is pushing it toward further consolidation with a goal of more than 50 million ton annual capacity by 2010. It is hoped that these consolidations will help alleviate the overcapacity situation throughout the Chinese iron and steel industry by eliminating many smaller firms and thus, will improve industry efficiencies and competitiveness.

Products, Services, and Corporate Leadership

Tangshan Iron & Steel Co. Ltd. is a manufacturer of steel products for sale within the People's Republic of China, as well as internationally. The firm engages in a full line of production processes from smelting and pressing ferrous metal, rolled steel, and metal products such as steel sheets and bars, wire rods, cold-rolled and hot-rolled steel plates, medium and thick steel plates, deformed steel bars, round steel bars, and other medium-sized steels. The firm also engages in the repair of electrical machineries, the supply of oxygen, and metallurgical technological services.

Following the merger of Tangshan with Handan Iron & Steel Corp., Wang Yifang (board chairman and general manager of Tangshan Iron & Steel Co. Ltd.) was named director of the Hebei Iron and Steel

Corp. and Liu Rujun (chairman of Handan Iron and Steel Corp.) was named deputy director of the Hebei Iron and Steel Corp. As of 31 December 2008, the company had nine major subsidiaries and six affiliates, which manufacture and sell steel materials, lime, coke, galvanized plates, aluminum and zinc alloy plates, iron concentrate, coal chemical products, and industrial gas, among others, as well as projects construction and international trading.

Officers of Tangshan Iron & Steel Co. Ltd. include: Wang Yifang (chairman), Yu Yong (vice chairman and general manager), Wang Zilin (vice chairman), Wang Junjie (chief accounting officer), and Guo Yong (secretary).

Business Strategies and Future Development Plans

In its short history, Tangshan Iron and Steel Co. Ltd. has been a success on a number of fronts. With 2008 sales of $57.7 billion, it generated a profit of $4.15 billion in difficult economic times. The firm will continue to focus on improved efficiency and capacity as a means to boost productivity. It is the goal of the firm, as well as the Chinese government, to increase the efficiency and competitiveness of the company on both a national and international scale.

Tangshan Iron and Steel Co. Ltd. finds itself in a strong position within the new Hebei Iron & Steel Group (Hebei Steel). With the merger of Handan Iron & Steel, Chengde Xinxin Vanadium and Titanium, and Tangshan Iron and Steel, only Tangshan Iron and Steel will remain listed on the Shenzhen Stock exchange. With the additional assets of subsidiaries Wuyang Iron & Steel and Xuanhua Iron and Steel merged with the assets of Tangshan Iron and Steel Co. Ltd., Tangshan Iron and Steel Co. Ltd. is in a position to produce in excess of 30 million tons of products annually.

In many ways, the future development plans for Tangshan Iron and Steel Co. Ltd. depend on how successful the merger with Handan Iron and Steel Co. Ltd. is in the next few years. It seems clear that Handan Iron and Steel Co. Ltd. will be a major player in the Hebei Iron and Steel Group. However, the leadership of Handan Iron and Steel Co. Ltd. does not wish to see their company's role in the group diminished. Although Handan Iron and Steel Co. Ltd. has less production capacity (produced 9 million tons of steel in 2007), it does have equipment that is comparable to that of Tangshan Iron and Steel Co. Ltd. (produced 22.75 million tons of steel in 2007). Therefore, the issue needs to be settled as to what role each of these firms will play within the Heibei Group and in the Chinese economy. The two firms' products and technologies overlap, potentially causing a dilemma as to how markets will be allocated. There may also be issues regarding how personnel and assets will be distributed between Handan and Tangshan. One thing remains clear: the Governor of Hebei Province intends to continue further restructuring of the steel industry as this is the stated wish of the PRC leadership.

Tangshan Iron & Steel Co. Ltd. does expect some difficult times in 2009. In late April 2009, management announced that it expects profits for the year to decrease by 50–100%, about RMB 100 million, compared to that of same period last year. The company cited the sharp decline of steel price as the main reason for this forecast. The declining profit announcement immediately followed an announcement that Tangshan Iron & Steel Co. Ltd. would pay no shareholder dividend for the year ended 31 December 2008. A balanced business operations focus will likely be seen between iron (5.6 million tons in 2008) and steel (5.9 million tons in 2008) at Tangshan Iron & Steel Co. Ltd. in the near future.

Key Roles Played in the Chinese and Global Economies

The path to efficiency and productivity in the Chinese steel industry seems to be one of consolidation through mergers and acquisitions, as the industry development policy encourages Chinese steelmakers to form larger groups. Its ultimate goal is to have one or two iron and steel groups with combined annual capacities of over 30 million tons, and several other firms producing annual yields of tens of millions of tons by 2010. The Hebei Group, of which Tangshan Iron & Steel Co. Ltd. is a leading player, is on target for the 30 million ton output level. Tangshan Iron & Steel Co. Ltd. will need to consider carefully the potential human cost of these mergers and acquisitions as it continues to embrace the Chinese industry development policy. As smaller firms are shuttered, more instances of social unrest could happen — such as the case of Anshan Iron & Steel in Liaoning Province, where a 10,000-employee layoff in 2008 led to demonstrations because former employees felt abandoned by the firm and by their government.

It is possible that Tangshan Iron & Steel Co. Ltd. will need to continue mergers and acquisitions just to survive the current Chinese and world-wide economic recession. The China Iron and Steel Association noted that the main Chinese iron and steel companies reported aggregate losses of $1.87 billion through November of 2008. Within the steel industry, the majority of firms compete on price. As such, larger firms with economies of scale possess the competitive advantage. The ability to obtain raw materials cheaply and produce at low cost will be critical in 2009 and beyond. Tangshan Iron & Steel Co. Ltd. faces a year where the benchmark price for iron ore as set by BHP Billiton Ltd. rose almost 100 percent in 2008. Tangshan Iron & Steel's negotiations may need to aim at 10 to 50 percent iron ore price reductions in 2009 if it is to be competitive in the global marketplace. The corporate leaders at Tangshan Iron & Steel Co. Ltd. anticipate that they will be able to compete more effectively on price, as the combined production capacities of the individual firms will greatly increase the overall capacity and therefore create greater economies of scale. Furthermore, the merged firms each had subsidiaries within the industry able to provide some raw materials. Also, Hebei Steel Group's unlisted subsidiary engages in mining operations — Hebei currently holds 1.04 billion tons of iron ore reserves as a result of these operations. Tangshan's subsidiaries engage in both mining and production of aluminum zinc alloys. These subsidiaries enhance Hebei's (and Tangshan Iron & Steel's) competitive advantage by providing raw materials to the firm.

James P. Gilbert

References

Alon, I and JR McIntyre (eds.) (2008). *Globalization of Chinese Enterprises*. New York: Palgrave Macmillan.

BusinessWeek (2009). Tangshan Iron and Steel Company Limited. investing.businessweek.com/research/stocks/snapshot/snapshot.asp?ric=000709.SZ. Retrieved on 24 August 2009.

Restructuring problems for China's steel industry (2008). *The Wire Association International, Inc.* www.wirenet.org/wji/current_detail.cfm?ID=3090. Retrieved on 24 August 2009.

Tangshan Iron & Steel merges with Handan to form China's largest steel maker (11 June 2008). *Forbes*. www.forbes.com/feeds/afx/2008/06/11/afx5103434.html. Retrieved on 24 August 2009.

Tangshan Iron & Steel Co. Ltd. to acquire stake in Aurox Resources (28 May 2008). *Reuters*. www.reuters.com/finance/stocks/keyDevelopments?symbol=AUOXF.PK&pn=1. Retrieved on 3 March 2009.

Tangshan Iron & Steel Co. Ltd. announces FY 2009 H1 net profit outlook (29 April 2009). *Rueters.com*. www.reuters.com/finance/stocks/keyDevelopments?symbol=000709.SZ. Retrieved on 5 August 2009.

Three-way merger creates another Chinese steel giant (30 December 2008). *The Deal.com*. www.thedeal.com/corporatedealmaker/2008/12/three-way_merger_creates_anoth.php. Retrieved on 21 August 2009.

TCL

Corporate Address and Contact Information

TCL Holdings Co.
8th Floor TCL Industrial Building
Huizhou, Guangdong Province 516001
People's Republic of China
Phone: (86)752-228-8333
Fax: (86)752-226-5428
www.tcl.com

TCL Holdings Co. Ltd. (TCL集团股份有限公司) is the second largest consumer electronic firm in China and the world's largest TV vendor. As a multinational firm of RMB 38.41 billion in sales, and RMB 659 million in profit, 27 million television units, 20 plants, four R&D centers, and 63,000 employees in 2008, TCL has a broad scope of global operations with 14 overseas factories, 6 design centers, and over 45 major sales agents around the world. The foreign market contributed 44.62% of the total revenue in 2008.

The name TCL comes from the English phrase "The Creative Life", which symbolizes the new contemporary lifestyle the company tries to represent.

Historical Development

Founded in 1981 under the municipal government of Huizhou, Guangdong Province, TCL is a locally controlled state-owned enterprise. Through innovative marketing during the early of 1990s, TCL become the top Chinese brand in the telephone and TV sectors. By the end of 1996, the net assets for TCL were about RMB 300 million. At that time, with support from the local government, TCL's CEO Li Dongsheng initiated a bold stock option sharing plan for his managers: if TCL management team achieve 10% returns on assets (ROA) or higher per year, the extra benefits would be shared by the shareholders, managers, and employees. This reform proposal not only helped government solidify TCL's state-owned assets but also greatly motivated managers to create more profits. Since 1997, TCL has achieved an average export growth rate of over 40% annually, and broadened its product offerings into personal computers and other segments of information industry.

In 2002, TCL launched another round of more aggressive restructure drive. After the local government sold 18% of its shares to overseas strategic investors including Japan's Toshiba and Sumitomo, Europe Royal Philips Electronics, Hong Kong's Nam Tai Electronics Inc., and Gold Peak, TCL listed its TV asset in Hong Kong, and went public with holdings company in 2004. Now the government only holds 35% of TCL shares, managers and employees have another 35%, while overseas investors own about 12%, and public shareholders hold the rest of the stock.

Since 1999, TCL has undertaken an ambitious internationalization program called the "Dragon and Tiger Plan". Its strategic intent is to join the rank of Global Top 500 with multiple global brands. In 2004, TCL acquired Alcatel's mobile phones business, and created a global joint venture TTE (TCL-Thomson Electronics) with Thomson Electronics Corp., the world's biggest TV maker. However, the expansion drive into the global market proved to be a costly move, as it seriously affected the profitability of TCL, resulting in two consecutive years of net losses in 2005 and 2006.

After putting some of its European subsidiaries through bankruptcy and sold TCL Low Voltage Electrical, TCL International Electrical and TCL Building Technology to Legrand France SA in 2005–2006, the company raised the necessary capital to go beyond its heavy loss, and then refocused on the Chinese domestic market. By quickly responding to the evolving domestic market of consumer electronics, TCL was able to seize the opportunities in the fast-growing liquid crystal display (LCD) TV market, and successfully returned to profit in 2007.

Main Products and Services

TCL engages in multimedia electronics, mobile communications, and digital electronics businesses worldwide. Its main products include home appliances; components, including modules, semiconductor chips, displays, and power supplies; and audio-visual equipment. TCL has emerged as one of the leading consumer electronics brand in China, competing with Qingdao Haier, Skyworth Digital, and global leaders Nokia and LG Electronics. Besides having a significant share of the Chinese market, the TCL brand is also widely recognized abroad.

In 2008, TCL sold 4.18 million sets of LCD TV, more than triple its 2007 level, against a capacity of 5 million units and total sales of 14.36 million TV sets posted in the year earlier. Sales from television and other audio and visual products accounted for more than 60% of the group's sales in the first three quarters of 2008. Furthermore, TCL Corp. plans to double its LCD TV production capacity to 10 million units by the end of 2009 to meet the rising domestic demand.

Overcoming the negative influences of the current global economic downturn, TCL sold a total of 13.73 million mobile phones in 2008, an increase of 15.3% from the previous year, as its sales volume still kept a stable pace of growth in both the overseas and the Chinese domestic markets. In the near future, as one of China's leading manufacturers in 3G core technology, TCL will focus especially on the fast-growing 3G sector in the domestic market.

In 2009, TCL also formed a joint venture with environmental service provider Guangdong O'meet Group, aiming at recycling abandoned household appliances in an eco-friendly and efficient way. By leveraging the recycling-technology from US chemicals giant DuPont, the venture seeks to capitalize the nationwide sales network of TCL and the environmental service firm's technological know-how on dismantling waste appliances for reuse. Although with huge market potential, its long-term impact on TCL operation is yet to be seen.

Corporate Structure and Leadership

The company makes television sets through its Hong Kong-listed unit, TCL Multimedia Technology Holdings, and mobile handsets via TCL Communication listed in Shenzhen.

As a key founder of TCL, Li Dongsheng holds the position of chairman and president. He is also the chairman of TTE Corp. since 2006. As a visionary leader, Li outlined his master plan for TCL in an article titled "Eagle Reborn" (Li, 2006): to be a sustainable market leader, TCL must learn from its lessons in global M&A, and further strengthen the company's HR capabilities; to improve the international competitiveness, TCL must aggressively promote its product and technical innovation based on "the strengths of design and quality"; with the goal of creating "end-to-end supply chains", TCL must implement process reform and innovation, improve global supply chain management capabilities, and build a culture of change and creativity signified by a "people-based, harmonious business environment". Only then TCL will be able to achieve its mission of success. Under Li's leadership, Liang Yaorong, a former executive in consumer electronics at Philips, was appointed CEO of TCL Multimedia in 2007, in charging TCL's core TV business.

After experiencing heavy losses of RMB 2 billion in 2005–2006, TCL was able to return to profitability in 2007, largely due to the optimization of asset structures, improvements in operational efficiency, comprehensive cost control management and independent innovation. In light of this episode, TCL took a large-scale reform in 2007 to adjust to the new development in international operations. The corporation was restructured into four major industrial groups and two main service networks. This "4+2" business structure, if fully implemented, and combined with a major shift from operational management to an investment holding management model, will likely have a great strategic significance for improving TCL's overall management capabilities and operational efficiency. After this reorganization program is completed, TCL's management structure will more closely follow the business's development strategy and the operational model of a large, diversified corporation.

Business Strategies and International Expansion

TCL's business growth plan moving forward includes the following five strategies: first, based on the domestic market and supported by the international market, and taking "3C consumer electronics" as its "blueprint", TCL will strive to become a respected and innovative global leader with healthy business and stable growth. Unlike its large-scale international joint venture (IJV) operation in 2004, TCL will refocus on the domestic market for its huge potential in LCD TV market. As TCL and other domestic players fight over the Chinese LCD TV market, their foreign rivals had been steadily losing market share from 64% in 2007 to 45% a year later; during the same time, TCL sales volume from LCD TV swell 233% in 2007 to 4.18 million in 2008, ranking the eighth place globally.

Second, TCL seeks to increase its overseas revenue from strategic original equipment manufacturer (OEM) in the developed market, as one of the growth areas for the company is to become an OEM supplier to the retail players. TCL is in talks with Reliance, Wal-Mart, and other chains to supply primarily color televisions, DVD players, and air conditioners for their private labels. Comparing to the gross margin of 22.3% in the domestic market, OEM gross margin is only 13.3%, but still better than 12.9% with its own brand in Europe and North America in 2007. So TCL implements design and manufacturing changes to cut costs and remain competitive in strategic OEM business, and it has since won the subcontract from South Korean Samsung.

In addition, TCL seeks to develop its brand in the emerging markets, where channels are consolidated and the brand profile is raised. TCL has gained market shares to become the third in Philippines, fourth in Vietnam, and fifth in Australia. TCL will continue to build its strong positions in key Southeast Asian markets, and ensure profitability before further expanding into new markets. Furthermore, in the communications business, TCL will use Alcatel brand to establish a more solid market position in the overseas market, and will keep the collaboration with key overseas operators.

Finally, TCL will attempt to build alliance with major brands to explore new business opportunities. In 2008, TCL made a strategic alliance with Intel to develop next-generation Internet-capable televisions. Through jointed research, development, and promotion of new televisions that are capable of accessing the Internet, providing more TV programs as well as opportunities for users to communicate and interact, the project may present huge market potentials for both Intel and TCL in the coming years.

Future Challenges

Although its high-end products have suffered a great loss in sales, the recent global financial crisis also presents TCL a growth opportunity in lower-priced products. While Japanese rivals were announcing layoffs, TCL started mass production of its LCD module in 2009, aiming at further controlling costs and increasing profitability. Upon the completion of its four production lines in April 2009, TCL will be able to produce 3 million LCD TVs and 2 million LCD components per year. The strategic move will likely help TCL keep its competitiveness in the global market. By 2010, the company is expected to sell 5 million LCD TVs. Looking forward, TCL will keep focusing on its global ambition, just as its ambitious leader envisioned, by "becoming the most respected and innovative enterprises around the world".

Sunny Li Sun

References

Knowledge@Wharton (2005). TCL's Dongsheng Li: We should control and own our brands. http://knowledge.wharton.upenn.edu/article.cfm?articleid=1168. Retrieved on 24 March 2009.

李东生 (2006). 鹰的重生, *TCL 动态* [Li, Dongsheng. Eagle reborn. *TCL Forum*. http://magazine.tcl.com/article.aspx?id=3268. Retrieved on 24 March 2009.

Li, PP (2007). Toward an integrated theory of multinational evolution: The evidence of Chinese multinational enterprises as latecomers. *Journal of International Management*, 13(3): 296–318.

Tabeta, S (2009). Ties, tactics underpin strong performances in slowing China. *Nikkei Weekly*, 9 March.

Tejal, A (2007). TCL eyes private label space in retail sector. *Business Standard* (Mumbai.), 15 June.

TONGLING NONFERROUS METALS

Corporate Address and Contact Information

Tongling Nonferrous Metals Group Holdings Co. Ltd.
Youse Plaza, West Changjiang Road
Tongling, Anhui Province 244001
People's Republic of China
Phone: (86)562-586-0016
Fax: (86)562-586-1313
http://www.TLYS.com.cn/english/, www.tnmg.com.cn

Tongling Nonferrous Metals Group Holdings Co. Ltd. (TLYS, 铜陵有色金属集团股份有限公司) engages primarily in the manufacture and processing of non-ferrous metals and chemical products. As a large state-owned enterprise, the company has 14,883 employees, and its major offerings are copper cathodes, gold, silver, steel balls, steel fine sand, vitriol, and copper products. TLYS' copper cathodes are applied in various fields of electric power, military industry, machinery, communication, construction, automobile, household appliance, and electronic, and the company distributes its products primarily in Eastern China. During the year ended 31 December 2008, TLYS obtained approximately 70% of its total revenue from its copper cathodes.

Corporate Development

TLYS is located in Tongling, Anhui Province. Known as "China's Ancient Bronze Capital", TLYS is one of the cradles of antique bronze culture, and the company also enjoys a favorable geographical location that closes to both Yangtze River and sea, with convenient transportation system in place.

As one of the earliest copper production bases in PRC, TLYS was put into production in June 1952. After more than half a century of development, TLYS has grown to become a large-scale enterprise that engages mainly in copper mining, mineral processing, smelting and refining, and copper products processing; the company also involves in trade, scientific research and design, machine building, construction and installation, shaft and drift construction, and tourism industry. As one of the large state-owned companies with preferential support from Anhui provincial government, TLYS is one of the 300 key enterprises that enjoy special supports in China. In August 1992, the company became the first stockholding enterprise in Anhui approved by the Provincial Commission for Economic Restructuring. Originally named Anhui Tongdu Development Stock Co. Ltd., it was renamed to Anhui Tongdu Copper Stock Co. Ltd. in 1996, and the company was listed on the Shenzhen Securities Exchange, which made it the first stock of the Chinese copper industry.

Since 1998, the company's main product, the copper cathode, has held the top spot in China's copper enterprises for five consecutive years, and TLYS became one of the 13 top copper refining enterprises in the world with 371.100 tons of copper cathode in 2004. In the following year, the company was ranked the 174th among the top 500 enterprises in China, and 98th among the large-scale Chinese industrial enterprises in terms of its sales revenue and total assets. On 19 September 2007, with the approval from Anhui government, the company was renamed to Tongling Nonferrous Metals Group Co. Ltd., and in 2008 TLYS was ranked 47th among the top 100 manufacturers in China.

As a state-owned and publicly listed company, TLYS is governed by a Board of Directors, with Wei Jianghong serves as the current chair and president. Fang Guotai is vice chairman and party secretary, other directors include Wang Renfa (CEO), Shao Wu (deputy manager), Wu Heping (secretary), Wu Xiaowei, Gong Huadong, Liang Keming, Chen Mingyong, Wang Libao (chief accountants), and Li Dongqing (chief engineer).

Main Products and Services

TLYS mainly engages in the copper mining, beneficiation, processing, smelting and refining, and copper products processing, and also involves in the machine building and chemical industry. Among its copper products are cathode copper, brass sheet (strip), brass (flat) wire, copper rod, brass bar, copper and brass tubes, anode phosphor copper, pure copper powder, and electrical wire and cable. The company also produces noble metals such as gold, silver, and fine silver powder. Its products from chemical industry include vitriol, dimethyl carbonate, propylene glycol, titanium white powder, copper sulfate, silver nitrate, and medical capsule. TLYS' machine series include special ceramics filter, high-pressure circular drill rig, multi-purpose service vehicle, and TCY LHD loader among others.

TLYS has first-rate technologies and products. Its highly pure copper cathode is a well-recognized product in China under the brand name of *Copper Crown*, which along with another brand *Jintun* has been registered in London Metal Exchange (LME), and begun to be known around the world. Other products, such as oxygen-free copper rod, round copper enameled wire, chalcanthite, plastic cables, and wires are listed as name brand products of Anhui Province. TLYS' continuous mining technology and equipment for underground mine have received the Blue Ribbon Award of the National Advancement in Science & Technology.

Competitors and Growth Strategies

Since the majority of its products are distributed in Eastern China, TLYS competes mainly with other metal manufacturers in the country, among them: Jiangxi Copper Co. Ltd., Yunnan Copper Co. Ltd., Hunan

Nonferrous Metals Holding Group Co. Ltd., and Anhui Xinke New Materials Co. Ltd. In 2008, TLYS reaped sales revenue of RMB 37.342 billion, and gross profits of 2.327 billion. Its total assets were RMB 19.277 billion, total equity of 5.811 billion, and 1.294 billion shares outstanding at of 31 December 2008.

During the current 11th Five-Year Plan (2007–2012), TLYS has formulated its overall developing strategy of "innovating, adjusting, reorganizing, and reconstructing", with the aims of "promoting main industry, separating and restructuring the subsidiary industries, standardized and effective managing, and developing both enterprise and employees". In order to become a modern enterprise with global competence, the company has sought to continue its structural reform and accelerate its development.

Although TLYS focuses primarily on the Chinese market, it has endeavored to play a more important role in the global metal industries in recent years. TLYS is one of the top 100 enterprises that has license to engage in foreign trade, and ranks the 175th among the top 500 enterprises in China in terms of total volume of imports and exports. Its international trade volume reached US$2.829 billion in 2007. Over the years, the company has established economic, technical, and trade cooperation relationship with more than 30 countries and regions around the world, and dozens of its products have been exported to over 10 countries and areas such as Japan, Germany, the United States, and Singapore. TLYS cooperated with some of the well-known companies in many sectors such as raw materials, products, and technologies, among them: BHP Corporation of Australia, Outokmpu Corporation of Finland, Sumitomo Corporation of Japan, KGHM Corporation of Poland, etc.

Qun Du

References

Reuters (2009). Tongling Nonferrous Metals Group Holdings Co. Ltd. http://www.reuters.com/finance/stocks/overview?symbol=000630.SZ. Retrieved on 10 August 2009.

Tongling Nonferrous Metals Group Holdings Co. (2008). About Us. http://www.TLYS.com.cn/english/. Retrieved on 10 August 2009.

Tongling Nonferrous Metals Group Holdings Co. (2009). 2008 Annual Report. http://www.tdty.com/eWebEditor/UploadFile/200942782337938.doc. Retrieved on 10 August 2009.

TPV TECHNOLOGY

Corporate Address and Contact Information

TPV Technology Limited
Harcourt House
21st Floor, Room 2108
39 Gloucester Road, Wanchai
Hong Kong
Phone: (852)2858-5736
Fax: (852)2546-8884
http://www.tpvholdings.com

TPV Technology Limited (TPV, 冠捷科技有限公司) is the world's largest display manufacturer. Selling over 47.6 million computer monitors in 2008, TPV holds a 28.5-percent share of the global computer monitor market. In addition to its dominant position in computer monitors, TPV surpassed Toshiba as the fifth largest manufacturer of LCD TVs. TPV's production operations in Poland and Brazil have been solid examples of the growth in Chinese outward FDI. TPV's strategies have provided strong contra cyclical performance in the global economic downturn of 2008–2009, providing a solid foundation for continual strong growth the firm has maintained throughout its history. While profits fell dramatically (down 46 percent) in the ravaged economic climate of 2007, output continued to grow with sales increasing 9.4 percent to US$9.2 billion.

Historical Development

TPV was founded in Fujian, China in 1990 as Top Victory Electronics, the first manufacturing plant of Taiwan-based Admiral Overseas Corporation (AOC), which had been originally established in 1967 by the Admiral Corporation. Although its initial expertise was based on CRT displays, TPV moved quickly to master flat panel display technology, entering that market in 2002 and becoming an OEM supplier for SONY, Philips, HP, Viewsonic, TCL, and other manufacturers.

In 2005, TPV took over Royal Philips Electronics' OEM monitor business as well as the manufacturing of Philips monitors and entry-level flat TV products. In return for a 15-percent equity position, TPV had vaulted to the number one PC monitor manufacturer with annual volume of over 35 million units. In addition to its monitor product line, by 2006, TPV was producing more than 2.6 million units of flat TVs and was the sixth largest manufacturer in the world (behind Samsung, SONY, Philips, Sharp, and LG).

In December 2008, TPV entered into an agreement with Philips for an exclusive license to use the Philips trademark to produce and sell monitors worldwide for five years. This agreement allows TPV to extend its reach to the end market with an established brand.

TPV Technology has continued to maintain its singular focus and has stayed within the boundaries of the display field. The firm has implemented measured movements from cathode-ray tubes, to LCD monitors on a contract basis, to monitors under the AOC, A-Mark, Envision, Maya, and Topview brands, to flat panel TVs (both as an OEM supplier and under AOC brands). TPV's newest extension within the display field is the ability to directly market LCD TVs to the end market using the established Phillips brand.

Corporate Structure and Leadership

At the helm of TPV is Dr. Jason Hsuan, Chairman and CEO, who joined TPV in 1990 as the company opened its first manufacturing facility in mainland China in Fuqing. Prior to joining TPV, Hsuan, who holds a master degree in systems engineering from Boston University and doctorate from the Polytechnic Institute of Brooklyn, had gained 20 years of experience in well-known multinational enterprises, including General Electric and PepsiCo.

In terms of ownership structure of TPV, as of May 2009, the two largest equity positions are held by Koninklijke Philips Electronics (27.3%) and China Great Wall Computer Shenzhen (26.6%), a subsidiary of state-owned China Electronics Corporation Group. Meanwhile the Chi Mei Optoelectronics has 7.1%, and the Brilliant Way Investment holds another 5.1% of TPV shares.

TPV's leadership features two significant departures from the Code on Corporate Governance Practices Governing the Listing of Securities on the Stock Exchange of Hong Kong Limited. The first is that Hsuan's dual role as Chairman and CEO does not comply with Code provision A.2.1, which stipulates that the roles of the chairman and chief executive officer should be separated, and not be performed by the same individual. Secondly, while Code provision A.4.1 stipulates that non-executive directors should be appointed for a specific term, subject to re-election, the company's non-executive directors are not appointed for a specific term. In its 2008 annual report, while these deviations are acknowledged there is also a commitment to not bring the organization into compliance with what are identified as "recommended best practices" based upon the organizations belief that the current model provides more consistent leadership, increased planning effectiveness and execution of long-term business strategies.

Business Strategies

Throughout its history, TPV's strategy has demonstrated a consistent devotion to "staying close to the knitting" by maintaining a steady concentration on displays. During its early growth, TPV sought market share by building cost leadership as an OEM monitor manufacturer pursuing the requisite output for the required scale efficiencies. However, rather than maintaining a direct path toward the always illusive goal of long-term cost leadership, TPV side-stepped and began producing its own monitor design as well as entering the LCD TV market.

While on the surface either or both of these entries into competitive markets might seem questionable, each contained hidden strategic esthetics. In both the monitor and TV markets, TPV was no ordinary late entry, but in fact moved into precise strategic niches in both markets.

In the monitor market, although lacking an established brand, TPV was not just another OEM supplier, but rather a fully capable ODM manufacturer. In addition, none of the market leaders was solely a dedicated monitor company. It was only matter of time before a recognizable market name would withdraw to refocus in other areas. Such was the case with Phillips in 2005 and TPV moved quickly, acquiring a high profile brand identity and thus negating its only significant weakness.

In the television market, TPV was again the sole focused display company and its AOC family of brands were uniquely re-enforced by the company's manufacturing prowess. As the competitive market began reacting to decreases in average selling price, the demand for outsourcing increased. TPV wielded a double-edged competitive sword. On the one hand, it enjoyed the inherent cost advantage of self-sourcing over out-sourcing. On the other hand, significant revenue and the ability to further increase manufacturing scale were afforded by the company's position as a major display driver to the market.

This upward strategic/operational spiral continued to accelerate through the 2008–2009 economic downturn, as other firms struggled to improve outsourcing efficiencies, TPV was able to focus on upstream integration, gaining the expertise necessary for further self-sourcing and expanded bundling to the OEM market. Furthermore, the company's R&D efforts have been focused on design of more generic circuitry that allows for a reduction of component suppliers while simultaneously increasing yield of production set-ups.

An important event during this period was the small misstep suffered by TPV's failed entry into digital frame production. From a firm much more practiced at success, TPV demonstrated its strategic abilities and moved decisively out of the market with no significant financial impact. As TPV continues its efforts toward technological integration, each step provides potential foundations for additional product offerings. As it quickly tested the digital frame markets, exploratory test moves into notebooks and/or netbooks are foreseeable.

In TPV's 2008 annual report, Hsuan stated, "Although we have no control over the macro environment, we are in full control of our business." In TPV's case that situation seems more than acceptable.

Neil Slough

References

Dorsch, J (2009). TPV Technology Limited. Hoover's Company Reviews.

LCD TV Association (2007). *LCD TV Matters*, Volume 1(2). http://www.veritasetvisus.com/LCDTVA/LCDTVA-2,%20Fall%202007.pdf. Retrieved on 30 June 2009.

Lau, J (2009). TPV Technology. *Polaris Capital*. www.polariscapital.net/downLoad.aspx?files=16200936722.pdf. Retrieved on 30 June 2009.

TPV Technology Limited (2009). *Annul Report 2008*. http://www.tpvholdings.com/cms_attachment/LTN20090423650.pdf. Retrieved on 30 June 2009.

WAHAHA

Corporate Address and Contact Information

Wahaha Group
No. 160 Qingtai Street
Hangzhou 310009
People's Republic of China
Phone: (086)571-8603-2866
Fax: (086)571-8684-6000
http://en.wahaha.com.cn
whh@wahaha.com.cn

Located in Hangzhou, Zhejiang Province, Wahaha Group Co. Ltd. (杭州娃哈哈集团有限公司) is a privately held company founded in 1987. It has about 20,000 employees and more than 100 subsidiary companies located in 27 provinces, with Zong Qinghou as the chairman and CEO of the corporation. Focusing mainly on the Chinese food and beverage industry, its products range from dairy products, water, tea, and soft drinks, to canned food and health care products. Wahaha is China's largest private soft drinks company with total assets about RMB 17.8 billion. It ranked third on the list of top 50 Most Valuable Privately held Chinese Brands in 2007 according to *Hurun Report*. In 1996, Wahaha entered a joint venture with Danone to form five new subsidiaries, which resulted in a long-running legal dispute with the French Firm on the ownership of some of the non joint-venture products that is still ongoing.

Historical Development

Wahaha means "laughing child" in Chinese. It was started by Zong Qinghou in 1987 in the Shangcheng School District of Hangzhou. Two years later, Zong established a plant called the "Hangzhou Wahaha Nutritional Foods Factory" to produce liquid nutrient for children, one of the first such products developed in the nation. With the support of the Hangzhou municipal government, this factory soon merged with the Hangzhou Canned Food Factory. With about 2,000 employees on payroll and negative net assets in balance sheet, Hangzhou Wahaha Group Corporation was formed in 1991 to start scale operation.

In 1992, Wahaha launched the Wahaha Food City Co. Ltd. in Hangzhou, which was renamed in 2001 to ZHI. In 1994, the company set up its first branch factory in Chongqing. In 1995, Zong and Danone negotiated a joint-venture agreement and the *Memorandum of Understanding* (MOU) was reached on 28 March 1996. Under the brand name of Wahaha, according to the agreement, Danone and Peregrine had invested some US$70 million in five joint-ventures with Wahaha, and in 1998 Danone became the majority stakeholders when they bought over Peregrine's stakes. With the new capital, Wahaha brought world-class production lines from overseas into its operations. Through effective use of foreign investment and technologies, Wahaha marched into the new century with its well-established national brand. By 2000, Wahaha Group has become the largest private company in the Chinese beverage industry with total assets of RMB 4.4 billion.

However, the marriage soon went sour and Wahaha and Danone were in a public dispute. In April 2007, after charging that Wahaha had sold some similar products using the Wahaha brand, Danone demanded to have a stake in those products as well. Consequently, the company has launched some of its new products using different names and logo, among them: Nutri-Express Drink, Wahaha Smoothie, and U-Yo Milk Coffee. On 7 June 2007, Danone filed suit against Wahaha in the United States, and facing the pressure Zong resigned as chairman. Nevertheless by the end of year, both companies agreed to put aside their legal dispute and continued with the negotiations. In February 2009, the California superior court has ruled that the legal dispute should be resolved in China as the United States has no jurisdiction on Danone and Wahaha.

Corporate Structure and Leadership

Since its founding in 1987, Wahaha has become one of the China's leading companies under the leadership of Zong Qinghou. Born in 1945 and with little formal education, Zong had a clear vision of the fast-growing beverage and food industry in China, and was remarkably successful in marketing his nutrition products and beverages to the country's rising middle class. After jointed force with Danone, Wahaha's businesses enjoyed a period of rapid growth, expanding into more than 40 subsidiaries in 16 provinces. In 1998, Zong launched Future Cola to compete with Coca Cola and Pepsi. With his vision, dedication and hard work, Zong has turned Wahaha into the largest beverage manufacturer in China; and Zong himself has been regarded as one of the most influential and successful entrepreneurs of the current Chinese economic reform. The presence of Wahaha was even felt in the United States, Europe and Southeast Asia. By 2008, *Forbes* magazine ranked Zong as China's 16th richest man with an estimated personal wealth of USD 1.3 billion.

Hangzhou Wahaha Group Co. Ltd. is owned by Zong Qinghou (29.4%), Zhejiang Wahaha Industries Joint-Stock Co. (ZHI) (26.4%), and the Shangcheng District Government (46%). The Hangzhou Wahaha Guangsheng Investment Co. was established in 2003. Among its subsidiaries or associates are the Hangzhou Wahaha Children's Clothing Co., Changsha Wahaha Beverages Co., Harbin Shuangcheng Wahaha Foods Co., and Jian Wahaha Beverages Co. In terms of joint-venture companies, Wahaha holds 39%, ZHI (10%), and Danone (51%) in majority of the joint-venture businesses.

Zong's shares are controlled by British Virgin islands-registered Ever Maple Trading Ltd. The offshore companies include the British Virgin Islands' Golden Dynasty Enterprise Ltd., Gold Factory Developments Ltd., Platinum Net Ltd., Sunworld Enterprises Ltd., Great Base International Ltd., Bountiful Gold Trading Ltd., Wintell Enterprises Ltd., Samoa, the Mega Source Investments Ltd., and Honour Bright Investments Ltd.

Main Product and Service

Wahaha main products consist of milk and yogurt drink, mineral water, carbonated soft drinks, fruit juice, isotonic drinks, tea, porridge, canned food, and health products. Its top selling products are bottled water and vitamin-enhanced milk drinks, followed by tea, mild drinks, fruit juice, and yoghurt.

In 1998, Wahaha started making its own cola production called Extreme Cola and Future Cola. In 2002, Wahaha entered in children's clothing business, and in the following year it began to market and sell milk products in the United States. By 2004, Zong was listed among the Top 10 Most Influential Private Business Owners in China by *Hurun Report*. Wahaha has since grown to be one of the best brands in China, and the corporation has become one of the largest employers and top tax revenue producers in the region.

Wahaha has total revenue of RMB 15.2 billion in 2005, and operating income of RMB 3.2 billion. The companies had non-joint venture total assets of RMB 5.6 billion and profit of RMB 1.04 billion in 2006. In 2007, Wahaha had produces 6.89 million tons of beverages with sales revenue of RMB 25.8 billion and RMB 5 billion in profit and tax. According to the China Beverage Industry Association (CBIA), in 2008, Wahaha has generated 55.57% of the CBIA's overall production, 65.84% of its revenue and 73.16% of its profit tax. In 2009, Wahaha plans to produce RMB 50 billion for its operating revenue and projects an increase to RMB 100 billion in three to five years.

Challenges and Business Strategies

Wahaha's main competitors in the soft drink market are Coca Cola, Pepsi, Uni-President Enterprise Corp., and Tingyi (Cayman Islands) Holding Corp, and its ongoing challenge is to convince the general public that the domestic cola is as good as Coca Cola and Pepsi, and to increase its cola sales at a competitive price.

Wahaha core strategy in promoting company products is to reduce its cola prices and defeat the competitive imitations. In order to strengthen its sale volume, Wahaha has employed three main marketing strategies: advertisement — marketing it as a national product including TV commercials; selective focus on the regions for its main products, as it was found that water and colas are in high demands in the urban and rural areas, respectively; use celebrities to promote its products such as tea drinks, bottled water, and Future Cola.

To cope with the current economic slowdown, Wahaha concentrates on its core businesses of food and beverage. In specific, the company has relied on a "co-distribution system" to improve its risk-management capabilities. Wahaha's future plan is to monitor closely the business trend and adopt swiftly as the demands and industry conditions change. Despite the recession, Wahaha still expects to see its annual sales increase by ten percent as compared to 2008. Looking forward in the next few years, when the market conditions are expected to improve, the company is planning to further implement the scientific management in its operations, refocus globally, and expand into medical and health care products on top of its current core beverage and food businesses.

Loi Teck Hui and Quek Kia Fatt

References

Danone and Wahaha vie for the last laugh (11 June 2007). *South China Morning Post*, p. B3.

Danone setback in Wahaha dispute after US court ruling (3 March 2009). http://www.flex-news-food.com/console/PageViewer.aspx?page=22372&str=. Retrieved on 14 April 2009.

Dickinson, SM (2007). Danone vs. Wahaha. *China Economic Review*. http://www.chinaeconomicreview.com/cer/2007_09/Danone_v_Wahaha.html. Retrieved on 14 April 2009.

Hangzhou Wahaha Group Corporation, Mindbranch. http://www.mindbranch.com/listing/product/R231-541.html. Retrieved on 14 April 2009.

Hangzhou Wahaha Group. *Wikipedia*. http://en.wikipedia.org/wiki/Hangzhou_Wahaha_Group. Retrieved on 3 April 2009.

Miller, MM (2009). Wahaha: The Chinese beverage company's expansion is no laughing matter. *China Business Review*. http://www.chinabusinessreview.com/public/0409/company_profile.html. Retrieved on 14 April 2009.

Wahaha presents Chinese business wisdom amid economic crisis (9 February 2009). *Reuters*. http://www.reuters.com/article/pressRelease/idUS144017+09-Feb-2009+PRN20090209. Retrieved on 14 April 2009.

Wang, Z. Wahaha, Danone start trademark arbitration (7 January 2009). *China Daily*. http://www.chinadaily.com.cn/bizchina/2009-01/07/content_7373492.htm. Retrieved on 14 April 2009.

Zong Qinghou (2009). In *Biographical Dictionary of New Chinese Entrepreneurs and Business Leaders*, W Zhang and I Alon (eds.), pp. 267–269, Cheltenham, UK: Edward Elgar.

16 Zong Qinghou (29 October 2008). *Forbes*. http://www.forbes.com/lists/2008/74/chinarichest08_Zong-Qinghou_NW67.html. Retrieved on 14 April 2009.

WEICHAI POWER

Corporate Address and Contact Information

Weichai Power Co. Ltd.
26 Minsheng Road
Weifang, Shandong Province
People's Republic of China
Phone: (86)536-819-7777
http://www.weichai.com

Weichai Power Co. Ltd. (潍柴动力股份有限公司) is founded by Weifang Diesel Engine Factory together with domestic and foreign investors. Weichai Power is a modern corporation as well as the major enterprise in the PRC specializing in the research and development, manufacturing, and sales of diesel engines. The company's products are widely applicable to different markets, including heavy-duty vehicles, coaches, construction machines, vessels, and power generator.

Historical Development

Weichai Power was established on 23 December 2002, which Weichai Factory injected its operating assets and liabilities relating to the manufacture and sale of WD615 and WD618 engines and cash, along with other investors that contributed capital. The history of Weichai Factory could be traced back to 1953, when the plant was founded as one of the first diesel engine manufacturers in the PRC. From the 1950s to the early 1980s, Weichai Factory developed and manufactured various medium-speed diesel engines with an output of 51kW–99kW. In 1984, the State Development and Planning Commission and State Economic Planning Commission specified Weichai Factory as one of the designated manufacturers of Steyr WD615 diesel engines. In addition, the company also received government approval to produce diesel engines for heavy-duty vehicles. In October 1989, Weichai's production line was tested and accepted by the relevant governmental authorities, and its production of WD615 engines for use in heavy-duty vehicles also commenced in the same year.

From 1990 to 1994, Weichai Factory successfully developed and launched various series of WD615 Engines for use in power generators, construction machines and vessels. In 1995, Weichai Factory received ISO9001 accreditation. In the same year, the company also entered a contract to import the

WD618 technology from Steyr. In October 1999, Weichai Factory acquired Chongqing Weichai and thereby increased its production capacity of WD615 Engines. In May 2000, WD618 Engines for use in heavy-duty vehicles were launched in the market. A year later, Weichai Factory successfully developed and launched its WD615 and WD618 Euro I engines. In 2002, Weichai Factory further upgraded its WD615 series to Euro II Standards. After Weichai Power was established, the company's WD618 Engines successfully achieved Euro II compliance. In August 2003, the company received the approval from the Bureau of Science and Technology of Shandong Province as a new high-technology enterprise. On 1 March 2004, Weichai Power passed the British ISO/TS16949 quality administration system authentication, the first company to do so in the Chinese internal-combustion diesel engine industry. Ten days later, Weichai Power (2338) debuted strongly on the Hong Kong Stock Exchange. In March 2005, Weichai Power produced its first EURO III compliant large power diesel engine, the Landking.

Corporate Structure and Main Products

Weichai Power Limited is owned by Weichai Holding Company. It was listed as an H-Share company in Hong Kong before it moved back to China's A-Share market. CEO and Chairman Tan Xuguang is also the Chair of the Board of Weichai Holding Company. Tan joined Weichai in 1977 and rose through the ranks to become the general manager of the factory in the ensuing years. He is the driving force behind Weichai's dramatic growth and diversification strategies. With over 32,000 employees worldwide, the company is governed by a 16-member Board of Directors.

Weichai Power has a nationwide service network with 37 company-owned service centers and 480 licensed service centers in the PRC. The company, specializing in the manufacture of high-speed, heavy-duty diesel engines, is one of the main diesel engine manufacturers in the PRC. Weichai's core products include WD615 and WD618 diesel engines, which are widely used in heavy-duty vehicles and coaches, construction machine engines, vessel engines and power generator engines. Currently, the revenue from the sales of WD615 Euro I Engines constitutes most of the sales of the company. In 2008, the company's aggregate sales of heavy-duty truck engines reached approximately 197,000 units, representing a year-on-year increase of 30.37%, 19.29% higher than the average of the industry. The company's market share in the 14 tons (and above) gross weight heavy-duty truck market reached 36.5%, representing an increase of 4.1% over last year. Shaanxi Heavy-duty Motor Company Limited, a subsidiary of the company, reported an aggregate sale of approximately 64,000 units of heavy-duty trucks, representing an increase of 6.81% over last year. Shaanxi Fast Gear Co. Ltd., another subsidiary, reported an aggregate sale of approximately 465,000 units of gearboxes, representing an increase of 7.98% over the previous year.

Business Strategies

As the dominant leader in its industry, Weichai Power has been pursuing a best-cost strategy. Comparing to its domestic competitors, Weichai enjoys considerable scale advantage in production and technological advantage in new product development. Furthermore, since after-sales services network is critical in diesel engine business, it is very difficult for foreign competitors to match Weichai's network of 37 service centers throughout China.

Diversification is another characteristic of Weichai's corporate strategy. After the acquisition of Xiang Huoju Auto Group, Weichai owns Shanxi Heavy Truck Group, Xiang Huoju Sparks Plug Limited, Shanxi Fast Gear Limited, and Mudanjiang Fotong Auto AC Limited, etc. Consequently, Weichai Power expanded its business lines while building a dominant position in each of the market segments covering commercial vehicles, auto components, and power assembly.

Unlike many domestic Chinese auto firms, Weichai Power has invested and supported its own R&D capabilities. Besides several national-level technology centers and power labs in China, Weichai has established its European R&D center in Austria. As a result, multiple new diesel engines with independent intellectual property were developed by Weichai and are being installed in heavy trucks. In terms of the company's globalization effort, Weichai has established 10 oversea sales offices to serve the international market, and has exported to countries such as India, Vietnam, Russia and other countries in Middle East, and Southeastern Asia.

Tom Tao

References

China Automotive Yearbook (2005, 2006, and 2007). China Automotive Technology Center. Tianjin: China.

Wang, D (2007). Weichai Power: Poised to be the biggest general power equipment base. Guolian Security.

Weichai Power Co. Ltd. (2009). Annual Report 2008. http://www.weichai.com/public/upload/20090429he.pdf. Retrieved on 20 June 2009.

Weichai Power Co. Ltd. History and Development. http://www.weichai.com/e_about/channel/about_03.shtml. Retrieved on 20 June 2009.

WUHAN IRON & STEEL

Corporate Address and Contact Information

Wuhan Iron & Steel Co. Ltd.
Qingshan District
Wuhan, Hubei Province 430083
People's Republic of China
Phone: (86)27-8680-7873
Fax: (86)27-8630-6023
http://www.WISCO.com.cn/

Wuhan Iron & Steel Co. Ltd. (WISCO 武汉钢铁股份有限公司) is located in Wuhan, capital city of Hubei Province. The company's principal activities are manufacturing and selling hot-rolled plates, cold-rolled carbon steel and silicon steel products. Other activities include developing metallurgy product technology and manufacturing metallurgy sub-products and steel extend products. The company also has subsidiaries and affiliates involved in manufacturing gas, non-ferrous metal products and coke, providing capital services, and mining coal. The firm has an annual capacity of 10 million tons of iron and 10 million tons of steel. WISCO enjoys a favorable Wright Quality Rating of ABA1. In 2008, the firm had sales of $73.34 billion, and currently is ranked third among China-based firms on annual production capacity and sixteenth in the world.

Historical Development

Construction on Wuhan Iron & Steel complex began in 1955, and in 1957, it received assurance from the government that raw material would be available for the plant. Chairman Mao officially opened the facility in September 1958, and production started at Wuhan Iron & Steel with a merger of Liuzhou Iron & Steel and Echeng Iron & Steel companies, which was the first of the big blast furnace manufacturers with open-hearth construction in China. Three years later, WISCO complex was completed. By 1967, the Wuhan Iron Steel Corporation was producing about 40 percent of China's 12 million tons of steel per year.

In 1992, Fitch assigned a BBB-rating to WISCO. At this point, the company was the third largest steel producer in China. Shortly thereafter, WISCO found itself at the heart of a philosophical dilemma: should 80,000 of its 120,000 workforce be laid off, thus breaking the "three irons" of iron salary (inflexible wages), iron chair (permanent jobs for officials), and iron rice bowl (lifetime jobs for workers)? In early 1992, state officials called on state factories to do just that. But when violence broke out in Wuhan, it appeared that officials saw this change as unrealistic, as there was no social security system in place to care for the laid off workers. Of interest here is that many of the 120,000 employees at WISCO did not work in the steel business; for example, some 8,000 employees were schoolteachers and administrators who ran 40 schools.

WISCO's problems got worse in 1994, when the firm found itself with $575 million accounts payable by customers for delivered goods. A cash flow crisis forced the company to delay crucial investments in new equipment, as it needed to find a way to pay $345 million in arrears to its suppliers. Management elected to place 70,000 employees into eight subsidiary companies and thus, reduce their payroll. Those were difficult times for WISCO and for China, as the economic reforms were under extreme pressure and the China economy experienced two straight years of 13 percent growth.

Late in 1997, a merger transpired between WISCO and two large central China steel firms: Daye Iron & Steel Co. and Hubei Iron & Steel Co. In the same year, the firm brought on line production of high-speed wire rods for steel corded fabrics, a remarkable accomplishment since previously all this material was imported into China. In 2002, WISCO twice raised its profit targets due to a strong economy and increasing orders for its steel products. Early in 2003, the firm found itself as the fourth largest steel producer in China. It then undertook an aggressive program to expand its production capabilities and improve product quality.

Late in 2003, WISCO acquired the assets of WC, an iron & steel products manufacturer. To help assure raw material availability for the complex, WISCO entered into a joint iron ore venture agreement with BHP Billiton, the world's largest mining company, and agreed to a strategic partnership with Pingdingshan Coal Co. Ltd. in late 2004. The company continued its expansion with a late 2005 joint-stock venture with Guangxi Liuzhou Iron and Steel, and CITIC Pacific agreed to sell a half stake in its magnetite ore facility to WISCO in 2006. In 2007, Kunming Steel was merged into Wuhan Iron & Steel Co. Ltd. To eliminate outdated production capacity and improve competitiveness, WISCO won approval to link-up with Guangxi Liuzhou Iron & Steel Co. Ltd., and purchased Panzhuhua Iron & Steel in 2008.

Main Products, Corporate Structure, and Leadership

WISCO has many interests, but is primarily engaged in the manufacture of iron and steel products. It makes both hot-rolled products (including hot-rolled plates, medium thick boards, heavy sections, high speed wires, steel rods, and steel billets) and cold-rolled products (including cold-rolled plates, coating boards, and cold-rolled silicon steel products). The bulk of its production is used domestically. More than a third of China's hot-rolled coil steel for automobile and appliance manufacturers is supplied by WISCO. The company has complete processing equipment to manufacture plate and sheet products, as it is composed of mining, coking, sintering, smelting, and rolling facilities. Thus, the firm is able to produce for sale coke, refractory, chemical products, powder metallurgical products, copper-sulfur-cobalt concentrated ore, granulated slag, oxygen, and rare gases.

Wuhan Iron & Steel Co. Ltd. and the holding company the Wuhan Iron & Steel (Group) Corporation are backbone enterprises under the State Council of the People's Republic of China. The company has approximately 83,700 employees, of which 19,000 are directly involved in the main steel business at its headquarter facilities. WISCO is made up of twenty wholly owned affiliated companies, seven share-holding companies, four branch companies, two factories directly under WISCO's leadership, two collectively owned enterprises, one listed share holding company, i.e., Wuhan Iron and Steel (Group) Corporation, limited.

WISCO's leadership team includes: Deng Qilin (chairman), Peng Chen (vice president and chief accountant), Wang Jiong (vice president and secretary, party committee), Shao Weimin (vice president and chief engineer), Li Fushan, Wang Ling, Hu Wangming, and Jia Baojun (vice presidents).

Business Strategies

Wuhan Iron & Steel Co. Ltd. is guided by the 11th Five-Year Plan of the PRC and the "Three representatives" — advanced social productive forces, advanced culture, and the interests of the overwhelming majority. The PRC's official policy states that by 2010, the top 10 producers of crude steel output must account for 50 percent of the total output for the country. This percentage must rise to 70 percent by 2020. WISCO has the capacity of 20 million tons (annual) and hopes to achieve 30 million tons by 2010. Thus, a strategy of growth by acquisition is inevitable. However, this growth strategy is threatened by the current economic woes within China and around the world. Achieving the 50 percent goal for the top 10 producers might prove more difficult than anticipated. In 2006, the total production share was 34.66 percent, down from the 46.25 percent achieved in 2001 for these top 10 producers.

WISCO has increased its mergers and acquisitions in an attempt to meet the 2010 goal. The company has also employed a strategy of increasing production of high value-added products, and worked to assure raw materials availability by developing partnerships such as the agreement to acquire a 23-percent share of MMX Sudeste Mineracao SA in Brazil (2009), and iron mine arrangement with Consolidated Thompson Iron Mines Ltd. in Canada (2009).

To comply with the national steel production policy outlined above, WISCO needs strong cash flow. To that end, the company was successful in mid-2008 in signing an agreement with a consortium of nine foreign banks for a low-interest loan of $169 million. WISCO is reticent to divulge specific development plans, but it is clear from the recent international mergers and acquisitions that it seeks to move into a position of greater international influence. The firm hopes to improve its competitiveness through high-quality outputs, improved production through scientific production methods and R&D in the areas of new technology.

Key Role Played in the Chinese and Global Economies

It seems clear that China's stimulus package is meant to assist the top five steel groups (of which WISCO is one) to reach a production capacity of 50 million tons of steel per year. This stimulus does not appear successful to date, as the Chinese steel industry has been in the red since October 2008. This is a direct result of the domestic and international financial crisis that is slowing new construction. The question may be whether exports can stimulate demand for WISCO's steel products. International automobile production and large construction projects are being cut just at a time when the firm would like to expand its market. Tariffs on Chinese steel imports are also being employed by Western nations. Meanwhile, the Chinese government has cancelled value-added tax rebates and levied a 5-percent to

10-percent export tax on 83 types of steel products, making WISCO's products less competitive on the international market. By April 2009, feeling the effects of the weakening domestic and global economy, WISCO fell to fifth place among Chinese Steel firms based on market value, and net profits declined 20.48%.

Nevertheless, as one the largest steel producers in China, WISCO enjoys the cost advantages gained through economies of scale. Further, as one of the state-owned enterprises destined to survive the governmental restructuring of the Chinese steel industry, WISCO is quite likely to emerge from the current crisis in a much stronger position, both domestically and globally. WISCO management hopes to build high-quality steel products that are internationally famous and to reach a rank of a top 500 enterprises in the world. The company leadership strives to be innovative in their scientific research, product offerings, and market competitiveness.

James P Gilbert

References

Chan, C (2008). Wuhan steel pays $180Am for half of Centrex mines. *South China Morning Post*, 19 December.

Steel companies follow global trend (5 September 2008). *China Daily*. english.peopledaily.com.cn/90001/6493577.html. Retrieved on 6 June 2009.

Tyler, PE (1994). Facing cash flow problems, China's Marxist industries try diversification. *New York Times*, 5 May. www.nytimes.com/1994/05/05/world/facing-cash-flow-problems-china-s-marxist-industries-try-diversification.html. Retrieved on 8 August 2009.

WuDunn, S (1993). Wuhan journal; Layoffs in China: A dirty word, but all too real. *New York Times*, 11 May. www.nytimes.com/1993/05/11/world/wuhan-journal-layoffs-in-china-a-dirty-word-but-all-too-real.html. Retrieved on 8 August 2009.

Wuhan Iron and Steel (2009). Company Profile. http://www.wisco.com.cn/wisco_en/brief/aboutus.shtml. Retrieved on 8 March 2009.

Zhang, W and I Alon (2009). *Biographical Dictionary of New Chinese Entrepreneurs and Business Leaders*. Northampton, MA: Edward Elger.

XIAMEN C&D

Corporate Address and Contact Information

Xiamen C&D Inc.
7F Seaside Building, 52 Lujiang Road
Xiamen, Fujian Province 361001
People's Republic of China
Phone: (86)592-226-3333
Fax: (86)592-211-2185
http://www.chinacnd.com/web/en/home, http://xiamencd.en.china.cn/
pub@chinacnd.com

Xiamen Construction & Development Inc. (厦门建发股份有限公司), known as Xiamen C&D, is a modern service-oriented enterprise headquartered in Xiamen, Fujian Province, People's of Republic of China.

Xiamen C&D is primarily engaged in supply chain operation, real estate development, and industrial investment. As of 31 December 2008, the company had seven major subsidiaries, mainly engaged in the development and operation of real estate, the operation of exhibition, the import and export trading, the processing and sale of paper products, as well as the loading and unloading, dispatching, packaging, and storage of cargos.

Corporate Development

On 16 June 1998, Xiamen C&D Inc. was listed on the Shanghai Stock Exchange (600153). After more than 10 years of development, Xiamen C&D has grown to become a modern service enterprise with core business in supply chain operations. In addition, the company also engages in real estate development, property lease, and industry investment. In 2008, the total amount invested by the company stood at RMB 15.8 billion in assets, with net assets standing at RMB 5.1 billion.

Xiamen C&D Corp. Ltd., the parent company of Xiamen C&D Inc., was founded in 1980 with the establishment of the Xiamen Special Economic Zone. After nearly 30 years in business, Xiamen C&D Corp. has developed into a large-scale investment management group in Fujian Province engaging in trading and logistics, real estate development, and tourism and hotels. In 2008, Xiamen C&D Corp. was ranked 147th of the top 500 Chinese enterprises, the 48th of the top 500 Chinese service enterprises, and the 3rd in logistics, warehousing, transportation, and distribution services.

Recently, Xiamen C&D has been named as an AAA credit-standing enterprise, and ranked among China's top 100 listed companies for consecutive years. As an indication of its strong competitive advantage in service industry, the company has been included as a composite stock of the Shanghai and Shenzhen 300 Index, SSE 180 Index, and SSE Dividend Index. In addition, Xiamen C&D ranked first among the top 300 enterprises in the tertiary sector (import and export) of Fujian Province in 2008. Moreover, its Paper & Pulp Co. Ltd. ranked 2nd in the wholesale industry, Xiamen C&D Automobiles Co. Ltd. ranked 13th in the retail industry, and Xiamen Candour Co. Ltd. ranked 46th in the import and export industry of Fujian Province in 2008.

The governance structure of Xiamen C&D includes shareholders conference, Board of Directors, and general manager. Wang Xianrong, a specialist in the industry, is the chairman of the company.

Main Products and Services

Xiamen C&D's main areas of business over the past decade include: supply chain operation, real estate development and property leasing, and industry investment, which are outlined below.

Supply chain operation

With years of experiences, sound business network and logistics facilities, Xiamen C&D has built an excellent reputation in the industry, as the company has the capability to provide its clients with comprehensive supply chain operation services from the purchasing of raw materials and parts, transport, storage, distribution of finished products right down to delivery to the ultimate client. Since becoming a listed company, Xiamen C&D's business has increased at an impressive speed year by year. The company's annual turnover exceeded the RMB 20 billion mark for the first time in 2006, and its main import and export products have achieved a considerable scale and hold a large market share. For successive years, its import and export trade volume has ranked high among China's top 500 foreign trade enterprises.

Real estate development and property leasing

The company's real estate development and property leasing business is primarily handled by the Lianfa Group Co. Ltd. A subsidiary of Xiamen C&D, Lianfa Group has developed and constructed over 1.7 million square meters of real estate space, including residential buildings, all-purpose factories, hotels, office buildings, and shopping centers. In addition, Lianfa has almost 400,000 square meters of property and factory space available for rent. As a part of its campaign to develop the Lianfa brand outside of its home province of Fujian, Lianfa Group has procured and developed land in Nanchang, Guilin, and Nanning. In recent years, the company has been awarded Grade-A qualification in real estate development, and is ranked among China's top 100 real estate enterprises as well as one of the top 10 most valued real estate brands in Southern China. Lianfa currently has 1.5 million square meters of land in reserve for the construction of housing projects, of which 500,000 square meters are located in Xiamen. With nearly 260,000 square meters for the development of industrial factory space, this land has enormous potential value.

Industry investment

Xiamen C&D has made industry investments based on its core business in supply chain operation. In recent years, the company has invested substantially in the development and launching of an Enterprise Resources Planning System (ERP), which acts as a highly effective control platform for management in which logistics flow, capital flow, and information flow are fully integrated. Moreover, Xiamen C&D also invests in infrastructure industries that can help the company to increase the core competitiveness of its supply chain operation, which include international expos, wharfs, and resources, etc.

Xiamen C&D holds a 40% stake in Sichuan Yongfeng Paper Industry Inc., a major state-level enterprise in the industrialization of agriculture business. The company has recently launched a pulping project occupying an area of over 109 acres with 120,000-ton annual output. The RMB 870 million undertaking is regarded as one of the key technological transformation projects in the nation, which will adopt newly developed chlorine-free bleaching technology and DCS Informational Automatic Control Systems, and its pulping technologies are among the most advanced in the world.

Among other industry investments, Xiamen C&D has a 20% stake in Xiamen Zijin Tongguan Mining Investment Development Co. Ltd., and holds a controlling stake in Monterrico Metals. A UK listed company, Monterrico Metals has a huge copper-molybdenum reserve in Whitney, Peru, which boasts nearly 7 million tons of copper deposits. In addition, Xiamen C&D holds a 20% stake in Xiamen Shipbuilding Industry Co. Ltd., which is a large scale shipbuilding enterprise with some of the best production facilities in China. The company's 30,000-ton class multifunctional-container ship series has been named as one of the "Global Top 10 Best Ship-types", and its 4900 PCTC (Pure Car/Truck Carrier) is also regarded as the best of its kind in terms of load capability and technical sophistication that has been built so far in China.

Future Growth Strategies

In the past 10 years, guided by business philosophy of "professional, efficiency, quality, and commitment", Xiamen C&D has gradually formulated its scientific development strategy. Under its group development framework, the company seeks to cultivate sustainable profitability, establish unique enterprise culture, and develop a talent team with high comprehensive capability and dedicated spirit. Despite the recent dip in net profit, the company has remained committed to its main tenets, which consist of providing clients with professional services, ensuring good profit returns for shareholders, offering ample opportunities for the development of employees, and creating public value. By creating win-win opportunities, Xiamen C&D believes its clients will grow along with the company, and shareholders will reap substantial rewards in the long run. In appreciation for the good business environment offered by the city for its growth and development, Xiamen C&D has adopted a social responsibility strategy by actively supporting public welfares for the poor people and the educational causes, sponsoring local sport programs, helping children with congenital heart disease, etc.

In the future, Xiamen C&D will endeavor to provide professional, efficient, and credible services, and to develop in harmony with its clients, shareholders, employees, and society as a whole. The company will seek further expansions based on its business strength, the employee quality, management system, and established brand. As stipulated in its new three-year plan, Xiamen C&D will emphasize on developing the core industries, implementing the strategy of talents, expanding the investment benefits and reforming the inadaptable business components.

With the maturing market economy and rapid development in the 21st century, enterprises in China are facing both opportunities and challenges. Xiamen C&D as a stable, practical and progressive business is confident about its future development. While still based in Xiamen, the company in the coming years plans to look to the whole country and project to the rest of world. By seizing various market opportunities, Xiamen C&D will make great efforts to establish itself as a large-scale investment conglomerate with great reputation in China and globally competitive capacity in the international market.

Hao Jiao

References

Xiamen C&D Inc. (2009). 2008 Annual Report. http://www.chinacnd.com/web/en/investrelate/timebulletin. Retrieved on 21 July 2009.

Xiamen C&D Inc. (2009). Company Profile. http://www.chinacnd.com/web/en/aboutcdc/resume. Retrieved on 21 July 2009.

YUNNAN COPPER

Corporate Address and Contact Information

Yunnan Copper Company Limited
Wang Jia Qiao
Wuhua District
Kunming, Yunan Province 650102
People's Republic of China
Phone: (86)871-839-0844
Fax: (86)871-310-6735
http://www.yunnan-copper.com

China's hunger for resources over the last two decades, based on its energy-hungry economic model, has led the nation to seek more intensively for natural minerals that it can exploit both within China and abroad, through acquiring assets in countries with rich deposits such as Canada, Australia, or some

African countries. Yunnan Copper Company Limited (YCC, 云南铜业股份有限公司) typifies these two impetuses — a state-owned company, with a long history, which has developed major projects in one of the most deposit rich areas of China, but which has also been linked with acquisitions abroad, and whose main executives in the last few years have been dismissed and imprisoned for massive corruption cases.

Historical Development

Because of its importance in the local economy, Yunnan Copper Company receives a huge amount of political and state support, with targets set by both the central and provincial government. In that sense, it is highly typical of large state-led, resource-sector industries. YCC started its history as Yunnan Smelting Plant, founded in 1958 as part of the First Five-Year Plan, which ran from 1953. Attempts to increase productivity and capacity in this area in the period of strong central control of industry from 1960 onwards were superseded in 1998 by the introduction of greater financial discipline into the company via a partial listing on the Shenzhen Stock Exchange, China's second main stock market after Shanghai. It has subsequently issued further share offers from 2005 to 2008.

Despite its recent success, in last few years YCC experienced a major upheaval in the corporate development. In 2008, after a period of investigation, Zou Shaolu, the then chairman of the company, along with two deputy managers Yu Weiping and Wang Jianwei, was indicted for corruption. In the end, Yu was sentenced to death by the Kunming Intermediate People's Court in February 2009 for accepting bribes of more than USD four million and embezzling more than RMB 41 million. He was also found guilty of misappropriating RMB 27 million of company funds, which he then lent on to others. Chairman Zhou was found guilty of taking RMB 19 million in bribes from 2003 to 2007, but was spared the death sentence, reportedly because he had admitted his guilt during investigation. Wang, the other deputy manager, was sentence to 20 years in jail for accepting RMB 4 million in bribes. Liu Caiming was named as the new chairman in 2008, with He Yu as general manager and Gao Lidong as CFO.

Main Products and Services

The state-owned Yunnan Copper Company Limited is the third largest copper producer in China, ranking seventh in the top 50 China nonferrous metal industry corporations. In 2004, the company ranked number 343 in China's Top 500 Companies. Its headquarters are in Kunming, the capital of Yunnan province, in southwestern China, an area rich in natural resources, and close to the mining areas where most of the company's raw materials come from. Its core business is the manufacturing, processing, and sale of electrolytic coppers, other processed products, chemical industry products and non-ferrous metals. *Tiefeng* is one of the brand names YCC produces goods under. Major products include highly purified copper cathode, copper wire billets for electrical purpose commercial sulfuric acid, copper rod, bare copper wire, gold, silver, platinum, palladium, selenium, tellurium, bismuth, copper sulfate, and crude nickel sulfate. In addition, YCC also deals with zinc, and is involved in the research, construction, and design services for production plants.

In 2007, the Yunnan Provincial Enterprise Association, a government organization, ranked YCC's parent company, Yunnan Copper Group, the province's second strongest company after tobacco giant Hongta Group. YCC itself employs approximately 20,000 people and recorded sales of RMB 39.2 billion that year. In 2008, the company had a net profit of RMB 1.96 billion, and sales of RMB 34 billion, a drop compared to the previous year due to lack of demand toward the end of the year because of the global economic slowdown. The market capitalization of the company in 2008 was USD 2.7 billion, with a total of 125 million shares. According to the company, in 50 years till 2008, YCC has produced 2.5 million tons of copper cathodes, 45 tons of gold, and 2,500 tons of silver, and paid RMB 4.5 billion in taxation.

Corporate Structure and Business Strategies

Since 1998, YCC has operated as a subsidiary of Yunnan Copper Industry (Group) Company Limited. In February 2007, the China Aluminum Corporation (Chinalco) paid USD one billion for a controlling 49% stake in Yunnan Copper Industry Group Company, the biggest such acquisition that year. YCC itself also explores for and develops minerals in China and overseas, investing in Laos, Burma, and Australia. In November 2007, YCC took a 21.2-percent stake in China Yunnan Copper Australia Ltd., which listed on the Australian Stock Exchange in 2008, aiming to make this YCC's main investment abroad. This has been part of the broader issue of China seeking access to resources abroad, under its "Go Global" policy started in 2001.

Even with the disruption of the last few years, YCC will likely remain on track for long-term growth, as it operates in one of the key sectors, with major assets, and significant government support, both at local and national level. One area where it is stepping into new ground is its activities abroad. Here, its interests in Australia in particular are worth watching, aiming to secure supply of badly needed commodities through the outright purchase of foreign companies. The government of Australia has, as of 2009, welcomed this, though the case of China Aluminum (Chinalco) taking an almost 19% stake in the British-Australian Mining giant Rio Tinto has already attracted talk by some politicians within Australia of the country being too keen to sell of its assets to a potential competitor, and a partner whose demands are at the moment not clear.

Looking forward, YCC strives to further develop its abundant resource reserves and implement advanced technology and logistic management into its operations. By 2010, YCC expects to reach an annual output of 500,000 tons of copper cathodes, 300,000 tons of intensive processed products, 300,000 tons of copper in copper concentrates produced by its own mines, with an annual turnover of RMB 19 billion, of which the annual import/export turnover will be USD one billion, and after-tax profits of profits of RMB one billion. In the future, its goal is to become the second in China's copper industry, and rank among the top ten in the world's copper industry.

Kerry Brown

References

Brown, K (2008). No reverse gear: China's overseas investment, an economic and political analysis. *CLSA China Strategy*. http://www.kerry-brown.co.uk/files/clsa_paper_final.pdf. Retrieved on 28 May 2009.

Chinalco pays USD1 billion for stake in Yunnan Copper (2 November 2007). *China Daily*. http://www.chinadaily.com.cn/bizchina/2007-11/02/content_6333238.htm. Retrieved on 28 May 2009.

Jiang, K and X Hu (2008). Energy and environment in China. In Song, L and Woo, WT (eds.). *China's Dilemma: Economic Growth, the Environment and Climate Change*. Canberra: ANU E Press.

Yunnan Copper executive sentenced to death for accepting bribes (13 January 2009). *Go Kunming*. http://www.gokunming.com/en/blog/item/775/yunnan_copper_executive_sentenced_to_death_for_accepting_bribes. Retrieved on 28th May 2009.

Yunnan Provincial Government (2005). Introduction of Yunnan Copper (2 July). http://www.eng.yn.gov.cn/yunnan English/146648462866251776/20050702/435190.html. Retrieved on 28 May 2009.

ZHONGXING TELECOMMUNICATION EQUIPMENT (ZTE)

Corporate Address and Contact Information

Zhongxing Telecommunication Equipment Company Limited
ZTE Plaza
Hi-Tech Road South
Hi-Tech Industrial Park
Nanshan District
Shenzhen, Guangdong Province
People's Republic of China
Phone: (86)755-2677-0000
http://wwwen.zte.com.cn/en/

Based in Shenzhen, Zhongxing Telecommunication Equipment Company Limited (ZTE, 中兴通讯) is a global provider of telecommunications equipment and network solutions. Founder Hou Weigui is the architect of ZTE's business strategy; though often characterized as a sober and mild mannered engineer, Hou has big ambitions for his company. Under Hou's leadership, ZTE became the first Chinese company to compete in the international high-tech markets. Convinced that only enterprises competing with their self-developed technologies could stay on top of the market, ZTE was one of the very few indigenous enterprises that opted for independent research rather than technology transfer through Sino-foreign joint ventures in its early development phase.

Corporate Development

ZTE's predecessor, a semiconductor company bearing the same name, was established in 1985. Zhongxing Semiconductor Co. Ltd. restructured itself using the "state-owned and privately managed" mechanism in 1993 and became a telecom equipment maker. The company's 51% of the stocks was owned by an affiliate of the Ministry of Aerospace and Shenzhen Guangyu Industrial Co. Ltd., and a privatized corporation Zhongning-Weixian Telecommunication Equipment Co. Ltd. owned the rest of the stocks. In 1997, ZTE was listed on the Shenzhen Stock Exchange with 55.01% of the company's total stocks; the other 44.09% were retained by the state-owned entities and the company's senior management. ZTE is China's largest publicly traded telecommunications equipment maker.

ZTE positions itself as a comprehensive telecom solution provider; its products include core networks, wireless networks, access, services, and terminals (i.e., handsets and data cards). In 2008, network infrastructure accounted for 65% of ZTE's incomes and mobile handsets 22%. ZTE hopes to grow the handset unit to eventually generate half of the company's revenues, partly because handset sales tend to create more opportunities for networks business.

Although ZTE is not China's biggest high-tech company, it has been hand picked as one of the 520 key large state-owned enterprises and designated a "National Innovative Enterprise". ZTE captures Chinese leaders' attention because it shunned the low-tech assembly business model early on and has been striving to move up the value-added ladder by developing its own technologies. During a visit to Shenzhen in April 2009, Premier Wen Jiabao singled out ZTE as a role model for other Chinese companies and exclaimed that "innovations ... win dignity for Chinese enterprises and Chinese people". While ZTE's national champion status provides it with a powerful patron, the company's success can be attributed to a good understanding of its relative strengths, such as a low-cost structure, R&D capabilities, and good relationships with telecom operators, and exploiting them effectively. Pragmatic and disciplined, ZTE has grown steadily by avoiding direct confrontations with stronger rivals and focusing on businesses the latter is not interested in.

To begin with, ZTE differentiates itself from its bigger and brasher local rival Huawei Technologies by not making wild bets on any individual opportunities. ZTE has a strict policy that forbids an over reliance on a single technology and it has always pursued a multi-product R&D strategy. ZTE's "strategic choice making" is based on advance tracking and elastic investments, this market-driven R&D strategy intends to help the company minimize risks without losing opportunities. ZTE's decision to invest in all three probable 3G mobile standards paid off handsomely in 2009 when China announced it would deploy more than one technology standard for its 3G networks.

International Expansions

ZTE had, nonetheless, suffered for years before it got to enjoy these payoffs. The repeated postponement in issuing 3G mobile licenses by the Chinese government prolonged the business of 2G mobile telephony and its dominance by global giants while impeding ZTE's 3G networks sales and recouping related R&D expenses. ZTE was thus compelled to venture abroad. As a result, overseas income as a share of total income expanded from 12% to 61% between 2003 and 2008. To establish its foothold, ZTE stays away from markets already saturated with powerful multinational rivals but targets less developed economies that prefer low-cost solutions. ZTE's lower cost structure enables it to out-bid industry leaders; ZTE's home base in China also affords it a better understanding of how to operate in developing countries. For the cash-strapped customers, ZTE also arranges vendor financing; its national champion status does help it easily secure credit lines with state-controlled banks in China. In addition, ZTE is flexible in ways that global giants will not, such as providing customized value-added solutions, because the latter cannot make money unless a certain scale threshold is met.

ZTE's dealings are equally flexible in the developed markets. The company has been pursuing an "MTO" (multinational operators) strategy since 2005. ZTE intends to persuade telecom service operators that already buy networks from it to buy handsets too. Without established brands, ZTE offers to customize mobile handsets for the operators. ZTE takes the white label approach (i.e., dropping the ZTE brand in favor of the operators'), but market leaders normally will not consider this option because they can make more money on their branded products. Operators eager to build their revenues and loyalty with their users respond to customization favorably. ZTE also benefits by cutting R&D time and saving substantial marketing expenses. Meanwhile, ZTE can learn about customer tastes in these foreign markets, cement its relationship with operators, and build up scale for its own handset business.

Growth Strategies and Future Challenges

Building on these advantages, ZTE can expect stellar growth in the near future. ZTE is especially confident about achieving double-digit revenue growth in 2009.

First, the construction of China's 3G mobile networks will be an important growth engine in the next three years. Thanks to its policy of investing in multiple products and technologies, ZTE is capable of handling both CDMA 2000 and TD-SCDMA technologies and it has emerged a major winner in China Unicom and China Mobile's tenders. For a new technology such as TD-SCDMA, network interoperability and communication between network and handset are critical; since ZTE develops all products in-house, it should have a significant advantage over network-only or handset-only rivals.

Second, ZTE's head start in developing economies, where much of the growth in the telecoms industry is happening, will give it clout. Saturation in wealthy markets is pushing operators to expand in emerging markets; ZTE gets a rare opportunity to inch into mainstream markets through cooperation with global operators in specific areas and regions. In a recessionary climate, ZTE's readiness to provide vendor financing may help it win business among cash-strapped operators looking to finance their network rollouts.

Third, customized phones will go mainstream in the 3G era in China and elsewhere. Being an early mover, ZTE has enormous advantages. Coupled with the demise of former industry stalwarts such as Nortel and Motorola, ZTE Chairman Hou Weigui sees the financial crisis as an opportunity for ZTE to overtake multinational vendors. However, while ZTE has ample reasons to be optimistic, challenges lie ahead.

ZTE has been growing in the shadows of the giants. Low-end models for emerging markets can only be a take-off point for its overseas businesses. To really grow, ZTE must compete successfully in key markets in America and Europe. However, advancing to the high-end markets will be difficult because of its lack of brand appeal and experience in selling directly to consumers. Whether ZTE's turning down the opportunity to buy Motorola's ailing handset unit or insisting on building its own brand is wise remains to be seen.

ZTE also suffers from a size disadvantage. Although ZTE is growing rapidly and its ranking has been rising fast on both the networks and the handset leagues, these achievements must be put in perspective. As industry consolidation since 2006 leaves fewer players in the market, ascending to a higher position will be easier but the gap between the merged giants and ZTE will be more pronounced than ever. ZTE's revenues remain much smaller than those of the top tier vendors. As a result, ZTE's strong commitment in R&D — as expressed in share of revenues spent on R&D — disguises the fact that ZTE's actual R&D budget pales in comparison with those of the giants. As 3G mobile equipments have very high thresholds in capital investment and technology such as software development, the 3G terminal market will likely be dominated by the companies with the strongest financial might.

In the past, ZTE could get by with a small R&D budget because the R&D inputs were abundant and cheap in China. Compared to multinational vendors reluctant to conduct research in China, ZTE rapidly built up engineering and independent R&D at home. This turns out to be a fleeting advantage because multinational vendors are now moving big chunks of manufacturing as well as R&D to China. As such, ZTE's cost advantage is no longer what it was. On the contrary, ZTE's own foreign direct investment drive has just begun. For a company with its roots in a developing economy, ZTE's long-term competitiveness lies in its ability to simultaneously leverage core competences at home and explore new opportunities abroad in an integrated fashion.

Finally, while the national champion status has afforded it prestige and advantages, ZTE must guard against complacency. ZTE's state-bank backed loans keep the lending risks off its balance sheet, but it must be aware of moral hazard and restrain from lending indiscriminately. Similarly, being awarded the largest TD-SCDMA equipment orders does not necessarily imply that domestic players will be favored in China's 3G market. The government's determination to promote TD-SCDMA will likely attract more competitors onto the battlefield. ZTE must turn its early mover advantages into sustainable ones; it will be a race against time.

Carmencita Cheung

References

Beutler, B (2007). Electronic business top R&D spenders. *Electronic Business*, 24 July.

Hao, Z (2008). Chinese firms take 10% of global 3G handset market. *China Daily*, 21 May.

Leander, T (2007). ZTE: National champion. *CFO Asia*, 16 May.

Luo, Y and RL Tung (2007). International expansion of emerging market enterprises: A springboard perspective. *Journal of International Business Studies*, 38: 481–498.

Wu, Y (2008). ZTE's second chance. *China Business Feature*, 10 January. http://www.cbfeature.com/special_coverage/news/ztes_second_chance/ztes_second_chance. Retrieved on 8 June 2009.

ZTE (2009). Premier Wen Jiabao visits ZTE headquarters. 23 April. http://www.zte.com.cn/pub/en/press_center/news/200904/t20090422_171116.html. Retrieved on 8 June 2009.

List of Abbreviations

ABS	American Bureau of Shipping
ADR	American Depository Receipts
ADS	American Depositary Shares
AIA	American International Assurance
AIG	American International Group
AISC	American institute of Steel Constructions
AISCO	Anyang Iron & Steel Company
AM	Aftermarket Manufacturer
AMAX	Asia Mediterranean American Express
ANSC	Angang New Steel Company Limited
AOC	Admiral Overseas Corporation
AQSIQ	Administration of Quality Supervision, Inspection, and Quarantine
ARPU	Average Revenues Per User
ASEAN	Association of Southeast Asian Nations
AST&L	American Society of Transportation and Logistics
ATM	Automated Teller Machine
BAIC	Beijing Auto Industrial Corporation
BASF	Badische Anilin und Soda Fabrik
BBVA	Banco Bilbao Vizcaya Argentaria
BCF	Billion Cubic Feet
BHP	Broken Hill Proprietary Company
BOCOM	Bank of Communications
BOC	Bank of China
BOCI	Bank of China International
BOCG	Bank of China Group
BOD	Board of Directors
BP	British Petroleum
BRS	Barry Rogliano Salles
BSI	British Standards Institution
BTT	Beijing-Tianjin-Tangshan
BV	Bureau Veritas
BYD	Build Your Drams
CAAC	Civil Aviation Administration of China
CAGR	Compound Annual Growth Rate
CBIA	China Beverage Industry Association
CBRC	China Banking Regulatory Commission
CBU	Completely Built-Up
CCB	China Construction Bank
CCCC	China Communications Construction Company

CCP	Chinese Communist Party
CCS	China Classification Society
CCTV	China Central Television
CDMA	Code Division Multiple Access
CE	Conformité Européenne
CEA	China Eastern Airlines
CEC	China Electronics Corporation
CEO	Chief Executive Officer
CFA	Chartered Financial Analyst
CFO	Chief Financial Officer
CHALCO	Aluminum Corporation of China Limited
CHD	China Huadian Corporation
CHEC	China Harbor Engineering Corporation
CHINALCO	Aluminum Corporation of China
CIGAML	China Insurance Group Assets Management Ltd.
CIIH	China Insurance International Holdings Company Limited
CIMC	China International Marine Containers (Group) Ltd.
CIRC	China Insurance Regulatory Commission
CIRe	China International Reinsurance Company Limited
CIS	Commonwealth of Independent States
CITIC	China International Trust and Investment Corporation
CMA-CGM	Compagnie Maritime d'Affrètement Compagnie Générale Maritime
CMBC	China Merchants Bank Corporation
CNACG	China National Aviation Company Group
CNHTC	China National Heavy Duty Truck Group Co. Ltd.
CNOOC	China National Offshore Oil Corporation
CNPC	China National Petroleum Corporation
CNY	Chinese Yuan
COSCO	China Ocean Shipping Company
CPIC	China Pacific Insurance (Group) Company
CRBC	China Road & Bridge Group
CREC	China Railway Group Limited
CRECG	China Railway Engineering Corporation Group
CRH	China Resources (Holdings) Co. Ltd.
CRM	Customer Relationship Management
CRT	Cathode-Ray Tube
CSA	China Southern Airlines
CSEC	China Shenhua Energy Company Limited
CSC	China Shipping Container Lines Company Limited
CSG	Changjiang National Shipping Group
CSP	Continuous Strip Production
CSR	Corporate Social Responsibility
CTL	Certification in Transportation and Logistics
CWGC	China Worldbest Group Co. Ltd.
DCS	Distributed Control Systems
DCSA	Digital China System Access Holding Limited

DFMC	Dongfeng Motor Corporation
DHL	Dalsey, Hillblom and Lynn (Worldwide Express)
DMS	Dealer Management System
DSL	Digital Subscriber Line
DWT	Deadweight Tonnage
EASA	European Aviation Safety Agency
EBITDA	Earnings Before Interest, Taxes, Depreciation and Amortization
e-CMMS	e-enabled Components, Module, Move, and Service
EMEA	Europe, the Middle East, and Africa
EMS	Electronics Manufacturing Services
EMS	Environmental Management System
EPC	Engineering, Procurement, and Construction
ERP	Enterprise Resources Planning
EU	European Union
EV	Electric Vehicles
EVA	Ethylene Vinyl Acetate
FAA	Federal Aviation Administration
FCR	Fiscal Cash Register
FDI	Foreign Direct Investment
FPC	Factory Production Control
FYP	Five Year Plan
GAAAA	Global Airline Alliance Adherence Agreement
GAAP	Generally Accepted Accounting Principles
GB	Guo Biao (Chinese National Standard)
GE	General Electric
GL	Germanischer Lloyd
GM	General Motors
GPRS	General Packet Radio Service
GSM	Global System for Mobile
GWCSS	Great Wall Computer Software and Systems Incorporation Limited
HACCP	Hazard Analysis and Critical Control Point
HEV	Hybrid Electronic Vehicle
HIPDC	Huaneng International Power Development Corporation
HKD	Hong Kong Dollar
HNC	Hunan Nonferrous Metals Company
HNG	Hunan Nonferrous Metals Holding Group
HP	Hewlett-Packard
HPEC	Harbin Power Equipment Company
HPEGC	Harbin Power Plant Equipment Group Corporation
HPI	Huaneng Power International
HSA	Head Stack Assembly
HSBC	Hong Kong Shanghai Banking Corporation
HSC	Hemopoietic Stem Cells
IADB	Inter-American Development Bank
IATA	International Air Transport Association
IBC	Industrial Bank Co.

IBM	International Business Machines
ICAO	International Civil Aviation Organization
ICBC	Industrial and Commercial Bank of China
IDC	Internet Data Center
IDG	International Data Group
IJV	International Joint Venture
ING	International Nederlands Group
IP	Internet Protocol
IPO	Initial Public Offering
IPP	Independent Power Producers
ISO	International Organization for Standardization
IT	Information Technology
JAW	Jinan Automobile Works
JCC	Jiangxi Copper Company Limited
JISCO	Jiuquan Iron & Steel (Group) Co. Ltd.
JIT	Just-In-Time
JORC	Australasian Joint Ore Reserves Committee
JV	Joint Venture
KFC	Kentucky Fried Chicken
KPI	Key Performance Indicators
LCD	Liquid Crystal Display
LCV	Light Commercial Vehicles
LED	Light-Emitting Diode
LG	Life's Good
LLC	Limited Liability Company
LME	London Metal Exchange
LPG	Liquefied Petroleum Gas
LR	Lloyd's Registers
M&A	Mergers & Acquisitions
MBA	Master of Business Administration
MII	Ministry of Information Industry
MMBOE	Million Barrels of Oil Equivalent
MMS	Multimedia Message Service
MNC	Multinational Corporation
MOR	Ministry of Railway
MOU	Memorandum of Understanding
MPT	Ministry of Posts and Telecommunications
MSC	Mediterranean Shipping Company
MTO	Multinational Operators
MW	Megawatts
NAIC	North American Industry Classification
NBA	National Basketball Association
NDRC	National Development and Reform Commission
NEC	Nippon Electric Company
NISCO	Nanjing Iron & Steel United Company Ltd.
NPC	National People's Congress

NPL	Non-Performing Loan
NRT	National Retail Transportation
NYSE	New York Stock Exchange
OAO	Otkrytoe Aktsionernoe Obschestvo
ODM	Original Design Manufacture
OEC	Overall Every Control and Clear
OEM	Original Equipment Manufacture
OHSAS	Occupational Safety & Health Management System
OMP	Osteoblast Milk Protein
OTC	Over-the-Counter
OTO	One to One
P&C	Property and Casualty
PCTC	Pure Car/Truck Carrier
PDP	Plasma Display Panels
PGS	Petroleum Geo-Services
PHS	Personal Handyphone System
PICC	People's Insurance Company of China
POS	Point of Sale
POSCO	Pohang Iron and Steel Company
PRC	People's Republic of China
PSOM	Products Support and Outsourcing and Maintenance Services
PTA	Purified Terephthalic Acid
PVDC	Poly-Vinylidene Dichloride
QDII	Qualified Domestic Institutional Investor
R&D	Research and Development
RMB	Renminbi (Chinese Currency)
ROA	Returns on Assets
ROAE	Return on Average Equity
ROI	Return on Investment
RTG	Rubber Tired Gantries
SAB	South African Breweries
SAIC	Shanghai Automotive Industry Corporation
SAR	Special Administrative Region
SARS	Severe Acute Respiratory Syndrome
SASAC	State-owned Assets Supervision & Administration Commission
SBU	Strategic Business Units
SEHK	Hong Kong Stock Exchange
SEPCO	Shandong Electricity Power Corporation
SEZ	Special Economic Zones
SGM	Shanghai General Motors
SIC	Standard Industrial Classification
SITIC	Shandong International Trust and Investment Corporation
SKU	Stock Keeping Unit
SMEs	Small- and Mid-sized Enterprises
SMS	Short Message Service
SMTC	Shanghai Material Trading Centre Company Limited

SOE	State-Owned Enterprises
SPC	Shanghai Petrochemical Corporation
SPDB	Shanghai Pudong Development Bank
SSE	Shanghai Stock Exchange
SSPC	Sinopec SenMei Petroleum Company
SUV	Sport Utility Vehicle
SVW	Shanghai Volkswagen
SWOT	Strengths, Weaknesses, Opportunities, and Threats
SZSE	Shenzhen Stock Exchange
TCL	The Creative Life
TD-SCDMA	Time Division-Synchronous Code Division Multiple Access
TEU	Twenty-Foot Equivalent Units
TFFP	Trade Finance Facilitation Program
3C	China Compulsory Certification
3C	Computers, Communications, and Consumer Electronics
3G	Third-Generation
TISCO	Taiyuan Iron & Steel (Group) Co. Ltd.
TLYS	Tongling Nonferrous Metals Group Co. Ltd. (Tongling Youse Jinshu)
TPAM	Taiping Asset Management Company Limited
TPI	Taiping Insurance Company Limited
TPL	Taiping Life Insurance Company Limited
3PLs	Third-Party Logistics
TRB	Taiyuan Railway Bureau
TTE	TCL-Thomson Electronics
UCBH	United Commercial Bank Holdings
UHT	Ultra High Temperature
UPS	United Parcel Service
USD	US Dollar
VAR	Vacuum Arc Remelting
VAS	Value-Added Services
VC	Venture Capital
VIC	Very Important Clients
VLCS	Very Large Container Ships
WAP	Wireless Applications
WCDMA	Wideband-CDMA
WISCO	Wuhan Iron & Steel Co. Ltd.
WLAN	Wireless Local Area Network
WMS	Warehouse Management System
WTO	World Trade Organization
YCC	Yunnan Copper Company Limited
YOY	Year-over-Year
YPC	Yangzi Petrochemical Co.
ZPMC	Shanghai Zhenhua Port Machinery Company
ZTE	Zhongxing Telecommunication Equipment Company

List of Contributors

Mohammad Faisal **Ahammad**, Nottingham Business School, Nottingham Trent University, UK
China Merchants Bank

Matt **Amick**, Walt Disney Company, USA
China Vanke, Shanghai Construction, Suning Appliance Chain Store Group

Dong **Bian**, EM Lyon Business School, France
Beijing Shougang, China International Marine Containers, Shanghai Electric Group

Kerry **Brown**, Chatham House, UK
Fosun International, Shanghai Material Trading Center, Shanghai Zhenhua Port Machinery, Yunnan Copper

Tays Torres Ribeiro **Chagas**, Ouro Preto Federal University-UFOP, Brazil
Anyang Iron & Steel, Handan Iron & Steel, Nanjing Iron & Steel, Panzhihua New Steel & Vanadium

Hao **Chen**, University of Texas at Dallas, USA
China Life Insurance, CPIC (China Pacific Insurance), Ping An Insurance

Carmencita **Cheung**, City University of Hong Kong, HK
Foxconn International Holdings, Sichuan Changhong Electric, ZTE

Victoria **Chu**, University of California, San Diego, USA
Bank of China, China Mengniu Dairy, Daqin Railway

Nik **Dholakia**, University of Rhode Island, USA
Sinotrans

Kevin **Ding**, Rutgers University, USA
Henan Shuanghui Investment & Development

Qun **Du**, University of Central Florida, USA
Bengang Steel Plates, JISCO, Tongling Nonferrous Metals

Terence **Egan**, Central University of Finance and Economics, China
China Minmetals Corporation, Industrial Bank, Sinofert Holdings

Quek Kia **Fatt**, Monash University Sunway Campus, Malaysia
CITIC, China CITIC Bank, CITIC Pacific, China Communications Construction, Wahaha

Marc **Fetscherin**, Rollins College, USA
Dongfeng Motor Group, Qingdao Haier, Shanghai Automotive

Marco Antonio Tourinho **Furtado**, Ouro Preto Federal University-UFOP, Brazil
Anyang Iron & Steel, Handan Iron & Steel, Nanjing Iron & Steel, Panzhihua New Steel & Vanadium

James P **Gilbert**, Rollins College, USA
Angang New Steel, Hunan Valin Iron and Steel, Maanshan Iron & Steel, Tangshan Iron & Steel, Wuhan Iron & Steel Processing

Douglas N **Hales**, University of Rhode Island, USA
Sinotrans

Hui **He**, James Madison University, USA
Datang International Power generation, Inner Mongolia Baotou Steel Union, PICC Property & Casualty

Mareike **Hoffschmidt-Fetscherin**, Rollins College, USA
China Aviation Oil (Singapore), China Railway Group, Shanghai Petrochemical

Regina Lujin **Huang**, East China University of Science and Technology, China
Laiwu Steel, Shanxi Taigang Stainless Steel

Loi Teck **Hui**, Loi & Mokthar Consulting, Malaysia
CITIC, China CITIC Bank, CITIC Pacific, China Communications Construction, Wahaha

Hao **Jiao**, Fudan University, China
China Coal Energy, China Insurance International Holdings, Hunan Nonferrous Metals, Xiamen C&D

Thomas D **Lairson**, Rollins College, USA
Baidu, Chery, Huawei, SINA

Thomas KP **Leung**, Hong Kong Polytechnic University, HK
Aluminum Corp. of China, China Shenhua Energy, COSCO

Zicheng **Li**, Lingnan College, China
China Shipping Container Lines

Song **Lin**, Central University of Finance and Economics, China
China Minmetals Corporation, Industrial Bank, Sinofert Holdings

Adrian Xueyuan **Liu**, Wuhan University, China
China Resources, Digital China, GOME Electrical Appliances Holding

Kevin **Lowe**, University of North Carolina at Greensboro, USA
Huaneng Power International

Margaret **Minnis**, Pepperdine University, USA
Air China, China Southern Airlines, Jiangxi Copper

Michael J **Miske**, Esq. Dawson & Clark, USA
CNOOC, Liuzhou Steel

Michael A **Moodian**, Chapman University, USA
Air China, China Southern Airlines, Jiangxi Copper

Maria **Nathan**, Lynchburg College, USA
Hunan Nonferrous Metals

Wei **Qian**, New Tigers Consulting Ltd., Canada
Dongfang Electric, Great Wall Technology, Harbin Power Equipment

Bing **Ren**, Nankai University, China
BYD Auto, Lenovo Group

Jinghong **Shao**, Nankai University, China
BYD Auto

Amir **Shoham**, College of Management, Israel
Datang International Power Generation, Inner Mongolia Baotou Steel Union, PICC Property & Casualty

Yinhua **Shu**, Wuhan University, China
Digital China

Neil **Slough,** Milwaukee Area Technical College, USA
Gree Electrical Appliances, Guangdong Midea Electric Appliances, TPV Technology

Sunny Li **Sun**, University of Texas at Dallas, USA
BYD Auto, Lenovo Group, TCL Holdings

Xue **Tang**, Wuhan University, China
China Resources

Tom Qingjiu **Tao**, Lehigh University, USA
Beiqi Foton Motor, Sinotruk, Weichai Power

Kenny Shiqiang **Wang**, Unionknopf (Shanghai) Limited, China
Jinan Iron & Steel, Laiwu Steel, Shanxi Taigang Stainless Steel

William **Wei**, Grant MacEwan University, Canada
China Petroleum & Chemical, PetroChina, Sinochem International

Keith L **Whittingham**, Rollins College, USA
China Mobile, China Telecom, China Unicom

Zhiwei **Yang**, Wuhan University, China
GOME Electrical Appliances Holding

Wenxian **Zhang**, Rollins College, USA
Baosteel, China Construction Bank, Henan Shuanghui Investment & Development, Huadian Power International, Huaneng Power International, Shanghai Construction

Yifang **Zhang**, Pepperdine University, USA
Air China, China Southern Airlines, Jiangxi Copper

Miao **Zhao**, Roger Williams University, USA
Sinotrans

Sixian **Zhou**, Nankai University, China
Lenovo Group

Xiaorong **Zhu**, Zhejiang University, China
Bank of Communications, China Minsheng Bank, Industrial & Commercial Bank of China

Zhiqun **Zhu**, Bucknell University, USA
China Eastern Airlines, Shanghai Friendship Group, Shanghai Pudong Development Bank

About the Editors

A Chinese native and graduate of Peking University and Southern Connecticut State University, **Wenxian Zhang** is Professor of Rollins College in Winter Park, Florida, where he joined the rank of Arts and Sciences faculty since 1995. He has team-taught courses on Chinese history and cultures and frequently taken students on field study trips to China, and is the recipient of the 2009 Cornell Distinguished Faculty Service Award at Rollins College. In addition to the *Biographical Dictionary of New Chinese Entrepreneurs and Business Leaders* (Edward Elgar, 2009), he has published many articles on information studies, international librarianship, historical research, and Chinese business management. (wzhang@rollins.edu)

Ilan Alon is the George D. and Harriet W. Cornell Chair of International Business at Rollins College, Executive Director of Rollins China Center, and visiting scholar and Asia fellow in the Harvard University Kennedy School of Government. He has published 20 books, over 100 peer-reviewed articles and chapters. His most recent five books on China include *Chinese Culture, Organizational Behavior and International Business Management* (Greenwood, 2003); *Chinese Economic Transition and International Marketing Strategy* (Greenwood, 2003); *Business and Management Education in China: Transition, Pedagogy and Training* (World Scientific, 2005); *The Globalization of Chinese Enterprises* (Palgrave-Macmillan, 2008); and *China Rules: Globalization and Political Transformation* (Palgrave-Macmillan, 2009).

Dr. Alon is a recipient of the Chinese Marketing Award, a dual award from the Tripod Marketing Association (China) and the Society for Marketing Advances (USA), and the prestigious Rollins College McKean Award for his work on education in China. He has taught courses in top Chinese MBA programs including Shanghai Jiao Tong University, Fudan University, and China Europe International Business School. He is also an international business consultant, with experience in China as well as other countries, and a featured speaker in many professional associations. (ialon@rollins.edu; ilan_alon@ksg.harvard.edu).